*Wilfrid Sellars*

# Philosophy Now

## Series Editor: John Shand

This is a fresh and vital series of new introductions to today's most read, discussed and important philosophers. Combining rigorous analysis with authoritative exposition, each book gives a clear, comprehensive and enthralling access to the ideas of those philosophers who have made a truly fundamental and original contribution to the subject. Together the volumes comprise a remarkable gallery of the thinkers who have been at the forefront of philosophical ideas.

**Published**

Donald Davidson
*Marc Joseph*

Michael Dummett
*Bernhard Weiss*

Saul Kripke
*G. W. Fitch*

Thomas Kuhn
*Alexander Bird*

David Lewis
*Daniel Nolan*

John McDowell
*Tim Thornton*

Robert Nozick
*A. R. Lacey*

W. V. Quine
*Alex Orenstein*

Richard Rorty
*Alan Malachowski*

John Searle
*Nick Fotion*

Wilfrid Sellars
*Willem A. deVries*

Charles Taylor
*Ruth Abbey*

Peter Winch
*Colin Lyas*

**Forthcoming**

David Armstrong
*Stephen Mumford*

Nelson Goodman
*Daniel Cohnitz & Marcus Rossberg*

Thomas Nagel
*Alan Thomas*

Hilary Putnam
*Max de Gaynesford*

John Rawls
*Catherine Audard*

P. F. Strawson
*Clifford Brown*

Bernard Williams
*Mark Jenkins*

# *Wilfrid Sellars*

## Willem A. deVries

To my siblings, Chris and David

First published in 2005 by Acumen

Acumen Publishing Limited
15a Lewins Yard
East Street
Chesham
Bucks HP5 1HQ
www.acumenpublishing.co.uk

ISBN: 1-84465-038-3 (hardcover)
ISBN: 1-84465-039-1 (paperback)

**British Library Cataloguing-in-Publication Data**
A catalogue record for this book is available
from the British Library.

Designed and typeset in Century Schoolbook
by Kate Williams, Swansea.
Printed and bound by Cromwell Press, Trowbridge.

# *Contents*

# *Preface*

This is *not* the overview of his philosophy that Sellars would have written. His own summary of his philosophy would have been more complex, deeper in insight, more profound, but it would also have been difficult, dialectical and in need itself of an interpretation. Sellars's works are subtle, nuanced and incredibly rich, but initially so forbidding that many are discouraged and turn away. The purpose of this book is to overcome that initial barrier by providing a reliable and intelligible map of the logical space of Sellars's reasoning that can be used until one feels enough at home to begin to explore in detail its native expression in his own works.

Even so, I have not been able to explore *everything* in his philosophy in detail. For instance, Sellars developed a complex and subtle treatment of freedom and determinism that I have not had space to examine. Sellars's historical essays are both valuable interpretations of the philosophical tradition, and philosophically rich in their own right; I have not touched them. Nor have I been able to treat all the details of his nominalism, his philosophy of science or his theory of practical reason, even though there are chapters devoted to those topics.

I have sometimes included lengthy quotations, for several reasons.

- Although Sellars has a reputation as a very obscure, even turgid writer, he had moments of profound lucidity. On those occasions he should speak for himself.
- His obscurity often results from structural opacity: many sentences or paragraphs seem opaque because one does not see what they are doing there. Relocated into a narrative where they

fit in right on the surface, rather than deeply, darkly and dialectically, the passages shine.
- Including substantial passages from a number of different papers will, I hope, encourage readers to tackle a wider range of Sellars's papers and not confine themselves to only his most well-known works.

I have preserved original emphasis in all quotations unless otherwise noted. Citations are given in the text using abbreviations. In the case of Sellars's works, these abbreviations have become standard. A list of them is included after this preface.

Some readers may be annoyed that the topics for which Sellars is most well known are treated later rather than earlier in this book, but to understand Sellars's treatments of knowledge and mind completely, one must see them in their full context in his philosophy. Readers may, of course, skip to the chapters that interest them, but I hope those who take the path I have charted here will be rewarded with a richer and deeper understanding of the motivations and the arguments that underpin Sellars's epistemology and philosophy of mind.

I have both institutions and people to thank. Of the people, I owe the largest thanks to two friends: Timm Triplett, whose driving desire to understand Sellars (admittedly, in order to refute him), forced me to raise my own understanding of Sellars dramatically; and Jay L. Garfield, a friend since graduate school in Pittsburgh, who has read most of the manuscript and given me invaluable advice and support throughout my career. Jay Rosenberg, the current Dean of Sellars Studies, also read and commented on the whole manuscript. He has also offered encouragement and support for many years, for which I am profoundly grateful. Paul Coates also read the whole manuscript, and I have also received comments on various parts of the manuscript from Sue Cox, Johannes Haag, Paul McNamara, Joseph Pitt and Aaron Schiller. I presented several chapters to the Propositional Attitudes Task Force in Northampton, MA, where I received helpful comments and argument from Ernie Alleva, Bert Bandman, John Connolly, Owen Freeman-Meyers, Alan Musgrave and especially Murray Kiteley, also a Sellars student and a long-time friend. Bruce Aune has long been helpful to me. I have also struck up a valuable friendship with James O'Shea, who is writing a book to compete with this one. We decided against showing each other our manuscripts, but have helped each other track down quotations and think through various puzzles in the texts. Everyone interested in

Sellars owes Andrew Chrucky an immense amount; the labour he has put into the "Problems from Wilfrid Sellars" website has saved all of us a tremendous amount of work. Earlier papers of mine, bits and pieces of which show up scattered through this book, have been read at Virginia Tech, the University of East Anglia, the European Society for Philosophy and Psychology, University College London, the University of Sussex, the University of Manchester, the University of Liverpool, University College Dublin, Trinity College Dublin and the University of Hertfordshire. My thanks to all who raised questions and challenges on these occasions. My colleagues at the University of New Hampshire have always been supportive of my work and deserve my grateful acknowledgment for making my professional life there a joy. I have had help proofreading from Jennifer Bulcock, Roger Eichorn and Aaron Schiller. And I owe thanks to Steven Gerrard at Acumen, and John Shand and Kate Williams, who have been supportive and helpful throughout the process.

The institutions I should like to thank are: the philosophy programme at the University of London and its director, Tim Crane. I began work on this material while a Visiting Fellow there, and London is an extremely exciting place to do philosophy. A sabbatical as well as a grant from the Faculty Scholars Program at the University of New Hampshire made an immeasurable difference in my ability to complete this manuscript on time, so I thank the University very much for its support. Small grants from the UNH Center for the Humanities and the College of Liberal Arts at UNH enabled me to get some research assistance (thank you, Dave Turner) to check quotations and assemble a bibliography. I am finishing the revisions of the manuscript under the auspices of a Fulbright Distinguished Lectureship at the University of Vienna, for which support I am very grateful.

And, of course, there's the family, which is what the whole shebang is ultimately all about. Besides being my wife, Dianne has helped me write firmer prose. And I welcome the newest member of my family, my grandson Benjamin Kaplan.

Willem A. deVries
Northwood, NH, USA
Vienna, Austria

# *Abbreviations*

AAE "Actions and Events" (1973).
AD "Acquaintance and Description Again" (1949).
AE "Abstract Entities" (1963).
AMI "Aristotle's Metaphysics: An Interpretation" (1967).
APM "Aristotelian Philosophies of Mind" (1949).
AR "Autobiographical Reflections: (February, 1973)" (1975).
ATS "The Adverbial Theory of the Objects of Sensation" (1975).
BBK "Being and Being Known" (1960).
BD "Berkeley and Descartes: Reflections on the 'New Way of Ideas'" (1977).
BEB "Belief and the Expression of Belief" (1970).
BLM "Behaviorism, Language and Meaning" (1980).
CAE "Classes as Abstract Entities and the Russell Paradox" (1963).
CC "Conceptual Change" (1973).
CDCM "Counterfactuals, Dispositions, and the Causal Modalities" (1957).
CDI "Reflection on Contrary to Duty Imperatives" (1967).
CE "The Concept of Emergence" (1956).
CHT "Comments on Mr. Hempel's Theses" (1952).
CIL "Concepts as Involving Laws and Inconceivable without Them" (1948).
CLN "Sellars' Notes for The Ernst Cassirer Lectures" (1979, published 2002).
CM "Comments on Maxwell's 'Meaning Postulates in Scientific Theories'" (1961).
CMM "Comments on McMullin's 'Matter as a Principle'" (1963).

CPCI "Conditional Promises and Conditional Intentions (Including a Reply to Castaneda)" (1983).

DKMB "The Double-Knowledge Approach to the Mind–Body Problem" (1971).

EAE "Empiricism and Abstract Entities" (1963).

ENWW "Epistemology and the New Way of Words" (1947).

EPH *Essays in Philosophy and its History* (1974).

EPM "Empiricism and the Philosophy of Mind" (1956).

FCET *Form and Content in Ethical Theory*, The Lindley Lecture for 1967.

FD "Fatalism and Determinism" (1966).

FMPP "Foundations for a Metaphysics of Pure Process", the Carus Lectures (1981).

GE "Grammar and Existence: A Preface to Ontology" (1960).

GEC "Givenness and Explanatory Coherence" (1973).

GQ "Gestalt Qualities and the Paradox of Analysis" (1950).

I "... this I or he or it (the thing) which thinks", the 1970 Presidential Address, American Philosophical Association (Eastern Division) (1972).

IAE "On the Introduction of Abstract Entities" (1975).

IAMB "The Identity Approach to the Mind–Body Problem" (1965).

IIO "Imperatives, Intentions, and the Logic of 'Ought'" (1956).

IIOR "Imperatives, Intentions, and the Logic of 'Ought'" (1963).

IKTE "The Role of Imagination in Kant's Theory of Experience", the Dotterer Lecture (1978).

ILE "The Identity of Linguistic Expressions and the Paradox of Analysis" (1950).

IM "Inference and Meaning" (1953).

IRH "The Intentional Realism of Everett Hall" (1966).

ITM "Intentionality and the Mental" (1957).

ITSA "Is There a Synthetic A Priori?" (1953, rev. 1956).

IV "Induction as Vindication" (1964).

KBDW "On Knowing the Better and Doing the Worse" (1970).

KMG *Knowledge, Mind, and the Given: Reading Wilfrid Sellars's "Empiricism and the Philosophy of Mind"* (DeVries & Triplett 2000).

KPT *Kant and Pre-Kantian Themes: Lectures by Wilfrid Sellars* (2002).

KSU "Kant's Views on Sensibility and Understanding" (1967).

KTE "Some Remarks on Kant's Theory of Experience" (1967).

KTI "Kant's Transcendental Idealism" (1976).

KTM    *Kant's Transcendental Metaphysics: Sellars' Cassirer Lectures and Other Essays* (2002).

LCP    "On the Logic of Complex Particulars" (1949).

LRB    "Language, Rules and Behavior" (1949).

LSPO    "Logical Subjects and Physical Objects" (1957).

LT    "The Language of Theories" (1961).

LTC    "Language as Thought and as Communication" (1969).

ME    *The Metaphysics of Epistemology: Lectures by Wilfrid Sellars* (1989).

MEV    "Mental Events" (1981).

MFC    "Meaning as Functional Classification (A Perspective on the Relation of Syntax to Semantics)" (1974).

MGEC    "More on Givenness and Explanatory Coherence" (1979).

ML    "Meditations Leibnitziennes" (1965).

MMB    "Mind, Meaning, and Behavior" (1952).

MMM    "Hochberg on Mapping, Meaning, and Metaphysics" (1977).

MP    "Metaphysics and the Concept of a Person" (1969).

NAO    *Naturalism and Ontology, the John Dewey Lectures for 1973–74* (1980).

NDL    "Are There Non-deductive Logics?" (1970).

NI    "Notes on Intentionality" (1964).

NPD    "A Note on Popper's Argument for Dualism" (1954).

NS    "Naming and Saying" (1962).

OAFP    "On Accepting First Principles" (1988).

OAPK    "Ontology, the A Priori and Kant" (1970).

OM    "Obligation and Motivation" (1951).

OMP    "'Ought' and Moral Principles" (1966).

OMR    "Obligation and Motivation" (1952).

OPM    "Ontology and the Philosophy of Mind in Russell" (1974).

ORAV    "On Reasoning About Values (1980).

P    "Particulars" (1952).

PANF    "The Paradox of Analysis: A Neo-Fregean Approach" (1964).

PH    "Phenomenalism" (1967).

PHM    "Phenomenalism" (1963).

PP    *Philosophical Perspectives* (1967).

PPE    "Pure Pragmatics and Epistemology" (1947).

PPHP    *Philosophical Perspectives: History of Philosophy* (1977).

PPME    *Philosophical Perspectives: Metaphysics and Epistemology* (1977).

PPPW    *Pure Pragmatics and Possible Worlds: The Early Essays of Wilfrid Sellars* (1980).

PR "Physical Realism" (1955).
PRE "Presupposing" (1954).
PSB "Putnam on Synonymity and Belief" (1955).
PSIM "Philosophy and the Scientific Image of Man" (1962).
QMSP "Quotation Marks, Sentences, and Propositions" (1950).
RA "Reply to Aune" (1967).
RAL "Reason and the Art of Living in Plato" (1973).
RC *Review of Ernest Cassirer, "Language and Myth"* (1948–49).
RCA "Review of C. West Churchman and Russell L. Ackoff, *Methods of Inquiry: An Introduction to Philosophy and Scientific Method*" (1951).
RD "Reply to Donagan" (1975).
RDP "Reply to Dennett and Putnam" (1974).
RET *Readings in Ethical Theory* (1952).
RM "Reply to Marras" (1973).
RMSS "Raw Materials, Subjects and Substrata" (1963).
RNWW "Realism and the New Way of Words" (1948).
RP "Review of Arthur Pap, *Elements of Analytic Philosophy*" (1950).
RPA *Readings in Philosophical Analysis* (1949).
RPH "The Refutation of Phenomenalism: Prolegomena to a Defense of Scientific Realism" (1966).
RQ "Reply to Quine" (1973).
SC "The Soul as Craftsman" (1967).
SCE "Substance, Change and Event" (1934).
SE "Science and Ethics" (1967).
SFA "Substance and Form in Aristotle" (1957).
SK "The Structure of Knowledge: (I) Perception; (II) Minds; (III) Epistemic Principles" (1975).
SM *Science and Metaphysics: Variations on Kantian Themes* (1967).
SMG "Sellars and the 'Myth of the Given'" (Alston 2002).
SPB "Some Problems about Belief" (1969).
SPR *Science, Perception and Reality* (1963).
SRI "Scientific Realism or Irenic Instrumentalism: A Critique of Nagel and Feyerabend on Theoretical Explanation" (1965).
SRLG "Some Reflections on Language Games" (1954).
SRPC "Some Reflections on Perceptual Consciousness" (1977).
SRT "Is Scientific Realism Tenable?" (1976).
SRTT "Some Reflections on Thoughts and Things" (1967).

SSIS   "Science, Sense Impressions, and Sensa: A Reply to Cornman" (1971).

SSMB   "A Semantical Solution of the Mind–Body Problem" (1953).

SSOP   "Sensa or Sensings: Reflections on the Ontology of Perception" (1982).

SSS   "Seeing, Seeming, and Sensing" (1974).

TA   "Thought and Action" (1966).

TC   "Truth and Correspondence" (1962).

TE   "Theoretical Explanation" (1963).

TTC   "Towards a Theory of the Categories" (1970).

TTP   "Towards a Theory of Predication" (1983).

TWO   "Time and the World Order" (1962).

VR   "Volitions Re-affirmed" (1976).

VTM   "Vlastos and 'The Third Man'" (1955).

VTMR   "Vlastos and 'The Third Man': a Rejoinder" (1967).

## Chapter 1

# Sellars's philosophical enterprise

> The aim of philosophy, abstractly formulated, is to understand
> how things in the broadest possible sense of the term hang
> together in the broadest possible sense of the term.
>
> (PSIM in SPR: 1)

Twentieth-century analytic philosophy is distinctive, in part, because
it treated philosophy as piecework. Philosophy, it was thought,
consists of puzzles, each of which could be attacked on its own and
solved or dissolved, usually either by paying attention to the way
language is used or by constructing a formalism that clarifies an ideal
of language. Some very valuable philosophical work was accomplished
in this way, but it leaves many hungering for a broader view: a philosophy that attempts to see the world as a whole and understand how it
all hangs together.

Wilfrid Sellars, almost alone, was both analytic and systematic. He
utilized the full panoply of analytic tools and methods, including careful attention to ordinary language and the sophisticated deployment
of formalisms, but he did so in the service of a unified vision of the
world and our place in it. Because of its systematicity, Sellars's philosophy is both more difficult to grasp initially and more rewarding in
the long run than that of any other analytic philosopher.

Sellars exercised a profound influence on American philosophy in
the latter half of the twentieth century. Some of his influence was
institutional: Sellars was an important figure in several of the leading
philosophy departments in the US (Universities of Minnesota and
Pittsburgh, and Yale University); he co-founded, along with his
colleague, Herbert Feigl, the first American journal expressly devoted

to analytic philosophy, the well-regarded *Philosophical Studies*; and he co-edited several anthologies that were, in their day, canonical.[1] Sellars was also an inspiring teacher; even those students who disagree with him philosophically still hold him and his philosophical efforts in the highest regard. But his true measure is his philosophical work: a wide-ranging collection of essays and lectures dealing with virtually every aspect of philosophy.

Analytic philosopher that he was, Sellars was also a sensitive and thoughtful interpreter of the history of philosophy, making important contributions to our understanding of Plato, Aristotle, the early moderns, and especially Kant. He also willingly engaged non-analytic philosophers in fruitful discussions, triangulating their positions by reference to the historical philosophical background shared by all.[2] Breadth of vision and historical depth are likely to keep Sellars's work relevant for many years to come, however philosophical fashion may shift.

This chapter has three sections: a brief overview of Sellars's background and biography to place his work in context; a discussion of Sellars's understanding of the role and methodology of philosophy; and, finally, a discussion of Sellars's most basic substantive philosophical commitments. This is all preliminary orientation; substantive, critical engagement awaits the later chapters.

# A life in brief

The emphasis in setting Sellars in context has to be on the richness and depth of his training in philosophy. He absorbed influences from many different traditions, melding and transforming them into a unique vision. Sellars, born in Ann Arbor, Michigan, on 20 May 1912, was an early and rabid reader. His father, Roy Wood Sellars, was a significant philosopher in his own right, teaching at the University of Michigan from 1905 until his retirement in 1950, and remaining philosophically active for several decades after that. Roy Wood published numerous books and articles and was one of the leaders of the Critical Realist movement in the early twentieth century. There are only two essays of Wilfrid's in which he discusses his father's work at some length, but there can be no doubt that his father's influence was profound.[3] Father and son shared, for instance, deep commitments to naturalism, to the rationality and ontological probity of scientific method, and to a complex analysis of perception.

Never a terribly social person, Sellars made friends with difficulty, but the friendships he made were long-lasting. Although born in the Midwest, his upbringing was cosmopolitan: when he was nine, the family spent a year in New England, a summer at Oxford, and the subsequent year in Paris, where Sellars attended the Lycée Montaigne. He then attended the high school run by the University of Michigan's School of Education, becoming deeply interested in mathematics. Although he took a summer course in mathematics at the University of Michigan after his high-school graduation, he postponed his full-time entrance to accompany his mother and sister back to Paris in September 1929 (his father would follow in the spring). He enrolled in a science-orientated programme at the Lycée Louis le Grand, and it was there that he had his first encounter with philosophy, for, according to his own testimony, he had not discussed it previously with his father. Sellars's original encounter with philosophy was twofold: he took a survey of philosophy course at the *lycée*, which we can assume dealt with the canonical writers of the Western tradition, and he acquired friends with whom he read and discussed "Marx, Engels, Lenin, and, in general, the philosophical and quasi-philosophical polemical literature which is the life blood of French intellectuals" (AR: 275), his principal influences being Boris Souvarine and Leon Trotsky. When his father arrived in spring 1930, Wilfrid began discussing philosophy seriously with him, quickly losing the pseudo-Hegelian jargon of Marxist *Naturphilosophie*, but retaining sympathies with Hegelian forms of social and historical interpretation. After his year in Paris, Sellars spent another six months in Munich, learning German and attending classes at the university.

Sellars returned to Michigan in 1931 and commenced his formal studies in philosophy. The University of Michigan, then as now, had an excellent philosophy department, including C. H. Langford and DeWitt Parker. Alongside more home-grown influences from his father's Critical Realism and other American philosophical movements, Sellars was also impressed by the analytic methodology of G. E. Moore and the logic of Russell and Whitehead, especially as extended by Langford and C. I. Lewis. Although modern logic seemed incredibly powerful, most attempts to capture philosophically interesting concepts and principles in the logical forms then available seemed "wildly implausible" to him. Nevertheless, he "regarded the strategy as a sound one and believed that the crucial question concerned the manner in which the technical apparatus of *Principia* would have to be fleshed out in order to do justice to the conceptual

forms of human knowledge" (AR: 282). Lewis and Langford's treatment of the logical modalities seemed a paradigm case of such enrich-
ment. Sellars wanted to extend their strategy to the causal modalities
as well. Since he was still in the grips of an empiricist abstractionism
at the time:

> The result was an immediate sympathy with the causal realism
> of C. D. Broad and, later, W. C. Kneale. Yet I was puzzled by what
> it could mean to say that necessity (logical or causal) was in the
> world, which, it seemed, must surely be the case, if modal concepts
> are genuine concepts and any modal propositions true. Was nega-
> tion in the world? I was tempted by the approach to negation
> which grounds it in a "real relation of incompatibility", and it was
> years before I sorted out the confusions (and insights) involved.
> Was generality in the world? I saw this as one aspect of the
> problem of universals, which was never far from my mind. It can
> be seen that my early reading of the *Tractatus* had had but little
> effect. (AR: 282–3)

Sellars went through the University of Michigan quickly, for he was
able to demonstrate by examination that he had already covered some
of the required courses. He then went to the University of Buffalo,
where he studied Kant and Husserl with Marvin Farber. Besides
becoming well versed in Husserlian phenomenology, Sellars took
inspiration from Farber's naturalism and came to believe that important structural insights usually stated in non-naturalistic terms could
nonetheless be reconciled with naturalism. He took an MA there with
a thesis on time titled "Substance, Change and Event" (1934).

Sellars won a Rhodes Scholarship and enrolled in the Philosophy,
Politics and Economics degree course at Oriel College, Oxford, in
autumn 1934. W. G. Maclagan was his tutor, and the Oxford Realists
John Cook Wilson, H. A. Prichard, and H. H. Price were among his
major influences.[4] Sellars came to favour Prichard's deontological
approach to ethics over Moore's ideal utilitarianism. The rise of
emotivism, however, kept him from slipping into ethical realism,
although he felt that emotivism was wrong-headed. Still, there was
something to it and "[s]omehow intuitionism and emotivism would
have to be *aufgehoben* into a naturalistic framework which recognized
ethical concepts as genuine concepts and found a place for intersubjectivity and truth" (AR: 285). By this time Sellars had abandoned
his earlier empiricist abstractionism and was starting to grope his way
towards a functional theory of concepts that makes "their role in

reasoning, rather than a supposed origin in experience, their primary feature" (AR: 285). Once more working through Kant, this time under the direction of Price, proved important. It was at this point that Sellars saw:

> that by denying that sense impressions, however indispensable to cognition, were themselves cognitive, Kant made a radical break with all his predecessors, empiricists and rationalists alike. The 'of-ness' of sensation simply isn't the 'of-ness' of even the most rudimentary thought. Sense grasps no facts, not even such simple ones as something's being red and triangular. Abstractionists could think of concepts as abstracted from sense, because they thought of sensation in conceptual categories. This enabled me to appreciate that Kant wasn't attempting to prove that in addition to knowing facts about immediate experience, one also knew facts about physical objects, but rather that a skeptic who grants knowledge of even the simplest fact about an event occurring in Time is, in effect, granting knowledge of the existence of nature as a whole. I was sure he was right. But his own question haunted me. How is it possible that knowledge has this structure? The tension between dogmatic realism, and its appeal to self-evident truth, and transcendental idealism, in which conceptual structures hover over a non-cognitive manifold of sense, became almost intolerable. It wasn't until much later that I came to see that the solution of the puzzle lay in correctly locating the conceptual order in the causal order and correctly interpreting the causality involved.                                                          (AR: 285)

Sellars took a first-class degree at the University of Oxford in 1936, which became in due course an MA and was to be the last degree he earned. In autumn 1936 he commenced work at Oxford on a DPhil, attempting a thesis on Kant under the direction of T. D. Weldon. Although Sellars knew what he thought was wrong with other interpretations of Kant, he could not articulate his own interpretation clearly enough. Abandoning his studies at Oxford, he enrolled in the PhD programme at Harvard University in autumn 1937, taking courses with C. I. Lewis, W. V. O. Quine, R. B. Perry, and C. L. Stevenson, among others. He passed his preliminary examinations in the spring of 1938. That summer he married Mary, an English literature student from West Yorkshire, whom he had met at university in Oxford.

In autumn 1938, Sellars began his teaching career at the University of Iowa, where he was responsible for all the history of philosophy courses. He never did return to graduate school or finish his PhD, and he suffered a significant writer's block during the early years of his career. At Iowa, Sellars continued working out his own slightly idiosyncratic, but sweeping, coherent and powerful interpretation of the history of philosophy, a foundation on which he would build throughout his career. He also formed a lifelong friendship with Feigl, originally a member of the Vienna Circle.

The Second World War interrupted Sellars's career, taking him to Rhode Island to serve in Naval Intelligence anti-submarine warfare. After the war, Sellars moved to the University of Minnesota, rejoining Feigl, who had moved there several years earlier. Realizing a need to break the log jam and start publishing, Sellars struck a bargain with his wife, an aspiring short-story writer, that they would write for ten hours a day, no matter how little they produced. After 17 drafts, his first completed work, "Realism and the New Way of Words" (1948) was done, and the floodgates were open. Having found a writing method, he wrote prolifically thereafter.

The rest of Sellars's career can be followed in his essays. He left Minnesota to become a visiting professor at Yale in 1958, moving there as a tenured professor in 1959. He did not, however, remain at Yale long: the department became factionalized, and Sellars felt that the internal politics were obstructing his ability to do philosophy. In 1963 he moved to the University of Pittsburgh, which quickly assembled a number of rising stars in philosophy and became one of the leading departments in the US. Sellars remained at Pittsburgh until his death in 1989, although he visited and lectured at a number of other universities. He also accrued a number of honours, giving the John Locke Lectures in 1965, the Matchette Foundation Lectures in 1971, the John Dewey Lectures in 1973 and the Carus Lectures in 1977, and served as President of the Eastern Division of the American Philosophical Association in 1970.

Sellars was always a systematic philosopher, and each of his essays is a perspectival glimpse of a more thoroughly worked-out, broader philosophical position. This seems to encourage some readers to think that Sellars's philosophical position was not itself amenable to change. In fact, Sellars's "system" was never set in stone. While his fundamental commitments did not waver, he revisited major portions of the system repeatedly, revising and refining his positions throughout his career.

# Philosophy: its role and methods

Sellars's considered statement on the place of philosophy among the disciplines of the intellect is contained in his inaugural lecture at Pittsburgh, "Philosophy and the Scientific Image of Man" (1962), reprinted as the initial essay in *Science, Perception and Reality* (1963). There is not much direct argument in the paper, perhaps, but it is a compact presentation of the underlying framework that pervades his thought. The major themes that emerge are the following:

• Philosophy is universal in scope.

> The aim of philosophy, abstractly formulated, is to understand how things in the broadest possible sense of the term hang together in the broadest possible sense of the term. Under "things in the broadest possible sense" I include such radically different items as not only "cabbages and kings", but numbers and duties, possibilities and finger snaps, aesthetic experience and death. To achieve success in philosophy would be, to use a contemporary turn of phrase, to "know one's way around" with respect to all these things, not in that unreflective way in which the centipede of the story knew its way around before it faced the question, "how do I walk?", but in that reflective way which means that no intellectual holds are barred. (PSIM in SPR: 1)

• Philosophy's ultimate aim is *practical*; a form of *know-how*.

> Knowing one's way around is, to use a current distinction, a form of "knowing how" as contrasted with "knowing that".
> (PSIM in SPR: 1)

• Philosophy is distinct from any special discipline, although it presupposes such disciplines and the truths they reveal.

> Philosophy in an important sense has no special subject-matter which stands to it as other subject matters stand to other special disciplines. (PSIM in SPR: 2)

• Philosophy is reflective, both in the sense that it is second-order knowledge that puts all our other knowledge into perspective, and in the sense that it must itself be pursued reflectively.

> It is this reflection on the place of philosophy itself, in the scheme of things which is the distinctive trait of the philosopher as contrasted with the reflective specialist; and in the

7

absence of this critical reflection on the philosophical enterprise, one is at best but a potential philosopher.

(PSIM in SPR: 3)

- Philosophy cannot be called *analytic* in a sense that contrasts to
*synthetic.*

... while the term 'analysis' was helpful in its implication that
philosophy as such makes no substantive contribution to what
we know and is concerned in some way to improve the manner
in which we know it, it is most misleading by its contrast to
'synthesis'. (PSIM in SPR: 3)

For Sellars, philosophy is neither a pure *a priori* enquiry to be
conducted without regard to our empirical knowledge of the world, nor
just another special science or a discipline ultimately to be replaced by
the sciences. Rather, Sellars viewed philosophy as an ongoing enterprise of understanding how we fit into the world of which we are a part.
Philosophy is essentially dialectical: it presupposes that we live in a
world in which we act and of which we have some knowledge, so it
always engages *in medias res,* and yet it is reflective and critical, so no
element of our current conceptual framework is absolutely beyond
question – we must remain open to new experience and new ways of
organizing experience. Philosophy ought not presuppose that there is
a static, once-and-for-all vision of humanity-in-the-world, for two
reasons: we are constantly learning new things that necessitate
revisions in our overall view, and there is no reason to think that the way
we fit into the world is itself static. The unitary vision of how things hang
together functions only as a regulative ideal in Sellars's philosophy.

There is, of course, plenty of room for disagreement about how things
hang together that shows up in arguments concerning, *inter alia,* the
respective reality of universals and particulars, the nature of causation,
the relation between mind and body, or the nature and existence of God.
But modern philosophy, in Sellars's eyes, is faced with a distinctive
challenge, for unlike our ancient and medieval predecessors, the modern
philosopher "is confronted by two conceptions, equally public, equally
non-arbitrary, of man-in-the-world and he cannot shirk the attempt to
see how they fall together in one stereoscopic view" (PSIM in SPR: 5).
The alternative pictures of humanity-in-the-world that Sellars has in
mind are *radically* different. Their difference is not, for example, the
difference between Platonic realism and nominalism, nor even between
the rationalistic approach typical of philosophy and a mystical or anti-

rational approach to the world, all of which count as differences *within* one of the alternative pictures. Rather, in Sellars's view:

> the philosopher is confronted not by one complex many-dimensional picture, the unity of which, such as it is, he must come to appreciate; but by two pictures of essentially the same order of complexity, each of which purports to be a complete picture of man-in-the-world, and which, after separate scrutiny, he must fuse into one vision. (PSIM in SPR: 4)

These are the *manifest* and the *scientific* images of humanity-in-the-world.

This distinction has now taken on a life of its own, although the terms are not always used in accordance with Sellars's original intention. Often, the distinction is treated as a relatively superficial distinction between common sense and what science tells us, where science simply gives us a finer-grained account of things in the world. It is important to see that the distinction reaches much deeper in Sellars's view; science does not give us just a finer-grained account of things, preserving in other respects the categorial structure of the manifest image, but it is also in the process of developing a distinctive categorial structure of its own.

To appreciate this claim, I should say a word here about the notion of a category, a subject to which we shall return in detail in Chapter 3. Categories have traditionally been conceived of as the highest genera into which things (in the broadest sense of the term) fall. Thus, a list of categories is also an ontology, telling us what kinds of things there are in the world. Aristotle's list, for example, includes substance, quality, quantity and relation. For Sellars, however, the traditional view rests on a naive conception of the relation between thought and reality; he takes a more Kantian view, according to which categories classify the kinds into which our concepts fall. According to Sellars, Kant treats the categories as the most generic functional classifications of the elements of judgements (see TTC in KTM: 329). Sellars, however, does not assume that there is one clear-cut set of categories stamped on human thought. Rather, Sellars applies the term to sets of linguistic forms subject to a distinctive set of syntactico-semantic rules. For example, since there are distinctive linguistic forms associated with the physical–mental distinction, Sellars thinks of that distinction as categorial. So conceived, a list of categories gives us the fundamental structural elements of the world-story we construct to make the world intelligible. As in many classificatory systems, the full meaning of the categorial distinctions drawn becomes apparent only in the context of the whole system.

The manifest image has a distinctive categorial structure, the analysis of which has been the lifeblood of philosophy since its inception, and which is not itself *manifest* in the sense of *evident*. Cartesian dualism and Aristotelian hylomorphism are both candidate analyses of fundamental categorial structures in the manifest image. Sellars himself frequently engages in the analysis of the categorial structure of the manifest image, for its own sake and in order to better understand how it relates to the scientific image. (Sellars holds that with regard to the manifest image, "[t]he Aristotelian–Strawsonian reconstruction is along sounder lines" than the Cartesian, for instance [MP: 252; in KTM: 307].)

The scientific image of the world is, in Sellars's view, neither a mere extension of, nor a finer-grained version of, the manifest image. Although the enterprise of science takes off from the manifest image, it threatens to break free from those roots; scientists are constructing a conceptual framework for describing and explaining the world that need not retain even the basic categorial scheme of the manifest image. The wave–particle duality in quantum physics is perhaps the most well-known categorial divergence from the manifest image in current science, but there is little reason to believe that it is the only one or even that it is the most radical divergence the sciences will develop. Since the scientific image *aims* to be complete (Sellars is under no illusion that it is currently complete), it constitutes, in effect, a challenge to the manifest image, threatening to displace it altogether.

What are the characteristics of these two images? Both are clearly idealizations, ideal types or constructs meant to cast light on a more complex reality. Although Sellars says that the manifest image is "the framework in terms of which, to use an existentialist turn of phrase, man first encountered himself – which is, of course, when he came to be man" (PSIM in SPR: 6), this characterization misleads by implying that the manifest image is primitive and unsophisticated. But in Sellars's view the manifest image is quite sophisticated: millenia of experience and reflection have refined it both empirically and categorially.[5] It has been refined empirically by inductive inferences and is in this sense itself a scientific image. For instance, the Boyle–Charles law that correlates changes in the pressure, temperature and volume of gases (all observable factors) fits perfectly well *within* the manifest image.

What Sellars excludes from the manifest image is any use of postulational methods; postulating unobservable, theoretical entities in order to explain the behaviour of observables is the distinctive move that makes possible the development of an alternative image capable of challenging the manifest image. Although I described the confrontation between the manifest and scientific images as peculiar to the modern era, this is not strictly true. We can find early attempts to employ theoretical entities already among the Greeks, for example, in Democratean atoms.[6] But it is only in the modern era that the use of postulational methods has been so systematically and successfully employed that we can begin to see a broad-ranging, coherent and yet detailed framework being developed that could begin to pose a systematic challenge to the manifest image out of which it is growing. The full story is complex, for the observable–unobservable distinction is not itself eternally fixed, so there is, in fact, a complex dialectic involved in the development of the scientific image.

It is incontrovertible that the scientific image develops out of the manifest image. Is it *founded* upon the manifest image in a way that its displacing the manifest image would cut its own foundation out from beneath it? Sellars claims not: the scientific image is grounded *methodologically* but not *substantively* on the manifest image. The development of the manifest image is a necessary historical prerequisite for the development of the concepts and methods essential to the sciences, but there is no good reason to grant the manifest image ontological priority over the scientific image. A leitmotif that runs through a great deal of Sellars's writing is that what is prior in the order of knowing need not be prior in the order of being, and that certainly applies in his view to the relation between the manifest and scientific images.

One fundamental difference between these two images concerns the basic objects countenanced in each. An object is basic in a given framework if it is neither a property nor a structure of anything more basic in the framework. In the manifest image, there are "mere" physical objects, living things, animals and persons. In Sellars's view, it is important to understand that persons are basic objects in the manifest image. He does not believe that it is built into the manifest image that persons are structures with two parts, body and soul or mind, each of which is fundamentally independent of the other. In fact, Sellars thinks that persons are the *primary* objects of the manifest image, in the sense that the manifest image conception of a mere physical object is in some sense a truncation of the concept of a person, a paring down of the rich conceptions of character and causation that apply to persons.[7]

It is not yet clear what the basic objects of the scientific image will be, although Sellars argues in his Carus Lectures for the primacy of what he calls "absolute processes". But it is clear that in the scientific image, persons are *not* basic particulars, but are complex objects that are structures of whatever is basic in that framework. We should expect that the categorial structure of the framework being developed by science will diverge in some significant ways from the categorial structure of the manifest image (however we end up construing it). This means that finding a "synoptic vision" in which the manifest and the scientific images are unified cannot be an easy task, for it will not be the case that the scientific image just extends the manifest image into the microworld or cosmos. Nor will it be the case that: "[t]he categories of the person might be reconstructed without loss in terms of the fundamental concepts of the scientific image in a way analogous to that in which the concepts of biochemistry are (in principle) reconstructed in terms of sub-atomic physics" (PSIM in SPR: 38).

I shall not wade into the details of Sellars's attempt to reconcile the two images here, but it is important for understanding Sellars to see that this project underlies and informs all his philosophical endeavours. It is particularly important to see that the manifest image "has in its own way an objective existence in philosophical thinking itself, and indeed, in human thought generally", and that "since this image has a being which transcends the individual thinker, *there is truth and error with respect to it, even though the image itself might have to be rejected, in the last analysis, as false*" (PSIM in SPR: 14, original emphasis). This is important because there are two different points of view to be discovered in Sellars's writings. Some of his essays are thoroughly within the manifest image, seeking to explore and delineate the conceptual structure constitutive of the image. This is most clearly true of his essays on ethics, such as "On Knowing the Better and doing the Worse" (1970); his essays on meaning, such as "Meaning as Functional Classification" (1974); and many of his historical essays, such as "Aristotle's Metaphysics: An Interpretation" (1969). Other essays revolve around issues raised by the clash between the manifest and scientific images, even if that clash remains in the subtext of the essay, and this can generate confusion in the reader. For instance, in several places Sellars proclaims that the primary being of colour is as a property of physical objects in space and time.[8] Yet Sellars also argues that ultimately we will come to posit, within our physical theory itself, a set of entities, sensa, that will be the final ontological resting place for colours. These claims are compatible because Sellars holds that it is true *in the manifest image* that colours are primarily properties of physical objects, but that this is one of the respects in which the developing scientific image challenges (and ultimately overrides) the manifest image, forcing us to relocate colours in the scientific image into another ontological category. Because of this, Sellars can also simultaneously claim that a sense-datum theorist who believes it possible to *analyse* a commitment to sense data out of our ordinary perception talk is just wrong and misunderstands the logic of perception talk, and that we nonetheless have good reason to believe that there are sensa, which are very like sense data but not quite the same, for Sellarsian sensa are *not* items discoverable by analysis of the concepts constitutive of the manifest image. The reader of Sellars's essays has to be aware of whether the point of view of the essay is inside or outside the manifest image.

Later we shall return to explore Sellars's views on the clash between the manifest and the scientific images and how he proposes to unify them. Here, I wish to highlight some important aspects of Sellars's philosophical methodology. As already pointed out, Sellars does not think of philosophy as a purely analytic endeavour, whether *a priori* or empirical. He mentions in several different places that in good philosophy, analysis and synthesis are both requisite. But talk of analytic and synthetic methods is itself fairly superficial: there is no univocal or well-defined method (or set of methods) of analysis in philosophy. What would count as a synthetic method in philosophy is even less clear. Once we leave behind this relatively useless vocabulary, we can give a substantive description of Sellars's philosophical methodology. Although philosophy is distinguished from the special sciences by having no distinctive subject matter, it is an explanatory and interpretive discipline, and it shares with other such intellectual disciplines certain methodological features. Most important, for our purposes, is that philosophers are theory-builders and, like most theory-builders, they use *models* drawn from more familiar territory to inspire and formulate their theories.

Readers of Sellars's articles sometimes feel frustrated because, after working through a difficult and complex essay, they cannot identify a clear-cut argument to be found in the essay supporting well-articulated claims. Often his articles are not aimed at providing a set of arguments to establish some thesis, supplemented by another set of arguments aimed against the thesis's opponents (although such argumentation does occur in his articles). Rather, his articles are aimed at getting us to see an issue a certain way, to persuade us of the fruitfulness of a certain model of an issue, on the basis of which we can begin to formulate an explicit theory.

Examples of this general methodology abound in Sellars's work. The most important case, perhaps, is his treating the notion of *speech* as a *model* to be used in understanding human thought. In his classic essay "Empiricism and the Philosophy of Mind" (1956), he attributes use of this model to his mythical genius, Jones, who uses it to develop a theory of thoughts as internal, subjective, intentional states. But it is perfectly evident in other works that he (Sellars) also employs the notion of speech as a model, the use of which helps us theorize more adequately about the nature and status of thought. In "The Structure of Knowledge" (1975), for instance, Sellars explicitly labels the model of speech that he employs "verbal behaviourism", "a useful tool which will help us understand some of the features of thinking, and of our awareness of ourselves as thinking beings" (SK II §9: 319). In another example, Sellars proposes that Kantian intuitions be thought of on the model of demonstrative phrases, for example, "this red cube facing me edgewise", never as a pure demonstrative ("this"), but always as a "this such". He then tries to clarify the status and structure of intuitions by utilizing this model and exploring its implications.

Sellars is, of course, quite well aware that the models he utilizes are simplified idealizations and inevitably will prove inadequate. Through exploration of such inadequacy, we can be led to new, more adequate models. In this regard, Sellars's philosophical methodology is consonant with, although not identical to, the methodology of the sciences. There are no laboratory tests or statistical data models relevant to the issues philosophy deals with, and in that sense its methodology is more comparable to that of linguistics, where more or less complex (and even highly formal) models are tested against the intuitions of native language users in order to make explicit the structural features of the language. As Sellars sees philosophy, there are two tasks the philosopher faces: (i) making explicit the structural features of the manifest image, the conceptual framework that has informed humanity's encounter with the world since it first became self-reflective and fully human; and (ii) exploring the new image of the world that is slowly and systematically being constructed by the sciences. This latter task involves both making explicit the structural features of this emerging framework and thinking through its relations to the manifest image out of which it grows and which it also comes to challenge.

Sellars's articles are therefore often not straightforward argumentative defences or criticisms of particular philosophical theses, but explorations of the adequacy of certain models and considerations of the extent to which they usefully illuminate a philosophical puzzle. The arguments that appear concern particular shortcomings of certain models or the relative advantage of one model over another. In fact, as Sellars sometimes emphasized in his classroom lectures (but I cannot recall his ever having put in print), at the highest level in philosophy there is no argument; one paints the best, most coherent picture one can of how things hang together and hopes that its power to illuminate, to help us know our way around, answers our questions and needs, and withstands the tests of time, experience and reflective scrutiny. Argument is relevant to the scrutiny of the picture's coherence and structure, its adequacy to specific aspects of our experience, and its relative advantage or disadvantage in comparison to other pictures. There is no argument directly for or against the overall picture: what premises would it start from?

This is one of the reasons many people have found reading Sellars so rewarding, although difficult: his essays always have more in mind than a particular thesis. This aspect of his philosophical activity has often been described in terms of his being a systematic philosopher, but that characterization can be misleading. He is not systematic in the sense that he believes there is some *a priori* structure or ordering of philosophical claims that it is the philosopher's job to unfold (either in *more geometrico à la* Spinoza or *more dialectico à la* Hegel). He is systematic in the sense that he approaches philosophical problems not as independent, individual cases in principle amenable to piecemeal treatment, but as always constituted within a larger context and requiring not resolution by the establishment of some particular thesis, but the development of a more insightful or more adequate model that permits us to see how the particular phenomenon or puzzle fits within a larger, coherent whole.

## Sellars's substantive philosophical commitments

Sellars's deepest philosophical commitment is to naturalism. Naturalism is itself a problematic term, of course. Just what it means in the mouths of different philosophers varies considerably, and Sellars treats the term with some diffidence. But naturalism of one kind or another runs in the family, at least since his father's work

*Evolutionary Naturalism* (1922). In the Introduction to *Naturalism and Ontology* (1980), Sellars says a few words to explain his growing connection to both pragmatism and naturalism over the course of his career:

> As for Naturalism. That, too, had negative overtones at home. It was as wishy-washy and ambiguous as Pragmatism. One could believe *almost* anything about the world and even *some* things about God, and yet be a Naturalist. What was needed was a new, nonreductive materialism. My father could call himself a Materialist in all good conscience, for at that time he was about the only one in sight. I, however, do not own the term, and I am so surprised by some of the views of the *new,* new Materialists, that until the dust settles, I prefer the term 'Naturalism,' which, while retaining its methodological connotations, has acquired a substantive content, which, if it does not entail scientific realism, is at least not incompatible with it. (NAO: 1–2)

Standardly, naturalism has both an ontological and an epistemological and/or methodological component, and, as we see above, Sellars wants both aspects in play.

Ontologically, everything that exists is in nature, but 'nature' is as ill-defined as 'naturalism' itself. Naturalism is at least a rejection of the spooky or supernatural, but it has also been interpreted to be a rejection of Platonic forms, of Cartesian minds and/or of Kantian noumena, and Sellars would agree with these rejections. For Sellars, naturalism includes the thesis that everything that exists is an element in the spatiotemporal causal nexus. He rejects, therefore, any kind of purported causal or metaphysical dependence on something outside space and time, such as God, souls, forms or other pure intelligibles.

Epistemologically, naturalism is often construed as a commitment to seeing the empirical methods of the natural sciences as paradigms of knowledge acquisition, but there are non-naturalistic interpretations of those methods. Perhaps it is better to see the epistemological dimension as a commitment to the idea that the acquisition of knowledge is itself a natural process within the causal order. Some naturalistic philosophers interpret this to mean that the study of knowledge (epistemology) must itself then be construed as the empirical study of knowledge acquisition. Thus, cognitive psychology ultimately replaces epistemology. This seems to carry along with it a rejection of any *a priori* or normative constraints on (or within) the knowledge acquisition process, for any *a priori* or normative element in the process would itself be immune to empirical investigation. This is *not,* however, how Sellars sees it. Rather, he believes that he is able, within his philosophy, to show how any *a priori* and/or normative elements essential to knowledge can be (non-reductively) accommodated within a broadly naturalistic framework. He is thoroughly committed to the normativity of epistemology.

Conjoined with his naturalism is an equally strong realism, another inheritance from his father. 'Realism' is another multivalent word in philosophy; here it is intended in its epistemological sense. Sellars worked throughout his career against the idea that our knowledge of the physical world is mediated by an independent or prior knowledge of something non-physical, whether it be something explicitly mental or something neither mental nor physical, as in a neutral monism. Like his father, he was convinced that a proper analysis of perception was philosophically essential, and he devoted a number of essays to the topic, defending what has to be seen as a descendent of his father's Critical Realism. That is to say, Sellars's realism is not a naive realism, although it has claim to be called a direct realism, because while it posits sensations as *causal* intermediaries in perception, our epistemic relations to objects are direct, that is, non-inferential. Sellars's theory of perception is addressed in greater detail in Chapters 5 and 8.

There is another, ontological, sense of realism that constitutes a core commitment for Sellars: scientific realism, the point at which his epistemological realism and his naturalism come together. Existence is ultimately existence in the spatiotemporal causal nexus, and science is the way it is best known, because science is a self-correcting endeavour that is constantly refining itself both methodologically and substantively and is aimed at knowledge of the natural world. Conversely, science is the most highly refined process of knowledge acquisition we have; science gives us knowledge of objects in physical space-time, so we have every reason to believe that the objects science locates in space-time are really real. "In the dimension of describing and explaining the world, science is the measure of all things, of what is that it is, and of what is not that it is not" (EPM: §41, in SPR: 173; in KMG: 253). Of course, acknowledges Sellars, current science is still very much in progress. Although it is rational to endorse as real whatever entities the best science available to us is committed to, we must also recognize that it is in the very nature of science to be subject to revision. Therefore, at any particular point in time, our ontological commitments are provisional. Our *ultimate* ontological commitment is to the entities recognized by the Peircean ultimate scientific framework: a regulative ideal in which all possible empirical questions can be answered; the framework that has achieved explanatory completeness. Sellars is unabashed about his scientific realism, although it has served as a major focal point for his critics. Arguments developed by Sellars to support his scientific realism will be examined in more detail in Chapter 6.

Another pervasive and fundamental Sellarsian commitment is to nominalism. This is, in his eyes, deeply connected with his naturalism, as he makes clear in *Naturalism and Ontology*. Nominalism is not forced by scientific realism; indeed, some have thought that scientific realism requires recognition of some abstract entities. Quine, for instance, thinks of himself as a nominalist because he denies the existence of meanings, propositions and the like, yet Quine also insists that one cannot do without classes for they are necessary to mathematics and the mathematical aspects of science. Sellars, however, attempts to construct a much more arid ontology than Quine: he recognizes only the individuals acknowledged by the ultimate scientific framework. But Sellars works very hard to show that nothing important is lost in his form of nominalism. His analysis of meaning and other semantic properties legitimizes our common semantic intuitions without committing us to meanings and propositions as abstract entities. His analysis of the logical, deontic and causal modalities similarly legitimizes our common intuitions about the operation of such notions, again without commitment to abstracta. Sellars even develops an original analysis of predication (based on clues he finds in Wittgenstein's *Tractatus*), demonstrating that predication itself is also nominalistically respectable, even though Platonists have argued since Plato himself that the predicative nexus could be made sense of only by positing abstract entities. These analyses are discussed in much greater detail in Chapter 4.

A different kind of fundamental commitment found in Sellars is his Hegelian conviction that virtually every important voice in the chorus of Western philosophy has something to teach us. Although Sellars often wrote essays on historical figures and movements in philosophy because they provided a convenient foil by which he could put forward his own views, those essays are worth reading even for those with no particular interest in Sellars's philosophy because he takes such pains to isolate and expose the important insights by which philosophy has grown. When he considers opposed positions, it is almost never the case that he simply sides with one against the other. There will always be important truths lying within each position that only a subtle dialectic can tease out and reconcile.

For instance, Sellars is widely known for his attack on empiricism, particularly the logical empiricism that was ascendant during his schooling. Yet his attack on empiricism is as much an attack on its traditional rival, rationalism, and his famous attack on foundationalism is as much an attack on traditional conceptions of its rival, coherentism. He works tremendously hard to develop and defend nominalism, but a large part of that effort is devoted to showing how to account for most of what the Platonist wants to say.

And it is in this spirit that we can now look at the last set of fundamental commitments that shape Sellars's philosophy. Naturalism, realism and nominalism adumbrate a fairly radical position in Western philosophy, although certainly not one without antecedents. (Besides Roy Wood Sellars, Hobbes springs to mind, for instance.) Such radicals are often identified as nay-sayers, for they deny much of the metaphysical architecture that, to the Platonic tradition, has seemed absolutely essential to the analysis of the world and our place in it; indeed, they often deny the possibility of metaphysics. Within metaphysics Sellars is one of these nay-sayers, but, unlike many of his predecessors, Sellars does not want to dismiss the metaphysical claims of the Platonic tradition as mere nonsense, nor does he reject the metaphysical project itself. Rather, he wants to construct a metaphysics in which the truths behind the Platonist's claims can be appreciated. Here is how Sellars put it in one of his earliest papers:

> [C]lassical rationalism ... made explicit the grammar of epistemological and metaphysical predicates, but – owing to certain confusions, particularly with respect to *meaning* and *existence* – came to the mistaken conclusion that philosophical statements were factual statements, albeit of a peculiar kind. Classical empiricism, on the other hand, argued that these statements were common or garden variety factual statements, and usually put them in the psychological species. Rationalism gave the grammar, but contaminated it with platonizing factualism. Classical empiricism threw out the platonizing, but continued to factualize, and confused the grammar of philosophical predicates by attempting to identify them with psychological predicates ...            (ENWW: 646)

Essentially, Sellars believes that once we reject the error common not only to classical rationalism and empiricism, but also to their ancient and medieval forebears – namely, that philosophical statements are factual statements – we can employ Sellars's nominalistic analysis to do away with any Platonistic implications of our philosophical statements while still appreciating the truth and wisdom, or the falsehood and folly, contained in such statements.

Let's be clear what kinds of statements are under discussion here. Among the candidates for such statements would be:

> Red is a property.
> Redness is an individual.
> Objects are just bundles of properties.
> Every change presupposes an enduring substance.
> 'Every event has a cause' is a synthetic *a priori* truth.
> Every experience is someone's experience.
> If the world is deterministic, then there is no free will.

Sellars would not endorse all of these claims, but he insists that in order to bestow or withhold endorsement justifiably, one must understand them properly. If philosophical statements are not factual, what are they, and what job do they perform? Sellars employed a multi-stage strategy. He claims that, in the first instance, such statements are "material mode" versions of claims that, formally, belong in the metalanguage, a stratagem learned from Carnap.[9] In such material-mode sentences, the vocabulary employed apparently belongs to the object language – for example, 'property', 'substance', 'individual' – but functions as disguised syntactic metalanguage. Thus, the first sentence in our list is treated as equivalent to "'Red' is a predicate".

This is, however, only the first step, for it does not guarantee an escape from factualism. Some assertions in the metalanguage are *factual* assertions; historical or descriptive linguistics contains many such assertions. But that is not what the philosopher is doing when she makes claims such as the above. In the philosopher's mouth such claims inevitably have a prescriptive, normative force: they formulate rules. Thus, the propositions that philosophers tend to be most interested in ought to be seen as attempts to articulate in the material mode the rules that govern or are being proposed to govern what we say or think about the world and ourselves. Most philosophers, in Sellars's view, have not been adequately aware of the fundamentally normative thrust of their assertions or their discipline.

So, in Sellars's view, the philosophical claims listed above are all, at heart, rules for using words or concepts. The consequences of this view are important. The justification of philosophical claims takes forms unlike the justification of factual claims; it is, at heart, a kind of practical reasoning. Theoretical reasoning is important in the process, in so far as one needs to work out the coherence and conse-quences of different proposed rules and rule-sets. Ultimately, how-ever, philosophy is practical, aimed at *know-how*, even if reflective, intellectually comprehended know-how.

There is a great deal of work Sellars needs to do to make this posi-tion respectable; clearly, no philosopher (except maybe Carnap) thinks of his or her project as literally providing rules for a particular language. When Sellars characterizes philosophical propositions as metalinguistic, he does not mean that they are in the metalanguage of some particular language (such as English or Swahili). So he needs to provide for a metalanguage that is no particular language's metalan-guage, while also laying out the parameters of the practical reasoning philosophers engage in: that is, what are the practical goals for prescribing rules for the use of words or concepts? These topics are examined in Chapters 2 and 3.

Effectively, then, Sellars takes the intelligible order supposedly discovered in the Platonic analysis of reality and relocates it not only into the metalinguistic, but into the realm of the practical and the normative. This preserves a sense for the metaphysical doctrines constitutive of the Platonic tradition, but without commitment to Platonic metaphysics itself, for Sellars is an anti-realist about norms. Normative sentences instruct, recommend or command action, but they are not factual or descriptive and do not commit us ontologically. Norms, we shall see, are ultimately dependent on human valuings; they have no existence apart from the socially constituted forms of human activity. Thus Sellars can make room for traditional meta-physics even within his naturalism.

The metaphysical, Platonic tradition in Western philosophy reveals a great deal of the architecture of the conceptual framework with which humanity encounters the world. The tradition thought it was reveal-ing the very structure of the world, but in Sellars's view that is ultimately a job for the empirical sciences. The elaboration of the scientific image is therefore a challenge not only to the manifest image, but also to what Sellars calls *philosophia perennis*, the philosophical endorsement of the manifest image as *real*. Platonist speculation remains valuable, however, for it reveals important features of the conceptual framework that embodies our collective know-how for getting around in the world. Traditional metaphysics is thus absolutely worth examining. Engaging in apparently metaphysical disputes is a crucial way to understand our conceptual framework, so Sellars throws himself with gusto into such arguments.

Sellars always has his eye on an even larger picture. The conceptual framework that science is developing must be unified somehow with the conceptual framework by which we live our daily lives. In his view that unification will accord science ontological primacy but will have to preserve the practical (that is, normative) concepts found in the manifest image. Science has nothing really to say about our practical lives: it provides the facts, laws, and connections we need in deliberation, but it cannot ultimately tell us what is good or right, what is an appropriate end of human activity. The real heart of the manifest image that cannot be replaced by science is the grammar of the practical. Even theoretical philosophy is, at heart, an investigation of the practical; it is the examination and rational choice of the best conceptual framework.

# Chapter 2

# *Sellars's philosophy of language*

Like most Anglo-American philosophers of the twentieth century, Sellars's reflections on language sit at the heart of his philosophy. Understanding language is absolutely essential in metaphysics: it holds the key both to the nominalism–Platonism debate and to a proper understanding of the nature of mind, especially the intentionality of thought. Consequently, it is also crucial in epistemology and the philosophy of science, for it is essential to understanding the mind's cognitive relation to the world. Sellars's treatment of meaning, in particular, is so central to his thought that it seems the best place to begin our detailed investigation of his philosophy.

A focus on language has been a major theme throughout contemporary Anglo-American philosophy. Rorty, for instance, makes a well-known distinction between ideal language and ordinary language theories.[1] The ideal language approach sees constructing an ideally perspicuous language as a central task for philosophy. From such an ideal language we could read off important insights in metaphysics and epistemology. This strain of philosophical enquiry into language stems from Frege, Russell and the early Wittgenstein (especially in their logical atomist phase) through Carnap and Tarski, to Quine and David Lewis. However, the goal of an ideally perspicuous language seems elusive at best, and the relation of this ideal language to the rich multiplicity of the daily linguistic activities of ordinary people is very problematic.

Ordinary language approaches, in contrast, assume that ordinary language is perfectly "in order" and focus on the careful examination of language structures and usage. Valuable insights about the diversity of linguistic forms and practices can be gleaned from this point of view. Ryle, P. F. Strawson, J. L. Austin, and late Wittgenstein are paradigms of this approach to language.

Sellars does not fit easily into either camp. His philosophy of language shows the influence of both these schools, as well as influences from the pragmatist tradition of Peirce and Dewey and even medieval thinkers such as Ockham. Sellars shares the ideal language theorist's belief that ordinary language often hides the real logical form of utterances, the uncovering of which is a job of the philosopher. He even invents formalisms to represent perspicuously what he claims is really going on in some aspect of language. The formalisms he offers are idealized *models* of fragments of the rich, multidimensional texture of ordinary language. But in his insistence on the need to respect the variety of linguistic functions and forms we see the imprint of ordinary language philosophy. For Sellars, language is inextricably entwined with human life and human action and cannot be properly understood independently of the communal "form of life" to which it belongs. He is happy to use the techniques and formal abstractions of ideal language theory, but they must be combined with a sensitivity to actual use, particularly the pragmatics of language.

Sellars differs from the paradigms of both ideal and ordinary language philosophy in his emphasis on linguistic change. He does *not* assume that ordinary language is already perfectly in order, that is, that philosophers confronting philosophical puzzles need only uncover the underlying order in language to resolve or dissolve the puzzle. Nor does he assume that the ideal language at which the intellectual disciplines aim can be determined *a priori*. The precise form of an ideal language is something we must negotiate with the world. Philosophy is a theoretical rather than therapeutic endeavour for Sellars. Language is constantly developing in the face of our encounters with the world and must therefore change to reflect changes in the world and to accommodate changes in our knowledge. Science, in Sellars's view, is a systematic and rigorous attempt to revise our language in response to controlled encounters with the world. Cumulatively, these revisions are potentially radical. The languages we have today are unlikely to accommodate everything we shall discover about the world or about ourselves without undergoing significant change. They have already changed in important ways. Sellars thinks that many of the philosophical puzzles we face today are symptoms of language being put under stress by our encounters with the world. Not knowing what to think about the mind–body problem is not knowing what to say about it, and this is in large part a function of the fact that we do not yet have a reflective understanding of how to meld the mentalistic and physicalistic languages we have (somewhat independently) developed. One of the jobs of philosophy is to identify such puzzles, understand their origin, and suggest appropriate resolutions. And this, in turn, requires a proper understanding of language.

## A bifocal view of language

Sellars aims to construct a naturalistic, nominalist, epistemologically realistic treatment of language that respects its centrality to all our conceptual activity. This means that any interpretive or semantic theory has to be compatible with the fact that language exists in the actual linguistic behaviour and interaction of people in the causal, spatiotemporal realm.

The most direct way to satisfy these commitments in a philosophy of language would seem to be a project of naturalization: construct the theory of language, including such concepts as *grammatical sentence, reference, meaning, inference, verification* and *presupposition*, as an *empirical*, psychological theory. But this is not the strategy Sellars chooses. Indeed, in his earliest articles, the "factualism" of many of his philosophical predecessors is one of Sellars's targets. He deems the kind of naturalization project Quine made familiar to be just a form of empiricist factualism, indeed, a form of the psychologism that Frege, Russell and even Husserl were fighting.[2]

Such an approach, Sellars believes, does violence to the fact that languages have an internal structure determined by *rules* constitutive of the language. While a language is realized empirically in a specific set of linguistic behaviours, these always underdetermine the language, and any number of other linguistic behaviours could also have realized the *same* language.[3] The purely empirical investigation of language would not allow us to distinguish a *rule* of language from a *law* of nature. A thoroughly empirical, naturalistic and behaviouristic investigation of our linguistic behaviour might, at best, reveal complex causal generalizations. Such causal generalizations could support subjunctives about what could have been said, but this would not constitute discovering or even formulating the rules constitutive of the language, nor would the subjunctives necessarily be those authorized by the rules of the language. In Sellars's view, the investigation of language cannot be reduced to a purely empirical research programme without neglecting the formal, ideal, normative dimension

25

of language, for rules are *normative* and concern correctness, whereas causal generalizations are purely *descriptive*. There is no empiricist or physicalist analysis of the normative metalinguistic concepts essential to an adequate theory of linguistic structure and function. He concludes that although the normative concepts linguists use and the truths about language formulated therewith must ultimately be unified with the concepts and truths of an empirical science of behaviour, they cannot simply be identified.

Sellars's philosophy of language allows for two separable enquiries: an investigation of the structures of language considered as a formal, ideal system of rule-governed token manipulations, and an investigation of how such a system is tied to or realized in the empirical linguistic behaviour of a community. Let us begin by considering the internal structures of language. At this level, the philosophy of language is both a *formal* and a *normative* enquiry: formal in its concern with the formation and transformation rules of idealized symbol structures, and normative in its concern with the *rules* constituting such structures. Some further historical context helps put Sellars's approach to these questions into perspective.

A history of analytic philosophy in the twentieth century might well describe it as beginning with a focus on philosophical syntax – conceived of as the study of the formation and transformation rules of a self-contained language – and applying and utilizing the structures developed in modern mathematical logic to philosophical puzzles. In the 1930s, with the work of Carnap and Tarski, the focus shifted to philosophical semantics, where semantics is understood as the formal study of the relations between language and the world. It was in this atmosphere that Sellars began his philosophical career, and in his early works he portrays his philosophical project as pushing philosophy into what had to be its next phase: philosophical (or as Sellars then called it "pure") pragmatics.[4] Pragmatics was conceived of as the study of not just the language–world relation, but also of the language–language user–world triad.[5] Early on, Sellars thought of pragmatics as "the attempt to give a formal reconstruction of the common sense notion that an empirically meaningful language is one that is about the world in which it is used" (PPE: 187). Such a language must be at least epistemologically useful to its speakers; ergo, philosophical pragmatics attempts to give a formal reconstruction of such concepts as *verification, confirmation* and *observation sentence*.

Sellars is not engaged in philosophy of language purely for its own sake, but sees it as methodologically useful in metaphysics and epistemology. While he lacks the logician's interest in formal languages as such, he is interested in formal languages with characteristics distinctive of human language, namely, those that (i) are about the world in which they are used,[6] and (ii) contain their own metalanguages (i.e. contain the resources to talk about themselves). These two characteristics entail that the theory reconstruct not just such syntactic concepts as grammaticality, but also semantic and pragmatic concepts such as *predication, reference, meaning, inference, verification* and *linguistic rule*.

Although human languages serve as their own metalanguages, Sellars holds that the concepts of object language and metalanguage apply to distinguishable levels of discourse. Many philosophical puzzles have been generated by confusing the two. As noted in Chapter 1, Sellars thinks such confusion, aided by the presence of the "material mode" of the metalanguage, has been endemic in philosophy.

Sellars is very clear that in discussions of the formal structure of language the philosopher is always working in the metalanguage, and as such is unable to address directly questions about the relations between words and things. Discussion of the real relation between language and the world must occur in the object language, wherein language has to be considered a fact in the world, not a formal or ideal structure. Linguistic *types* have to be embodied in physical *tokens* that can then participate in real-world relations and interactions. Such real-world relations are *natural* relations, that is, spatiotemporal, often causal relations investigable by empirical methods. Linguistic tokens as physical structures are called "natural linguistic objects" by Sellars, and the concept of a natural linguistic object plays a significant role in Sellars's philosophy of language.

## A theory of 'meaning'

Sellars makes some interesting points about syntax – namely, the dispensability of predicates (see Chapter 4) – but he never indulges in syntactic investigations for their own sake. He returns repeatedly, however, to the topic of meaning, which plays a central role in both his metaphysics and his epistemology.

Unlike his contemporaries Davidson and Dummett, in his approach to meaning Sellars examines actual meaning claims quite closely.[7] On the surface, such claims seem to be relational in form. Take, for example:

'Brother' means *male sibling*
'*Rot*' (in German) means *red*
'*Schnee ist weiss*' (in German) means *snow is white.*

Some classical theories of meaning take this surface feature very seriously. A couple of well-known texts on semantics, for instance, name four common theories of meaning: the referential theory, the ideational theory, the behaviourist theory and the functionalist theory.[8] In at least the first three, the fundamental thrust of the "theory" is to tell us what the "meaning relation" is and what it relates. In the referential theory, for instance, the meaning of an expression is the object, event or phenomenon in the world that the expression "picks out" or refers to. Obviously, this is a bad theory of meaning, for it cannot account for the truth of

'*Einhorn*' (in German) means *unicorn.*

There are no unicorns, so the referential theory either treats '*Einhorn*' as meaningless, or, if it gives it some arbitrary object as its meaning, cannot distinguish '*Einhorn*' from '*Kobold*' (in English, gremlin). The referential theory also does a terrible job with the logical words; what do 'not', 'or' and 'if' refer to? The behaviourist and ideational theories of meaning fare no better.

Sellars rejects all such approaches to meaning, for he insists that meaning is not a relation. Although he defends a version of a functionalist or use theory of meaning, he does not offer a theory that asserts a relation between a word and a functional role. Meaning claims *appear* to have a relational form '*aRb*', but this is *mere* appearance; their logical form is not relational at all.

Consider a meaning statement such as, "'*Rot*' (in German) means *red*". We have to worry about the status of all three essential parts, the subject term, the object term and the verb. The subject term, "'*rot*'", is a singular term, but Sellars rejects the idea (which he believes many philosophers have fallen prey to) that it is the name of an abstract entity, the German word '*rot*' as a universal that can (and does) have many instances.[9] Instead, he proposes that we interpret it as a distributive singular term. Distributive singular terms are grammatically singular but distribute their reference across an entire class.[10] Sellars's stock example was "The lion is tawny". A double use of distributive singular terms is available in "In chess, the bishop moves on the diagonal". Distributive singular terms need not be formed with the definite article; they can also be formed with 'an' or 'any', for example, "A trauma victim needs to be monitored for symptoms of shock". Distributive singular terms are roughly equivalent to plurals. "The lion is tawny" is close in meaning to "Lions are tawny"; "The Bishop moves on the diagonal" is close to "Bishops move on diagonals". Obviously, the equivalence is only rough, because the plural formulation can accept an explicit universal quantifier that specifies more precisely the relation between the extensions of the subject and predicate terms. "Lions are tawny" is vague on whether lions are universally, generally, typically or merely occasionally tawny. "The lion is tawny", where 'the lion' is used distributively, requires, to my ear, at least typicality.

Sellars construes the subject term of a meaning claim to be a distributive singular term, the reference of which is not a linguistic *type* as abstract entity but is instead distributed over the class of *tokens,* thus avoiding any reference to abstracta. "'*Rot*' (in German) means *red*" is, therefore, in Sellars's view, roughly equivalent to "'*Rot*'s (in G) mean *red*".

Next, let us consider the object term in our sample meaning claim. '*Red*' is not *used* in its normal sense at all: no colour is being attributed or denied to anything by it. Nor is it being *mentioned*, at least not as the particular English word it is. If we translate the sentence into French, we would translate '*red*' into French as well: "'*Rot*' (en Allemagne) veut dire *rouge*." This demonstrates a third way that Sellars proposes an expression can occur in a sentence, namely, as an interlinguistic "illustrating sortal". In other words, Sellars claims that "'*Rot*' (in G) means *red*" conveys to a speaker of English that the German word '*rot*' plays a role in German that is relevantly similar to the role that '*red*' plays in his background language, English.

Notice, Sellars is *not* saying that "'*Rot*' (in G) means *red*" is synonymous with or should be analysed as "'*Rot*' (in G) plays a role relevantly similar to the role '*red*' plays in English". The latter sentence is, indeed, a complex relational statement. It can be translated into French or Swahili with no significant problem; the statement would convey to the French or Swahili speaker that two words, '*rot*' and '*red*', play similar roles in German and English, respectively, but it would not inform them what those words mean. Knowing that two words have the same meaning is not the same as knowing what they mean.[11]

Suppose the '*red*' in "'*Rot* (in German) means *red*" is an interlinguistic illustrating sortal. What does that really mean, and how does this offer an illuminating analysis of meaning claims? Sortals are kind terms; they attribute, not just simple properties, but complex structures that are often difficult to analyse. 'Cat', 'dog' and 'pre-Raphaelite' are sortals. They are object-language and non-illustrating sortals. A *metalinguistic* sortal attributes membership in some linguistic kind, for example, adverb or noun. An *illustrating* sortal is formed from an example of the kind in question. Thus in our sample sentence 'red' serves as an example of the kind to which '*rot*' is being assigned. 'Red', in our sample sentence, is an unusually formed common noun.

That also tells us what to make of 'means'. According to Sellars, 'means' is a specialized form of the copula; claims about meanings are not relational in form, they are monadic predications. In the end, then, Sellars thinks that "'*Rot*' (in G) means *red*" is fundamentally like "Weimaraners are dogs", but with a predicate formed in an unusual way.

Sellars introduced a special technical device, dot-quotation, in order to make this more perspicuous. Dot-quotation forms a common noun that has in its extension every item in any language that functions in a relevantly similar way to the quoted expression. Thus, ·red· is a common noun that picks out all terms that function in any language like the English word 'red'. ·Red· is an illustrating sortal.

Sellars's claim, in a nutshell, is that the true logical form of "'*Rot*' (in German) means *red*" is "'*Rot*'s (in German) are ·red·s." "According to this analysis, *meaning is not a relation* for the very simple reason that 'means' is a *specialized form of the copula*" (MFC: 431).

## Expressions and their uses

The fact that expressions have meanings is no more ontologically troublesome for Sellars than the fact that garden tools have uses.[12] It is natural to ask what counts as the function of an expression: what is it about the use of an expression that determines its meaning? Sellars points to three important roles that linguistic expressions play that can determine their meanings:

- language-entry transitions, in which a speaker responds to perceptible (or introspectible) objects, events or situations with linguistic activity;
- intralinguistic moves, in which a speaker's linguistic activity tends to occur in patterns or sequences that accord with various transition rules of the language (especially valid inference rules); and

• language-exit transitions, in which a speaker responds to certain kinds of linguistic episodes (e.g., "I shall now write my philosophy paper") with appropriate behaviour (in this case, sitting down and starting to write the paper).[13]

The first thing to notice is that no expression has meaning independent of the linguistic system to which it belongs. Like Quine and Davidson, Sellars goes beyond the Fregean dictum that words have meaning only in the context of a sentence, for he asserts that words have meaning only in the context of an entire language. This excludes certain primitive forms of empiricism that try to ground the meaning of words or ideas in isolable acts of ostensive definition or abstraction (see Chapter 5).

A great deal more can be said about each of the three kinds of roles expressions can play. Consider language-entry transitions. Not every expression will figure often in language-entry transitions. The meaning of expressions in the "observation language", expressions that describe the observable and/or introspectible characteristics of objects and events, will depend to a significant degree on how the expressions are used in language-entry transitions. Other expressions, such as 'transfinite', may only rarely, if ever, show up in language-entry transitions.[14]

There are several reasons, however, for thinking that intralinguistic moves occupy a pre-eminent role for Sellars. For instance, consider exclamations such as "Alas!" Such terms certainly have meaning, and they have correct translations into other languages ('Alas' is *'hélas'* in French, 'Oy vay' in Brooklyn). Sellars's treatment of meaning accounts for this. Yet we do not think of these as expressing *concepts* or as having significant descriptive content because they do not commit us to any particular inferential moves in the language game.[15]

The most significant reason to emphasize intralinguistic moves is that languages are a proper subset of representational systems, and all empirically usable representational systems also have entry and exit transitions. Even a fairly simple thermostat can possess an empirically usable representational system in this sense. In as much as Sellars thinks of both formation and transformation rules as intralinguistic, it is the intralinguistic moves (the syntactic structures and inference patterns available in the language) that distinguish languages from other forms of representational systems.[16] It is especially important to Sellars that human languages are rich enough to contain or generate their own metalanguages. But it is important not to take too narrow a view of the formation and transformation rules of a language; they should not be confined to the strictly formal rules that are codified in textbooks on symbolic logic. In particular, Sellars insists that we have to employ the notion of a *material principle of inference* as well as the familiar notion of a formal principle of inference, such as *modus ponens.*

An expression's contribution to good inferences plays the most significant role in determining its meaning. This doctrine is a familiar one as applied to the logical constants, such as *and, either-or* and *if–then,* the meanings of which are determined by the formally valid inferences in which they occur. Sellars contends in "Inference and Meaning" (1953) that "material transformation rules determine the descriptive meaning of the expressions of a language within the framework established by its logical transformation rules" (IM: 336). The inference from "*x* is red" to "*x* is coloured" is formally invalid, but it is clearly a good inference. Sellars holds that it is not an enthymeme in which the premise $(\forall x)(\text{red } (x) \supset \text{coloured } (x))$ is left out; rather, there is an extralogical or material rule of inference in our language that is partially constitutive of the meaning of 'red' and 'colour' and that licenses this inference. The example he uses in "Inference and Meaning" is the material inference from "It is raining" to "The streets will be wet". This is significant, for the connection between rain and wet streets is not genus–species or determinate–determinable, but cause and effect. Sellars thinks that the meaning of our terms is infused with material inferences that reflect the place of the object or characteristic in nature as grasped by the framework the language embodies. Every meaningful empirical language is effectively an outline of a complete *world-story.* Causal laws, in this view, are material mode expressions of (proposed) material rules of inference, not descriptive statements of fact. We shall return to this conception of law in Chapter 6.

The argument in "Inference and Meaning" rests on the claim that without invoking the notion of such material rules of inference, there is no appropriate explanation of subjunctive conditionals, which in Sellars's view make explicit such material rules of inference. This aspect of Sellars's philosophy has been worked out in great detail for some forms of language by Robert Brandom in *Making It Explicit.*[17]

A word of warning: Sellars's notion of a material rule of inference is not a mere throwaway. Although we cannot fully explore the notion here, it will return: it plays a role in his ontology, his epistemology and his philosophy of science. Brandom's work shows how rich a notion it can be when used wisely.

## "Stands for" and "refers"

The above description of Sellars's treatment of claims about meanings is the tip of the iceberg. After all, statements about the meaning of expressions are only one way to specify the semantic value of linguistic expressions. Consider,

> *'Dreieckig'* (in German) *stands for* triangularity.
> *'Der Ball ist rund'* (in German) *stands for* (the proposition) that the ball is round.
> *'Venedig'* (in German) *refers* to Venice.

These appear in their surface grammar to be relational statements and are treated by Sellars as metalinguistic statements containing a distributive singular term as the subject, a specialized form of the copula and an illustrating sortal following the verb.

However, there are other differences that need to be accounted for. In sentences with the 'stand for' locution, for instance, the term on the right-hand side of the verb is clearly a noun that appears to name an abstract entity, either a universal or a proposition. Sellars makes several interpretive moves in this case.

> In general, I suggest that so-called nominalizing devices which when added to expressions, form corresponding abstract singular terms, thus '-ity,' '-hood,' '-ness,' '-tion,' '-that ...', etc., are to be construed as quoting contexts which (a) form meta-linguistic functional sortals and (b) turn them into distributive singular terms.
> (NAO: 80)

That is, these nominalizing devices serve the function of dot-quoting. Thus, the two 'stand for' sentences become, respectively:

> The *'dreieckig'* is the German ·triangular·.
> The *'Der Ball ist rund'* is the German ·the ball is round·.

These, in turn, are equivalent to

> *'Dreieckig'*s are German ·triangular·s.
> *'Der Ball ist rund'*s are German ·the ball is round·s.

Thus, the 'stand for' locution is just another way of giving a functional classification of certain inscriptions or sound patterns.

But we can ask, as does Sellars, "Why are there *two* semantical statement forms, involving the pseudo-predicates 'means' and 'stands for' respectively, which have, in the last analysis, the same reconstruction?" (NAO: 82). His answer is that 'stands for' is useful because its (surface) structure suits it better to make evident the relation to truth implicit in such sentences. Consider, for instance,

'*Der Ball ist rund*' (in German) means *the ball is round.*

As noted, the phrase 'the ball is round' occurs in an odd way in this sentence, neither straightforwardly used nor straightforwardly mentioned. It:

> does not have the clear cut surface grammar of a referring expression, though the context
> — is true
> is a predicative one and calls for a subject which does have this surface grammar. (NAO: 82)

There is indication in the surface grammar of a meaning claim that the expression on the right-hand side is clearly a metalinguistic referring expression that would be equally at home as the subject of a truth claim. In the 'stands for' locution, the expression on the right-hand side has the surface form of a noun (phrase) that can serve in such capacity.[18] Although the 'means' and the 'stands for' locutions are ultimately identical, the presence in our language of both:

> illustrates the subtlety with which surface grammar reconciles pressures which arise from the fact that however intimate the connection between meaning and truth, the *immediate* function of meaning statements requires a surface grammar which highlights the rehearsing *use* of expressions, whereas the *immediate* function of truth statements requires a surface grammar of *reference* and *predication.* (NAO: 83)

In Chapter 4, a good deal more time is devoted to this analysis of 'meaning' and 'standing for', for it is crucial to Sellars's nominalism.

Many eyebrows will no doubt have been raised at the suggestion that 'refers' is to be given a treatment strictly parallel with meaning. Reference is supposed by many to be the relation that pins language to the world, and the temptation to construe reference claims as statements of a relation between expression and object is very difficult to resist. But Sellars argues that a sentence such as "'*Venedig*' (in German) refers to Venice" is clearly in the metalanguage. We cannot, then, consistently interpret the term on the right-hand side of it to be an object-language term being given a normal use. So Venice is not, in this sentence, really being referred to at all. Thinking that it is confuses

the object-language and metalanguage levels within a complex natural language and opens the gates to further philosophical confusions.
Sellars also cannot treat reference claims as having the same depth grammar as meaning claims. The reason for this is not difficult to see. While we can say that both

> *'Venedig'* (in German) refers to Venice

and

> *'Venedig'*s are the German ·Venice·s

are true, we can't say that both

> *'Die Königin der Adria'* (in German) refers to Venice

and

> *'Die Königin der Adria'*s are German ·Venice·s

are true. The first member of each pair is, indeed, true. The analysis that works with meaning will not work with reference. *'Venedig'* and *'Die Königin der Adria'* both refer to Venice, but there are significant enough differences in their uses that it is highly implausible that they are functionally similar enough to consider them both ·Venice·s. For instance, although they are both singular referring expressions, *'Venedig'* is, like 'Venice', a proper name, whereas *'Die Königin der Adria'* (the queen of the Adriatic) is a definite description. Reference is extensional, not intensional like meaning. To accommodate this, Sellars introduces a quantification into his reading of the 'refers' locution.

> We introduce a variable 'S' (read 'sense') which takes as its substituends common nouns formed by dot quoting. . . . We also introduce the form
> $S_i$ is materially equivalent to $S_j$
> examples of which would be
> ·Rational animal· is materially equivalent to ·featherless biped·
> which is true if and only if
> $(x)$ $x$ is a rational animal $\equiv x$ is a featherless biped
> and
> ·Plato· is materially equivalent to ·the teacher of Aristotle·
> which is true if and only if
> $(f)$ $f(\text{Plato}) \equiv f(\text{the teacher of Aristotle})$ (SM III §63: 84)

Our sample sentences, "'*Venedig*' (in German) refers to Venice" and "'*Die Königin der Adria*' refers to Venice" are analysed, respectively, as

> For some S, *'Venedig'* (in German) stands for S, and S is materially equivalent to ·Venice·

and

> For some S, *'Die Königin der Adria'* (in German) stands for S, and S is materially equivalent to ·Venice·.

These sentences are both true. The quantification over senses combined with the extensionalist notion of material equivalence makes Sellars's analysis of the reference rubric extensional.[19]

Given Sellars's other philosophical commitments, this analysis might be surprising, for it involves quantifying over senses, which seems to conflict with Sellars's nominalism. But there are two responses to this charge. First, although we are instructed to call the things quantified over 'senses', Sellars does *not* treat them as abstract objects. The substituends are "common nouns formed by dot quoting". If we further analyse the analysans of our last sample sentence, making everything explicit, we would get

> For some ·S·, *'Die Königin der Adria'*'s are German ·S·s (namely, ·the queen of the Adriatic·s), and ·S· is materially equivalent to ·Venice·.

All we are committed to here is the existence of functionally classifiable expressions of languages. Secondly, discussed in Chapter 4, Sellars rejects the notion that quantification, and particularly quantification in the metalanguage, is the measure of existential commitment. He therefore also rejects the idea that his analysis of reference locutions violates his nominalism.

# Relating language and world

Sellars is resolute in treating the traditional semantic terms 'means', 'stands for' and, perhaps most significantly, 'refers' as metalinguistic expressions by which we classify object-language expressions with respect to their functional role. None of these terms names or describes a language–world relation. One advantage of this approach is that semantic theory itself makes no ontological commitments to anything other than the expressions it talks about. But does this approach have the crushing disadvantage that it cuts language off from the world altogether? Surely language and the world are related to each other. Semantics certainly *appears* to be about that language–world relation.

Given Sellars's non-relational analysis of semantic vocabulary, how are we to understand the relation between language and world?

Sellars provides for language-world relations aplenty, although they need to be the right kinds of relations. What relationship, if any, is there between the words 'Venice' and '*Venedig*' (in English and German, respectively) and that city at the head of the Adriatic Sea? In denying that meaning and reference are relations, Sellars certainly does not mean to deny that there are relationships – and *real* relationships at that – between (tokens of) the expressions and the city. Yet the way many philosophers have spoken about meaning and reference implies that meaning and reference are themselves particular, specific, real relations that can hold between two or more entities. That is part of what Sellars is denying. Talk of *the* meaning relation or *the* reference relation is nonsense.

In accordance with Sellars's basic nominalistic naturalism, he believes that what I alluded to above as *real* relations are relations between items in the spatiotemporal, causal nexus. Real relations need not be themselves spatiotemporal or causal relations; for instance, one rose may be more red than another or more odorous. But at least the relata are real items in space-time and there is some network of spatiotemporal or causal relations that underlies the "more red" relation. There are, for instance, no *real* relationships to Santa Claus, unicorns or square circles; similarly, the relationships detailed in pure mathematics are not *real*, although they often have real analogues in the spatiotemporal order. Nor are there *real* relations between rules or norms and events or objects in the world. In order to understand how language relates to the real world, we have to understand how language really relates to the world, that is, what kinds of *real* relations there are between languages and the world. And this means considering language not as a formal structure constituted by normative formation and transformation rules, but as a manifold of events and objects in space-time causally interacting with other spatiotemporal events, whether linguistic or not.

So, in Sellars's view, there are most certainly relations between 'Venice' and Venice, 'Socrates' and Socrates, 'red' and red things. But it is simply useless and misleading to say that there is *a* (univocal) relation, the reference relation, between these items, especially since it is true that 'Pegasus' refers to Pegasus. The *real* relations between 'Venice' and Venice, 'Socrates' and Socrates, 'red' and red things are not relations between expression *types* and items in the real world, for expression types are not items in space-time. Rather, the real relations between 'Venice' and Venice and so on are relations between expression *tokens,* particular spatiotemporal events or objects, and the real-world item. These relations are extremely complex, and there is enough play that, although *some* singular terms (how many? which ones?) in the language must have tokens that participate in such real relations to the things they "denote", it is not necessary that all singular terms participate in such real relations to the things we say they denote. Thus 'Pegasus' can refer to Pegasus, even though tokens of 'Pegasus' do *not* bear the kinds of real relationships to Pegasus that tokens of 'Secretariat' bear to Secretariat.

So what are the real relations between language and world that tie them together? Here is a "first instalment of the explanation" Sellars gives in *Science and Metaphysics* (1967):

(1) Non-demonstrative referring expressions must themselves belong to the 'natural' order and be connected with objects in a way which involves language entry transitions, intra-linguistic moves (consequence uniformities) and language departure transitions (willings-out-loud).

(2) There must be a relatively stable, if skeletal, framework of propositions (involving these referring expressions) which describe the spatio-temporal location of these objects with respect to each other' [*sic.*].

(3) A proper part of this skeletal framework must "specify location of the language user in his environment".

(4) Rehearsings of this skeletal framework must gear in with the use of demonstratives to "specify the location with respect to *here-now* of the objects with which the referring expressions are correlated".[20]                      (SM V §30: 125–6)

According to condition (1), non-demonstrative referring expressions such as 'Venice' must be items in a language that is used responsively in the world. The language must make provision for the potential use of the term in numerous language-entry transitions, such as "Ladies and gentlemen, we are now arriving in Venice; will all passengers please disembark", or "Look out of the window, Daddy; is that Venice?". The language must also provide for uses in intralinguistic moves, for example, "Venice is west of Trieste; Milan is west of Venice; so Milan is west of Trieste". This example also illustrates (2), the requirement that the language provide for the descriptions of the relative spatiotemporal locations of objects referred to. The language must also have provision for language-departure transitions, where an example would be the announcement "I've decided to take my wife to Venice for our twentieth anniversary," followed (ultimately) by a trip to Venice (or at least efforts to arrange such a trip). The language must allow users to locate themselves in the general and stable spatio-temporal framework it provides for description of objects in the world: "I live in New England, and I visited Venice in the spring of 2002". In addition, the language must contain demonstrative or indexical expressions that enable it to express the relations between the current situation of language use and objects talked about: "I'm in New England now, so Venice is to the east". The language-entry sentences used above to illustrate requirement (1) are also examples of (4).

The overall picture here is that *uses* of the language, *tokens* of linguistic expressions, must correlate with objects and events in the world in certain ways. These correlations are *real* relations, uniformities between the production by language users in certain situations of certain tokens and objects or events in space-time.[21] It is crucial to see that the correlations Sellars is pointing to here are *not* to be identified with a reference or meaning relation. Equally important, these correlations are not (generally) rule-followings. By this I mean that one could think there is a "rule of language" that, for instance, "In English, one ought to call Venice 'Venice'" or "In German, one ought to call Venice '*Venedig*'", and that it is in virtue of these rules that 'Venice' or '*Venedig*' refers to Venice.[22] In some sense, of course, there are rules concerning what things are to be called, but upon analysis, statement of these rules will, naturally, turn out to be in the metalanguage, and thus be no more statements of language-reality connections than meaning or reference claims. The real connections between tokens of 'Venice' and the city at the head of the Adriatic are not forged by our following rules of action in using the linguistic tokens.

Now that the issue of linguistic rules has been raised, let us meet it head on, for it forms a major theme that runs through a number of Sellars's essays.

## Language and rules

Emphasis on the rule-governedness of language has been a constant theme in twentieth-century Anglophone philosophy. Sellars clearly thinks it has afforded important insights, but he recognizes that it harbours significant dangers as well. The notion of a rule is very complex. An inadequate appreciation of the kinds of rules and the different ways in which our behaviour can be rule-governed leads to substantial philosophical error: rationalistic apriorism, reductive descriptivism,[23] or even the myth of the given.[24] Sellars needs a conception of rules and rule-governed behaviour that satisfies two criteria: (i) it must not reject or neglect the normativity or prescriptive force of rules in favour of empirical regularities; and (ii) it must not reify rules or normativity into abstract or ideal existences that we grasp in some non-empirical intuition. Both approaches oversimplify, either forcing a naive naturalism or rejecting naturalism altogether.

Because the topic of rules raises the question of the being of the normative, it goes to the very heart of Sellars's philosophy. Indeed, the question of the being of the normative is, I believe, *the* fundamental question within Sellars's philosophy. The deeper issues concerning the place of the normative in the world, however, will have to await the final chapter of this book. To begin to make sense of the complex issues raised by rules, here I will confine myself to the specific application to language of the distinctions Sellars draws.

Rule-governed behaviour stands in contrast to several other forms of activity. On the one hand, it contrasts to the merely chaotic, in which there is no regularity at all. On the other hand, it is equally to be distinguished from *law*-governed activity, in which there is exceptionless regularity in accordance with a law of nature. Rule-governed behaviour must exhibit regularity, but that regularity need not be absolutely exceptionless: breaking the rule must be possible. Of course, the mere fact of some generally reliable (although not absolute) uniformity does not entail the presence of rule-governed activity. In order to be rule-governed, the activity must occur or take the form it has *because of the rule*. Here is the crux: how does the rule enter into the explanation and/or generation of the activity?

The paradigm of rule-governed behaviour that many people seem to operate with might be called rule-*obeying* behaviour. In rule-obeying behaviour, (i) there is a conscious subject who possesses an awareness of a rule that is applicable in the circumstances the subject takes herself to be in, and (ii) the rule has motivational force (directly or indirectly) for the subject, as a consequence of which (iii) the subject forms an intention to perform the action dictated by the rule, which intention then causes the subject to behave accordingly. Notice, this is a recipe for *action*, not just behaviour. Stopping for a red traffic light late at night at a deserted intersection because it is the rule (and one knows it is the rule) that one stops for red traffic lights would be a paradigmatic case of rule-obeying behaviour. Notice the cognitive complexity involved in action: in paradigmatic rule-obeying behaviour, both the rule and the circumstances are present and operative via an explicit *awareness* of them. The first point Sellars makes about rule-governed behaviour, and linguistic behaviour in particular, is that it *cannot all* be of this paradigmatic rule-obeying kind.

We have to ask what a rule actually is and, correlatively, what constitutes an awareness of a rule.

> A rule ... finds its expression either in what are classified as non-declarative grammatical forms, or else in declarative sentences with certain special terms such as 'correct,' 'proper,' 'right,' etc., serving to distinguish them from generalizations.     (LRB: 299)

However it may be expressed, is the rule *itself* something linguistic, or is it something non-linguistic? This question is crucial, for if rules themselves are linguistic entities, and rule-following presupposes an *awareness* of the rule followed, then there is a serious problem confronting the notion that linguistic activity is rule-governed behaviour. In particular, a linguistic conception of rules of language seems to make it impossible to explain how one could ever learn a first language.

> *Thesis.* Learning to use a language (L) is learning to obey the rules of L.
>
> *But,* a rule which enjoins the doing of an action (A) is a sentence in a language which contains an expression for A.
>
> *Hence,* a rule which enjoins the using of a linguistic expression (E) is a sentence in a language which contains an expression for E – in other words, a sentence in a *meta*language.
>
> *Consequently,* learning to obey the rules for L presupposes the ability to use the metalanguage (ML) in which the rules for L are formulated.
>
> *So that* learning to use a language (L) presupposes having learned to use a metalanguage (ML). And by the same token, having learned to use ML presupposes having learned to use a *meta*metalanguage (MML) and so on.
>
> *But* this is impossible (a vicious regress).
>
> *Therefore,* the thesis is absurd and must be rejected.
>
> (SRLG in SPR: 321)

Taking rule-obeying behaviour to be the form of all rule-governed behaviour makes it impossible to think of rules as fundamentally linguistic in form, on pain of the vicious regress sketched above. An

alternative would be a view of rules as real but non-empirical structures (permissions, demands or prohibitions) "out there" in the world
and available to our cognitive processes via some form of intuition.[25]
As real non-empirical structures, rules would be independent of
language, although representable in language. But this metaphysically realistic alternative, Sellars argues, cannot succeed, for the
notion of awareness itself is embedded in and makes sense only inside
a system of normative demands or rules. We cannot offload all the
normativity on to "real structures in the world" that are independent
of awareness itself.

> It may be an over-simplification to identify reasoning, thinking,
> being aware of possibilities, connections, etc., with playing a
> *language* game (e.g., French, German), but that it is playing a
> game is indicated by the use of such terms as 'correct', 'mistake',
> etc., in commenting on them.                (SRLG in SPR: 324)

Ultimately, Sellars contends, the "game" of reasoning – at least as
played by human beings – within which awareness plays its role cannot
be fully explicated without bringing language back into the picture.

Still, in true Sellarsian fashion, Sellars finds something importantly
right about this realistic suggestion, for the metaphysical realist:

> sought to offer us an account in which learning a game involves
> learning to do what one does *because doing these things is making
> moves in the game* (let us abbreviate this to 'because of the moves
> [of the game]') where doing what one does *because of the moves*
> need not involve using language about the moves. Where he went
> astray was in holding that while doing what one does because of
> the moves need not involve using language about the moves it
> does involve *being aware* of the moves demanded and permitted
> by the game, for it was this which led to the regress.
>                                              (SRLG in SPR: 325)

Therefore, Sellars sketches a form of rule-governed behaviour that is
not rule-obeying behaviour, a form of rule-governed behaviour in
which things are done *because of the rules*, but not because of an
*awareness of the rules*.

This form of rule-governed behaviour is a species of what Sellars
calls "pattern-governed behavior":

> The key to the concept of a linguistic rule is its complex relation
> to pattern-governed linguistic behavior. The general concept of
> pattern governed behavior is a familiar one. Roughly it is the

concept of behavior which exhibits a pattern, not because it is brought about by the intention that it exhibit this pattern, but because the propensity to emit behavior of the pattern has been selectively reinforced, and the propensity to emit behavior which does not conform to this pattern selectively extinguished.

(MFC: 423)

Notice that the concept of pattern-governed behaviour applies generally to the behaviour of organisms and is a readily available element in the scientist's repertoire of explanatory devices. An organism exhibiting some pattern-governed behaviour can nonetheless be described as acting *because of the rules*, even though the organism has no awareness of those rules, if the organism acquired that pattern of behaviour *because* that pattern conforms to the rules.

If patterned governed behavior can arise by "natural" selection, it can also arise by purposive selection on the part of trainers. They can be construed as reasoning.

Pattern-behavior of such and such a kind *ought to be* exhibited by trainees, hence we, the trainers, *ought to do* this and that, as likely to bring it about that it *is* exhibited.　　(MFC: 423)

Again, there is nothing particularly linguistic in this notion of rule-governed patterned behaviour: animal trainers can have in mind a set of rules they want their animals to follow and train them accordingly. The subsequent behaviour of the (successfully) trained animal will be, in the appropriate sense, rule-governed behaviour, although the animal has no awareness of the rules as such.

There is, however, a difference between the rules that govern the animal and the rules that the self-conscious trainer is following, which Sellars marks as a distinction between an *ought-to-do* and an *ought-to-be*. In other places, Sellars calls these "rules of action or performance", and "rules of criticism" respectively.[26] Rules of action tell us what to do in given circumstances and assume that we have the cognitive and conative structures to recognize the circumstances and the rule and then apply the rule. Rules of criticism make no such assumptions: they endorse a state of affairs as to be realized (*ceteris paribus*). It ought to be the case, for instance, that one's dog comes when called, stays when ordered to and so on. "Come when called" is not a rule the dog follows by learning the rule as such, recognizing the circumstance and applying the rule. The dog is *trained* to come when called; that is, the trainers, themselves recognizing the "ought-to-be", selectively reward or punish behaviours until the requisite pattern of behaviour is ingrained. The *trainers* are often following rules of action (such as "do not hit the dog" or "decrease frequency of reinforcement slowly as the desired behaviour becomes more regular"), but the dogs are not.

Two quick points: if we did not conform to a large number of ought-to-be's, including patterns of linguistic behaviour, we would not be in a position to be agents, followers of ought-to-do's; any rules of action presuppose a groundwork of rules of criticism. And this applies equally well to linguistic rules. There are linguistic rules of action,[27] but the primary being of linguistic rules is as rules of criticism.

> It can scarcely be over-emphasized that to approach language in terms of the paradigm of *action* is to make a commitment which, if the concept of action is taken seriously, and the concept of rule is taken seriously, leads to (a) the Cartesian idea of linguistic episodes as *essentially* the sort of thing brought about by an agent whose conceptualizing is not linguistic; (b) an inability to understand the rule-governed character of this conceptualizing itself, as contrasted with its overt expression. For if thought is analogous to linguistic activity to the extent implied by Plato's metaphor "dialogue in the soul," the idea that overt speech is *action* and its rules *rules of action* will generate the idea that all inner speech is *action* and *its* rules *rules of action*, which leads to paradox and absurdity without end. (LTC: 98)

Just as importantly, *ought-to-be*'s imply (for agents) *ought-to-do*'s.[28] Rules of criticism have no grip on the world except in so far as agents undertake actions that bring the behavioural patterns into line with them. Full command of a rule-governed system requires awareness of the rules.

> One isn't a full-fledged member of the linguistic community until one not only *conforms* to linguistic ought-to-be's (and may-be's) by exhibiting the required uniformities, but grasps these ought-to-be's and may-be's themselves (i.e., knows the rules of the language.). (LTC: 101)

But there seems to be an obvious problem with Sellars's line of reasoning here. Sellars argues that linguistic activity cannot be action *all the way down*. But does he not also need to argue that it cannot be action *all the way back*? Rules of criticism imply rules of action. If there are no agents around to bring the world into conformity with the ought-to-be's, those ought-to-be's have no grip on reality at all. Training youngsters to exhibit correct linguistic patterns still requires agents acting on rules of action, agents who are aware of the rules as such. Sellars's story may explain how individual persons can come to have knowledge of a language without already knowing a language, and thus resolve the problem for the conception of language as a rule-governed activity quoted above from "Some Reflections on Language Games" (1954). But it still leaves mysterious the origin of language itself. Individual language learners learn their language from others who already know it and who have a metalanguage available in which to state the rules of the language. How did language get started in the first place, before anyone could be said to know the language already?

How language originated is a question to which no one has a satisfactory answer, and Sellars never addresses it directly. It is not hard to sketch the rough outlines of the story Sellars would have to tell. The evolutionary development of an increasingly complex representational-*cum*-communication system within the species reaches a point of complexity that permits reflexive metarepresentations. Language about language comes to be possible. Given the utility of the system, people come to care about it and cultivate it. The structures and functions of the items in the evolved representation–communication system can thereby transform from being *normal* (present because naturally selected) to *normative* (present because selected by the linguistic community in virtue of "the way things are done"). We are unable to fill in the blanks in this sketch, but no rival story is any more plausible. That hardly constitutes a ringing endorsement of the story, but it will have to do. Perhaps further work in evolutionary psychology will cast more light on this topic.

We have seen that the linguistic rules cannot be primarily rules of action. This means that the fundamental linguistic moves, the language-entry transitions, basic intralinguistic moves, and language-departure transitions mentioned above are not only "*acquired* as pattern governed activity, they *remain* pattern governed activity. The linguistic activities which are perceptual takings, inferences and volitions *never* become *obeyings* of *ought-to-do* rules" (MFC: 424). This is significant because, in Sellars's view, empiricism has tended to treat observation or perception reports as *actions*, governed by rules of action. "Now, certain overly enthusiastic regulists have spoken of the 'sense meaning rules' of a language, arguing that the hook-up of an empirically meaningful language with the world is a matter of rules of linguistic usage" (LRB: 301). This is echoed in Part VIII of "Empiricism and the Philosophy of Mind":

Thus, it has been claimed, not without plausibility, that whereas *ordinary* empirical statements can be *correctly* made without being *true,* observation reports resemble analytic statements in that being correctly made is a sufficient as well as necessary condition of their truth. And it has been inferred from this – somewhat hastily, I believe – that "correctly making" the report "This is green" is a matter of "following the rules of the use of 'this', 'is', and 'green'." (EPM: §33, in SPR: 166; in KMG: 245)

If this rule-following is rule-*obeying*, it requires that there be some form of pre-linguistic awareness or recognition, which brings us "face to face with givenness in its most straightforward form" (EPM: §34, in SPR: 167; in KMG: 246). So Sellars takes it to be of the utmost philosophical importance to recognize that the correctness involved in observation reports, in simple inferences and in acting out one's volitions is not the correctness of obeying an ought-to-do, but that of an ought-to-be. We establish, via our training, a set of causal dispositions, the structure of which is, on the whole, endorsed by our linguistic community. The consilience of our *de facto* causal dispositions with the normatively endorsed or correct patterns of linguistic responses is what ties world and language together, and the actualizations of these causal dispositions are not rule-obeying behaviour. Our linguistic responses to the world have a double life: they are, given our training, simply *caused* by our encounter with the world; at the same time, they generally conform to the rules constitutive of the language. Thus are the real and the logical orders knit together.

## Truth

There are two other important elements in Sellars's treatment of the language–world relation: *truth* and *picturing.* The influence of pragmatism is clear in Sellars's treatment of truth, but the notion of picturing, he claims, sets his treatment apart from classical pragmatism. To begin with, it is clear that truth is a semantic concept and subject to a treatment parallel to that of all the other semantic conceptions: truth, as a property of sentences, propositions or propositional mental contents does not name or describe a language–world relation, known as 'correspondence'. If there is something to the correspondence theory of truth, it is not that there is some univocal real-world relation that holds between sentences and states of affairs in virtue of which sentences are true. Part of the attraction of the correspondence theory of truth is accounted for by Tarski's semantic theory of truth.[29] However, Sellars believes that there is something to the correspondence theory above and beyond the semantic theory, and this element Sellars calls 'picturing'.

But first, more about truth. It has been customary since Tarski to emphasize the importance of T-sentences in the theory of truth:

That snow is white is true ≡ snow is white.

It is important, according to Sellars, to understand the role of such sentences.

26. Now it is clear, I take it, despite rumblings on the horizon, that such equivalences ... thus

That snow is white is true ↔ snow is white

do not formulate identities of sense. On the other hand, they *are* conceptually necessary. The account of this conceptual necessity I wish to recommend is that these equivalences "follow" from the "definition" of truth in that for a proposition to be true is for it to be assertible, where this means not *capable* of being asserted (which it must be to be a proposition at all) but *correctly* assertible; assertible, that is, in accordance with the relevant semantical rules, and on the basis of such additional, though unspecified, information as these rules may require ... 'True', then, means *semantically* assertible ('S-assertible') and the varieties of truth correspond to the relevant varieties of semantical rule.

27. From this point of view,

The ·snow is white· is true

has the sense of

The ·snow is white· is S-assertible

and the implication

That snow is white is true → snow is white

is not an element in an *extensional* definition of 'true', a recursive listing of truth conditions, as, in effect, it is on Carnap's account, but is rather a consequence of the above *intensional* definition of 'true', in the sense that the assertion of the right-hand side of the implication statement is a *performance of the kind authorized by the truth statement on the left.*          (SM IV §§26–7: 100–101)

This passage requires some unpacking. First, the "semantical rules" Sellars speaks of are the rules of criticism, the ought-to-be's, that define the standard against which linguistic activity is judged to be correct or incorrect. Thus, the "semantical rules" include not only rules of grammar and the logical rules of inference, but the rules – the ought-to-be's – that govern language-entry and -exit transitions, and those intralinguistic moves governed by material rules of inference. In other words, according to Sellars, to say of a sentence that it is true is to say of it that it would be a piece of ideal linguistic behaviour, linguistic behaviour in which everything goes right and is above criticism.[30]

Secondly, when Sellars speaks of "varieties of truth" he has in mind the distinctions between empirical, logical, mathematical, ethical and other such varieties of truths. Consider the following sentences:

Bill deVries is over 6 feet tall.
$2 + 2 = 4$
It is *prima facie* wrong to cause pain.

Sellars's position is that there is a generic sense of 'true' that applies to all these sentences, namely, that they would be ideal pieces of linguistic behaviour that conform to all the relevant rules. But the relevant rules differ. For example, the ought-to-be's governing perceptual reports are relevant to the correctness of the first, but not the second sentence above.

Thirdly, 'true', as a semantic predicate of sentences, is clearly in the metalanguage, and its principal force is *practical*: its use conveys authority to assert the expression of which it is predicated. Thus, the primary role of 'true' is captured, according to Sellars, in inferences such as

That Bill deVries is over 6 feet tall is true.
So, Bill deVries is over 6 feet tall.

or

'$2 + 2 = 4$' is true.
So, $2 + 2 = 4$

and

$2 + 2 = 4$
So, '$2 + 2 = 4$' is true.

Basically, since true sentences would be semantically ideal linguistic performances (abstracting from such directly pragmatic speech-situation-relative considerations as relevance and concision), one has the authority to assert such sentences.

Truth, on this account, is as non-relational as all the other semantical properties and "relations" Sellars has dealt with. That gives rise to qualms about the adequacy of his treatment of truth. Does Sellars end up relativizing truth entirely to one's language? Must we say that "The Earth is the centre of the universe" is true in Ptolemaic Greek and therefore as true as any sentence can be?

As a first response, Sellars recognizes a use of 'true' that is not language-bound.

> 23. In drawing his contrast between the 'absolute' and the 'semantical' sense of 'true', Carnap had in mind the distinction between the use of 'true' just illustrated ["That Socrates is wise is true"] and that which is found in
>
> 'Socrates est sage' (in F) is true
>
> where reference is made to a specific language. From the stand-point of our analysis he mistakenly infers from the absurdity of
>
> That Socrates is wise is true in English
>
> that the expression 'that Socrates is wise' here stands for a *non*-linguistic entity. According to our account, *that Socrates is wise* is *inter*-linguistic rather than *non*-linguistic, its inter-linguistic character being constituted by the use of 'that' to form a singular term which we have reconstructed as 'the ·Socrates is wise·'. Our concern, therefore, is with the contrived statement,
>
> The ·Socrates is wise· is true.          (SM IV §23: 99–100)

Thus, for Sellars, truth is not *language*-relative, but it is tied to a conceptual scheme that can be realized in different languages.

Secondly, Sellars does not regard languages or conceptual schemes as fixed entities, frozen in time. Languages – and perforce the rules that constitute them – change, and the changes are not merely random or irrational. Sellars recognizes this important fact by defining a sense of 'true' that can be applied across conceptual schemes. This involves identifying families of counterpart propositions, namely, sets of propositions that are relevantly similar in function within their respective schemes. Our own conceptual scheme, however, occupies a privileged position for us.

> Notice, however, that however many sophisticated senses of 'true' may be introduced, and however important they may be, the

> connection of truth with *our current conceptual structure* remains
> essential, for the cash value of S-assertibility is assertion by us *hic
> et nunc.* SM V §53: 134)

This cross-conceptual-scheme conception of truth can also be
extended to make sense of the Peircean notion of an *ideal* language
and/or conceptual framework.[31] While it may have been the case that
assertions of the centrality of the Earth in the universe seemed
unexceptionable to Ptolemy's linguistic community, translated into
our language they no longer hold water. *We* are certainly not committed to "It is true that the Earth is the centre of the universe". Although
we are committed to those propositions that belong to the framework
with which we confront the world, we can nevertheless recognize that
our framework is fallible and that a great deal of it is destined to be
revised or replaced in time.

Peirce's assertion that "the opinion which is fated to be ultimately
agreed to by all who investigate, is what we mean by the truth, and the
object represented in this opinion is the real"[32] has been widely
criticized because it is unclear whether there is a unique final theory
towards which enquiry will converge. Sellars, however, suggests a
solution to this problem.

> 75. Notice that although the concepts of 'ideal truth' and 'what
> really exists' are defined in terms of a Peircean conceptual struc-
> ture they do not require that there ever be a Peirceish community.
> Peirce himself fell into difficulty because, by not taking into
> account the dimension of 'picturing', he had no Archimedean point
> outside the series of actual and possible beliefs in terms of which
> to define the ideal or limit to which members of this series might
> approximate. (SM V §75: 142)

# Picturing

Sellars's notion of picturing has not received a great deal of attention
and has been criticized even by some of his more orthodox interpreters,
including Jay Rosenberg.[33] My interpretation of picturing, however,
gives that notion a recognizable and valuable role and shows that
Sellars was again presciently anticipating subsequent developments
in epistemology and philosophy of mind. Briefly, I argue that Sellars's
claim that there must be, in any empirically meaningful language, a
set of terms (in particular, referring expressions) the use of which

constructs a *picture* of objects and their relations in the world, is equivalent to the claim that the occurrence of some linguistic tokens (whether in speech or thought) forms a system of events that bears a complex multidimensional isomorphism to the objects and events in the world of the language user. Sellars's picturing requirement plays a role in his semantic theory parallel to the role he gives to the reliability requirement on observation reports in his theory of knowledge (see Chapter 5).

But that is not the only role picturing plays for Sellars. It also plays a role in his ontology, which makes it more difficult to spell out the notion of picturing at this point, in as much as we are only at the beginning of our examination of his thought and have not yet discussed any of the details of his ontology or his epistemology. Sellars's conception of picturing is inspired by Wittgenstein's use of the notion in the *Tractatus*; unfortunately, using Wittgenstein's original conception to illuminate Sellars's adaptation of it is an explanation *obscurum per obscurius*.

The first thing to note is that the picturing relation does not hold between every kind of statement and the world: only first-order, matter-of-factual atomic statements picture. This requires a distinction between atomic and molecular statements, which Sellars takes to be "a familiar one, easy to indicate, but difficult to refine" (SM V §10: 119). Clearly, atomic statements contain no logical words, no quantificational structure. In a subject–predicate language they are configurations of names and predicates; in Jumblese – the artificial language Sellars invented, inspired by Wittgenstein's *Tractatus* – which dispenses with predicates altogether in favour of different ways of writing and arranging names, atomic sentences would be quite literally configurations of names. The picturing relation, as Sellars interprets it, is not a relation between facts, as Wittgenstein originally held, but a relation between objects in the causal, natural order.

> If picturing is to be a relation between objects in the natural order, this means that the linguistic objects in question must belong to the natural order. And this means that we must be considering them in terms of empirical properties and matter-of-factual relations, though these may, indeed must, be very complex, involving all kinds of constant conjunctions or uniformities pertaining to the language user and his environment. Specifically, although we may, indeed must, know that these linguistic objects are subject to rules and principles – are fraught with 'ought' – we abstract from this knowledge in considering them as objects in the natural

order. Let me introduce the term 'natural-linguistic object' to refer
to linguistic objects thus considered.                    (TC: 212)

The basic form of claims about linguistic pictures is:

[natural-linguistic objects] $O_1'$, $O_2'$, ... , $O_n'$ make up a picture of
[objects] $O_1$, $O_2$, ... , $O_n$ by virtue of such and such facts about $O_1'$,
$O_2'$, ... , $O_n'$.                    (TC: 215; NAO: 118)

Thus, if it is the case that

'John is next to Harry' pictures John as next to Harry

the sentence involved is treated as a (complex) natural object – a
particular object or event in space-time consisting of a configuration
of sounds or marks – which bears the picturing relation to the configuration of objects John-next-to-Harry. Notice that 'picture', in Sellars's
treatment, is a first-order, object-language expression, not a disguised
copula or a metalinguistic property or relation. Picturing is neither
meaning nor standing for.

If atomic sentences can picture objects and configurations of objects,
then structures of atomic sentences, considered as natural-linguistic
objects, can form complex *maps* of parts of the environment by occur-
ring in patterns that correspond (modulo some projection relation) to
the properties and relations among the objects in the environment.
This use of 'map' is clearly an extended use: the structure of atomic
sentences need not be a *spatial* structure, unlike common road maps
and atlases. Furthermore, it might well be *dynamic* in the sense of
representing the *temporal* dimension as well, allowing it to map configurations of objects over time, not just at a time. But this is a use of
'map' increasingly familiar to us with the proliferation of computer-
based or digital maps around us. The digital maps one buys on a CD-
ROM or downloads from the Internet are not the only examples, either:
a computer simulation of some event, for example, a traffic accident or
a weather pattern, is a map of that event (a dynamic one) in our sense.
Such a simulation, of course, includes more than just the map, for the
program's lines of code represent the relevant laws of nature, and these
are not part of Sellars's 'map'. His map consists only of those statements or declarations in the computer that track where the objects are
at different times, what properties they have, and how they are inter-
related. The role of laws will be discussed in Chapter 6.

Recall Sellars's "first instalment of the explanation" of the "job of
referring expressions" in a base language from *Science and Metaphys-*

*ics* (SM: 125–6), quoted above (p. 38). Any set of representations that conforms to those requirements will, effectively, be or contain a *map* of the environs. In this regard, it will picture the world.

Several things follow from Sellars's position. First, there must be some kind of "projection relation" that specifies how the configurations of objects in the map are related to the configurations of objects they represent. It will be, in the case of the linguistic and/or mental maps possessed by human beings, mind-bogglingly complex. But it provides a standard of correctness for the linguistic activity of human beings that is distinct from truth as such, yet, according to Sellars, is essential to the notion of an empirically meaningful language. Given such uniformities, the occurrence or non-occurrence of certain statements in certain situations will be "normal", not in the full-blown normative sense of *true*, but as the projection of the world into the medium of a language.

Secondly, it takes a whole system to represent in any interesting sense. A dot in the middle of an otherwise blank page could be said to represent New York, but without some other structures present in the "map" relating to New York and its environs in some systematic way, the assertion seems empty. In his late essay "Mental Events" (1981), Sellars elaborates the concept of animal representational systems, in part to clarify further the relation between language and mind. We shall explore this in greater detail in Chapters 7 and 8, on the mental, but it is clear that Sellars believes our linguistic representations are themselves built upon a primitive animal representational system that more or less systematically maps the immediate environment of the organism, although the map in such an animal representational system is not a *linguistic* map. The mapping function, however, is essential to any empirically useful representational system and will therefore also be performed within the linguistic representational system that is the peculiar possession of human beings.

With the notion of an animal representational system and the protocognitive maps such systems contain, Sellars clearly makes contact with work in both cognitive science and contemporary philosophy of mind that seeks to explain important mental phenomena by reference to systematic relations between the internal states of organisms and the conditions in the world they represent.[34] There are different ways to fill in the details; Sellars's notion of picturing is similar to such attempts to naturalize meaning and the mental.[35] But the dissimilarity cannot be ignored: Sellars does not identify picturing and meaning and does not attempt a reductive naturalization of meaning or intentionality. The naturalistic core provided by picturing is a necessary but not sufficient condition of using an empirically meaningful language. Nevertheless, Sellars claims that the picturing relation is "a mode of 'correspondence' *other than truth* that accompanies truth in the case of [elementary] empirical statements" (TC: 222). The notion of picturing is the residue of the correspondence theory of truth above and beyond what is explained by the semantic theory of truth.

Last but not least, Sellars relies on this notion of picturing in an attempt to give real bite to Peirce's notion of an ultimate and ideal language and/or conceptual framework. Sellars holds that we can make good sense out of the notion that one language can be more adequate than another, and, in particular, that one language can permit a more adequate picturing of objects than another.

> 68. It should be noted that statements to the effect that one linguistic system generates more adequate pictures of these objects than another, though in one sense a "meta-linguistic" statement, is an object language statement …
> 69. Let us now go one step further and conceive of a language which enables its users to form *ideally* adequate pictures of objects, and let us call this language Peirceish. Indeed, let us conceive of the conceptual structure which would be common to English Peirceish, French Peirceish, and even Mentalese or inner episode Peirceish. (SM V §§68–9: 140)

Ideally adequate pictures, one assumes, would at a minimum be pictures that were accurate or correct at any arbitrary level of resolution, the frame of which could also be expanded arbitrarily.[36] It is not clear what other standards of adequacy are operative here. In this sense, we might suppose that a US Geological Survey map is more adequate than an ordinary roadmap, in that it contains all the information the roadmap contains *and more.*

But it is far from clear to me that there is a well-defined notion of final and ultimate adequacy, even if the picturing relation is naturalistic and not semantic, for adequacy seems fundamentally interest-relative. For instance, a thick tome of US Geological Survey maps would be quite a bad thing to use on a cross-country drive, whereas a standard road atlas is geared to that purpose. There are many different maps of the Earth, depending on the projection used, and no one map is optimal for all purposes. All flat maps distort in some way or other, and a globe, which does not distort shapes, areas, distances or bearings, is inconvenient, even inadequate, for many purposes. Could there be a map adequate for *all* purposes? Since purposes themselves can conflict, the presumption, it seems to me, is against such an ideally adequate map.

Sellars's notion of picturing gets one outside the circle of beliefs only in the sense that whether an utterance and/or inscription correctly pictures the world is an *object language* question in a way that the question about whether an utterance and/or inscription is true is not. For according to Sellars the question about the truth of an utterance is, initially, a question about its S-assertibility. Whether a statement, which could be an ethical claim as well as an empirical claim, is S-assertible is a matter of rules and roles. It is a role of first-level, atomic, matter-of-factual statements to picture.

> [E]ven within this level essential distinctions must be drawn if we are to grasp the difference between the *primary* concept of factual truth (truth as correct picture), which makes intelligible all the other modes of factual truth, and the *generic* concept of truth as S-assertibility, which involves the quite different mode of correspondence bound up with illustrating propositional expressions and the truth performance ... in terms of which the "correspondence" statement (i.e. equivalence statement)
>
> That 2 plus 2 = 4 is true $\leftrightarrow$ 2 plus 2 = 4
>
> is to be understood. (SM V §9: 119)

In general, we pronounce sentences true when they are authorized by the rules of the language game, but an empirically meaningful language game must contain a subgame, the rules of which effectively require the construction of a map, a representation of the world related to the world in naturalistically respectable ways. The requirement that this part of language be naturalistically related to the world imposes a serious constraint. For one thing, it means that abstracta cannot be pictured, for there are no naturalistic relations to abstract entities. This consequence will be explored further in Chapter 4. It also entails that mental acts are not among the ultimate ontological constituents of the world.

> 78. The concepts of ideal matter-of-factual truth and of what there really is are as fraught with subjunctives pertaining to conceptualization as the idealists have ever claimed. But *no* picture of the world contains *as such* mentalistic expressions functioning *as such*. The indispensibility and logical irreducibility of mentalistic discourse is compatible with the idea that in *this* sense *there are no*

> *mental acts.* Though full of important insights, Idealism is, there-
> fore, radically false. (SM V §78: 142–3)

This consequence will be explored more fully when we examine Sellars's philosophy of mind.

Any empirically meaningful language must be embodied in structures in the world, parts of which bear a non-intentional representation relation to the rest of the world. But, of course, there is much more to any language, for languages contain, among other things, logical operators, and logical operators do not represent in this pre-intentional- or information-theoretic sense. These issues will be explored more fully when we examine Sellars's views on laws, mentality and ethics.

## Chapter 3

# Categories, the a priori, and transcendental philosophy

The basic formal and material relations between language and the world were the topics for Chapter 2. There are, however, also important structural features of languages and the more abstract conceptual frameworks they embody that need to be examined before we begin to look at Sellars's substantive views in metaphysics and epistemology. These features include categorial structure, the conception of *a priori* truths, and the possibility of specifying transcendental conditions for empirically meaningful languages in general.

## Categories

The ontologist asks, "What is there?" An answer at the level of individual detail ("Well, there's me, my coffee cup, the dog sitting at my feet, the tree I see outside the window ...") is not the point. Rather, the ontologist seeks to know what *kinds* of things there are. But moving to kinds rather than individuals is of little help if *every* kind counts. ("Well, there are people, coffee cups, dogs, trees ...") Traditionally, then, philosophers have sought to construct or discover a set of *highest* or *most general* kinds, and called them 'categories'. The notion of a category, however, has not been fixed and well-defined over the history of philosophy. Because they are *highest* kinds, there is something ultimate in the notion of a category: things of different categories have nothing in common, save perhaps certain transcategorial characteristics shared by everything, regardless of kind (e.g. being and identity). The serious category theorist also seeks an *exhaustive* set: a kind for everything and everything in its kind.

If the common thread among the various notions of a category is that they are highest kinds, we have to ask: "Highest kinds of *what*?" Aristotle thought of categories as the highest kinds of being, that being which is "said in many ways".[1] There is a strong tradition of categorial realism in Western philosophy, reaching back to the Greeks. On this view, a proper theory of the categories limns the fundamental structure of the world itself, or, in Plato's phrase "carves nature at the joints".[2] One might therefore find the highest genera by starting with a representative sampling of things in the world and climbing the genus–species ladder by successive abstraction.

> Fido is a dachshund.
> Fido is a dog.
> Fido is an animal.
> Fido is a corporeal substance.
> Fido is a substance.[3]

We arrive at a highest kind when there is no further rung in the ladder. This technique has fairly restricted conditions of application, however, for it seems to work only when the subject is a singular referring expression and the predicate a common noun or kind-term. As Sellars points out, the sequence

> $x$ is red.
> $x$ is coloured ...

does not seem to go anywhere. Instead, we get to what has seemed the appropriate category via an alternative sequence:

> $x$ is a red.
> $x$ is a colour.
> $x$ is a perceptual quality.
> $x$ is a quality.

Sellars asks, *vis-à-vis* this sequence, "What sort of item could $x$ be?" (TTC in KTM: 324). Perhaps we should say the sequence begins not with "$x$ is a red", but with "red is a colour." In both cases, however, we ignore the fact that 'red' is primarily an adjective. That each sequence is grounded in the referent of some noun ("$x$ is a red" or "red is a colour") encourages us to think of each sequence as revealing a hierarchy of properties inhering in some thing. Reification, then, seems unavoidable. We seem led ultimately to the notion that there are things that are qualities, relations, *abstract entities* of various kinds. In the context of a categorial realism, especially, we seem driven straight into a Platonic realism, according to which abstract individuals are generally on a par with substances and concrete individuals.

This is not a result with which a naturalist should be content, and Sellars thinks the first move out of this situation was taken by the late medieval philosophers.

> 17. The first major breakthrough in the theory of categories came, as one might expect, in the late Middle Ages, when logic, like knighthood, was in flower. A new strategy was developed for coping with certain puzzling concepts which were the common concern of logicians and metaphysicians. This strategy is illustrated by Ockham's explication of such statements as
>
> (A) Man is a species
>
> Roughly, he construes it to have the sense of
>
> (B) ·Man· is a sortal mental term ...          (TTC in KTM: 326)
>
> 23. What all this amounts to is that to apply Ockham's strategy to the theory of categories is to construe categories as classifications of conceptual items. This becomes, in Kant's hands, the idea that categories are the most generic functional classifications of the elements of judgments.          (TTC in KTM: 329)

Sellars thoroughly endorses this Ockhamite–Kantian move to a categorial conceptualism; the connection it draws between language and thought or conception enables him to utilize the concepts and distinctions developed in his philosophy of language in the explication of the nature of thought. Thus "Kantian 'categories' are concepts of logical form, where 'logical' is to be taken in a broad sense, roughly equivalent to 'epistemic'" (KTE in KTM: 274). Combined with Sellars's functionalist or conceptual-role theory of meaning, "To say of a judging that it has a certain logical form is to classify it and its constituents with respect to their epistemic powers" (KTE in KTM: 274).

The purely formal logical inferences into which a judgement can enter reveal only a small part of its "logical powers" in this broader sense, for its *epistemic* powers include such things as being an appropriate observation response to certain situations, being good or weak evidence for other judgements, having implications for certain intentions one has, and the like. For example, whatever the strictly *logical* powers of the judgement "The needle is in the red zone", the judgement is an appropriate *perceptual* response to certain situations and (in one such situation) is strong *evidence* that the car is overheating, that something is wrong with the car, that one should stop driving the car or risk major damage. The material inferences that were said in Chapter 2 to constitute the specific meaning of an expression would certainly be included in the expression's 'epistemic powers', as Sellars understands the term. But, of course, not *all* of the material inferences pertaining to an expression will figure into its logical or categorial form, for the notion of a category is that of a highest kind.

> 24. If judgings qua conceptual acts have "form," they also have "content." Of all the metaphors that philosophers have employed, this is one of the most dangerous, and few have used it without to some extent being taken in by it. The temptation is to think of the "content" of an act as an entity that is "contained" by it. But if the "form" of a judging is the structure by virtue of which it is possessed of certain *generic* logical or epistemic powers, surely the content must be the character by virtue of which the act has *specific* modes of these generic logical or epistemic powers.
>
> (KTE in KTM: 274–5)

That there are, for example, causal or spatiotemporal implications connected with many expressions is, on this view, part of their categorial form; *which* causal or spatiotemporal implications an expression contributes to the judgements it occurs within is a matter of the particular meaning of that expression.

Given the relationship that Sellars postulates between the structure of thought and the structure of language, the concepts that appear in an ideal and general theory of the structure and function of usable, human languages would also apply to human conceptual thought. Notice, however, that Sellars never tries to construct a final theory of the categories that claims to offer a systematic and exhaustive exposition of the highest genera and species of linguistic-conceptual items. Kant's own theory of the categories expands and improves the traditional Aristotelian theory in some interesting ways – namely, the addition of the modalities – but it is fairly obviously inadequate, a fact exploited and addressed by Hegel.[4] We can see why Sellars never even tries to offer a complete theory of the categories, despite his obvious yearning to be systematic and his lack of metaphysical modesty. One reason is that a perfectly general theory of the structure and function of human language, a theory adequate not only to the semantics but also the pragmatics of all possible human language, is still far in the future. Moreover, since Sellars is well aware of the creativity of human linguistic activity, the subject may be in principle open-ended: it is far from clear that the linguistic-conceptual changes that occur in the course of human history must occur entirely within a rigid and unchangeable framework.[5]

Those familiar with the categorial speculations of the philosophical tradition will note that there is something odd about this reason for shying away from offering a full-blown theory of the categories. Traditionally, categories have been thought to be both a fixed set, not susceptible to change or development (although our appreciation of them may be), and discoverable by pure, *a priori* methods. Sellars's statements imply at least that the fixedness of the categories is not a sure thing. And if they are not fixed, how *a priori* can our knowledge of them be?

We are thus led to ask about Sellars's position on another basic philosophical conception: the *a priori*. Since Sellars often portrays his project as a transposition into contemporary terms (with improvements) of the Kantian project, we would like to know not just about the *a priori*, but also about the *synthetic a priori*.

## The *a priori*, synthetic and otherwise

Sellars's systematic statement on the synthetic *a priori* was originally produced in 1951, the same year as Quine's attack on the analytic–synthetic distinction.[6] While Quine's discussion has coloured almost all treatments of the analytic or the synthetic since, it seems to have had no impact on Sellars's discussion, even though Sellars later revised his essay for publication. Sellars's principal target is C. I. Lewis, and he neither attacks nor defends the distinction between the analytic and synthetic *per se*. He is conscious that neither the analytic–synthetic distinction nor the *a priori–a posteriori* distinction has been clearly and univocally defined in the historical tradition. He can utilize the distinctions to make important points, however, while respecting their most common characterizations.

Sellars is not as distrustful of these distinctions as Quine. Unlike Quine, Sellars believes that there is a relatively unproblematic role for the notion of meaning. Quine thinks the very notion of meaning involves commitment to shady entities that cannot be given well-defined criteria of identity; therefore we should, if possible, abandon the notion of meaning itself. But Sellars shows us a perfectly respectable (even nominalistically respectable) treatment of meaning. Meanings themselves may well be vague, but meaning talk is classificatory, and there is nothing unusual or dangerous about vague classifications *per se*. If there were, we would have to deny the existence of the bald and the tall, the short and the fat. The entities in question, linguistic tokens, are as determinate as they need to be. Sellars thus sees no need to call the very idea of the analytic–synthetic or the *a priori–a posteriori* distinctions into question, although his position implies that these distinctions are not the sharp-edged distinctions the logical positivists assumed they were.

Sellars adopts a narrow reading of the analytic in his treatment, so that a proposition counts as analytic only if "when defined terms are replaced by their definientia, it becomes a substitution instance of a truth of logic" (ITSA in SPR: 298). Thus, the synthetic is that which is neither logically true nor logically false.

Sellars recognizes that the notion of the *a priori* is not entirely univocal across the tradition. He isolates four different (although related) senses that have been given to the term: "(1) It is knowledge of *necessary* truth; (2) It is *certain* knowledge; (3) It is knowledge *independent of experience*; (4) It is knowledge of truth *ex vi terminorum*" (ITSA in SPR: 318). Ultimately, Sellars believes there is good reason to hold that these notions coincide, and does not think it crucial to pick one over the others, but in his consideration of the notion of synthetic *a priori* knowledge, he focuses on the fourth conception of the *a priori*. This is, perhaps, a bit odd, since many regard the notion most central to the *a priori* to be the third sense, independence of experience, and the notion of truth *ex vi terminorum*[7] has also been taken as a definition of the analytic (it is, in fact, recognized by Sellars as the "broader sense" of 'analytic'). Given Sellars's choices here, we seem to lose the sense that one distinction (analytic–synthetic) is clearly *logical* and the other (*a priori–a posteriori*) clearly *epistemic,* but Sellars has already shown a tendency to elide that boundary. Nonetheless, Sellars's choices keep the analytic–synthetic distinction separate from the *a priori–a posteriori* distinction, for the analytic–synthetic distinction is always at heart a matter of *formal* truth, while the *a priori–a posteriori* distinction is, we can say, aimed at *material* truths.

It is this notion of material truth that holds the key to Sellars's position on the synthetic *a priori*. Remember that, according to Sellars, the conceptual content of an expression is determined by its contribution to the good inferences in which the expression figures. The relevant set of inferences are not all formal inferences: every descriptive term is involved in a set of material inferences. Furthermore:

where 'x is B' can be validly inferred from 'x is A', the proposition 'All A is B' is unconditionally assertable on the basis of the rules of the language. Our thesis, then, implies that every primitive descriptive predicate occurs in one or more logically synthetic propositions which are unconditionally assertable – in short, true *ex vi terminorum*; or, as it was put at the end of the preceding section, true by implicit definition. But a logically synthetic proposition which is true *ex vi terminorum* is, by the conventions adopted at the opening of the chapter, a synthetic *a priori* proposition.                                              (ITSA in SPR: 317)

Given this position, one might think of Sellars as a kind of super-Kantian: not only are there synthetic *a priori* propositions, but there are a great many of them, at least as many as there are primitive descriptive predicates in the language. If the example provided earlier of a material rule of inference is a good one, namely that "x is coloured" can be validly inferred from "x is red", then the proposition "All red things are coloured" counts as a synthetic *a priori* proposition in Sellars's view. One uncomfortable upshot of Sellars's position is that causal laws ought then also to be synthetic *a priori* truths. Sellars treats them as *proposed* synthetic *a priori* truths, provisional until either they are discarded in the march of science or we achieve a final Peircean framework that enables us to produce a determinate picture of any kind of worldly process.

Of course the most philosophically interesting such propositions are those at the highest levels of abstraction. Those are precisely the propositions that formulate categorial truths, and they are also the propositions by which we make explicit the fundamental extralogical forms of inference and the fundamental conceptual forms available in our language or conceptual framework.

This endorsement of the synthetic *a priori* may not make all defenders of the notion happy. Unlike Kant, Sellars believes that although there will necessarily be synthetic *a priori* propositions in each linguistic-conceptual framework, there need not be a single synthetic *a priori* proposition that is an element of all possible languages or conceptual frameworks. Kant thinks there is one and only one conceptual framework incumbent upon all humanity; Sellars sharply disagrees.

[I]f one means by synthetic *a priori* knowledge, knowledge which is logically synthetic, yet true *ex vi terminorum,* then, indeed, there is synthetic *a priori* knowledge. If one means by it, synthetic knowledge to which there is no significant alternative, then synthetic *a priori* knowledge is a myth, a snare, and a delusion.

... For not only can we be *caused* to modify out [*sic.*] linguistic frame, we can deliberately modify it–teach ourselves new habits– and give reasons for doing so. Now the use of a conceptual frame is the awareness of a system of logical and extra-logical necessities. The essence of scientific wisdom, therefore, lies in being tentative about what one takes to be extra-logically necessary.

(ITSA in SPR: 319)

In this respect, Sellars is more Hegelian than Kantian, for he recognizes that the synthetic *a priori* truths and even the set of categories we operate with are, potentially, dynamic, changing under the impact of both experience and reflection. Chapter 6 will look more closely into the methods by which categorial frameworks can be changed.

## The transcendental task of philosophy

We are now in a position to revisit Sellars's conception of philosophy and his distinction between the manifest and the scientific images. One of the tasks of philosophy is clearly interpretive: we utilize a complex and sophisticated linguistic-conceptual framework in dealing with the world, but we cannot be said yet to have a thoroughly reflective comprehension of that framework. Coming to a reflective grasp of the categorial framework that has developed over the millenia of human history is one of the endeavours that constitute philosophy. Indeed, it is not an established fact that there is only *one* categorial framework to be found in human history.

Another of the tasks of philosophy is speculative. As discussed, Sellars holds that alternative conceptual frameworks are possible. For example, scientists routinely attempt to reconstruct our current framework via theoretical research and controlled experiment, striving to generate new, rival frameworks. The philosopher's interpretive tools and skills help in understanding the relation between the new developments in science and the manifest image. Since the scientific image is still in relative infancy, it is incumbent upon the philosopher to expend some effort speculating on further possible developments and their meaning. Sellars is one of the few twentieth-century analytic philosophers who actually took this speculative aspect of philosophy seriously, as we shall see in his treatment of sensation.

There is an objection to all this talk about conceptual frameworks that merits a look, as voiced by Davidson in his essay "On the Very Idea of a Conceptual Scheme".[8] Davidson's argument (whether one accepts it or not), however, does not gainsay Sellars's use of the notion of a conceptual scheme. Davidson has two targets in mind: "1) the idea that we can distinguish between an unconceptualized content given in experience and an organizing scheme, and 2) the idea of radically incommensurable basic views of the world".[9] Sellars is potentially a target in the first sense: he does believe that sensation constitutes a level of unconceptualized "content" distinguishable from the conceptual. But we are not far enough along to deal with this charge adequately. The sense in which such content is "given" is crucial.

Davidson's second target, which he also describes in terms of a belief in the possibility of mutually untranslatable languages, is also a target of criticism for Sellars. To consider some form of activity linguistic is to think of it as capable of semantic characterization. But semantic characterizations, according to Sellars, classify the relevant activity as belonging to some linguistic kind relevantly similar to a recognizable linguistic kind in a background language. To be a language at all, the putative linguistic activities would have to play a role in the lives of the (putative) speakers analogous to the role our language plays in our lives (e.g. permit communication, mutual adjustment of plans, representation of the world, etc.) *and yet* those putative linguistic activities would be able to share *nothing* in common with the functions played by the activities of our language. This just seems incoherent.

Sellars, like Davidson, believes that linguistic-conceptual activity takes place within a shared world and context of needs that necessarily allow some comparisons to be made between the linguistic-conceptual activity of others and our own. These boundary conditions make possible a kind of transcendental argumentation that echoes Kant.

40. To construe the concepts of meaning, truth, and knowledge as metalinguistic concepts pertaining to linguistic behavior (and dispositions to behave) involves construing the latter as governed by *ought-to-bes* which are actualized as uniformities by the training that transmits language from generation to generation. Thus, if logical and (more broadly) epistemic categories express general features of the *ought-to-bes* (and corresponding uniformities) which are necessary to the function of language as a cognitive

instrument, epistemology, in this context, becomes the theory of this functioning – in short *transcendental linguistics*.

41. Transcendental linguistics differs from empirical linguistics in two ways: (1) it is concerned with language as conforming to epistemic norms which are themselves formulated in the language; (2) it is general in the sense in which what Carnap describes as "general syntax" is general; i.e., it is not limited to the epistemic functioning of historical languages in the actual world. It attempts to delineate the general features that would be common to the epistemic functioning of any language in any possible world. As I once put it, epistemology, in the "new way of words" is the theory of what it is to be a language that is about a world in which it is used. (KTE in KTM: 281)

Which ought-to-be's are "necessary to the function of language as a cognitive instrument" is, of course, not immediately evident. But it is the job of philosophy, as both an interpretive and a speculative enterprise, to develop theories about such matters. Sellars's own readings of the history of philosophy give us glimpses of how he thinks past philosophers have contributed to the task of transcendental analysis.

Transcendental philosophy, on this view, is neither insight into a special realm that transcends experience nor a unique methodology reserved only for philosophers. It is reflection on the most general norms and structures constitutive of cognitive engagement with the world. Every reflective or methodologically self-conscious confrontation with the world will have a transcendental "moment" – a level at which the discerning eye can recognize the operation of a particular conception of these norms and structures in the empirical behaviour of persons.

## Chapter 4

# *Sellars's nominalism*

## Whose nominalism?

The debate over the ontological status of abstracta and concreta is as old as philosophy itself. Each age prosecutes the case using its own methods and its own terms, beginning in ancient times as an argument over the status of universals and particulars, and lately broadening to include classes, propositions and possible worlds. Sellars is convinced that any naturalistic philosophy must also be nominalistic, for the heart of naturalism is the commitment to the primacy of the causal order, and abstracta are causally impotent. Some of Sellars's illustrious contemporaries, most notably Quine and Goodman, also proclaim themselves nominalists, but in Sellars's view, their nominalism is fundamentally flawed – Quine, at least, countenances some abstract entities such as classes – but also, and more importantly, their methodology is mistaken. Yet these supposed nominalists have determined the terms and principles that have dominated contemporary ontology. To understand Sellars's nominalism, one has to put much current ontological orthodoxy into question.

Nominalists have sometimes been quite puritanical, in that they have wanted to impose strict limits on what we can say and to rule out characteristically Platonistic turns of phrase as nonsense, but that is not the approach Sellars takes. He believes he can show that most of the things responsible Platonists want to say can be reconstructed using his tools and remain *true,* although shorn of their obnoxious ontological commitments.[1] Saving what the Platonist wants to say without giving in to ontological excess leads Sellars at times to sound as if he is not, in fact, a thoroughgoing nominalist.

For instance, in "Abstract Entities" (1963) he remarks that one could draw:

> a distinction between a generic sense of 'abstract entity' in which the lion and the pawn as well as triangularity (construed as the ·triangular·) and that two plus two equals four (construed as the ·two plus two equals four·) would be abstract entities as being ones over and against manys; and a narrower sense of abstract entity in which qualities, relations, sorts, classes, propositions and the like are abstract entities ...                   (AE in PP: 233)

This passage sounds as if Sellars is objecting to some but not all abstract entities and has no intention of abjuring abstracta generally. And indeed, Sellars's critics took him to task for claiming to be a nominalist but really only trading in some abstracta in favour of others. Similarly, in *Naturalism and Ontology* (1980), Sellars actually claims at one point to be defending a form of ontological realism, albeit "a cagey form" of it (see NAO: 43). Such passages need to be treated as unfortunate slips intended to express Sellars's belief that he really can preserve the logical structure of a great deal of Platonism in a nominalistically acceptable form. I interpret him to be a thoroughgoing nominalist who believes that abstract entities do not *really* exist. Nonetheless, much of what we say in apparent reference to abstract entities is true, once we see that the *apparent reference* to abstract entities is just that. Platonistic *talk* is not incompatible with nominalism.[2]

## Quantification and ontology

Most contemporary ontology is conducted in the shadow of Quine's dictum that "to be is to be the value of a variable"[3] and his corresponding claim that quantification is the touchstone of ontological commitment. Sellars rejects this approach to ontology. Sellars is not denying that existence claims often take the forms "There are *K*s", or "There is an *H*": for example, "There are lions"; "There are no unicorns"; "There are numbers"; and "There is a house in New Orleans they call 'The Rising Sun'". It does not follow, however, that quantification is itself the touchstone of existence. "Classical quantification theory plays a key role in contemporary ontology and hence requires a no-holds-barred scrutiny to determine whether its hands are clean" (NAO: 28).

There are two separable lines of argument by which Sellars hopes to show that classical quantification theory has "dirty hands".[4] His first argument is an external critique of classical quantification theory, which starts from a presumption that is extrinsic to the theory, namely, naturalism, and argues that the classical interpretation of quantification is inconsistent therewith. His second line of argument is an internal critique that looks at the informal readings logicians typically give of quantifier formulae; he argues that these readings so misconstrue the grammar of the sentences that ontological commitment seems unavoidable where none in fact is made.

## Quantification and naturalism

Sellars is perfectly willing to accept that "There are lions" can be paraphrased as (or is for current purposes equivalent to) "Something is a lion", which is standardly captured *in more logico* as

$(\exists x)(x$ is a lion$)$.

In these sentences, as in all simple sentences, there is both a reference and a characterization of the referent. The reference, however, is *indeterminate* and seems to include *all* the objects in the domain, although not in the same way as in the sentences

Everything is a lion.           $(\forall x)(x$ is a lion$)$.[5]

The currently popular view is that the indeterminate reference of quantification is the basic medium of reference. This inclines one to think that sentences focus such indeterminate reference on one or more particulars in virtue of the predicates that occur in them.[6] "Determinate reference is the focussing of indeterminate reference" (NAO: 10). But, Sellars asks, *how does* indeterminate reference itself work?

The common assumption that quantifiers are the most basic referential device in language, when taken seriously, leaves us searching for an understanding of how they can accomplish this task.

The variable 'x' is said to range over objects. But it is not clear what it is for a variable to 'range' over objects. Is there a "word–world" connection between variables and items in the extra-linguistic realm of stones and tigers? If so (and the answer must surely be "yes") is this 'ranging' – which is clearly the counterpart of the indeterminate reference of 'something' – to be explicated in terms of determinate reference or is it to be taken as a basic mode of reference?                                                    (NAO: 8)

A Tarski-style treatment of quantification, which assumes a "satisfaction" relation between words and objects, is just fine for *formal* purposes, but it is insufficient for and does not meld easily into a naturalistic treatment of language. "Explicating" reference via a telephone-directory-style listing works for the formal semanticist, but it does not show us what kind of *real* connection there may be between language and the world; it does not help the psycho-linguist at all. If quantification is the primitive and fundamental medium of reference, then reference remains, from the point of view of naturalism, a mystery.

Sellars does not balk at the notion of indeterminate reference. Indeed, he recognizes that it is a necessary element of any useful language. But if the indeterminate reference of the quantifier is the *fundamental* form of reference, then it is extremely difficult to construct a theory of reference that is compatible with a respectable naturalism. Such a treatment of the quantifier:

> amounts to nothing more nor less than the idea that the word 'something' has a connection, unmediated by determinate references, with all objects – and by 'connection,' as will become evident, I mean a genuine relation to be captured by psycho-linguistic theory.

(NAO: 8)

What are the alternatives that would explicate the indeterminate reference of quantification in terms of determinate and naturalistically acceptable reference? Sellars mentions two alternatives. The first, which he recognizes as inadequate, was nonetheless canvassed in the early days of modern logic: equate the existential quantifier with a (possibly infinite) disjunction. The second alternative, which points in the direction Sellars wants to go, considers the truth-conditions for an existentially quantified sentence such as "Something is a lion," and points out the following:

> 'Something is a lion' is true ≡ some statement which makes a determinate reference to an object and classifies it as a lion is true.[7]

Thus Sellars espouses a substitutional approach to quantification.[8] But he recognizes that it is not unproblematic. The most prominent problem is that the resources of any natural language are always limited: not everything has a name. So we cannot:

> construe the phrase 'some statement which makes a determinate reference to an object' as referring to statements containing one or other of a list of such expressions in current usage. Such a

proponent must rather rely on the fact that a language not only consists of more than the grammatical strings which are actually deployed at any one time (which is obvious), but also of more than the grammatical strings which are available for deployment. It also includes, in a sense difficult to define, the resources by which the language could be enriched through being extended in specific ways. (NAO: 7–8)

As shown in Chapter 2, Sellars treats 'reference' *strictu sensu* as a term in the semantic metalanguage. Despite his talk in the passages from *Naturalism and Ontology* about a "word–world connection", he cannot maintain that reference is some particular object-level relation between words and objects. Unfortunately, he occasionally writes in *Naturalism and Ontology* as if this is what he meant, but such passages must be read as shorthand for a longer story. Sellars has a theory of picturing, according to which there are atomic, empirical sentences that *picture* objects and their configurations in virtue of a naturalistic isomorphism in certain contexts between the occurrence of those sentences (which are specific configurations of names) and the configuration of objects they picture. Picturing relations provide the naturalistic basis for the determinate reference of basic names, even though Sellars refuses to *analyse* reference as picturing. The point is that although reference is *analysed* in terms of the classificatory force of reference statements, the empirical meaningfulness of a language requires that some of the occurrences of its sentences constitute a partial picture of the world. The semantic *analysis* of reference is not yet an *explanation* of reference. The naturalist needs to be able to offer *both* an analysis and an explanation of reference. Taking quantification to be primitive and fundamental makes a naturalistic explanation of reference mysterious. Sellars's approach, in contrast, permits a complete theory of reference that contains an *analysis* and *explanation* of reference that is compatible with the naturalistic commitment to the priority of the causal order and also with the nominalistic commitment to the priority of individuals.

Sellars's standard for measuring ontological commitment affects the strategies he employs to argue for nominalism and the problems he encounters along the way. His standard of ontological commitment is as follows:

[A]mong the forms by the use of which one most clearly and explicitly asserts the existence of objects of a certain sort – I am not concerned with singular existence statements, which raise their own problems – are the forms 'There is an N', 'Something is an N' and 'There are Ns', and ... the logistical counterpart of these forms is

(24) (Ei) i is an N

where 'i' is a variable taking singular terms of a given type as its values, and 'N' is an appropriate common noun.

(GE in SPR: 256)

This remains sketchy, for which types of singular terms and which kinds of common nouns are "appropriate" must be specified. While Sellars allows for some framework relativity here, countenancing a mathematician's claim while doing mathematics that there is a prime number between 100 and 200, the ultimately basic singular terms and the appropriate common nouns are those used in our *empirical* language, especially those that occur in atomic sentences at the picturing level.

## Reading quantifiers

The second line of argument Sellars directs against classical quantifier theory is internal, although in a slightly peculiar way. He does *not* claim that there is some technical error in the formal treatment of quantifiers by Tarski or other luminaries of logic. Rather, he claims that the informal reading that is given to quantifier formulae "generates puzzles as soon as its auxiliary role is overlooked, and it is made the focal-point of philosophical reflection on quantification and existence" (GE in SPR: 250). The standard informal readings of sentences involving quantifications of predicates, propositions and such tend not to respect the grammatical categories of the expressions quantified. Rather, they tend to transform the *apparent* structure of the sentence so as to treat the quantified expressions as singular terms (which they are not), thus falsely encouraging the notion that they involve commitment to the existence of predicative or propositional entities. Sellars believes that we have been seduced by such informal readings: quantification itself is not the touchstone of ontology.

A preliminary note before I try to summarize this line of argument: Sellars does not assume that "$S$ is $f$" (e.g. "John is tall") has the same logical form as "$S$ is an $f$" or "John is a human". In the first sentence form ('$x$ is $f$'), the place of '$f$' is generally filled by an adjective, whereas in the second sentence form ('$x$ is an $f$'), the place of '$f$'

is generally filled by a common noun. In elementary logic courses, the difference between these sentence forms is often treated as superficial and unimportant, but that is *not* what Sellars thinks.

To begin Sellars's argument, assume there is a sentence of the form

(1)  $S$ is $f$

which we generalize to

(2)  $(\exists f)(S \text{ is } f)$.

The informal reading typically given (2) is

(2i) There is an $f$ such that $S$ is $f$.

What are we to make of the first occurrence of the variable in (2i)? It is tempting to assume that it takes common nouns as substituends, for that would be the case in most uses of the phrase 'an $f$'. (Consider, for comparison's sake, such sentences as "There is an otter over there, just about to slide into the pool" or "There is a school bus stopped in the other lane; you have to stop".) But there is a difficulty, for if the first '$f$' in this informal reading takes a common noun substituend, so should the second. If (2) is the existential generalization of something like "John is tall", we must either reject the idea that the second occurrence of the variable takes common nouns as substituends or we must treat 'tall' as a common noun. Taking the latter route, the original sentence ought to read "John is a tall". It seems natural, perhaps automatic, to adapt this latter sentence into "John is a tall thing", but then we are forced to regard "$S$ is an $f$ thing" as the basic logical form of simple adjectival attributions.[9] Furthermore, we must then also adapt (2i) to read

(2icn)  There is an $f$ such that $S$ is *an $f$* (thing).

And it gets worse, for, having made this move, parity of reasoning forces us to read the *first-order* quantification

(3)  $(\exists x)\ x$ is tall

as

(3i) There is an $x$ such that $x$ is tall.

This may appear commonplace until we realize that if the variable in the construction "there is an $\alpha$" is treated as a common noun variable, the second occurrence of the variable in (3i) must also be treated as a common noun variable. And that does not work.

    \*(3i')   There is a man such that man is tall.

    \*(3i'')  There is an otter such that otter is swimming.[10]

The variable in (3i) is supposed to be an *individual* variable. Sellars suggests that the obvious move is to hold that there are two things going on in the construction "there is an α": there is an implicit common noun categorizing the relevant variable in addition to the occurrence of the variable itself. So (3i) should be read as

    (3ict)   There is an individual, $x$, such that $x$ is tall

and (2i) should be read as

    (2ict)   There is a quality, $f$, such that $S$ is $f$.

This move works well for the individual variable, but it generates still more difficulties with the predicate variable, for if it makes sense to say "there is a quality, $f$, ...", then it ought to make sense to say "$f$ is a quality". But in this case '$f$' is now serving as a proper name, certainly not as an adjective. With some predicate terms, however, this is less obvious, for example, colour words. "Red is a quality" and "White is a quality" both seem acceptable, and their subject terms do not seem different in form from the adjectives 'red' and 'white'. But with other (indeed, most) terms, it is obvious that the root predicate term has to be transformed in category in this new context. Consider the example "John is tall".

    \*Tall is a quality.

In order to get it right, the latter must be transformed into "Tallness is a quality". Platonism is knocking at the door, for the idiom of quantification seems to force the naming of abstracta. Correspondingly, (2ict) sounds fine when applied to 'white':

    (2ictw) There is a quality, white, such that $S$ is white

but not when applied to 'tall' or 'rectangular':

    \*(2ictt) There is a quality, tall, such that $S$ is tall.

    \*(2ictr) There is a quality, rectangular, such that $S$ is rectangular.

The first '$f$' in (2ict) should take singular terms as substituends, but the second should take adjectives. How can we bring these two variables back into line with each other? One way is to take them both to be singular-term variables by rewriting (2ict) as

    (2platonic)   There is a quality, $f$-ness, such that $S$ has $f$-ness.

And now Platonism seems unavoidable. Via a series of relatively insensible steps, a simple adjectival attribution has been transformed into a relation between entities, one of which is abstract, for (2platonic) seems to have the form and the kind of commitments exhibited by "There is a pet, Fido, such that Jones possesses Fido".

Sellars insists that we do not have to accept the appearances here: "one no more has to construe '(Ef) S is f' (2) as saying 'there is a quality, f-ness, such that S has f-ness' ... than we have to construe 'S is white' ... as *really* saying 'S has whiteness'" (GE in SPR: 251). Thus goes Sellars's diagnosis of the (faulty) line of reasoning that seems to generate Platonism from predicate quantification in simple adjectival constructions. He constructs parallel diagnoses concerning kind terms and propositions that will not be rehearsed here. His conclusion is that:

> there is no *general* correspondence between *existentially quantified formulae* and *existence statements*. Only in those cases where the variable which is quantified is a variable of which the values are singular terms will a quantified formula be the counterpart of an existence statement. Nor is this all; not even all (so-called) existential quantification over singular term variables has the force of an existence statement. For the latter involve common nouns or expressions having the force of common nouns.
>
> (GE in SPR: 255)

## Quantificational liberalism

If quantification is the measure of ontological commitment, and one hopes to be a nominalist, then quantifying over anything other than singular referring terms poses a problem. Indeed, Quine and his followers abjure all such quantifications. Although the move from "John is thin" to "Someone is thin" $[(\exists x)Tx]$ is unobjectionable, they do not want to allow the move from "John is sick" to "John is somehow" $[(\exists F)Fj]$, or from "Jones is tall and Smith is tall" to "Jones is something and so is Smith" $[(\exists F)(Fj \ \& \ Fs)]$, much less from

> Jesse ran fast and Ralph also ran fast

to

> Jesse ran somehow and Ralph also ran *thathow*.

But Sellars has no problem with any of these and asserts that none commit us ontologically. Indeed, Sellars suggests that we could (in fact, *should*) adopt and be happy with a set of quantifiers that would be grammatically marked for easily keeping track of the proper grammatical categories for their substituends, for example, 'something', 'somehow', 'somesort' and 'somethat'.

| | |
|---|---|
| ($\exists x$) $x$ is white | Something is white |
| ($\exists f$) John is $f$ | John is somehow |
| ($\exists K$) John is a $K$ | John is a somesort |
| ($\exists p$) $p$ or Tom is tall | Somethat or Tom is tall |
| ($\exists p$) Tom said that $p$ | Tom said somethat |

Such a convention would allow us to read formulae involving quantification with no significant temptation to see untoward commitments to ontological excess everywhere, as long as we remember throughout that these terms are not equivalent to 'some thing', 'some how', 'some sort' and so on. English does not have a *system* of such categorially marked quantifiers, but we do have some expressions of this kind. In general, we use 'something' with abandon, relying on the context to fix the grammatical category of the appropriate substituend. That is fine with Sellars, as long as it is not equated with speaking of some thing.

## The names of abstract entities

Quine's mistaken emphasis on quantification is rooted in the fact that existence claims do, in fact, usually make use of quantification. Sellars, however, insists that only quantifiers that take singular referring terms as substituends formulate existence claims. This puts the emphasis where Sellars thinks it ought to be: on the primacy of determinate, singular reference. Confining existential commitment to determinate singular reference (and generalizations thereof) does not by itself advance nominalism, for we certainly possess numerous determinate singular referential devices, the apparent referents of which are abstract entities. 'Triangularity', 'roundness' and 'courage' all apparently refer to abstracta. As seen in Chapter 2, Sellars offers us an analysis of the contexts in which many such terms occur, for example,

'*Dreieckig*' (in German) stands for triangularity

in which these terms do not act as proper names of abstract entities, but as distributive singular terms

'*Dreieckig*' (in G) stands for the ·triangular·

and ultimately play a classificatory function as common nouns,

'*Dreieckig*'s (in G) are ·triangular·s.

Yet abstract names are not used solely as the direct object of 'stands for'. For example, the good Platonist maintains that both of the following are true:

(a)  Triangularity is a universal.
(b)  Triangularity is an individual.

If both occurrences of 'triangularity' are replaced with the same distributive singular term:

(a′)  The ·triangular· is a universal
*(b′)  The ·triangular· is an individual

there is a problem: (a′) reduces directly to

(a″)  ·Triangular·s are universals

which is, taken out of the material mode completely,

(a‴)  ·Triangulars· are predicates.

This is true. Performing exactly the same transformation of (b), however, produces a falsehood, incorrectly reconstructing the Platonist's assertion. Sellars maintains that in order to properly reconstruct (b), we have to realize that in (b) the Platonist has climbed yet another rung on the linguistic ladder: The "deep form" of (b) is

(b″)  The ·the ·triangular·· is an individual constant

which is equivalent to

(b‴)  ·The ·triangular··s are individual constants

which is perfectly true.

Ontologically, the lesson is that apparent object-language names of abstracta are really metalinguistic (or metametalinguistic) distributive singular terms that commit us, at most, to the existence of tokens of the relevant kind, but not to the abstractum itself.

## A path not taken

At this point in the arguments of both "Grammar and Existence" and *Naturalism and Ontology*, Sellars devotes a good deal of space to diagnosing and rejecting the Fregean position that he attributes to Geach and Dummett, namely, that while

(1)  $S$ is $f$

does entail

(2f) There is something that $S$ *is*,

what we are committed to by this is not some *object* (for the proper substituend is not a name but a predicate), but a property or a concept, a non-object.[11] This part of Sellars's argument is more thoroughly and technically worked out in *Naturalism and Ontology* than in the earlier "Grammar and Existence", so it is obviously something to which he devoted considerable time. Given the constraints of this book, where Sellars's nominalism must be compressed into a single chapter, this is one piece of the picture I will skip. Besides, if one accepts the theory of predication at the very heart of Sellars's nominalism, the Fregean alternative has little attraction anyway.

The hard-core Platonist treats virtually all terms as name-like. In the Platonist's view, even predicate terms and propositional terms refer to objects, not the kind of objects referred to by the subject terms of atomic, empirical sentences, but different kinds of objects. The Fregean is uncomfortable with the idea that predicates and propositional terms are names and refer to objects, even if strange kinds of objects, so they are treated as non-names but are still thought of as referring, although to non-objects. Sellars offers us a radical alternative. Predicates are not at all like names, and they do not in any interesting sense refer. In fact, predicates are merely dispensable auxiliary symbols: a language without predicates is possible, although a language without names is not.

## A theory of predication

A theory of predication has to tell us what the basic linguistic structure of predication does and how it does it. Since subject–predicate structure seems universal and fundamental in language, the topic is as basic as can be in the philosophy of language. This section therefore provides an essential supplement to the treatment of Sellars's philosophy of language in Chapter 2.

## The persistence of the relational

Confronted with questions about what is "going on" in a sentence, or what it is for a sentence to be true, Western philosophical tradition has invoked a relational model of what lies behind the simplest assertion. Assuming, for the moment, that the copula in an atomic assertion of the form 'a is F' functions only as a tense marker, so that the modern functional notation of *Principia Mathematica* captures everything else essential to such an atomic sentence, then the traditional theory can be summarized in something like Figure 1.[12]

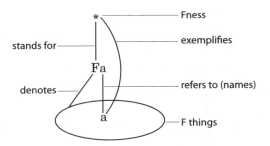

*Figure 1*

The precise terminology, of course, is not of great importance. The important lessons contained in Figure 1 are:

- Both 'F' and 'a' are taken to be singular referring expressions in some sense: 'a' refers to a particular, *a*, 'F' to the universal, Fness, although the reference relation in this case is called 'standing for'.
- 'F' has a double semantic role: it is the name of Fness (which is what all F things have in common), and it denotes F things.
- The linguistic expression 'Fa' signifies the fact that Fness and *a* stand in a particular relation, namely, the exemplification relation. In other words, the relation of a particular to the universal it exemplifies is expressed by a relation between tokens of the names of these entities.

The nominalist thinks this picture is seriously flawed because what is apparently an elemental fact, *a is F,* is turned into something quite complex involving relations to abstract entities. Furthermore, the nominalist can launch a very serious attack on this picture that Sellars mentions several times in his work: Bradley's paradox, which generates a vicious regress. Traditional theory analyses predication as the expression of a relation, exemplification, among entities, namely, a universal and one or more particulars, but relations are themselves predicative forms. So, if

Fa

is to be explicated by (or, is true because)

Exemplifies (a, Fness)

we still have a predicative form (now with more components, i.e. a higher adicity) in need of explication, and the theory seems then to offer the explication

Exemplifies (Exemplification, a, Fness).

But now something has gone wrong: exemplification was offered originally as an analysis of the predicative tie, but here it reoccurs in its own explication. Moving to orders of exemplification, so that first-order objects exemplify$_1$ first-order universals, but the 'relation' among such objects and exemplification itself has a different order, exemplification$_2$, is of no help, for this too would generate an infinite regress. The standard defence against Bradley's argument is to claim that exemplification is not a relation at all, it is something else with a very special status, a *tie* or a *nexus*.[13]

### *A non-relational interpretation of predication*

Sellars is convinced that the traditional theory of predication is unsalvageable. The very model it employs to try to make sense out of predication ensnares it in tangles it cannot resolve. Avoiding the troubles of traditional theories of predication requires a radical new model for understanding predication. A new model for predication, however, first requires a real *diagnosis* of what is wrong with the traditional model, not just noticing the puzzles it generates. Sellars sees in the traditional analysis of a predicative sentence, "a exemplifies Fness", not a first-order statement of a relation between a particular and an abstract entity, but a metalinguistic sentence in the material mode. Sellars applies to exemplification sentences the apparatus he applies to meaning statements. 'Exemplification' seems clearly tied to *truth* or *true of*. This sentence seems necessarily equivalent to

Fness is true of a.

Furthermore, 'Fness', rather than functioning in this sentence as the proper name of an abstract object, should be read as a material mode, distributive singular term. So our sample sentence can be rewritten as

That it is F is true of a

which yields

That a is F is true,

hence

·Fa·s are true

and finally

Fa.

Since the rewrite moves in this derivation can go in either direction, this derivation shows us why

Fa

is necessarily equivalent to

a exemplifies Fness,

but it also shows us how to begin to understand predication non-relationally. For, notice, in this derivation the "relation" of exemplification is analysed away: as a term, 'exemplification' signals the semantic assertibility of certain combinations of linguistic tokens. While this move frees us from a too-quick assumption that predication is to be understood in terms of some special relation, it does not yet point us towards a better understanding of predication. We must turn elsewhere for that illumination.

Sellars finds the inspiration for his new model of predication in a remark in Wittgenstein's *Tractatus*:

> 3.1432 Instead of, "the complex sign '*aRb*' says that *a* stands to *b* in the relation *R*", we ought to put, "*That* '*a*' stands to '*b*' in a certain relation says *that aRb*."

Like many of Wittgenstein's pronouncements, this claim is obscure, and, indeed, Sellars believes that the overwhelming majority of philosophers have missed its point.

## The dispensability of predicates

A paragraph ago, I claimed that Sellars analyses away the supposed relation of exemplification by treating exemplification sentences as being not object-language claims about relations between universals and particulars, but material mode metalinguistic claims about the truth or semantic assertibility of certain combinations of linguistic tokens. But this does not analyse away all relationality, for it leaves standing that there are *combinations of linguistic tokens*. We must then ask about the functions of the tokens that are involved in those combinations and the function of the combination itself. Is relationality still firmly present here? A natural temptation is to say that the function of the predicate terms is to stand for properties or relations, and that the combination of tokens functions to stand for or represent the exemplification relation, bringing us back where we started. As long as all sentences are thought of as combinations of linguistic tokens, sentences seem inescapably relational entities, and that relationality seems to play an indispensable role in the sentence's ability to perform its predicative function.

Sellars wants to release us from this picture. Sentences themselves are not necessarily combinations of linguistic tokens and therefore are not inescapably relational entities. Once we see this, we can begin to understand and appreciate the real role that relations among linguistic tokens play, and then it is easy to see that relations among linguistic tokens within a sentence are not in the least a reflection of any kind of relationality intrinsic to predication itself. If predication does not have a relational structure, then there is no need for any supposed relatum that is posited simply to fulfil this (nonexistent) relation.

The easiest way to convince people that sentences need not be combinations of linguistic tokens is to construct an example language in which this is the case, and that is precisely what Sellars does. He does not construct a *whole* language, but rather enough to provide an idea of how it might go. There are no predicate words, no verbs, adjectives, adverbs and so on in Sellars's language, which he calls 'Jumblese, only individual constants and individual variables'.[14] Sentences consist of names or variables written in a certain way or arranged in a certain pattern.[15] The Jumblese translation of 'a is triangular' might be

**a**

whereas 'a is round' might be

a.

The Jumblese translation of 'a is larger than b' could be

a b,

whereas 'b is larger than a' would then be

b<sub>a</sub>.

Jumblese might translate 'a is above b' as

a

b.

Clearly, in many respects Jumblese would be a difficult language: how
would it be spoken? Could there possibly be enough distinctive ways
of writing names and arranging them to be able to express all things
we would like a language to express? There would, however, be some
marvellous efficiencies in such a language. For instance, 'A, which is
round, is larger than b, which is triangular' could be expressed quite
concisely:

a b.

It is not essential to Sellars's argument that Jumblese be useable
in real life. His crucial arguments bring out the structure of certain
moves made by Platonists such as Bergmann to avoid Bradley's paradox and also show how structurally similar moves (discussed immediately below) can be made at a lower level to obviate the motivation
behind Platonism generally. Jumblese contributes by clarifying and
illustrating Sellars's claim that predicates are dispensable.

Suppose that Jumblese is a possible, although highly impractical,
language. What lessons are then to be drawn? Since there are no predicates in Jumblese, only variables and names of particulars, taking
Jumblese seriously should disabuse one of the notion that predicates
themselves are names. More important, since there are no predicates
in Jumblese, it shows us that predicates are, in fact, dispensable,
inessential to language as such. Jumblese thus hints at the real function of predicate terms, for we are now in a position to appreciate the
lesson Sellars takes from *Tractatus* 3.1432.

The Platonist thought that such sentences as

a exemplifies Fness          a stands in R to b

explicated the deeper form of

a is F          aRb.

In both cases the supposed explicans contains a new term, 'exemplifies' and 'stands in', respectively, that increases the adicity of the
predicate. This encourages the notion that the underlying structure is

*always* relational and more complexly relational than ordinary object-language assertions would otherwise seem. But Jumblese indicates that predicate terms are, in fact, dispensable. According to Sellars, Wittgenstein realized this when he wrote that "we ought to put *'That "a" stands to "b" in a certain relation says that aRb'*". The point is that at the highest level of abstraction, both the Jumblese sentence

ab

and the English sentence

a is larger than b

have the same logico-syntactic form. In Jumblese, it seems evident that all we have is a token of 'a' and a token of 'b' standing "in a certain relation" (in this case, *'a' written in a larger font and concatenated to the left with 'b'*). There is no *need* for there to be further tokens involved. The corresponding English sentence, however, must have the same fundamental logico-syntactic form. Thus, 'a is larger than b' is just a way of putting the name tokens 'a' and 'b' into a certain relation. The expression 'is larger than' plays no other role than to determine the specific relation in which 'a' and 'b' stand.[16] 'Is larger than' does not *name* a relation or even represent some relation that is an independent entity distinct from the sentence; it relates the 'a' and the 'b' in a certain way. For in the English sentence, 'a' and 'b' have the relation *concatenated to the left and right (respectively) with an 'is larger than'*.

Similarly, the monadic English sentence

a is round

and the Jumblese

a

have the same fundamental, non-relational form. The Jumblese sentence has the form *'a' written in a certain way (Century Gothic)*; the English sentence must also have that form. So 'a is round' is just a certain way of writing 'a', namely, writing 'a' *concatenated with an 'is round'*. Predicate expressions modify the characteristics of and relations between the names that occur in the sentences to which they belong. Those predicate expressions are, in principle, dispensable. They are, in fact, auxiliary symbols that have themselves no isolable referential function.

To draw an analogy within English, consider "Fred danced a tango while Ginger danced a waltz". How many "things" were present? Fred,

Ginger, a tango, a waltz, and two dancings? But the fact that 'danced' is dispensable, so that we need only write "Fred tangoed while Ginger waltzed", removes the temptation to think 'danced' is doing a separable job or designating something on its own. Sellars simply wants us to go one step further and realize that we could have written "𝔉𝔯𝔢𝔡 while 𝔊𝔦𝔫𝔤𝔢𝔯" to the same effect, so that 'tangoed' and 'waltzed' are just as dispensable and also not doing a separable job of designating something on their own.

Here is a slightly more technical way to conceive of the matter. In the face of Bradley's paradox about relations, to stop the threatening regress, the Platonist seems driven to hold that exemplification is not itself a relation. But Sellars shows us how to avoid the threat of a regress altogether via a non-relational analysis of predication.

> [T]he previous move of introducing a *privileged* non-name, 'exemplifies', to stop Bradley's regress was a clumsy attempt to capture the radical difference between expressing a relation by *using a relation word in addition to the names of the terms,* and expressing it by *relating the names of the terms.* (TTP: 305)

We not only express a relation among objects by relating the names of those objects, we express monadic properties of objects by endowing the names of those objects with particular *monadic* characteristics. The rules of language permit the construction of equivalent and apparently relational expressions of predication in the material mode of the metalanguage, such as exemplification sentences (and exemplification$_2$, exemplification$_3$, etc. sentences), but this amounts to a possibly infinite progress, not a vicious regress, in as much as exemplification sentences are not *explications* of predication sentences, but *elaborations* of them.

## The semantic contribution of predicates

The reader is probably still dissatisfied, for there is an irrepressible urge to say that 'red', 'triangular' and 'man' clearly do contribute *something* to the meaning of the sentences in which they occur; surely also that there has to be *something* "out there" in extralinguistic reality that corresponds to the contribution these terms make to sentences and that helps account for the truth-value of the sentences in which they occur. Sellars thinks both points are well taken.[17] But it would be a simple mistake to think that each of these *somethings* has to be either an *object* or a *Fregean entitative non-object*. Indeed, the something in question is simply *red objects, triangles* and *men.*

> 71. The "real relation" which underlies the fact that 'man' refers to men must surely be a real relation between the word 'man' and men, a relation to be formulated in terms of generalizations having subjunctive form, which specify uniformities in which expression-tokens (including sentences containing the word 'man') and extra-linguistic objects (including men) are involved ... 72. The point with which I shall conclude this chapter is that the generalizations in question do not, so to speak, *separately* relate 'red' to red things nor 'man' to men. They relate *sentential* expressions containing 'red' to red things and *sentential* expressions containing 'man' to men. For, after all, if our account of predication is correct, the kind of connection involved must also apply to the Jumblese dialect, *in which there are no predicative expressions.* (NAO: 60–61)

According to Sellars, we must take more seriously than Frege ever managed to do the primacy of the sentential. Predicates as such have no *real* relations to extralinguistic reality, but some of the sentences in which they occur do. We can abstract the function of the predicate from its occurrence in the primordial sentences that connect with reality, but it would be wrong to explain the truth of an atomic sentence as derivative from more primitive facts about the reference of its singular term, the reference of its predicative term, and the relation between those two referents. Predicates are, after all, expendable. Facts about the reference of predicates cannot be more primitive than nor presupposed by the semantic assertibility of the sentence itself, nor can the "real" relation of the predicate to the world be more primitive than the "real" relation of the sentence to the world.

If the predicate from a sentence cannot be extracted and treated as bearing a real relation to the world that is more primitive than the relation of the sentence to the world, why should we be able to do this with singular referring terms or individual constants? Sellars's position implies that sentences presuppose a respectably independent real relation between individual constants and objects. Two reasons for accepting this asymmetry between individual constants and predicate constants are that (i) individual constants are indispensable, unlike predicate constants,[18] and (ii) according to Sellars, "pace Wittgenstein, the extra-linguistic domain consists of *objects, not facts*" (NAO III §76: 61). Tokens of (basic) individual constants, objects in their own right, can bear "real" relations to their referents, for both are objects, things of the right kind to be "really" related to each other. Sellars does not think that there could be protolinguistic objects with a naming relation to real objects in the world that never figure into propositionally structured representations.

Sellars offers a correct diagram of the metaphysics of predication (Fig. 2).[19] 'INDCON' is a metalanguage variable that takes individual constants as substituends. The asterisk quotes in "is an *F*INDCON" are, like other quotation marks, a name-forming device, but the *-quotes form the name of the *sign design* illustrated between them. For instance, *fern* occurs in both English and German. Stylizing the languages into the notation of *Principia Mathematica* for the purpose of illustrating this point, *fern*INDCONs in English are the linguistic representations of ferns, whereas in German *fern*INDCONs are the linguistic representations of distant things.

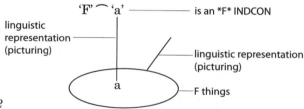

*Figure 2*

The linguistic representation relation in Figure 2 is introduced in "Towards a Theory of Predication" (1983) by Sellars as follows:

> 158. Let me now introduce the concept of *linguistic representation* and say, to begin with, that a singular term INDCON$_i$ is the linguistic representation (LR) (in L) of an object, $O$, if and only if by virtue of its role in L it stands in appropriate psycho-sociological-historical (PSH) relations to $O$. Thus we have
>
> INDCON$_i$ is LR (in L) of $O \equiv$ PSH(INDCON$_i$, $O$).
>
> (TTP: 318)

The linguistic representation relation cannot be the reference relation as construed in Chapter 2, for linguistic representation *is* a relation, and moreover a *real* relation, whereas supposed "semantic reference" is actually, in his view, not a relation, but a form of classification. Given his characterization of it, only existing objects can have linguistic representations; Pegasus cannot have one, because there is no object to which 'Pegasus' stands in appropriate PSH relations. Thus, it appears that the linguistic representation relation Sellars writes of in "Towards a Theory of Predication" is the picturing relation he has tried to characterize and defend elsewhere.

The diagram shows that 'a' has the LR relation to a, but 'F' has no particular relation to anything. Instead, *F*INDCONs have the LR relation to F things. But can this really be the *same* LR relation? The relata seem different enough for me to be unconvinced that there is one and only one LR relation with two different forms. If there are two different LR or picturing relations in question here, such that the relation between names and objects is not quite the same as that between sentences and characterized objects, this would not necessarily damage Sellars's overall point. Names relate to the world, and sentences relate to the world; it is unnecessary to hold that predicates relate independently to anything extra-linguistic.

# Review

It is time to look back and summarize Sellars's position. There are two major motivations for modern Platonic realism about abstracta. One is that abstract entities seem to be demanded by semantic theory, and a commitment to them is therefore implicit in the very fact of language. The other, not unrelated, is that the intentionality of thought involves a relationship between thinkers and abstract entities, a relationship often characterized in terms of awareness or perception. At the end of Chapter 4, we have finally assembled most of the tools Sellars uses to address these issues. Although we have not yet addressed the philosophy of mind, Sellars holds that intentionality and semantics are deeply connected, so the tools he develops to deal with the notion that language itself already commits us to abstracta can also be extended to the analysis of intentionality. Nor have we looked at all the detailed argumentation Sellars develops in response to specific cases or arguments. For instance, although Quine avows nominalist proclivities, he also claims that he cannot do without classes. Sellars has a very detailed analysis of talk about classes meant, *inter alia,* to disarm Quine's line of thought.[20] Similarly, many think that mathematics forces Platonic realism upon us, but the difficult problem of a Sellarsian reconstruction of mathematics is beyond the scope of this book.[21] Still, the outlines of Sellars's nominalism are clear.

Sellars has argued that the current standard of ontological commitment, being the value of a variable of quantification, is mistaken. It makes the indeterminate reference of the quantifier more primitive than any form of determinate reference, which is incompatible with naturalism, and it also gets the grammar of existence claims wrong. Sellars proposes a different standard: we are committed to the kinds of things we can explicitly name and classify in true, bottom-level, object-language statements.

In ordinary language we often talk about meanings, properties, propositions and so on, thus apparently committing ourselves to the existence of such abstracta. Sellars disarms such talk by analysing it as material mode metalinguistic speech about the functional role of expression-kinds. The only things we are committed to ontologically by such speech are expression tokens that participate in complex causal systems involving interactions between language users and the world.

A deeper worry motivates Platonic realism as well: that the most basic linguistic structure, predication itself, already involves a commitment to abstracta, for common explications of the predicative 'relation' make essential mention of properties, relations and such. Sellars aims to disarm this line of thought by offering a very different explication of predication, according to which it is not a relation at all, but a matter of qualifying and arranging names. At the most basic, atomic level, this means endowing the names with counterpart characteristics, enabling some atomic sentences to 'map' objects in the world.

## Ontology and modality

With an almost complete outline of Sellars's ontology before us, there is now one more essential piece of the puzzle to discuss: Sellars's theory of the modalities. Metaphysicians have often thought of the modalities as real, in the sense that they believe that there is something "out there": some objective, mind-independent aspect of reality above and beyond the particulars involved that makes modalized propositions true or false. Whether the emphasis is on the reality of the causal connection or the reality of possible worlds, modalities have often been an occasion for a vast inflation of the furniture of the world.

Hume's denial of the reality of necessary connections came as a genuine bombshell to many philosophers. But the problem of "real connections" confronts any nominalist who maintains that objects (particulars) and configurations of objects exhaust what there is, for then there seems to be no way to differentiate a mere accidental configuration of objects (or lack thereof) from either necessary or impossible configurations. A concern for the problem of "real connections" runs through Sellars's works, from "Concepts as Involving Laws and Inconceivable without Them" (1948) and "Language, Rules and Behavior" (1949) on, but his most complete treatment of the topic is in "Counterfactuals, Dispositions, and the Causal Modalities" (1957). In these works Sellars sketches a unified treatment of the modalities, logical, causal and deontic, that is consistent with his nominalism and his overall approach to matters of ontology.

This is an important topic for Sellars, for it touches on issues at the very heart of his philosophy: the status of laws in the empirical and formal sciences and their ontological import, and, even more important, the ontological status of norms. Sellars consistently hews to a starkly nominalist line in his treatment of the modalities. His inspiration is, once again, a line from the *Tractatus* 4.0312: "My fundamental idea is that the 'logical constants' do not represent".[22] Sellars takes seriously the idea that the modalities are made explicit in language as logical constants, whether as special sentence connectives (entailment) or as *operators* modifying a sentence. In either case, their function is not representational, where a representational function would be serving as a proxy for some entity in the world (whether one thinks of this as a referential function or as a picturing or mapping function).

Instead, Sellars thinks of modal expressions as (surprise!) terms that express in the material mode metalinguistic commitments and policies embedded in the language behaviour of the speakers. "The root idea behind modal connectives is *inferability* ..." (CDCM: 251). This applies rather unproblematically in the case of logical necessity.[23] Thus, a modal formula such as

$$\Box(p \supset p)$$

expresses an endorsement of inferences of the form

$p$
So, $p$.

Of course, we attach modal operators to statements that are not themselves conditionals, such as

$$\Box \sim (p \ \& \ \sim p).$$

But it is simple to construe this assertion as expressing the universal or unconditional assertibility of sentences of the form '~(p & ~p)' or, equivalently, a proscription against assertions of the form '(p & ~p)', which itself comes down to a proscription against asserting both 'p' and '~p'. An assertion such as

Coloured things are necessarily extended

expresses the general validity of material inferences of the form

x is coloured
So, x is extended.

Sellars generalizes this approach to the modalities to include the physical and deontic modalities as well, although in each case there are special considerations peculiar to the domain. Causal laws, for instance, are not merely universal generalizations: they support subjunctive or counterfactual conditionals. The traditional realist view is that they express necessary connections between events or states of the world. In Sellars's view, however, a causal law (say, that thunder is caused by prior lightning flashes) is an "inference ticket" that expresses our reasoned endorsement (on empirical grounds) of inferences of the form

Thunder here now                Lightning here now
So, lightning shortly before     So, thunder shortly.

The basic story is no different for more specific scientific laws, for example, $pV = nRT$ (the Boyle–Charles law). Such mathematically formulated laws allow us to formulate efficiently endorsement of a whole range of inferences. There is a great deal more to be said about the nature of causal laws and their relation to theoretical structures, induction and observation, but that will await our discussion in Chapter 6.

Sellars applies this general strategy to the deontic modalities as well, treating obligation and permission as modal operators that express endorsement of practical inferences and intentions from an appropriately universal point of view.[24] Again, the many complications of ethical discourse cannot be examined here.

One more general complication needs to be added before drawing ontological conclusions from this picture of the modalities. The modalities have been characterized as expressing (in the material mode) our commitments to certain patterns of connection among our assertions and intentions, but we are not limited to those patterns we currently and *de facto* endorse. For example, it makes perfect sense to say that there are causal connections that have not yet been discovered and obligations that have not yet been recognized; indeed, it would be foolish not to believe this. We know that the material inferences we currently recognize as valid are not *all* the inferences we ought to accept (i.e. those inferences consistent with our epistemic goals or the moral point of view), nor are they all inferences we are determined to hold on to, whatever new evidence shows up. The realms of causal laws and ethical principles are not themselves unstructured. For instance, the conservation laws in physics seem to have a somewhat privileged position and are more resistant to disconfirmation than many lower-level laws.

> It is therefore important to realize that the presence in the object language of the causal modalities (*and* of the logical modalities *and* of the deontic modalities) serves not only to express *existing* commitments, but also to provide the *framework* for the thinking by which we reason our way (in a manner appropriate to the specific subject matter) into the making of *new* commitments and the abandoning of old.                                        (CDCM: 302–3)

Nonetheless, since modal language is ultimately *really* in the metalanguage, it does not commit us ontologically to *real necessary connections, moral facts* or the reality of *normative properties*. Thus, Sellars thinks it essential to the language and thought of any reflectively rational creature that it be richly endowed with modal contexts. Yet nothing about those modal contexts represents any particular element in the world, for the world is simply the totality of particulars.

> Clearly, to use the term 'ought' is to prescribe rather than describe. The naturalistic "thesis" that the world, including the verbal behavior of those who use the term 'ought' – and the mental states involving the concept to which this word gives expression – can, "in principle," be described without using the term 'ought' or any other prescriptive expression, is a logical point about what is to count as a description *in principle* of the world. For, whereas in ordinary discourse to state what something is, to describe something as (e.g., a person as a criminal) does not preclude the possibility that an "unpacking" of the description would involve the use of the term 'ought' or some other prescriptive expression, naturalism presents us with the ideal of *pure* description of the world (in particular of human behavior), a description which simply says what things *are*, and never, in any respect, what they *ought* or *ought not* to be; and it is clear (as a

matter of simple logic) that neither 'ought' nor any other prescriptive expression *could* be *used* (as opposed to *mentioned*) in such a description.

An essentially similar point can be made about modal expressions. To make first hand use of the expressions is to be about the business of *explaining* a state of affairs, or *justifying* an assertion. Thus, even if to state that p entails q is, in a legitimate sense, to state that something is the case, the primary use of 'p entails q' is not to state that something is the case, but to explain *why q,* or justify the assertion *that q.* The idea that the world can, in principle, be so described that the description contains no modal expression is of a piece with the idea that the world can, in principle, be so described that the description contains no prescriptive expression. For what is being called to mind is the ideal of a statement of 'everything that is the case' which, however, serves *through and through, only* the purpose of stating what is the case. And it is a logical truth that such a description, however many modal expressions might properly be used in *arriving at* it, or in *justifying* it, or in showing the *relevance* of one of its components to another, could *contain* no modal expression.                     (CDCM: 282–3)

The "pure description" or "statement of 'everything that is the case'" that does *only* that is, in fact, the very notion of a *picture* of the world that keeps recurring in Sellars's work. Such a picture or map of the world contains no modal expressions and represents no "modal facts" in the world. It is Sellars's claim that being represented on the map is the standard of ontological commitment. Therefore, there is no commitment to the ultimate reality of necessary connections, possible worlds or obligations, however unavoidable such things are in the construction and utilization of the map.

## Chapter 5

# Knowledge and the given

Sellars wrote a number of essays dealing with epistemological issues,[1] but the principal texts where the issues are discussed in depth include "Empiricism and the Philosophy of Mind", "The Structure of Knowledge" and a series of essays in which he responds to Roderick Firth's "Coherence, Certainty, and Epistemic Priority", including "Givenness and Explanatory Coherence" (1973), "More on Givenness and Explanatory Coherence" (1979) and finally, the Carus Lectures for 1977, published as "Foundations for a Metaphysics of Pure Process" (1981).[2] Sellars's views in epistemology clearly evolved in the course of these twenty-plus years, but whether the changes are simply refinements of his early doctrines or major revisions, even disavowal of some of those doctrines, is a matter of some debate.[3]

Sellars's epistemology is complicated by the fact that he never wrote a purely epistemological essay. Especially in the major texts just mentioned, metaphysical issues, particularly those in the philosophy of mind, are inextricably interwoven with matters epistemological. This is no surprise, for Sellars thinks that one cannot prosecute epistemology without some metaphysical convictions about the nature of the world and the mind that knows it; for that matter, neither can one undertake metaphysics without at least a prototheory of knowledge to explain the authority of one's claims. Nevertheless, in this chapter I shall try to tease out the more purely epistemological aspects of Sellars's philosophy.[4]

# Some dimensions of empirical knowledge

Sellars's theory of knowledge is a complex attempt to balance competing insights in several different dimensions: empiricist–rationalist, foundationalist–coherentist, externalist–internalist, realist–phenomenalist–idealist. We need an understanding of these opposed positions to be able to understand the difficult balancing act Sellars is attempting. Whatever historical associations may exist among these positions (e.g. classical empiricists tended towards foundationalism, internalism and some form of phenomenalism), they are logically independent. Although Sellars is often characterized as an epistemological radical (anti-empiricist, anti-foundationalist), this is a historical accident dependent on the dominance of a particular brand of epistemology at the middle of the twentieth century. Sellars is really a centrist: he seeks a middle way that preserves the important insights to be found in each of these dimensions.[5]

The empiricist–rationalist dimension is complex, because these labels have been in place for the longest time and have several distinguishable positions associated with them. Sellars himself distinguishes between concept empiricism and judgement empiricism. Concept empiricism is the doctrine that there are simple concepts that can be understood independently of any other concepts and that are acquired directly by abstraction from sensory experience.[6] Judgement empiricism, in contrast, is the doctrine that there are no synthetic *a priori* truths. According to the judgement empiricist, every synthetic or ampliative judgement is contingently true and can be justified only on the basis of sensory experience; the only *a priori* knowledge we possess, and the only knowledge of necessary truths, consists of judgements that are true by virtue of the meanings of the terms involved. There are, correspondingly, two aspects to rationalism: concept rationalism, which denies that all our concepts are derived from experience; and judgement rationalism, which holds that there are synthetic *a priori* truths.

The foundationalism–coherentism dimension primarily concerns the structure of justification. The pure foundationalist holds that the epistemic status of a proposition depends on its position in an hierarchically structured system of justification that has, at its base, a set of *basic propositions* that have their epistemic status for that person independently of the epistemic status of any other propositions.[7] The epistemic status of basic propositions therefore must not derive from that of other cognitive states. The standard metaphor is that such non-derivatively warranted propositions form the *foundation* for the rest of our knowledge. Obviously, there are many different possible forms of foundationalism. What accounts for the non-derivative warrant of the basic propositions: the content of the propositions, the circumstances in which we acquire a belief in them, or some combination of the two? (Empiricism and rationalism agree that there must be basic propositions, but disagree strongly about which propositions are basic and why.) How strong is the non-derivative warrant: certainty, infallibility, incorrigibility, or something weaker, such as presumptive acceptability or being more reasonable than its contradictory? Coherentism, in its pure form, rejects the notion of basic propositions and a hierarchy of justification. Instead, coherentism proposes that the epistemic status of any proposition is always a matter of relations of mutual support in a complex web of propositions.[8]

Historically, there have been two ways to argue for foundationalism or coherentism. One is to actually try to carry out the programme, as Descartes does in the *Meditations*. Such efforts often get bogged down in matters of detail, so the principal arguments have been negative, arguments *against* the other theory. The argument against coherentism (and, therefore, for foundationalism) has been that unless there are basic propositions, justification would generate either an infinite regress, since there is no stopping point in the chain of justifications, or a vicious circle, since propositions would ultimately show up in their own justifications. The argument against foundationalism (and, therefore, for coherentism) has focused on the fact that few, if any, propositions really stand entirely on their own; if there are some that do, they are insufficient to ground the wealth of our knowledge.[9]

The externalist–internalist dimension concerns the extent to which a proposition's justification for a person must be understood by or cognitively available to that person. Cognitive availability can range from possible presence to consciousness to explicit knowledge of the justification as a justification. The extreme form of internalism would hold that whatever it is that justifies a proposition $p$ for a subject $S$ must be something $S$ knows and that $S$ must also understand or know *that* it justifies $p$. Justification would be solely a matter of relationships internal and patent to a subjectivity. Externalism denies this. Pure externalism places no demands on what the subject understands or is aware of. It is sufficient that some objective relationship hold between the subject's belief that $p$ and the state of affairs that $p$, whether the subject knows, believes or apprehends that relation to hold or not. For instance, the externalist might hold that *p* is justified for *S* if the fact that *p* is what causes *S*'s belief that *p*.

The realism–phenomenalism–idealism dimension concerns the status of the objects of our knowledge. A realist holds that the objects of knowledge exist independently of mind and the acts of knowledge themselves. In particular, realists affirm the mind-independence of physical objects while still insisting that they are knowable. Sellars's father was a well-known Critical Realist, and Wilfrid inherited a related realism from Roy Wood. Critical Realism differs from naive realism and neo-realism by insisting on the distinction between the *content* of a perceptual state and the *object* of the perception (which naive realism and neo-realism seek to identify). It differs from representational realism by insisting that the sensory content of a perception (as opposed to its intentional content) is merely the *means* to knowledge, not itself a separate object of knowledge whose representational relation to the distal object must be exploited in our knowledge of that distal object. The relations between idealism and phenomenalism are complex. Idealists deny the independence of the known from the knower; this means that the objects of knowledge are, in the idealist's view, themselves mental. Phenomenalism gives the *sensory* a special role; often the sensory is thought of as a realm of special objects, called sense data, to which we relate immediately in sensation. Some phenomenalists are also idealists, because they believe that sense data are themselves mental. But some phenomenalists hold that the sense data they identify as basic particulars are neither mental nor physical. Such philosophers are often called 'neutral monists'.

This list of the dimensions of epistemology makes no pretensions to completeness, but Sellars is explicitly concerned with each of these dimensions, and neglect of any of them skews the understanding of his epistemology. In Anglo-American philosophy of the mid-twentieth century, a phenomenalist, internalist, foundationalist empiricism – often identified with logical positivism – was dominant. Knowledge of empirical generalizations is always posterior to and justified inductively by the particularistic, sensuous knowledge at the foundation. In Sellars's view, this dominant picture is deeply flawed. It not only motivates a deep scepticism about the "external world" and other minds (which Sellars thinks is unjustified), but it thereby reinforces a dualism that makes a naturalistic approach to mind impossible. It also misunderstands how science fits into our overall knowledge structure; however highly the positivists may have said they valued science, they, in fact, treated it as a mere auxiliary that itself reveals nothing about the *nature* of things, but only the patterns of their occurrence.

Belief in foundationalism and the given is not, however, the only error Sellars thinks permeates mid-twentieth-century philosophy. Another crucial error he calls "factualism" in "Epistemology and the New Way of Words" (1947), "descriptivism" in "Language, Rules and Behavior", and later assimilates to a form of the naturalistic fallacy. Lately, Sellars's concern with this issue has regained prominence, as one of his modes of expressing it, namely, through references to "the logical space of reasons", has been picked up and amplified by philosophers such as John McDowell and Robert Brandom. A third error Sellars thought rampant concerned the nature and role of generalizations – both empirical and theoretical – in our knowledge.

Correcting these errors leads Sellars to a centrist position that he believes captures the insights of each camp and fits his brand of naturalism and nominalism: it clarifies both the epistemological and ontological status of science, and it comports with our current best understanding of ourselves as evolved, biosocial beings.

## Enter the given

The linchpin that held together the dominant epistemology is the notion of the given. Once one has accepted the idea that there *is* (or better, *must be*) a given at the basis of empirical knowledge, the other dimensions of knowledge are pretty much determined by *what* one takes to be given. What is a given? The concept of the given is meant to capture the idea that there is some level at which knowledge is a matter of direct, immediate encounter with its object and depends on nothing other than that encounter. This primitive encounter with the object of knowledge is then supposed to provide the foundation on which all other empirical knowledge rests. One of the major features of a given is its immediacy. Sellars agrees with the "givenists" that empirical knowledge is possible only if some empirical knowledge is immediate *in the sense that it is not inferred from other knowledge.*

But acceptance of a given commits one to more than a belief in the immediacy of some knowledge. What more? Two features seem crucial to a robust conception of the given:

- The given is *epistemically independent,* that is, whatever positive epistemic status our cognitive encounter with the object has, it does not depend on the epistemic status of any other cognitive state. Notice that epistemic independence does *not* follow from immediacy (not being inferred from other knowledge) unless the *only* form of epistemic dependence is actual inference.

- It is *epistemically efficacious,* that is, it can transmit positive epistemic status to other cognitive states of ours.

If there were items of immediate and independent knowledge that were unable to support other knowledge, they would be epistemic dead ends of no real significance in our broader empirical knowledge. This characterization of the given leaves indeterminate what the nature of the given is, what kind of positive epistemic status our apprehension of the given has, and what our relation to the given is supposed to be. Specifying such parameters generates different versions of givenism.[10]

## Some forms of the given

Although Sellars aims at "a general critique of the entire framework of givenness" (EPM: §1, in SPR: 128; in KMG: 205), he develops his argument by critiquing certain specific forms of the given. If he succeeds in creating a critique of the entire framework, it would be via a generalization of the moves he makes in specific cases. The criticisms he makes of particular forms of the given are quite complex and cannot be addressed in great depth in this chapter, so I shall look briefly at the particular cases he considers and extract from them the principal lessons to be learned.[11] We shall look at Sellars's critique of sense-datum theory, two versions of his response to appearance theories, his treatment of the notion of 'direct apprehension', and a form of the given identified in his late work. On the way, we shall also pause to consider his theory of concepts and concept acquisition.

### *Sense-datum theory*

Throughout much of the first half of the twentieth century, it was common to argue that in perception we are *directly* related, not to physical objects, but to sense data, and that the epistemological situation mirrors the ontological: any empirical knowledge we have is ultimately based on a direct knowledge of the sense data which are given to us. The most common arguments for sense data were arguments from illusion, hallucination or dreams: in such non-veridical experiences, we nonetheless experience *something*. If one hallucinates a pink elephant, must there not be something, somehow, somewhere pink? There were many internecine disputes about the exact nature of sense data and our relation to them. But central characteristics most sense-datum theorists focused on were that sense data are non-physical, inner, qualitative, intrinsically private, directly sensed and directly knowable objects.

The basic thrust of Sellars's discussion of sense-datum theories in Part I of "Empiricism and the Philosophy of Mind" is that there are numerous tensions in sense-datum theory that make sense data unsuitable to be the given. Four dimensions in which these tensions arise stand out:

- knowledge of fact versus knowledge of particulars;
- learned versus unlearned cognitive capacities;
- factualism about knowledge versus non-naturalism about knowledge; and
- inner episodes as causal intermediaries of empirical knowledge versus inner episodes as epistemic intermediaries of empirical knowledge.

To begin the discussion, it is important to distinguish objectual knowledge, which has the form

S knows O

where O is a noun phrase referring to some object or particular, from propositional knowledge, which has the form

S knows that p

where p takes propositions as substituends.

Sense data are particulars, and sense-datum theorists treat knowledge of these particulars – Russell called it "knowledge by acquaintance" – as foundational.[12] In Sellars's view, however, attributions of objectual knowledge amount to attributions of generalized propositional knowledge and even know-how, just as semantic reference is extensional, in his view, because it generalizes over intensions.[13] If Joe knows Tom, Joe has the ability to recognize Tom; perhaps he also knows various facts about Tom's history or character and so on. If Joe knows Paris, then Joe knows how to get around in the city, where things are and so on. In Sellars's view, knowledge of particulars always presupposes some propositional knowledge, and thus cannot itself be the independent foundation of all propositional knowledge.[14] Why should we believe this, though? Any reasonable epistemology has to account for our propositional knowledge (I know that the paper before me is white, that the Red Sox last won a World Series in 2004, that grass is green, that protons have a positive charge and so on), and the foundation of our knowledge has to be able to justify any non-basic knowledge we have. Justification is transmitted via inferential connections (deductive or inductive) between propositions. But objectual knowledge is inferentially sterile. For instance, since 'grass is coloured' follows from 'grass is green', my knowledge that grass is green justifies my knowledge that grass is coloured. But 'London' implies nothing, whether formally or materially, so my knowledge of London cannot justify any particular propositional knowledge. In short: non-basic justification is a matter of inference, but knowledge of particulars is inferentially sterile, so knowledge of particulars cannot provide the epistemically efficacious foundation of our knowledge.

Thus, Sellars thinks the sense-datum theorist must make a decision:

(a) It is *particulars* which are sensed. Sensing is not knowing. The existence of sense data does not *logically* imply the existence of knowledge, or

(b) Sensing *is* a form of knowing. It is *facts* rather than *particulars* which are sensed.

(EPM: §3, in SPR: 129; in KMG: 207)

The notion of knowledge by acquaintance allowed sense-datum theorists to avoid squarely facing this choice. But they still had to say something about the acquaintance relation. According to Sellars, many of them took sensing a sense datum to be a *purely factual* relation. Those who took sensing to be "a unique and unanalysable act" (EPM: §5, in SPR: 130; in KMG: 208), however, cannot account for the existence of a logical connection between *sensing a sense datum* and *having non-inferential knowledge;* and many of those who were willing to analyse the notion of sensing a sense datum did so in non-epistemic terms. "Typically it was held that for a sense content to be sensed is for it to be an element in a certain kind of relational array of sense contents ..." (EPM: §5, in SPR: 130–31; in KMG: 209).[15] Conflating the distinction between the epistemic and the factual is a very significant error, in Sellars's opinion.

Now the idea that epistemic facts can be analyzed without remainder – even "in principle" – into non-epistemic facts, whether phenomenological or behavioral, public or private, with no matter how lavish a sprinkling of subjunctives and hypotheticals is, I believe, a radical mistake – a mistake of a piece with the so-called "naturalistic fallacy" in ethics.

(EPM: §5, in SPR: 131; in KMG: 209)

Sellars is a naturalist, but not a reductionist. Truth is a *value*, and claims or attributions of knowledge are necessarily *evaluations* of the epistemological agent's condition. In Sellars's view, evaluative language, which always has prescriptive force, is very different in its logical grammar and its commitments from descriptive language; ignoring that important difference is the origin of many serious philosophical errors. Naturalism, for Sellars, is a thesis about the resources necessary to a complete description of the world; evaluations and prescriptions operate in a different dimension.

Another tension Sellars believes permeates sense-datum theories is summarized in an inconsistent triad:

A. *x senses red sense content s* entails *x non-inferentially knows that s is red.*
B. The ability to sense sense contents is unacquired.
C. The ability to know facts of the form *x is* φ is acquired.

(EPM: §6, in SPR: 132; in KMG: 210)

Sellars does not believe that all versions of sense-datum theory are subject to this tension, but if one accepts the empiricist rejection of innate ideas, the notion that all propositional knowledge involves the application of concepts, and the notion that knowledge of the characteristics of sense data is simply *given*, something that requires no learning on our part, then trouble is sure to follow.

Thus, Sellars suggests that there is really a common root to the three tensions in sense-datum theory we have so far identified: there are two distinguishable jobs for inner episodes in empirical knowledge, and the classical notion of a sense datum is a "crossbreeding" – really, a *confusing* – of them:

(1) The idea that there are certain inner episodes – e.g. sensations of red or C# which can occur to human beings (and brutes) without any prior process of learning or concept formation; and without which it would *in some sense* be impossible to see, for example, that the facing surface of a

physical object is red and triangular, or *hear* that a certain physical sound is C#.

(2) The idea that there are certain inner episodes which are non-inferential knowings that certain items are, for example, red or C#; and that these episodes are the necessary conditions of empirical knowledge as providing the evidence for all other empirical propositions.

(EPM: §7, in SPR: 132; in KMG: 210–11)

One is a role in the *causal chain* that produces observation knowledge; the other is a role in the *justification chain* of items of empirical knowledge. The sense-datum theorist assumes that one and the same set of inner episodes plays both roles. In the face of the tensions pointed out in the typical conception of sense data, however, there is every reason to reject such an assumption.

There are so many forms of sense-datum theory that it would be virtually impossible to refute them all in detail, and Sellars cannot claim a detailed refutation of all possible sense-datum theories. Nor are the arguments here reviewed, taken from Part I of "Empiricism and the Philosophy of Mind", the only arguments he launches against sense-datum theories. In "Phenomenalism" (1967) he adds another powerful argument, namely, that, despite their hopes, sense-datum theorists cannot reconstruct our putative common-sense knowledge of physical objects and perceivers on the basis of sense data and knowledge thereof because they cannot justify the kind of generalizations in the sense-datum framework that would justify assertions about public, physical objects.[16] Furthermore, despite his attacks on sense-datum theories, Sellars believes that such theories are correct about the need to postulate special, qualitative entities to explain appearances. What can be said, in summation, is that Sellars's arguments definitely put on the defensive any attempt to construe sense data as the given from which all other empirical knowledge derives its warrant.

## Appearance theories I

Another form of empiricist foundationalism Sellars spends considerable time on takes appearances – facts of the form "*X* looks *F* to *S*" – to be the given. Since appearance theories take knowledge of these facts about appearances to be basic, they cannot be charged with either illicitly conflating objectual and propositional knowledge or simply leaving unexplained how objectual knowledge could support propositional knowledge. What appearance theories share is the claim that people have direct access to facts about how things *seem* to them, and that this access affords us knowledge of such facts, knowledge that is both independent of other pieces of one's knowledge and provides the basis for our empirical knowledge of how things *are*. Appearance theories assume, however, that we can know how things *seem* entirely independently of knowing how they *are*.[17]

The argument Sellars aims at appearance theories is that they misunderstand the logic of appearance claims, and that, properly understood, it is clear that talk of what *is* the case is conceptually and epistemically prior to talk of what *seems* to be the case. Sense-datum theorists tended to treat appearance claims as statements of a triadic fact, one relatum of which is a sense datum. Appearance theorists, according to Sellars, tend to treat appearance facts either as dyadic relations between the subject of experience and a 'red appearance' or as "ultimate and irreducible" (EPM: §11, in SPR: 141; in KMG: 220). All three options are faulty construals of such claims, for appearance claims *are* analysable, but they are not relational, according to Sellars.[18]

First, Sellars points out that there are a couple of different forms that appearance claims can take. There is a difference, for instance, between

(QL) The ball over there looks red to me

and

(EL) It looks to me as if there is a red ball over there.

The first implies that there is a ball over there, while the second does not commit itself on that score. The first is a *qualitative looking,* the second is an *existential looking.*

Secondly, as Sellars sees these claims, it is wrong to put them on the same level as a normal observation report:

(OR) The ball over there is red.

Rather, they both belong in a group with

(SS) I see that the ball over there is red.

(QL), (EL) and (SS) are "on the same level" in the sense that, while (OR) is a straightforward observation report that locates an item of a specific kind in space and attributes a sensible property to it, (QL),

(EL) and (SS) include reference to an experience kind. In (SS), the experience is a *seeing*, which, according to Sellars, implies success: if one *sees* that the ball over there is red, then the ball over there is red. In (QL) and (EL), however, the experience is a *looking* or *being appeared to*, and this does not carry the implication of success. Yet it is also part of the logic of (QL), (EL) and (SS) that, from the point of view of the subject or experiencer, the experiences reported might well be indistinguishable. There need be no marks internal to the experience itself by which the subject can tell whether (QL), (EL) or (SS) is the best, most accurate report.[19]

The point of the idioms of looking and appearing is not to express the basis of our knowledge. Appearance statements have a dual role; they allow us to report the character of an experience while also assessing its epistemic status.[20] Thus, if I assert (SS), I am doing several things in that one act: I am reporting that I have an experience that makes the propositional claim "The ball over there is red", *and* I am endorsing that propositional claim.[21] If, in contrast, I assert (QL), I am still reporting that I have an experience that makes the propositional claim "The ball over there is red", but I am endorsing only the notion that there is a ball over there; I am withholding endorsement from the attribution of the quality red to it. In (EL) I am, once again, reporting that I have an experience that makes the propositional claim "The ball over there is red", but now I am withholding endorsement from the whole proposition, both the existence of the ball over there and its being red. The increased certainty of (QL) and (EL) compared to (OR) is not an indication that they are more primitive elements of the chain of justification, nor that we have a special and direct access to appearances that we do not have to physical objects, but simply a result of the fact that less is risked and bets are hedged in such sentences.

A quick caveat here. Sellars is perfectly aware that a perceptual experience cannot be reduced to the occurrence of some propositional claim, "not even if we add, as we must, that this claim is, so to speak, evoked or wrung from the perceiver by the object perceived" (EPM: §16, in SPR: 144; in KMG: 223). But just what more there is to an experience is a very long story for Sellars, one that takes us out of epistemology into philosophy of mind and metaphysics, a question that will be pursued in Chapter 8.

Because (QL) and (EL) are not on the same level as (OR) and introduce an extra factor, Sellars thinks they cannot legitimately be taken to be basic observation reports. Instead, they presuppose the intelligibility of observation reports directly about ordinary, perceptible physical objects in space and time, for, at the very least, the vocabulary we employ within the appearance context is still, by and large, the vocabulary of physical objects in space and time. Thus, the attempt on the part of some appearance theorists to define 'is red' in terms of 'looks red' is misguided.

x is red $\equiv$ x looks red to standard observers in standard conditions

is a necessary truth *not* because the right-hand side is the definition of 'x is red', but because 'standard conditions' means conditions in which things look what they are.

(EPM: §18, in SPR: 147; in KMG: 225–6)

Before we push further into Sellars's analysis of 'looks' statements, however, let us consider an objection to the "levels" to which Sellars assigns 'looks' statements. Many philosophers maintain that there is a sense of 'looks' that does not involve an epistemic assessment, but straightforwardly reports the intrinsic nature of one's experience. Daniel Bonevac claims

> We do not need to see '*x* looks green to Jones' and 'Jones sees that *x* is green' as being "on the same level" in the sense that both raise the question of endorsement and, thus, of truth. We can see 'looks' talk as prior to 'sees that' talk precisely in that it does not raise the question of endorsement. To recognize that *x* looks green to Jones, we need to recognize Jones's experience as being of a certain kind. To recognize that Jones sees that *x* is green, we need to do that *and* recognize that the experience is veridical, that is, that *x* is green.[22]

To the Sellarsian response that, in fact, we use 'looks' talk precisely when the question of endorsement is relevant, Bonevac responds that our perceptual experiences are normally veridical, and we count on this.

> *Looking* φ, from this perspective, is epistemically prior to *being* φ; our experience's being of a certain kind (*x*'s looking green, say) provides evidence – normally, accurate evidence, and the only evidence we require – that the object is φ ... Our experience constitutes evidence concerning the perceptual properties of the object; we defeasibly infer that the object has the properties it appears to have. So, normally, we do not bother to report that *x* *looks* green; we make the defeasible inference and report that *x* *is* green.[23]

This seems to get the phenomenology of observation reports wrong; I am certainly not *aware* that in my observational survey of the world, I am repeatedly jumping to defeasible conclusions from a prior and independent appreciation of my own subjective state. But such phenomenological considerations are far from conclusive.

But there are other points to be made in Sellars's favour. Bonevac argues that 'looks' talk need not concern endorsement; it is simpler than, and therefore epistemically prior to, 'sees' talk. But he has not argued that 'looks' talk is on the same level as 'is' talk. Indeed, Bonevac grants that 'is' talk is *logically* prior to 'looks' talk, merely on the grounds of the compositional structure of such claims.[24] Bonevac seems to think that the move from the logical priority of 'is' talk to its *epistemic* priority over 'looks' talk depends solely on the idea that 'looks' talk adds the complication of endorsement. Once he has denied that 'looks' talk must entail endorsement, he believes he can assert the epistemic fundamentality of 'looks' talk. However, endorsement is not the only difference in question: observation reports are less complex than appearance statements because they involve no reference to the subject of experience. The idea of a subject of experience makes a relatively late appearance in human cognitive development, as one would expect of something epistemically complex.

Sellars denies that sense-datum theorists can appropriately reconstruct physical object language in terms of sense-datum language, because the right kinds of generalizations will not be available. This criticism of sense-datum theories also applies to appearance theories. The uniformities among pure appearances can be formulated in ways susceptible to useful generalization only because we can utilize the language of physical objects in space and time.

> The very principles in terms of which the uniformities are selected carry with them the knowledge that these uniformities are *dependent* uniformities *which will continue only as long as these particular objects constitute one's environment*, and hence preclude the credibility of the generalization in [appearance] terms which abstract consideration might lead us to think of as instantially confirmed by the past uniformities.
>
> (PHM: 84, with an appropriate substitution)

If, indeed, the 'is' talk, which is logically simpler than 'looks' talk, cannot be given a reasonable epistemic rationale on the basis of 'looks' talk alone, then either it must be abandoned or the order of epistemic dependence must be reversed.

## Direct apprehension

Another, perhaps more general argument against a popular form of foundationalism is to be found in "The Structure of Knowledge" (SK III §§21–5: 338–9). It looks at the position of those philosophers who want to ground empirical knowledge in some form of *direct apprehension* of facts, unmediated by concepts.[25] Sellars says that such a position raises two serious problems:

> (1) What sort of entities are *facts*? Do they belong to the real (extra-conceptual) order? That 'fact' is roughly a synonym for 'truth', and 'true' is appropriately predicated of conceptual items (in overt speech or Mentalese) should give pause for thought. (SK III §22: 339)

He does not expand on this, but we can recognize that in his own ontology fact-talk is material mode metalinguistic talk about truths. If the given takes the form of a pre- or sub-conceptual apprehension of a fact, it would have to be both conceptual (quasi-linguistic), because of the relation between fact and truth, and non-conceptual (non-linguistic). We can see the tensions that beset sense-datum theories returning.

The second problem arises when we consider "(2) How is 'direct apprehension' to be understood?" For we can ask, "If the apprehend-*ing* is distinguishable from the apprehend*ed*, is it not also 'separable'? Might not apprehending occur without any *fact* being apprehended?" (SK III §23: 339). Many of the terms to describe this direct confrontation between the knower and the known derive from the models of sight or grasping. But both the root metaphors, *to see* and *to grasp,* are achievement terms and contrast not only with the abject failure to see or to grasp, but also with the mere *seeming to see* and *seeming to grasp.*

> Now the distinction between *seeing* and merely *seeming to see* implies a criterion. To rely on the metaphors of 'apprehending' or 'presence of the object' is to obscure the need of criteria for distinguishing between 'knowing' and 'seeming to know', which ultimately define what it means to speak of knowledge as a *correct* or well-founded *thinking* that something is the case ... If so, to know that we have apprehended a fact, we would have to know that the criteria which distinguish *apprehending* from *seeming to apprehend* were satisfied. (SK III §§24–5: 339)

The notion of direct apprehension of facts is, Sellars claims, "a merely verbal solution ... an *ad hoc* regress stopper" (SK III §25: 339) revealed as such by simply taking seriously the root metaphors it is based on.

Sellars's formulation deserves further clarification. Direct-apprehension theorists might agree with the idea that "to know that we have apprehended a fact, we would have to know that the criteria which distinguish *apprehending* from *seeming to apprehend* were satisfied". A direct-apprehension theorist could conceive of basic knowledge of facts in two ways. He could say it is my direct apprehension of the fact that *p* that justifies my knowledge that *p*, or he could say that my knowledge of my directly apprehending that *p* justifies my knowledge that *p*. If he chooses the first way, then all that is relevant to my knowing that *p* is that I directly apprehend that *p*: I do *not* need to *know* that I directly apprehend that *p*. If he chooses the second path, then knowledge of the direct apprehension is indeed relevant. It seems that Sellars's charge holds against the second path, but perhaps not against the first.

But I think Sellars's criticism is also valid against the first path. For even if it is just the direct apprehension of the fact that *p* that somehow justifies my belief that *p*, if apprehension is subject to standards and can sometimes *seem* to occur when in fact it has not, then the reasonableness of any belief I form on the basis of my (purported) apprehensions will be sensitive to my ability to spot seemings or misapprehensions. This, in turn, again implies that I must have *some* metaknowledge that I bring to bear in some way in forming and maintaining my beliefs, but this is incompatible with the epistemic independence of such factual knowledge.

## Atomism and concept acquisition

The theory of concepts and their acquisition is not really a digression from a discussion of knowledge, for any epistemology must contain a story about how we acquire concepts, what having and exercising a concept amounts to, and how these relate to the epistemic status of the exercise of concepts in particular acts of knowledge. Just as the Cartesian tradition has tended to assume epistemological foundationalism, so also has it tended to assume a similarly hierarchical structure for concepts. That is, it has assumed that there is some set of independent, primitively meaningful concepts in terms of which all our other concepts can be defined or out of which they can be constructed. The rationalists and the empiricists differed about which

concepts were basic and why they possessed primitive meaningfulness, but both assumed some such conceptual foundationalism.

Empiricists have traditionally held that we acquire our basic,
simple concepts by abstracting them from instances in experience.
Thus, we acquire the concept *red* by abstraction from experiences of
red. The primary existence of red, then, must be in *experiences of red*,
whether these are thought of as relations to a sense datum or as
apprehensions of something's looking red. The redness of a physical
object, then, must be in some sense derivative from or definable in
terms of the primary redness in experiences. But Sellars rejects this
picture of sensible qualities, at least as an analysis of the manifest
image:

> I shall begin my examination of 'X looks red to S at t' with the
> simple but fundamental point that the sense of 'red' in which
> things *look* red is, on the face of it, the same as that in which
> things *are* red. When one glimpses an object and decides that it
> looks red (to *me*, *now*, from here) and wonders whether it really *is*
> red, one is surely wondering whether the colour – red – which it
> looks to have is the one it really does have.
>
> (EPM: §12, in SPR: 141; in KMG: 220)

Combined with Sellars's analysis of 'looks', both the notion of ostensive
definition and the hierarchical structure of concepts is abandoned.

> For if the ability to recognize that x looks green presupposes the
> concept of *being green*, and if this in turn involves knowing in what
> circumstances to view an object to ascertain its colour, then, since
> one can scarcely determine what the circumstances are without
> noticing that certain objects have certain perceptible characteris-
> tics – including colours – it would seem that one could not form the
> concept of *being green*, and, by parity of reasoning, of the other
> colours, unless he already had them.
>
> (EPM: §19, in SPR: 147; in KMG: 226)

The point is this: suppose that in order to be able to recognize that
something *looks* green, I have to be able to recognize when things *are*
green. In order to do that, I must be sensitive to differences in observation conditions. But I can recognize either standard or unusual
observation conditions only by noticing characteristics of the various
things in my environment, among which we surely must include
colours. I cannot, therefore, be said to have the concept of something's
being green in isolation from concepts of being red, yellow, light, dark,

perhaps even such concepts as being in shadow, near a light source, in moonlight and so on. I may also have to be sensitive to disturbances in *me* as well as in my environment: am I awake and alert, have I been dabbling in too much alcohol or hallucinogens, am I colour-blind or wearing tinted sunglasses?

Given Sellars's functionalist theory of meaning and the tight connection he draws between meaning and intentionality, it is no surprise that he rejects the foundationalist theory of concepts. Concepts are states (or better, dispositions) of thinkers specified by their role in a complex language-like system of inference-like transitions that mediates between the subject's perceptual encounter with the world and its acting in the world. Thus we can say that Sellars adopts a form of the coherence theory of concepts.

More to the point, Sellars adopts a particularly aggressive form of the theory. After raising the problem in the preceding quotation, Sellars responds to it as follows:

> Now, it just won't do to reply that to have the concept of green, to know what it is for something to be green, it is sufficient to respond when one is *in point of fact* in standard conditions, to green objects with the vocable "This is green." Not only must the conditions be of a sort that is appropriate for determining the color of an object by looking, the subject must *know* that conditions of this sort *are* appropriate. And while this does not imply that one must have concepts before one has them, it does imply that one can have the concept of green only by having a whole battery of concepts of which it is one element. It implies that while the process of acquiring the concept of green may – indeed does – involve a long history of acquiring *piecemeal* habits of response to various objects in various circumstances, there is an important sense in which one has *no* concept pertaining to the observable properties of physical objects in Space and Time unless one has them all – and, indeed, as we shall see, a great deal more besides.
>
> (EPM: §19, in SPR: 147–8; in KMG: 226–7)

To the coherence theory of concepts, Sellars adds the requirement that concepts not be held *blindly*; to have a concept is not just to have a disposition that plays a role in a complex, inferentially articulated system that mediates one's interaction with the world, but also the subject and the system must be *epistemologically reflective* in that the subject exercises her concepts knowingly. Oddly, Sellars never explicitly defends this requirement in "Empiricism and the Philosophy of Mind".

Here is an argument in favour of epistemological reflexivity. In his epistemological discussions, Sellars tends to employ the relatively "thin" vocabulary of reports and responses rather than the "richer" vocabulary of beliefs. He seeks to avoid, as far as possible, extraneous Cartesian implications that might accompany words such as 'belief'. (After all, he grew up in an environment where the implications and use of 'belief' were a matter of great controversy between the Cook Wilsonians, the pragmatists, the logical positivists, etc.) But if one is focusing on the thin notion of a *response*, it is easy to see that it cannot be "sufficient to respond when one is *in point of fact* in standard conditions, to green objects with the vocable 'This is green'", for it might not be too difficult to build a simple machine that could do that. The epistemological reflexivity requirement rules out such a machine as a possessor of concepts; in fact it sets the bar quite high, for it effectively means that in order to have *any* concepts, one must be a complete knower in some sense. A "complete knower" in this sense is not an *ideal* knower, but an *achieved* knower: one with general, reliable, but not universal, success who is capable of self-correction when things go sideways. (Just what is essential to being a complete knower is a crucial question to which we shall return. Many think Sellars has set the bar too high here.)

## Appearance theories II

Sellars's adoption of a coherence theory of concepts opens up a new line of response from the appearance theorists. This line of response is adumbrated by Roderick Firth in "Coherence, Certainty, and Epistemic Priority" (although not as a response to Sellars in particular). Firth's overall purpose is to defend some of C. I. Lewis's objections to coherentism and thereby Lewis's foundationalism. Firth argues, in Part I of his essay, that a coherence theory of *concepts* is compatible with a Lewis-style foundationalist theory of *justification*. *Prima facie*, Firth admits, this is not clear:

> For if a philosopher maintains that 'The apple is red' can be analyzed as meaning "The apple would look red under such and such physical conditions," he is assuming that "looks red" is logically prior to "is red," i.e., that it is at least *logically* possible to have the concept "looks red" *before* we acquire the concept "is red." But if the coherence theory of concepts is correct, and we cannot fully understand "looks red" unless we possess the contrasting

concept "is red," then it would seem that it is *not* logically possible to have the concept "looks red" before we have the concept "is red".[26]

In Sellars's scheme, 'looks red' contrasts directly with 'is seen to be red', not 'is red', for, remember, both qualitative and existential lookings are on the same level as seeing statements.[27] Nevertheless, what is sauce for the goose is sauce for the gander. Sellars espouses a coherence theory of concepts, yet he wants to claim that the concept *is red* is conceptually prior to the concept *looks red*. If part of the meaning of these concepts is their mutual contrast, as it must be on Sellars's theory, then Sellars appears to be caught in his own net.

Firth himself thinks that the problem can be overcome, for even before learning the distinction between the adult concepts *looks red* and *is red,* a child applies the *word* 'red' "to things that *look* red to him whether these things are, as we should say, 'really red,' or whether they are merely made to appear red by abnormal conditions of observation".[28] Firth concludes "that it would not be unreasonable to assert that the child is using 'red' to express a primitive form of the concept 'looks red'".[29] It is a primitive form of *looks red* because the child does not understand its contrast to *is red,* but as long as the child retains this primitive conception when he acquires full adult conceptions of *looking* and *being red,* there is no direct threat to foundationalism from the coherentist interdefinition of the concepts of *looking red* and *being red.* "There is no inconsistency in maintaining that even as adults we continue to have *a* concept 'looks red' which is logically prior to our concept 'is red'".[30]

Interestingly, Sellars anticipated this line of thought. In a footnote added to the 1963 edition of "Empiricism and the Philosophy of Mind", Sellars remarks:

> The argument can admit a distinction in principle between a rudimentary concept of "green" which could be learned without learning the logical space of looks talk, and a richer concept of "green" in which "is green" can be challenged by "merely looks green." The essential point is that even to have the more rudimentary concept presupposes having a battery of other concepts.
>
> (EPM: §19, in SPR: 148; in KMG: 227)

Note two different points in Sellars's remark. First, Firth does not seem to be contemplating a thoroughgoing concept coherentism. Rather, he seems to assume that what the child's word 'red' expresses before he is inaugurated into the subtleties of the appearance–reality distinction is (i) a concept, (ii) capable of ostensive specification independently of other concepts the child might possess, and (iii) best understood as a form of 'looks red', not 'is red'. If Firth assumes that there are some purely ostensively specified concepts on which more sophisticated concepts rest, he has begged the question against Sellars, for Sellars has argued powerfully against ostensively defined concepts. Therefore Firth has not shown that a *thoroughgoing* coherence theory of concepts is compatible with a foundation of Lewisian expressive judgements.

Secondly, Sellars implies that if we do attribute a concept to the child before his realization of the appearance–reality distinction, it is a rudimentary form of *is red*, not *looks red*. This theme is picked up and made fully explicit in "The Lever of Archimedes":

> I want to argue that while there is, indeed, *a* concept pertaining to red which is prior to the pair of contrastive concepts, it is a concept of *is red*. It is not the concept of a *kind* of experience or a *manner* of experiencing, but of something which is an *object* of experience.                    (FMPP I §40: 10–11)

Again, as in the response to Bonevac, the point is that the concept of *looking F* is essentially more complex than the concept of *being F,* so the presumption must be that the latter is prior to the former.

There are deeper issues in this neighbourhood on the borderline between the epistemology and the metaphysics of sense. The metaphysical issues can be left to dangle until Chapter 8, but some epistemological issues concerning the Carus Lectures need to be addressed here.

### A different form of the myth?

In the Carus Lectures, Sellars characterizes the myth of the given as follows:

> If a person is directly aware of an item which has categorial status C, then the person is aware of it *as* having categorial status C.

> This principle is, perhaps, the most basic form of what I have castigated as "The Myth of the Given." ... *To reject the Myth of the Given is to reject the idea that the categorial structure of the world – if it has a categorial structure – imposes itself on the mind as a seal imposes itself on melted wax.*                    (FMPP I §§44–5: 11–12)

Some take this to be a major revision in Sellars's conception of the given.[31] Rejecting the myth of the given in *this* form, they believe, still leaves a great deal of the "framework of givenness" standing, namely, everything supposedly given that does *not* concern something's categorial status. Sellars is no longer a hero of the battle against foundationalism.

Is this Carus Lectures version, the rejection of a categorial given, a drastic change from his characterizations of the myth of the given in "Empiricism and the Philosophy of Mind"? Since Sellars himself attributes Protean forms to the myth, it is hard to tell. The Carus Lectures version certainly picks up themes already present in "Empiricism and the Philosophy of Mind":

> [W]e can easily take for granted that the process of teaching a child to use a language is that of teaching it to discriminate elements within a logical space of particulars, universals, facts, etc., of which it is already undiscriminatingly aware, and to associate these discriminated elements with verbal symbols.
>
> (EPM: §30, in SPR: 161–2; in KMG: 241)

Sellars clearly takes the "logical space" in question to have a certain categorial structure. So the formulation in the Carus Lectures is not just an entirely new tack on the myth, but by confining itself to the categorial level, it does seem to narrow significantly the meaning of rejecting the myth. In "Empiricism and the Philosophy of Mind", Sellars characterizes a form of the myth this way:

> One of the forms taken by the Myth of the Given is the idea that there is, indeed *must be*, a structure of particular matter of fact such that (a) each fact can not only be non-inferentially known to be the case, but presupposes no other knowledge either of particular matter of fact, or of general truths; and (b) such that the noninferential [*sic.*] knowledge of facts belonging to this structure constitutes the ultimate court of appeals for all factual claims – particular and general – about the world.
>
> (EPM: §32, in SPR: 164; in KMG: 243)

Rejecting this form of the myth seems to leave no room for claiming that such facts as that *the ball is red* or that *the ball appears red to me* could be given. Rejecting the myth as characterized in the Carus Lectures excludes knowledge only of facts about categorial status, for example, that red is a property of physical objects or a property of sense data or an adverbial property of certain mental acts. (And remember, in Sellars's view, such "facts" are really metalinguistic or metaconceptual classifications, and not directly "about the world" at all.)

The crucial question is whether Sellars, in the Carus Lectures, abandons his rejection of the givenness of particular facts, and now rejects only the givenness of "categorial facts". There is no reason to read the Carus Lectures in this way. Rather, Sellars focuses on a particularly significant form of the myth that he believes persists even in such sophisticated and critical thinkers as Firth and Chisholm. Sellars still labels what he distinguishes there as a *form* of the myth, not as the myth itself.

A relatively early precursor to the Carus Lectures characterization of the given is in "Scientific Realism or Irenic Instrumentalism", presented as a lecture in 1963 and published in 1965.

> [T]o reject the myth of the given is not to commit oneself to the idea that empirical knowledge as it is now constituted has no rock bottom level of observation predicates proper. It is to commit oneself rather to the idea that even if it does have a rock bottom level, it is *still* in principle replaceable by another conceptual framework in which these predicates do not, *strictly speaking,* occur. It is in this sense, and in this sense *only,* that I have rejected the dogma of givenness with respect to observation predicates.
>
> (SRI: 187; in PP: 353)[32]

Still, there are important questions raised here about what it really means for something to be given. As we shall see in Chapter 8, Sellars believes that our sensory capacities, including our sensory state spaces (e.g. the colour solid, location in which partially determines the identity of a visual sensation, the auditory space determined by pitch, tone, and timbre that defines sounds) are biologically determined. Furthermore, these capacities and the states in which they manifest themselves have evolved to "map" certain aspects of the world. The sensation of orange is – objectively – further from the sensation of blue than from the sensation of red, and this is determined by our biological apparatus. But is the fact that orange is more like red than like blue something just *given,* something we can just "read off" our experience itself? Surely we do not want to say that this is a fact that we learn solely by learning our language, such as the fact that brothers are male siblings. It does not seem merely to be a conventional truth or an analytic truth. Nor is it something we discover empirically by a process of hypothesis and confirmation. Knowing the structure of the

116

proper sensibles seems simpler than, and a prerequisite for, engaging in empirical confirmation. Yet if orange's greater similarity to red than to blue is not simply a *given*, do we not have to concede that it is either an analytic or an empirical truth?

As Gary Gutting points ou,[33] Sellars seems committed to the idea that, as a conceptual framework is replaced by a successor, although the first-order predicates in the successor framework are not *identical* to their predecessors, there must be second-order predicates in common between them. Otherwise we could not make sense of the idea that a predicate of the later framework is the successor to a predicate of the earlier framework. Referring to the passage from "Scientific Realism or Irenic Instrumentalism" (1965) quoted above, Gutting then asks whether this means that Sellars ultimately believes that these second-order predicates are simply given.

> Thus, for Sellars, the predicates of the observational framework play the role of an epistemological given only if it is required that *they themselves* must occur in any theoretical framework. However, this does not exclude the possibility of these predicates' making their influence felt (even if they are not present), via their second-order properties, on the new predicates of the theoretical framework. Rejecting the given only means rejecting immutably true descriptions of the world and immutably appropriate descriptive categories. Immutable *structures* (specified by second-order predicates) of descriptive framework are *not* rejected. Such structures are apparently Sellars's equivalent of Kantian categories.[34]

Should the friends of the given take solace in Sellars's position? Notice that no first-order descriptive statement about the world is epistemically independent. On the other hand, there must be some non-epistemic constraints on our theories. Here we begin to touch upon the metaphysics of the sensory. It currently seems impossible to ground the structure of colour space in objective facts about the electromagnetic spectrum or any other properties of the perceptible object to which we apply colour terms in the manifest image. If, however, there is a domain in the world, and in particular, within the sensitive organism, that exhibits the abstract properties of colour space, then we might be in a position to explain why colour space has the structure it does. We would then be in a position to explain why it is that orange is closer to red than to blue. That full story will unfold in Chapter 8.

## Midterm review

We have now looked at Sellars's critique of some of the more popular candidates for the empirical basis of our knowledge in a foundationalist framework. From these examples, a more general formulation of Sellars's challenge emerges.

1. The doctrine of the given is that any empirical knowledge that *p* requires some (or is itself) basic, epistemically independent knowledge (that *g, h, i, ...*), which is epistemically efficacious with respect to *p*.[35]
2. Epistemic efficacy – relations of epistemic support – is always a matter of inferential support, formal or material.
3. Inferential relations are always between items with propositional form.
4. Therefore, non-propositional items (such as sense data) are epistemically inefficacious and cannot serve as what is given.
5. No *inferentially* acquired, propositionally structured mental state is epistemically independent.
6. Examination of multiple candidates for non-inferentially acquired, propositionally structured mental states indicates that their epistemic status presupposes the possession by the knowing subject of other empirical knowledge, both of particulars and of general empirical truths.
7. Empirical knowledge that presupposes the possession by the knowing subject of other empirical knowledge is not epistemically independent.
8. All empirical knowledge is either inferential or non-inferential.
9. Therefore, it is reasonable to believe that no item of empirical knowledge can serve the function of a given.

This is not a knock-down argument. It is, in fact, inductive in the sense that it counts on the examination of cases to carry a good deal of weight. But most important, it offers no positive alternative. Philosophers have been moved to accept foundationalism because the alternative seemed hopeless: infinite regress or vicious circle. In order to allay the fears that drove philosophers to the given in the first place, Sellars needs to propose his own positive theory of empirical knowledge, and especially non-inferential empirical knowledge, for he never doubts for a moment that there is non-inferential knowledge. So, let us turn to the examination of Sellars's positive proposal for non-inferential empirical knowledge, after which we shall examine the status of epistemic principles in his epistemology.

## Observation knowledge

There must be non-inferential knowledge if there is empirical knowledge at all. Sellars's critique of the given leads him to maintain that the epistemic status of even our non-inferential knowledge must nonetheless depend on inferential relations to other pieces of knowledge. Justification is never atomistic. Obviously, in cases of non-inferential knowledge, such inferential relations must be cases of infer*ability*, not actual inference. But the uninferred, immediately known items that form the *de facto* epistemically efficacious basis of our empirical knowledge would have no epistemic status at all if they did not bear inferential relations to other items of our knowledge. So we shall first consider what these items are that are uninferred, endowed with positive epistemic status, and epistemically efficacious with respect to the rest of our empirical knowledge.

In "Empiricism and the Philosophy of Mind", as mentioned above, Sellars calls these items observation *reports*, even though in his use a report need not be an overt verbal performance. This is in part due the structure of "Empiricism and the Philosophy of Mind": Sellars wants to avoid as far as possible heavily laden mentalistic terminology, pending his subsequent discussion of the philosophy of mind in the later parts of the article. In his other epistemological writings, such as "The Structure of Knowledge", "Givenness and Explanatory Coherence", "More on Givenness and Explanatory Coherence" and "Foundations for a Metaphysics of Pure Process", he talks of observation *beliefs*. But observation beliefs, as he understands them, are occurrent states, episodic in nature, not standing dispositions, as are many of our other beliefs. This is unproblematic; what is of more concern is what is the right kind of *content* for a basic observation.

One lesson Sellars draws from his critiques of sense-datum and appearance theories is epistemological realism. There are, of course, varieties of epistemological realism ranging from the naive to the indirect. Sellars's position is that observation knowledge of physical objects is epistemically direct, but causally indirect. This means that the knowledge of physical objects that we acquire in observation is not inferred from more immediate knowledge of any other kind of thing, whether a sense datum or the state of our own minds.

119

The normal result of the perceptual process is knowledge of the world; that is the point of the perceptual faculty and why it makes sense to treat perception as an epistemically immediate relation to physical objects. Observation knowledge, however, clearly results from a highly complex perceptual process that must be taken into account in the explanation of perceptual failure, illusion, hallucination and so on. Observation knowledge is therefore causally indirect. Our ordinary understanding of perception provides for its causal complexity via the concept of a sensation: a non-conceptual state of a perceiver that accounts for such phenomena as illusion and hallucination. The causal dimension of perception will be pursued in much greater detail in Chapter 8.

There is another important point to understand about observation: there is no fixed set of characteristics of physical objects to which observations are limited. That is, there is no clear-cut or principled limit on the vocabulary that can appropriately appear in observation claims. We can form non-inferential observation beliefs about red balls before us, but, with adequate training, we can also make direct, non-inferential reports of the location of a quasar or an α-particle in a cloud chamber. Observation reports need only be reliable responses, whatever vocabulary is used. Sellars believes that there is a special vocabulary that we employ in "minimalist" observation claims, that is, observation claims in which we risk as little as possible without moving up (or back) a level and characterizing our *experience* rather than *the world*. This vocabulary is that of the "proper and common sensibles". We can make minimal objective (that is, object-oriented) observation reports by saying, for example, "There's something red, round and smelly over there".

Why do observation reports and/or beliefs possess positive epistemic status, according to Sellars? At first glance, it might look as if we get two different answers from Sellars. In "Empiricism and the Philosophy of Mind" he asks why an observation report has *authority* and answers, "Clearly, on this account the only thing that can remotely be supposed to constitute such authority is the fact that one can infer the presence of a green object from the fact that someone makes this report" (EPM: §35, in SPR: 167; in KMG: 247). If we construe having authority as having positive epistemic status, then Sellars seems to say that the report has its status because of what follows from it, which would be a case of the conclusion justifying the premises. In "The Structure of Knowledge", however, he seems to suggest a different story:

> Now to say that this [observation belief] that something is the case
> is epistemically *justified* or *reasonable* or has authority is clearly
> *not* to say that Jones has correctly inferred from certain premises,
> which he has good reason to believe, that there is a red apple in
> front of him. For we are dealing with a *paradigm* case of non-
> inferential belief. *The authority of the [belief] accrues to it in quite
> a different way. It can be traced to the fact that Jones has learned
> how to use the relevant words in perceptual situations.*
>
> (SK II §37: 324)

But the stories are not, in fact, different, though the formulations
highlight different aspects of the situation. The explanation of the
report's possession of *authority* in "Empiricism and the Philosophy of
Mind" is an explanation of the report's epistemic efficacy, but its
having positive epistemic status rests on its correctness.[36]

In Sellars's view, positive epistemic status attaches to observation
beliefs and reports because, given the process by which language is
learned, *they are likely to be true.* Observation reports and beliefs are
thus *reliable indicators* of the conditions reported or believed in; observation reports are like temperature readings or the pronouncements
some cars make about their condition ("Your door is open"). Thus,
Sellars installs what is fundamentally an externalist condition at the
very heart of his theory of empirical justification. There is no appeal
here to insight or some special kind of direct apprehension or to the
self-transparency of mental states. Chains of empirical justification
can properly start with observation reports and/or beliefs simply
because they are reliable indicators of their conditions, which licenses
an inference to the likely truth of their contents, from which other
things follow by either formal or material rules of inference.[37]

Yet this is not the end of the story. Sellars is not a reliabilist. After
all, a car may report reliably that the door is open, but it cannot be said
that the car really *knows* that the door is open. Reliable indication is
not sufficient for knowledge. The condition Sellars adds is that the
putative knower must also *know* that she is a reliable indicator of the
kind of condition reported. Again, the statement of this condition in
"Empiricism and the Philosophy of Mind" throws many readers off the
track:

> if the authority of the report 'This is green' lies in the fact that the
> existence of green items appropriately related to the perceiver can
> be inferred from the occurrence of such reports, it follows that only
> a person who is able to draw this inference, and therefore who has

not only the concept *green*, but also the concept of uttering 'This is green' – indeed, the concept of certain conditions of perception, those which would correctly be called "standard conditions" – could be in a position to token 'This is green' in recognition of its authority. In other words, for a *Konstatierung* 'This is green' to "express observational knowledge," not only must it be a *symptom* or *sign* of the presence of a green object in standard conditions, but the perceiver must know that tokens of 'This is green' *are* symptoms of the presence of green objects in conditions which are standard for visual perception.

(EPM: §35, in SPR: 168; in KMG: 247)

Once more an emphasis on the epistemic efficacy of the report rather than its positive epistemic status puts a non-standard twist to the thought. The statement in "The Structure of Knowledge" is, perhaps, more straightforward:

39. If we were to overhear him, and if we had reason to believe that none of these countervailing conditions obtain, *we* would be justified in reasoning as follows,

Jones has thought-out-loud 'Lo! Here is a red apple'
(no countervailing conditions obtain);
So, there is good reason to believe that there is a red apple in front of him.

Note that although this is an *inferential* justification of *our* belief that there is a red apple in front of Jones, it is a special kind of inference. It has the form:

The thought that-*p* occurs to Jones in a certain context and manner;
So, it is reasonable to believe that-*p*.

The same proposition, that-*p*, is mentioned in both the premise and the conclusion. But the first mention concerns the fact of its occurrence *as a propositional event* in a context to which the basic features of language learning are relevant. From this premise, the inference is drawn that the proposition in question is one which it is reasonable to believe.

40. We looked at the above example from the standpoint of an external observer. Let us now look at it from the standpoint of Jones himself. As we saw in the preceding lecture, to be fully a master of his language, *Jones must know these same facts about what is involved in learning to use perceptual sentences in perceptual contexts.* Thus, Jones too must know that other specifiable

things being equal, the fact that a person says 'Lo! Here is a red apple' is a good reason to believe that he is indeed in the presence of a red apple. Thus, Jones, *too,* can reason:
I just thought-out-loud 'Lo! Here is a red apple'
(no countervailing conditions obtain);
So, there is good reason to believe that there is a red apple in front of me.
41. Of course, the conclusion of this reasoning is not the *thinking* involved in his original perceptual experience. Like all justification arguments, it is a higher-order thinking.

(SK II §§39–41: 325–36)[38]

Jones must have sufficient other knowledge to be able to recognize that the production of an observation report or possession of an observation belief gives him reason to accept the report or retain the belief. But here is the problem as far as foundationalism is concerned: much of this other knowledge is itself *empirical* knowledge, and some of it is even *general* empirical knowledge. It includes empirical knowledge about his status as a language learner, knowledge about what conditions count as standard for observations of the relevant type, and knowledge of the particular conditions of this observation. This is incompatible with the standard empiricist picture, for our non-inferential knowledge is not atomistically independent of other knowledge. The classic empiricist idea that our knowledge is structured as a partial ordering from atoms of knowledge of particular observational fact to ever higher levels of empirical generalization is destroyed.

## The epistemic reflexivity requirement

We see here a broadening of the epistemic reflexivity requirement we encountered earlier in our discussion of Sellars's coherence theory of concepts. There, the requirement stipulated that concepts need to be employed knowingly; here we can understand the requirement to stipulate that observation reports need to be made knowingly.[39] But what does that mean? The epistemic reflexivity requirement is a keystone element in Sellars's epistemology, so care must be taken to do it justice. I will first discuss the motivations for the epistemic reflexivity requirement, then state more fully what the requirement really comes to and, finally, return to consider various objections that have been raised against it.

## Why the epistemic reflexivity requirement?

The epistemic reflexivity requirement is a major element of Sellars's theory of concepts and his theory of epistemic justification. Yet, as Alston points out "The author just lays it down",[40] without defending this important condition explicitly. What convinced Sellars that either we are already committed to the epistemic reflexivity requirement (an implication of some turns of phrase in "Empiricism and the Philosophy of Mind"), or that it simply did not require explicit defence? One line of thought is clear: although Sellars treats observation reports and beliefs as "thin" symbol occurrences, he does not accept externalism, and the epistemic reflexivity requirement is an internalistic require-ment that precludes fancy thermostats and talking vehicles from being knowers. But the epistemic reflexivity requirement is not the only way or the easiest way to do that, so we need to push deeper.

Sellars also regularly connects justification with having reasons: "Presumably, to be justified in believing something is to have good rea-sons for believing it, as contrasted with its contradictory" (SK III §2: 332). We need to reflect, therefore, on the notion of *reasons*. Reasons are primarily items that can function as premises in inferences.[41] So we return to the theme that knowledge is fundamentally propositional in form, and draw a corollary: only beliefs can justify beliefs. Being justi-fied in believing that *p* is not just a matter of there *being* good reason for it; one must *have* that reason. And to *have* a reason, one must, in some sense, understand it, which is itself already a form of knowledge.

The externalist would object to assuming a connection between justification and having reasons. Why, for *S* to be justified in believ-ing that *p*, is it insufficient that there *be* a reason to believe that *p*, even if *S* doesn't *have* that reason in the sense of understanding or being aware of it?[42] The reason to believe that *p* would have to be related to *S*'s believing that *p* in *some* way, say causally (otherwise *S*'s belief that *p* would seem to be entirely accidental), but neither the reason to believe that *p* nor the relation between the reason to believe that *p* and *S*'s belief that *p* need be cognitively available to *S*.

Sellars never addresses the externalist objection directly. When he wrote "Empiricism and the Philosophy of Mind", externalism as an explicitly formulated position was still a decade away. Even in his later work, Sellars does not pay attention to externalism as such. So we have to extrapolate his reasons for discarding a pure externalism almost out of hand. The key here is that externalism is a form of what Sellars variously calls "factualism", or "descriptivism" (recall the above quotation (from EPM §5), in which he likens attempts to analyse the epistemic in terms of the non-epistemic to the naturalistic fallacy). In a comment that seems recently to have spawned a small cottage industry of neo-Sellarsian epistemologists, Sellars says: "The essential point is that in characterizing an episode or a state as that of *knowing*, we are not giving an empirical description of that episode or state; we are placing it in the logical space of reasons, of justifying and being able to justify what one says" (EPM: §36, in SPR: 169; in KMG: 248). Epistemological characterizations of someone's state are *not* empirical descriptions. Sellars does not mean that we have some non-empirical access to cognitive states (either our own or of others). If I attribute knowledge, for example, of what time it is, to myself or to someone else, I do *not* do so on some non-empirical basis; clearly, any such attribution would have to be based on the empirical facts of the case. Thus, the emphasis in Sellars's denial is not on 'empirical' but on 'description'. 'Description' gets most of its punch from the contrast to 'prescription'. Consider Sellars's assertion quoted in Chapter 4:

> The naturalistic "thesis" that the world, including the verbal behavior of those who use the term 'ought' – and the mental states involving the concept to which this word gives expression – can, "in principle," be described without using the term 'ought' or any other prescriptive expression, is a logical point about what is to count as a description *in principle* of the world.      (CDCM: 282)

Sellars is denying that epistemic characterizations of episodes or states could ever, even in principle, be so fully unpacked that 'ought' or its cognates and prescriptive relatives would be eliminated. Epistemic characterizations of episodes or states are therefore not *reducible* to or *replaceable* by empirical descriptions, because there is an ineluctable prescriptive element in such characterizations. Among other things, this entails the rejection of any epistemological naturalism that would simply substitute the empirical psychology of belief fixation for epistemology.

Sellars is a naturalist, even though he rejects a Quinean epistemological naturalism. Naturalism, in Sellars's view, is a thesis about the descriptive resources of an empirically adequate language. Prescriptive or normative language does a different job from descriptive language. Epistemic terms are normative, not descriptive. It will also turn out that Sellars is a kind of anti-realist about norms; norms, as we saw briefly in Chapter 4 and shall discuss more thoroughly at the end of this book, do not show up in the final map of the world, although they are indispensable for its creation and use. Therefore, in Sellars's view, we are not committed to the *ontological* reality of norms, although we are most certainly committed to their *practical reality*. Sellars's anti-realism about norms is not in the least a subjectivism about norms, as will be made clear in Chapters 9 and 10.

So much for the negative part of Sellars's claim about epistemic characterizations. His positive claim is that such characterizations place their objects "in the logical space of reasons". *Any* characterization, epistemic or otherwise, occurs within the logical space of reasons in the sense that any characterization is open to challenge or defence, but it is important to see that it is not the epistemic characterization that Sellars is concerned with here, but the thing characterized. If one says that John knows that snow is white, it is John's state that is being placed in the logical space of reasons. Similarly, if one says that Fred just remembered where he put his keys, it is, again, a particular episode Fred has undergone that one is placing in the logical space of reasons. John's and Fred's states are what are eligible for challenge or defence.

Further, the logical space of reasons is not characterized by Sellars as merely the realm of the truth evaluable; he explicitly describes the logical space of reasons as constituted by actual and potential *justifications*. This introduces a significant pragmatic flavour, for several reasons. First, justification is primarily an *activity*; anti-Platonist that he is, Sellars takes it that talk about justifications must ultimately be cashed out in terms of people justifying. Secondly, the primary *object* of justification, according to Sellars, is itself also activity or, better, conduct. Sellars makes this clear in one of his early essays, "Language, Rules, and Behavior", where he explicitly asks, "what sort of thing, then, is a justification?" And especially, "What sort of thing does one who justifies justify?" He points out that one of the things we justify is *conduct*, but that we also justify *assertions*. Is there a relation between these two contexts of justification?

> Shall we say, then, that one does not justify a *proposition,* but the *assertion* of a proposition? – that one does not justify a *principle* but the *acceptance* of a principle? Shall we say that all justification is, in a sense which takes into account the dispositional as well as the occurrent, a *justificatio actionis?* I am strongly inclined to think that this is the case. (LRB: 295)

In "Language, Rules, and Behavior", Sellars has not yet made all the distinctions he needs to make, teasing apart *action* from other (equally evaluable) acts, or rules of action from rules of criticism. But he never abandons his emphasis on the activity or practice of justifying and the primacy of doings as the object of justification.

There are several important consequences: any knowledge attribution which locates some episode or state in the logical space of reasons thereby situates it in an ambience of social practices, and that episode is simply impossible without those practices. These practices are normatively constituted: they are defined by the norms or rules with regard to which our acts, whether actions or not, are right or wrong, correct or incorrect, and the practices are themselves subject to ongoing assessment in terms of higher ideals. The social practices within which a cognition is located are not arbitrary nor merely conventional: as practices of justification, they are ultimately responsible to the ideals of logical consistency and explanatory coherence. We cannot claim to have a detailed, much less a final and unchangeable, conception of the standards by which justification is secured and transmitted. A detailed implementation of the ideals of consistency and coherence must be worked out in practice itself in the course of the self-correcting enterprise of rational enquiry.

Sellars's distinction between rules of action (ought-to-do's) and rules of criticism (ought-to-be's) applies within the logical space of reasons. An observation report is correct as an instance of an ought-to-be. For example, it ought to be the case that English speakers are disposed to respond to red things by calling them 'red'. When we immediately respond to something red with 'red' (in thought or overt speech), we are not "following a rule" in the sense of somehow "noticing" the object's redness, and then (as a separable act) applying the (independently represented) rule "Call red things 'red'". Nonetheless, the behaviour is rule-governed in the sense that it occurs because there is an ought-to-be in the linguistic community that red things be called 'red', which informed the activities of our teachers, who brought it about that we conform our behaviour to the rule.

For some state to be a *knowing*, is, *inter alia,* for it to be in the logical space of reasons. For it to be in the logical space of reasons is for it to have a place or role in a rule-governed (social) practice of justification. While one might assume that individual states get located in the space of reasons piecemeal, one by one, that's not how Sellars conceives of it. For, as he notes, what is important about observation reports and/or beliefs is that they occur "in a certain context and manner". That is, they occur in an appropriate observation context and to someone on account of and in accord with a proper training in the ought-to-be's, the rules, of one's language. But, as Sellars notes in "The

Structure of Knowledge", justification is always a higher-order activity. Justifying what one says or thinks requires not just that one produce appropriate observation responses to the world, but also that one have the ability to take a higher-order stance towards those productions and be sensitive to their conformance with the rules governing the activity at hand (in this case, observation).

As we shall see more fully in Chapter 9, ought-to-be's can exist only if there are rule-obeying agents who can implement them by transforming them into and acting upon ought-to-do's. One is a fully fledged agent only if one is capable of obeying rules because the whole constellation of rule-governed behaviours can be sustained only by rule-obeying agents.

Sellars thinks that we cannot assess an individual state as a *knowing* independently from assessing the subject of that state as a *knower*. To return to the example of the talking car, the car's observation report, "The door is open", is a reliable response to the condition reported, but the car is not a participant in a rule-governed social practice of justifying or being able to justify what it says, and thus the car is not a knower, although its report can be evidence for our knowledge. Sellars says,

> If I reject the framework of traditional empiricism, it is not because I want to say that empirical knowledge has *no* foundation. For to put it this way is to suggest that it is really "empirical knowledge so-called," and to put it in a box with rumors and hoaxes. There is clearly *some* point to the picture of human knowledge as resting on a level of propositions – observation reports – which do not rest on other propositions in the same way as other propositions rest on them. On the other hand, I do wish to insist that the metaphor of "foundation" is misleading in that it keeps us from seeing that if there is a logical dimension in which other empirical propositions rest on observation reports, there is another logical dimension in which the latter rest on the former.
> (EPM: §38, in SPR: 170; in KMG: 250)

Clearly, it is important that the relations of epistemic dependence he is discussing be of two different types or "dimensions". Otherwise the charge of circularity (which he must still work to avoid, as we shall see) would be unanswerable. One of the "dimensions" – the bottom-up direction – is what one would expect: observation provides a basis from which we can, inductively, infer general empirical truths. But in the other direction, reports or beliefs can be construed as *knowledge* only if the subject who makes them is a knower who, as knower, commands a number of general truths and practices. Only in that case do they occur as items in the logical space of reasons.

In "Empiricism and the Philosophy of Mind", Sellars expresses this notion obscurely by referring to the *presuppositions* of knowledge.

> One of the forms taken by the Myth of the Given is the idea that there is, indeed *must be,* a structure of particular matter of fact such that (a) each fact can not only be non-inferentially known to be the case, but presupposes no other knowledge either of particular matter of fact, or of general truths.
>
> (EPM: §32, in SPR: 164; in KMG: 243)

The basic thrust of his doctrine is that in attributing any particular bit of knowledge to something, we already presuppose that the question of whether that thing is a knower has been answered in the affirmative.[43] The epistemic reflexivity requirement (ERR) is the fundamental criterion for being a knower, because it is the necessary condition for participating in the self-correcting enterprise of gaining empirical knowledge and the self-sustaining practice of following rules.[44] The epistemic reflexivity requirement thus constitutes Sellars's attempt to capture this other logical dimension in which observation reports rest on other empirical propositions.

## Problem 1: how high the bar?

One clear problem is that the epistemic reflexivity requirement seems to set the bar very high: too high, according to many of his critics. Sellars requires that knowers not only be reliable reporters of their environment, but also that they be participants in the practice of justification. It is dubious that animals and very young children meet this standard. If they do not, however, they have no knowledge at all, in Sellars's view. Although knowledge is commonly attributed to both animals and pre-linguistic children, in Sellars's view such attributions are either metaphorical or employ a different sense of knowledge.[45] We clearly need to spell out what kind of epistemic reflexivity Sellars calls for, especially because explicit reflection on one's epistemic situation is a relatively rare piece of human behaviour, and knowledge is not confined only to intellectuals.

It seems clear that epistemic reflexivity requirement is itself such a strong requirement that Sellars must intend only its weakest reading. The principal issue is whether the required metaknowledge must be explicit or can be implicit. If the knowledge of one's perceptual reliability that is required for observation knowledge has to be explicit and employed in each instance of observation, it is difficult to see how anyone could accumulate enough observation knowledge to ground any empirical knowledge at all. Similarly, if one's awareness of the external and internal conditions of observation had to be explicit and employed in each instance, observation knowledge would be at best a rare achievement.

But if the metaknowledge required by the epistemic reflexivity requirement need not be explicit, if the epistemic reflexivity requirement requires only that one have the knowledge in the sense that it shows up in one's actual epistemic and/or conceptual behaviour, things are quite different. People can know things they cannot formulate or defend explicitly. Even so, the case for attributing knowledge to them can be incredibly strong. Perhaps the best example is knowledge of the rules of a language. I know English, but just what it is that I know when I know English, I cannot say. English is presumably governed by a finite, complex system of rules, and knowing English is operating in accordance with those rules in one's understanding and production of language. But I cannot formulate all the rules of English; in the current state of linguistics no one can. Perhaps my knowledge of the internal and external conditions of perception and my knowledge of the reliability of my perceptual responses is like my knowledge of the syntax and semantics of my language.

The analogy with language is more than passingly apt. In understanding Sellarsian epistemology, it is important to see that he is here too, as well as in his philosophy of language (and his philosophy of mind, as we will see), a kind of functionalist. Syntactic, semantic, epistemic and even mentalistic descriptions are really, in his view, classifications of items in terms of their role in a complex, rule-governed system. The epistemic system differs from the general rule-governed linguistic system in that it has a specific, relatively easily identifiable goal – truth and accurate picturing – whereas the goal of the general system of language *cum* thought is to enable us better to cope with the world.

We are now in a position to penetrate a bit deeper into the motivation for the epistemic reflexivity requirement. In Sellars's view, describing someone as possessing a certain concept or as knowing that *p* is not at all like describing an object as fifty centimetres long. It is more like describing that person as having, say, a bishop (in chess) or (in chess, again) having her opponent in check. Such descriptions presume a background of rules that define and constitute the positions, objects and moves concerned. In none of these cases is the game-relative description analysable into or reducible to a description that makes no reference to the rules of the game: having a bishop is not analysable into or reducible to having a certain physical relation to an object of a certain physical kind. The physical objects and relations that might embody having a bishop are beyond number. Similarly, having a justified observation belief is not just a matter of standing in some particular relationship to some object or state of affairs; the context of rules is essential to the identity and individuation conditions of such a state.

It is not just the potential infinity of embodiments of such facts as having one's opponent in check or justifiably believing that there is a red ball before one that is crucial. Even more important is that there are normative, indeed, cognitive presuppositions packed into such descriptions. Making a move in chess is not just a matter of the translation in space-time of some object (leaving aside for the moment the fact that there need be no particular physical movement at all): a pigeon in the park could move a chess piece to another legal square, but that would not be a chess move, because it was not done *because of* or *with respect for* the rules. To be a chess move, the action must be done *with regard for the rules*. This does not mean that the chess player needs to be thinking about the rules either before or as she moves. The inexpert player may, indeed, have to worry explicitly about the legality of the moves she contemplates, but the Grand Master probably does not pause to consider such trivialities. The Grand Master tends simply to "see" or consider only the legal options (indeed, the "good" legal options) and chooses among them. But the Grand Master undoubtedly acts with regard for the rules. It is appropriate to say that a move is a chess move only if it is made *knowingly*. This is the turn of phrase used in the earlier discussion of the epistemic reflexivity requirement and the coherence theory of concepts, and it is apt here as well.

Lest we become too enamoured of the image of the Grand Master playing chess, an image that is just as revealing is that of the young child (say, around five years old) who has very little ability to formulate explicitly the rules of the language she is speaking, but clearly has significant command of them. Not only does she tend to understand much of what is said and to formulate her own utterances with regard for the rules, but in response to a clear violation of the rules she may well laugh and point out that one cannot say *that*. She is on the road to being a critical user of language and is becoming increasingly sensitive to the rules as normative constraints on linguistic behaviour. She is also becoming a *knowing subject,* a critical user of her own beliefs and responses. It takes time and experience before one becomes a sophisticated critical thinker capable of formulating (much less applying) explicitly rules in the knowledge game, and some people never make it that far. But all that Sellars intends to demand is that in order to have knowledge, one must be sensitive to the rules of the knowledge game, even if the knowledge of those rules remains thoroughly implicit. A guffaw at a rank improbability, a raised eyebrow at a dubious inference, a decision that someone must be joking to make a certain claim, a wrinkled brow and a question "What?" or a challenge "Why?": these can be the behavioural currency in which an otherwise inarticulate critical sense expresses itself. One must have the rudiments of a critical apparatus in place, however inarticulately, in order to be following rules.

Nevertheless, the bar of the epistemic reflexivity requirement is high. The degree to which animals are epistemically critical is an empirical question, but they are probably not Sellarsian knowers. The results of developmental psychology are still open to interpretation, but arguably young children do not satisfy Sellars's criteria for knowers until they are at least four years old.[46] Until then, we can justifiably attribute to young children at most a knowledge-analogue. That seems intolerable to many people.[47] In Sellars's view, treating them as knowers is a projection on the part of the adults that is essential for their becoming knowers.

## Problem 2: circularity

Since Sellars is proposing a non-foundationalist theory of justification, it is natural to worry whether it is viciously circular or regressive, the major problem with coherence theories. Sellars responds:

> all that the view I am defending requires is that no tokening by S *now* of "This is green" is to count as "expressing observational knowledge" unless it is also correct to say of S that he *now* knows the appropriate fact of the form *X is a reliable symptom of Y,* namely that (and again I oversimplify) utterances of "This is green" are reliable indicators of the presence of green objects in standard conditions of perception. And while the correctness of

this statement about Jones requires that Jones could *now* cite prior particular facts as evidence for the idea that these utterances *are* reliable indicators, it requires only that it is correct to say that Jones *now* knows, thus remembers,[48] that these particular facts *did* obtain. It does not require that it be correct to say that at the time these facts did obtain he *then knew* them to obtain. And the regress disappears.

Thus, while Jones's ability to give inductive reasons *today* is built on a long history of acquiring and manifesting verbal habits in perceptual situations, and, in particular, the occurrence of verbal episodes, e.g. "This is green," which is superficially like those which are later properly said to express observational knowledge, it does not require that any episode in this prior time be characterizeable as expressing knowledge.

(EPM: §37, in SPR: 169; in KMG: 248–9)

The regress is vicious only if the knowledge presupposed by observation knowledge must also be possessed by the subject *prior* to the observation knowledge. Sellars denies that. His picture, instead, is that we learn responses to the world and to other responses piecemeal, acquiring a repertoire of response dispositions that increasingly takes on the reflexive structure of the responses produced by a critical observer or thinker. This is similar to the neophyte in chess who learns, piecemeal, the moves available to each of the pieces. Until the moves of all the pieces have been learned, chess (even bad chess) cannot be played. As we acquire a sufficiently large core of responses and come to be comfortable with this structure and make it our own, describing our activities merely as responses to various stimuli ceases to be the best available characterization of what is going on. As a child develops, it is at some point in sufficient command of the rules of critical thought that a new vocabulary is appropriate: the vocabulary of making moves in the knowledge game, of justifying and being able to justify what we say or believe. If there is a circle here, it is a hermeneutic circle, not a vicious circle.

Sellars adequately disarms the charge of a vicious regress on the part of observation knowledge, but several philosophers have charged that he nonetheless falls to a regress concerning memory.[49] Memory is no less crucial a source of knowledge than perception, and Sellars's response to the circularity charge requires that people be able to remember things they did not know at the time, and were not even in a position to know. The kinds of things people would have to remember include episodes of having responded correctly to items of kind K and episodes of remembering correctly other things that happened, even though at the time they did not – could not – know they were responding or remembering correctly, because they were not then sufficiently reflective to be knowers at all.

Fales thinks that requiring general knowledge that one's memory is reliable introduces a new circularity, but if Sellars's response successfully disarms the circularity charge in the case of perceptual knowledge, I do not see why it does not also work for memory knowledge. Fales does nothing to show that there is something special about memory knowledge that evades Sellars's strategy, and it is simple to rewrite Sellars's response to the circularity charge, substituting 'memory knowledge' for 'observational knowlege' and making other appropriate changes, to generate a response to Fales's criticism that seems as adequate as the original response to the purported circularity of observational knowledge.

Sosa's challenge is more blunt: "[W]e cannot plausibly be said to remember particular earlier exercises of memory constitutive of a data bank which can later support our underwriting generalizations".[50] That is, at no time (and certainly not in a young knower-to-be) does one have a database of particular feats of memory adequate to support the general claim that one's memory is reliable. There are some obscurities in Sosa's argument that deVries and Triplett questioned in *Knowledge, Mind, and the Given*, but I want to pursue another line of response here. Both Fales and Sosa want their readers to focus on relatively narrow channels of justification individually – does perceptual knowledge always presuppose other perceptual knowledge? does memory knowledge always presuppose other memory knowledge? – in order to generate worries about vicious circles. This piecemeal approach, however, falsifies the actual conditions under which we grow into knowers. While Johnny may have trouble remembering large numbers of particular cases of good memory, he need not rely solely on his own memory resources for "data" to support his belief (or, better, his implicit assumption) that his memory is reliable. He can see the couch to be where his apparent memory places it. Perhaps more important, as he learns the concept of memory, his parents, siblings and friends confirm his memories, and laugh when he claims to remember fanciful imaginings. Constructing a conception of memory as a reliable source of knowledge is not something Johnny has to do alone; he is aided throughout by his community. What looks to be a vicious circle in a narrow justificational channel turns out to be a mere eddy in the many confluent currents of justification we can exploit. We shall come back to this in the next section's discussion of epistemic principles.

The central point remains that becoming a knower is not a change in one's empirical characteristics (although such changes necessarily accompany ascent to the company of epistemic agents); rather, it is a change in one's relation to the knowledge game. In the course of a young human being's development it becomes increasingly appropriate – indeed, increasingly necessary – to characterize his or her behaviour in terms of moves in the knowledge game made with regard for and because of the rules constituting that practice. There need be no determinate moment at which the child suddenly becomes a knower, a player in the game; indeed, we tend (generously) to construe even very early behaviours of children as appropriately characterized in highly cognitive terms.

## Problem 3: the status of epistemic principles

Sellars is a coherentist in that he believes that the epistemic status of any belief is a matter of its inferential connections to other beliefs. Foundationalists hold, in contrast, that there have to be some beliefs the epistemic status of which is non-inferential.[51] They clearly disagree about the right story to tell about particular empirical knowledge claims. But they also disagree about the story to tell about the epistemic principles that license acceptance of general knowledge, given particular knowledge. Firth and Chisholm, for instance, seem to treat such principles as synthetic *a priori*. Let us examine Sellars's treatment of such principles.

Sellars returned often to Firth's "Coherence, Certainty, and Epistemic Priority" because, in his attempt to give a sympathetic reconstruction of a coherence theory of justification, Firth comes so close to what Sellars saw as the truth, while remaining a convinced foundationalist. Firth puts the issue of coherentism this way: "warrant-increasing properties" are the characteristics of a statement that increase its epistemic warrant. These can be inferential or non-inferential. The foundationalist holds that there must be ultimately *non-inferential* warrant-increasing properties. Firth distinguishes two different kinds of *inferential* warrant-increasing properties. Statements have a *directly* inferential warrant-increasing property if they have the property of being validly inferable from certain other statements (what properties those other statements must have is a question for later). An empirical generalization, for instance, has the directly inferential warrant-increasing property of following by sound inductive principles from warranted observation statements.

But clearly not *all* warrant-increasing properties are of the directly inferential sort. For instance, for a statement concerning geology, the property of being believed by most of the fellows of the Geological Society of America (GSA) might be a warrant-increasing property: the fact that, say, the origin of natural petrochemical deposits from ancient organic materials is accepted by most fellows of the GSA might increase the warrant of the statement that natural petrochemical deposits originated from ancient organic material. But "being believed by most of the fellows of the Geological Society of America" is not an *inferential* property of that statement. How should coherentists, who emphasize the inferential, treat such cases? According to Firth,

> to preserve coherence as the ultimate court of appeal they would insist that such a non-inferential property can be a warrant-increasing property of a statement *S* only if a particular statement *about S* – the statement, namely, "If *S* has property *P* then *S* is [probably] true" – is validly inferable from (coheres with) certain other specified statements.[52]

Applied to our sample case, *S* is the statement "Natural petrochemical deposits originated from ancient organic material". So we must consider the warrant of the metastatement,

> MS If 'Natural petrochemical deposits originated from ancient organic material' has the property of being accepted by most fellows of the Geological Society of America, then 'Natural petrochemical deposits originated from ancient organic material' is probably true.

If we have evidence that in such matters the members of the GSA tend to believe true things, then MS would have *directly* inferential warrant from the generalization that is, in turn, *directly* inferentially warranted by that evidence. Leaving aside for the moment the question of the warrant of the evidence itself, let us say that in this case *S* has an *indirectly* inferential warrant-increasing property. We can see how the coherentist could hope that all the apparently non-inferential warrant-increasing properties can be brought into the coherentist fold: the coherentist holds that all apparently non-inferential warrant-increasing properties are, in fact, really only *indirectly* inferential warrant-increasing properties. So warrant and inference ultimately must go hand in hand.

But Firth does not think that the coherentists can pull it off. MS may well itself be inductively warranted. But he believes, along with C. I. Lewis, that there are other statements that are clearly not directly inferentially warranted and are not indirectly inferentially warranted either. Firth has in mind Lewis's expressive judgements, for example, "It looks as if I am seeing something red". Firth suggests:

> it would probably be close to the spirit of Lewis's position to maintain that in the last analysis a statement can now have for me only one warrant-increasing property that is not ultimately inferential—that compound property which consists in (1) purporting to characterize (and only to characterize) the content of my present experience, and (2) being a statement that I either now believe to be true or should now believe to be true if I had just decided whether it were true or false.[53]

Let us call this complex property Firth refers to 'PE'. Now, there clearly is a metajudgement in the neighbourhood:

> MEJ  If "It looks as if I am seeing something red" has the property PE, then it is probably true.

It is unlikely that MEJ is warranted all by itself: MEJ is probably warranted as an instance of a more general principle:

> MJ1  For any statement, if it has property PE, then it is probably true.

If Lewis-style expressive judgements refute coherentism, then, as Sellars points out:

> when Firth tells us that *PE*, the property of being exclusively about one's own experience of the present moment, is an *ultimately* non-inferential WP [warrant-increasing property], he means that *PE* is not only not an inferential property of the judgements in question, but that, unlike being believed by members of the GSA, it is not a WP by virtue of itself having an inferential property.                           (MGEC §49: 185)[54]

We are thus led to ponder why MJ1 is warranted. Sellars points out that it shares a great deal in common with those things Chisholm called epistemic principles, for example:

MJ3　If a person ostensibly perceives (without ground for doubt) something to be Φ (for appropriate values of Φ), then it is likely to be true that he perceives something to be Φ.

MJ4　If a person ostensibly remembers (without ground for doubt) having ostensibly perceived something to be Φ (for appropriate values of Φ), then it is likely to be true that he remembers ostensibly perceiving something to be.[55]

Now, the principle which licensed (MS), which I now formulate thus:

MJ2　Statements about general features of the earth's geology that are believed by most of the fellows of the Geological Society of America are probably true

is itself, as I noted, inductively supported. That is, it is a piece of empirical knowledge, even if it is *also* a criterion we use to assess certain kinds of empirical claims. There is no barrier in principle to empirical knowledge serving as a criterion by which other empirical claims are judged.

But what about MJ1, MJ3 and MJ4? Surely, the foundationalist claims, these could not be warranted by inductive inference from instances, because they are the very principles we need to apply to such instances in order to be able to use them as inductive evidence. MJ1, MJ3, and MJ4 differ importantly from MJ2. How are we to account for this without throwing up our arms and saying either that they differ from MJ2 in that they are basic and must be accepted without further justification (i.e., they are self-evident), or that the most we can say is "this or nothing": if MJ1, MJ3 and MJ4 are not justified for us, no empirical truth is justified for us? Sellars thinks that the former strategy "is too atomistic an interpretation of the authority of epistemic principles", while the latter is just "too weak" (MGEC §55: 186).

First, Sellars does not think that these principles face the question of their justification one by one. MJ1, MJ3 and MJ4 work together as elements of a coherent conceptual framework in which our ostensible introspective, perceptual, and memory judgements (IPM judgements) are treated as having similar epistemic status. One coherentist answer to the challenge of explaining why MJ1, MJ3 and MJ4 are warranted is simply that they are elements of an empirically well-grounded theory. This claim, so baldly put, lands us in a position where we are committed to both

(IPM1) We accept IPM judgements for the reason that they are elements of theory *T*

(IPM2) We accept theory *T* for the reason that it is supported by our IPM judgements.

But Sellars does not think this kind of coherentism gets one anywhere. It is unclear whether the circle here is necessarily vicious, given that theory *T* has a great deal of value in other areas, but there is a kind of vacuity to it. So Sellars grants that "*a* reason for accepting them is the fact that they belong to *T*, which we suppose to be an empirically well-confirmed theory" (MGEC §66: 188). But there needs to be something more, an independent reason still consistent with his brand of coherentism that makes it reasonable to be in a situation where one accepts both (IPM1) and (IPM2). Sellars believes he has a strategy to demonstrate that we have, indeed, this independent reason: the pragmatic turn relied on in his discussions of induction. As he notes, in those discussions, he does not touch the status of IPM judgements directly.

> If challenged, I would have appealed to something like MJ1, MJ3, and MJ4 and argued that they are true. If asked why it is reasonable to accept them, I would have argued that they are elements in a conceptual framework which defines what it is to be a finite knower in a world one never made ... To be one who makes epistemic appraisals is to be in this framework. And to be in this framework is to appreciate the interplay of the reasonablenesses of inductive hypotheses and of IPM judgements.
>
> (MGEC §§73–5: 189)

But this conceptual framework is unlike specific empirical theories, in that such theories can be adopted by a process of inductive reasoning, but this makes no sense for the broader conceptual framework we are now considering. With respect to this framework, we have to distinguish the genetic question about how we got into the framework in the first place from the justificational question, "Granted that we are in the framework, how can we justify accepting it?" That these are two different questions is something Sellars thinks the foundationalist has not understood properly: "Presumably the question 'How did we get into the framework?' has a causal answer, a special application of evolutionary theory to the emergence of beings capable of conceptually representing the world of which they have come to be a part" (MGEC §79: 190).

The answer to the second question, the question of particular interest to us here "lies in the necessary connection between being in the framework of epistemic evaluation and being agents" (MGEC §80: 190).

82. The answer is that since agency, to be effective, involves having reliable cognitive maps of ourselves and our environment, the concept of effective agency involves that of our IPM judgements being likely to be true, that is, to be correct mappings of ourselves and our circumstances.

83. Notice, then, that if the above argument is sound, it is reasonable to accept

MJ5:   IPM judgements are likely to be true,

simply on the ground that unless they *are* likely to be true, the concept of effective agency has no application.

(MGEC §§82–3: 190)

How does this response differ from the "this or nothing" response that Sellars rejected as "too weak"? The principal difference is in broadening the scope of the 'nothing' that confronts us. Rather than confronting us with a lack of justified beliefs, Sellars confronts us with the absence of *agency*. A sceptic can accept the absence of justified beliefs and still carry on, claiming that, justified beliefs or not, he still has to live and act in the world. But that response does not seem available to one who accepts the absence of agency, for what would it then be to "carry on"? In this sense, Sellars's answer seems stronger, although not significantly so. It is at least a coherentistic answer in turning away from the atomistic approach favoured by those who rely on self-evidence.

This last set of arguments goes by quickly, but we must return to Sellars's conception of induction, the laws of nature and the nature of theories in Chapter 6 to build up a more complete understanding of what he thinks is going on when we not only observe (and introspect, etc.) but begin to draw conclusions from our experience.

## Summary

Let me briefly recap this chapter's journey. We looked at a number of attempts to capture the notion of the given, all of which failed either the epistemic efficacy requirement or the epistemic independence requirement. Generalizing these arguments gives us good reason to look elsewhere for an account of knowledge.

The first move to make after rejecting givenness is a reassessment of the relation between the genetic or causal underpinnings of empirical knowledge and its justificational structure. Causal stories about our beliefs can be important parts of their justificational stories, but the causal story is never *ipso facto* justificational; there's no privileged point at which the move is made from the causal to the epistemic realm. There are causal patterns of interaction with the world that include states and episodes that are assessable in terms of our shared, public epistemic goals. The epistemic standards and rules by which we assess such states and episodes are not reducible to physical or, more generally, descriptively empirical characterizations or laws. The logical space of reasons must, however, be tied to, and indeed exploit, the causal patterns embodied in our behaviour. It does this by providing for entry and exit moves into the logical space of reasons: observation reports and/or beliefs, indexical beliefs or thoughts, intentions and volitions. Otherwise it is without being.

Cognition is part of an ongoing process of adjustment to the world, but it is more than mere adaptation, because it is rule-governed and goal-oriented. This is why it is appropriate to describe it normatively as a self-correcting enterprise.

## Chapter 6

# *Science and reality: induction, laws, theories and the real*

Natural philosophers have hitherto sought to understand 'meanings'; the task is to change them.           (CDCM: 288)

## From observation to law to theory

Empiricism assumes we can know some particular facts independently of others; we can collect such evidential facts and make non-deductive inferences to general truths; and, finally, we can develop theories that enable us to explain these general truths. Traditional empiricism also assumes that our knowledge hooks into reality via the given and, thus, that all our general 'abstract' knowledge is ultimately in the service of our interaction with the given. Science, the repository of our most general and most abstract knowledge, is treated as merely instrumental. Science develops ever more sophisticated methods to anticipate and plan for encounters with the given, but the given retains ontological priority over any posits science may propose.

Sellars does not accept any of this. His critique of the given and his view of observation knowledge disrupt this vision of a unidirectional march from the particular to the general and from the concrete to the abstract. Science, he believes, is the measure of what is real. This chapter explores how Sellars conceives of general and theoretical knowledge, his reasons for espousing scientific realism, and what he has to say about the nature and justification of induction.

# Laws as inference tickets

## *Generalizations versus lawlike generalizations*

A standing problem for empiricism is distinguishing adequately between true contingent empirical generalizations, such as "All the coins in my pocket are pennies" or "All the dinosaurs are dead", and *lawlike* empirical generalizations, such as "Whenever there's lightning there's thunder". "All the coins in my pocket are pennies" might be excluded from being lawlike because it contains an indexical reference to a specific, limited region of space-time. Cannot there be laws that are limited to specific regions of space-time or the objects in them, such as laws of plate tectonics or terrestrial biology? "All the dinosaurs are dead" has no such limitation built into it, but neither does it seem to be a *law*.

In more sophisticated logistical treatments of science, the tendency to formulate laws as universal generalizations in the first-order predicate calculus is a symptom of this problem. Put both "All the coins in my pocket are pennies" and "Unsupported bodies heavier than air near the surface of the Earth accelerate towards Earth at 9.8m/s$^2$" into the first-order predicate calculus, and there is no significant difference between them to account for the fact that only one is a lawlike statement.

> My point, of course, is not that we *couldn't* use '(x) Ax $\supset$ Bx' to represent lawlike statements. It is, rather, that given that we use this form to represent general statements which do not have a lawlike force, to use it *also* to represent lawlike statements is to imply that lawlike statements are a *special case* of non-lawlike statements. It is therefore particularly important to note that I am not claiming that all restricted generalizations, i.e. generalizations of which the subject term is a *localized* term, are unlawlike. It may, indeed, be true that all unrestricted generalizations *which we can have reason to assert* are lawlike. But not all lawlike statements which we can have reason to assert are unrestricted generalizations. And the logical form of even a restricted lawlike generalization is obscured rather than clarified by representing it by '(x) fx $\supset$ gx'. (CDCM: 297)

Unlike mere generalizations, lawlike statements *support counter-factuals* or *subjunctive conditionals*. If I accept the statements "The coin in my hand is a dime" and "All the coins in my pocket are pennies" I will *not* infer the statement "If the coin in my hand were in my pocket, it would be a penny". The generalization "All the coins in my pocket are pennies" is not lawlike. But if I accept the statements "The coin in my hand is a dime" and "Unsupported bodies heavier than air near the surface of the Earth accelerate towards Earth at 9.8 m/s$^2$", I may well infer (and have the *right* to infer) the statement "If I release the coin in my hand, it would accelerate towards Earth at 9.8 m/s$^2$".[1]

## Entailments, modalities and inference tickets

The distinction between lawlike statements and mere generalizations must be seen in the context of the long-standing debate between the empiricist regularity analysis of causation and the rationalist entailment analysis. For the empiricist, general causal claims and laws of nature simply assert universal, empirical, descriptive regularities. "Striking matches causes them to light" and "Lightning causes thunder" simply assert regularities found in nature. The empiricist hopes to explain the logical peculiarities of lawlike or causal sentences by their unrestricted nature, or even as a delusional appearance our habits trick us into. Although many philosophers, including the empiricists' rationalist opponents, hold that causes and laws describe *necessary connections*, the empiricist must deny any non-analytic necessities: regularity is all we get. Correspondingly, the "problem of induction" challenges us to explain and justify the right to assert uniformities that go beyond one's evidence.

The rationalist, in contrast, maintains that lawlike or causal claims assert the existence of a physical entailment relation between event kinds or properties. Unlike the entailment relations exploited or explored in logic and mathematics, physical entailment relations cannot be discovered by intuition; they must be understood (*seen*) via observation and experiment. For the rationalist, laws – in mathematics or the empirical sciences – state *necessities*. The rationalist construes the "problem of induction" as explaining and justifying our right to assert the existence of such necessities. Sellars thinks that the rationalist analysis better respects the logical grammar of the relevant form of discourse, in this case talk of laws, but is saddled with an undesirable metaphysics: 'real' causal connections and necessities. The empiricists have the metaphysics right, but they misconstrue the rich and complex grammar of the concepts with which we operate.

Sellars wants a treatment that will respect the rich texture of the language of laws without committing him to the metaphysical excrescences of rationalism. We should by now be very familiar with his general strategy: go metalinguistic, that is, construe lawlike statements not as first-order descriptive assertions in the object language, but as material mode expressions of metalinguistic claims. The metalanguage is a peculiar one, in that it is not tied to a specific object language. A causal law such as "Lightning causes thunder" is not tied to English, but it says something about ·lightning· and ·thunder· and thus only indirectly concerns lightning and thunder.

In Sellars's analysis of sentences concerning general causal connections and laws of nature, he outlines a general theory of the modalities that recognizes and accounts for the parallels among the logical modalities, the physical modalities and the deontic modalities. Let us review this treatment of the modalities, particularly the physical modalities.

> To make first hand use of [modal] expressions is to be about the business of *explaining* a state of affairs, or *justifying* an assertion. Thus, even if to state that p entails q is, in a legitimate sense, to state that something is the case, the primary use of 'p entails q' is not to state that something is the case, but to explain *why q*, or justify the assertion *that q*. (CDCM: 283)

Explaining and justifying are intrinsically connected with reasons and arguments, so wherever a modal expression is at hand, there is an implicit reference to or invocation of some reasoning or argumentation connected to the modally qualified claim. Being "about the business" of explaining or justifying is very vague: what is the connection between the modal expression and the argument? Explaining and justifying are linguistic activities that differ from the linguistic activity of describing. We necessarily use descriptions in our explanations and justifications, but something more than just description is going on whenever we explain or justify. And again, we have to ask: what more?

The modality (which, as far as Sellars is concerned, is built into the notion of causation) essentially signals that a valid inference rule is contextually operative. The regularity theorist, who discounts talk of natural necessities, thinks that the reasoning:

> Lo! There's lightning
> So, (in all probability) thunder will soon follow

is really enthymematic, for only formal rules of inference are countenanced. Fully spelled out, the reasoning would have to be

> Lo! There's lightning

Whenever there is lightning, thunder follows shortly
So thunder will soon follow.

In Sellars's view, however, the modal force of lawlike statements is a sign that they function as "inference tickets", whether there is present an explicit modal expression, an implicit modal expression (such as 'causes'), or a modalized construction such as the subjunctive conditional.

... the 'season inference ticket'

If anything *were* A, it *would be* B

is actually an *inference ticket,* and not, so to speak, a *letter of credit* certifying that one has a major premise and a *formal* inference ticket at home. (CDCM: 286)

Accepting the general causal statement "Lightning causes thunder" is accepting a standing licence to make the immediate inference

Lightning at location $l_1$ at time $t_n$
So, thunder around location $l_1$ at time $t_{n+m}$.

Causal statements and other lawlike statements differ significantly from accidental generalizations in that causal statements perform a different function within our linguistic system, one that is not purely descriptive but is importantly prescriptive. They express our recognition of a standing permission to make certain inferences.[2]

The actual inference from "lightning now" to "thunder shortly" is in the object language; the lawlike statement "Lightning causes thunder" that expresses the "inference ticket" is best thought of as in the meta-language, for it tells of the status of certain object-language sequences. The rationalist insistence on real necessary connections or physical entailments mistakes the *prescriptive* force of causal and lawlike sentences for a *description* of a metaphysically special entity.

Since Sellars attempts to have his cake and eat it too – preserve the rationalist conception of the logical grammar of causal and lawlike sentences without growing Plato's beard while simultaneously preserving the empiricist emphasis on the non-analytic character of the laws of nature without abandoning their modal character – he must avoid multiple dangers. General causal statements and laws of nature are supposed to be material inference tickets. But that seems to cast the net too widely. In the discussion in Chapter 2 of the notion of material inference, the inference from "X is red" to "X is coloured" was cited as an example. Presumably, "Everything red is coloured" is an inference ticket validating such transitions. But "Everything red is coloured" is not a *law of nature* nor a causal law. "Everything red is coloured" is a necessary truth and thus, like the laws of nature, possesses a modal character, although not the *same* modal character as the so-called laws of nature. Sellars does not spend time trying to make precise the distinction between those inference tickets expressed in the laws of nature and those expressed in conceptual truths. Presumably, the distinction rests on whether there is empirical backing for the inference ticket.

The empiricist might object: an entailment is something that one comes to know in virtue of understanding the language in which it is expressed. Admittedly, sometimes what one understands is an arm-chair *procedure*, so one's knowledge is dependent on the exercise of the procedure, without a need for empirical, that is, sensory, input. In short, entailments unpack what is already implicit in the relevant concepts or claims. But that cannot be what is going on in an empirical science and empirical laws.

> [T]he challenge is met by *drawing a distinction* and by *reflecting*, in the spirit of the later Wittgenstein, *on the idea of 'meaning.'* The distinction is between the *antecedent* 'meanings' of 'A' and 'B' in terms of which one formulates the evidence which points to a certain inductive 'conclusion' (actually the decision to espouse the inference ticket 'If anything were A, it would be B') and what one *subsequently* 'understands' by these terms when one uses them in accordance with this decision. The point of this distinction is that while one does not inductively establish that A P-entails B by armchair reflection on the *antecedent* 'meanings' of 'A' and 'B', to establish by induction that A P-entails B is to *enrich* (and, perhaps, otherwise modify) the use of these terms in such a wise that to 'understand' what one now 'means' by 'A' and 'B' *is* to know that A P-entails B.          (CDCM: 287)

The point is significant. The standard conception of the growth of empirical knowledge assumes that there is a basic vocabulary, the meaning of which is fixed – either by ostension or innately – and thus remains unchanged. Progress in understanding the world is made in one of two ways: (i) by discovering new generalizations formulable in the fixed vocabulary, or (ii) generating a new vocabulary that is at least partially definable in terms of the old, fixed vocabulary and which enables one to formulate generalizations otherwise too complex to express in the fixed vocabulary. In this standard picture, the fact that there is a basic set of terms that retain invariant meanings no matter how many further general facts are added to the knowledge base guarantees that scientific change is *progress,* because we do not have to worry that scientific change amounts to changing the subject.

Sellars, however, rejects the idea that any terms have a fixed meaning, either ostensively or innately, in the requisite sense. In his view, the meanings of terms are determined by their functions in the linguistic economy, especially their contributions to valid inferences. Discovering new laws in the course of experience, whether through explicit and self-consciously scientific methods or "by the seat of one's pants", is changing the intralinguistic moves into which the relevant terms figure, and that means changing their meanings. Science, for Sellars, does not aim to construct an adequate representation of the world given a fixed stock of basic concepts or terms; it aims to *change* our concepts and terms to enable us to anticipate, explain and plan ever better our interaction with reality. Science is the methodologically rigorous attempt to reform and extend the descriptive resources of language to better equip us in all those tasks that presuppose descriptive language. If the entailments discovered in logic and mathematics are things we can eventually "just see" because they are in some sense built into the concepts or terms already (and therefore not subject to empirical disconfirmation), physical entailments can be thought of as proposed connections among concepts or terms that, pending possible empirical disconfirmation, can be rationally attached to the concepts.

There are obvious objections to such a view. The explicit definition of a term such as 'gene' need not change as we develop the theory of heredity and come to understand some of its intricacies. Sellars grants this, but explicit definitions hardly exhaust meanings. As Mendel's simple model gets complicated by such things as distorted monogenic segregation, the concept of a gene does change, even though its explicit definition need not change. Such conceptual change is not unconstrained, at least to the extent that it is the result of a methodologically scientific process.

> [S]cientific terms have, as part of their logic a 'line of retreat' as well as a 'plan of advance' – a fact which makes meaningful the claim that in an important sense A and B are the 'same' properties they were 'before.' And it is this strategic dimension of the use of scientific terms which makes possible the reasoned recognition of what Aldrich has perceptively called "renegade instances," and gives inductive conclusions, in spite of the fact that, as principles

of inference, they relate to the very 'meaning' of scientific terms, a corrigibility which is a matter of 'retreat to prepared positions' rather than an irrational 'rout.' The motto of the age of science might well be: *natural philosophers have hitherto sought to understand 'meanings'; the task is to change them.*

(CDCM: 288)

A term such as 'mass' has a central core that may be merely structural, that is, certain second-order properties of the concept are preserved across the changes that the concept has undergone in its successive uses in Aristotelian, Newtonian and Einsteinian physics. Proposed revisions of the concept that would violate this core would not clearly be concepts of mass. Thus, there can be scientific change that does not merely change the subject.[3]

# Theories

Sellars's non-standard conception of laws is matched to a non-standard conception of theories. Through the early years of his career, the "standard" view of theories was that developed by the logical positivists, a view that has been devastatingly attacked over the past sixty years and is no longer the dominant conception, but still provides the touchstone against which contemporary theories of theories define themselves. Briefly characterized, the standard view is this.[4] A theory is a set of propositions, hopefully formalized as a pure (uninterpreted) axiomatic calculus in mathematical logic, containing (i) logical and mathematical terms and (ii) theoretical terms, some of which may be explicitly defined in the axiom system. The axioms formulate definitions and laws specifying relationships among the theoretical terms. There will also be (iii) theory-independent observation terms and a set of *correspondence* or *bridge laws* that specify relationships between the theoretical and observation terms, interpreting the abstract calculus.

Sellars plays off this standard view of theories in ways that often obscure how widely his own view diverges from the standard.[5] As we have already seen, Sellars does not think of laws as *really* object-language statements of general truths. Although *for some purposes* it may be convenient to construe a theory as an axiomatic formulation of a system of scientific laws, in Sellars's view it masks important aspects of theories as they are actually used. Some of the ways in which the logistic conception of theories misleads include:

- promoting a conflation of deduction and explanation, and a corresponding misunderstanding of the very nature of explanation;
- encouraging a neglect of the role of models and metaphors in theory development;
- promoting an instrumentalistic interpretation of scientific theories;
- encouraging a misinterpretation of the relation between observation and theory, and theoretical descriptions and their instances;
- promoting a misinterpretation of the nature and import of theoretical "identities"; and
- reinforcing the myth of the given.

If theories are uninterpreted axiomatic calculi, they will always be highly determinate and well formulated. But real theories are not like that. Focusing on a few examples that seem to fit this ideal, such as Newtonian or quantum mechanics, can entice one to ignore the real complexity and fuzziness of theory formation. Sellars emphasizes that most theories start with a *model* (not in the "model-theory" sense), that is, some domain with which we are already familiar and use as an analogy to help us develop concepts to grasp the problem domain better. The model can be something very prosaic: for example, thermodynamics can use elastic collisions of macro-objects like billiard balls as a model of its micro-domain. In the early days of nuclear physics, several different models for the atom were proposed, such as J. J. Thompson's "plum pudding" model or Bohr's planetary model. Every model has a more or less explicit commentary spelling out which aspects of the model domain "count" and which ones are discounted. But in the early stages of working out and testing a theory, it may be indeterminate which properties and/or structures of the model are taken to be analogous to properties and/or structures of the problem domain, and that remains something to be worked out empirically. As far as Sellars is concerned, a theory is present as soon as a model is proposed and used analogously to formulate concepts, test hypotheses and explore putative explanations in the problem domain.

So what is a theory, according to Sellars? One difficulty is that Sellars shifts in a cavalier way between talk of languages, talk of conceptual frameworks, and talk of theories. For instance, in his discussion of induction at the end of "Some Reflections on Language Games" (especially paragraphs 82ff.), he slides almost imperceptibly from talking of language games to talking of conceptual frameworks to talking of theories. Given the standard view of theories, this ignores important distinctions in kind. But in Sellars's view, there are deep commonalities among these, and the differences turn out to be fairly subtle. Languages and conceptual frameworks both consist of complex systems of norms governing the production and interaction of categorially structured symbolic episodes, where the content of episode-types is determined by their roles in that system. Whereas languages must be complete, "language games" can be partial, a fact Wittgenstein exploited brilliantly in the *Investigations*. Sellars is at home talking about similarly partial conceptual frameworks.[6] In several of his earliest papers, he argues that an empirical language must be tied to a "world-story". Essentially, a language cannot be entirely neutral about how things in the world tend to work: *every* empirical language must include material inference moves that embody commitments concerning the ways in which the world is articulated in space and time.[7]

For Sellars, languages are more specific than conceptual frameworks, in that speakers of different languages (e.g. French and English) can share the same conceptual framework, for example, a Cartesian framework or the conceptual framework of physical objects. But remember, concepts are, for Sellars, classificatory specifications of inferential roles. To say someone has the concept of snow is to say that she has a ·snow· available in her idiolect. To say that speakers of different languages share the framework of physical objects is to say that the expressions in their languages that are ·physical object·s function as similarly central, even irreducible, category terms in their languages.

Now, 'theory' for Sellars is very similar, but not entirely identical to 'language' and '(conceptual) framework'. It cannot be identical, for, recall, he views the manifest image as a conceptual framework and/or language, but *not* as a theory. The manifest image is not a theory for two reasons: (i) it was never *reasoned to*, but rather (originally) caused in us by essentially non-rational processes unlike the decision-making that is typical of theory adoption and therefore is not the product of induction;[8] and (ii) it is total, in the sense that there is no particular subject matter or domain it is concerned with explaining.

6. What would the conceptual framework of common sense be a theory *of*? Granted that common sense beliefs *within* this framework include proto-theories about specific subject matters capable, in principle, of being characterized without the use of the vocabulary of these proto-theories, what is the framework itself a theory of? A *trivial* answer is, of course, available namely, "Common sense objects and events." But this would be like

answering the question "What is atomic theory a theory of?" by saying "Atoms." A *false* answer is also available, namely, "Sense impressions."

7. If we distinguish, in the spirit of the classical account, between the 'internal' and 'external' subject matters of micro-theories, so that in the case of the kinetic theory of gases, for example, molecules and their behavior would be the 'internal' subject matter of theory, and gases as empirical constructs defined without reference to molecules its 'external' subject matter, then, as I see it the conceptual framework of common sense has no *external* subject-matter and is not, therefore, in the relevant sense a theory *of* anything.                    (SRI: 172–3, in PP: 338–9)

Sellars often refers to theories as frameworks, but when he uses 'theory' strictly, it is a framework that is rationally adopted via an inductive process in order to explain some delimitable (set of) phenomena.

One of Sellars's major objections to the "standard view" is that it badly misunderstands the relation between observation and theory and therefore also the relation between theory and reality. In the standard view, there is a "layer-cake" structure to theoretical explanation: particular observational facts are explained by empirical generalizations formulated in the observation language. Correspondence or bridge laws correlate observation language terms with theoretical terms, and by substituting their theoretical equivalents for the observation terms, equivalents of the empirical generalizations are derivable within the theory. In short, particular empirical fact is explained by empirical generalization, and empirical generalization is explained by theoretical law.

This standard view gives rise to a problem labelled by Hempel the "theoretician's dilemma".[9] The axioms of a theory, together with the bridge laws, generate equivalents to empirical generalizations, but it is those empirical generalizations that, in fact, do the explanatory work. The theory is, perhaps, a convenient tool in discovering new empirical generalizations and may streamline the calculations necessary in making predictions, but the theory is *not essential* to the explanatory enterprise. The theory itself, strictly speaking, is dispensable. If the theory is dispensable, then any commitments it makes – especially ontological commitments to micro-entities or other unobservable entities (e.g. fields, probability waves, etc.) – are also dispensable. The dispensable is not really real, so theoretical entities are *only* theoretical; scientific realism is false.

There are many potential difficulties with the layer-cake view. For instance, are the theoretical kinds cleanly delimitable in terms of the observation vocabulary? But Sellars does not base his rejection on this difficulty. First, he attacks the layer-cake reading itself, especially the idea that theories that postulate unobservable entities serve only to explain the empirical generalizations and not the particular facts themselves.

> To suppose that particular observable matters of fact are the proper *explananda* of inductive generalizations in the observation framework and of these only, is to suppose that, even though theoretical considerations may lead us to formulate new hypotheses in the observational framework for inductive testing and may lead us to modify, subject to inductive confirmation, such generalizations as have already received inductive support, the *conceptual framework* of the observation level is autonomous and immune from theoretical criticism. (LT: 40; in SPR: 121)

We can see here why Sellars thinks the standard view of theories tacitly reinforces the myth of the given. The layer-cake view is a kind of foundationalism applied to scientific theories.

Sellars diagnoses one reason for finding the layer-cake view attractive: namely, accepting "too simple ... a connection between explaining an explanandum and finding a defensible general proposition under which it can either be subsumed, or from which it can be derived with or without the use of correspondence rules" (LT: 39; in SPR: 120). Explanation and derivation are not identical, as a moment's thought about logic and mathematics will demonstrate. Forcing theories into the Procrustean bed of first-order predicate calculus encourages the confusion between explanation and derivation, doing significant violence to the logic of causal assertions. In Sellars's response in "Counterfactuals, Dispositions, and the Causal Modalities" (1957) to Goodman's puzzles about counterfactuals, he emphasizes that causal generalizations in their natural habitat have a great deal more structure to them than allowed by regimentations into first-order predicate logic: in such claims, there are categorial distinctions operating between the thing-kinds to which their subjects belong (or which are their subjects), the circumstances in which they are found, what is done to them and what they do in response. Real explanations do not simply subsume events or objects under logically general truths: they also place the objects or events into a rich system that provides classifications that permit distinctions among identifying and accidental traits, occurrent and causal properties, the active and the passive and so on, and provides a richly articulated set of material inferences (lawlike relations) among these disparate elements.[10]

Sellars's account of the relationship between theory and empirical generalization and between theory and particular matter of fact abandons the traditional layer-cake view. Theories explain particular empirical facts directly, not through the intermediary of empirical generalizations. Electron theory explains lightning; statistical thermodynamics explains heat transfer and the phenomena of boiling and freezing and so on; "that is, they explain why individual objects of various kinds and in various circumstances in the observation framework behave in those ways in which it has been inductively established that they do behave" (LT: 41; in SPR: 121). They do this by *identifying* the observable object with a system of theoretical objects. It is *because* a gas is a cloud of molecules that it behaves the way it does. What is the relation between theory and empirical generalization? Theories about observable things "explain empirical laws by explaining why observable things obey to the extent that they do, these empirical laws" (LT: 41; in SPR: 121).

If anything is made redundant or dispensable in the development of a postulational theory, it is the *empirical generalization,* not the theoretical generalization or the theoretical entities. The empirical generalization is never quite right, and a good theory of the phenomena will show us both why the empirical, observation-level generalization is as good as it is and how and why it is wrong.[11] Furthermore, the theory is not dispensable for another reason: what looks to be mere random variation among cases at the observation level is revealed to be itself lawful when seen from the perspective of the theory, and we are thus led to new generalizations that would remain opaque to us if we insisted on remaining at the observation level.

An example may help clarify this. Suppose that the Boyle–Charles law relating the pressure, volume and temperature of gases was developed on a purely observational basis. The observational data were limited, because extremes of temperature and pressure were very hard to achieve and to measure at that time. The Boyle–Charles law works well in non-extreme conditions, but the French physicist Henri Regnault discovered inaccuracies under extreme conditions in the mid-nineteenth century and proposed a revised equation. His equation, like the Boyle–Charles equation, implies that as $P$ increases (at a fixed temperature), $PV$ steadily decreases. Later in the nineteenth century, Johannes van der Waals developed a still more accurate equation in which this is not the case; he took the molecular theory of gases seriously and realized that as the pressure increases, a point will be reached at which the particles become too crowded, and the volume will shrink ever more slowly. *PV* will begin to rise with *P*. From the viewpoint of the observational framework, this looks like a big change in gas behaviour, a reversal of the curve uniting the (projected) data points. One could accept it as brute observational fact, but there are no deeper insights into this apparent change afforded by the observation framework. From the point of view of molecular theory, however, the change in the data curve seems only to be expected. There are many curves that will fit the data, whatever reasonable data there is. Taking theory seriously differentiates some curves from others in ways that lead to new insights that would not have occurred otherwise, insights that are intelligible only if the theory captures the structure of reality better.

> Roughly speaking, inductive procedures within the observation framework yield generalizations which are unstable not only in that they "break down" and "require modification," which is a truism, but that the modification requires the injection into the observation framework of what might be called an *image* of the theory ... It is not that the "physical thing framework" doesn't sustain *enough* inductive generalizations, but rather that what inductive generalizations it *does* sustain, it sustains by a covert introduction of the framework of theory into the physical thing framework itself. (SRT: 315)

Empirical generalizations at the observation level are increasingly infected with theory, not only because the possession of theory encourages us to make distinctions that would not be salient from the standpoint of a "pure" observation framework, but also because the development of theory often encourages new kinds of experiments and the development of new instruments to use in our observations. We enrich the observational data that our empirical generalizations cover with these new, instrument-based observations, but also thereby import into the observation framework the very theory on which the instrument is based.

After all, the distinction between the observation framework or language and the theoretical framework or language is not itself absolute or fixed. For Sellars, the observation–theory distinction is fundamentally a methodological distinction with no direct ontological import. Furthermore, it is a *malleable* distinction, in that it is not only possible but virtually inevitable that some theoretical terms come to play a reporting or observational role. We can learn to respond to the world *directly* in terms of our theory. The physicist can *just see* the alpha-particle track in the cloud chamber *as* an alpha-particle track, without independently noticing that it has a certain shape or texture and *inferring* that it is an alpha-particle track. In Sellars's opinion, the continued improvement of the (apparently) observation-level generalizations we rely on in our everyday activity increasingly relies on being informed with theory. Sellars thinks this points to a future in which theory comes to dominate, in which the observation reports we make and the empirical generalizations we use in navigating our way through the world are formulated in terms developed through systematic inductive processes.[12]

So, in Sellars's view, the observation-level generalizations play a methodologically important but ultimately dispensable role in theory formation. Via the development of postulational theories that improve our understanding of the world, we construct fragments of a larger conceptual framework, slowly bootstrapping ourselves into a framework sufficiently unified and broad enough to be capable of challenging the conceptual framework of common sense (the manifest image), at least in the dimensions of describing and explaining the world. That scientific framework, unlike the framework of common sense, will have been built painstakingly by careful inductive procedures, and it will justifiably claim our full endorsement. "[I]n the dimension of describing and explaining the world, science is the measure of all things, of what is that it is, and of what is not that it is not" (EPM: §41, in SPR: 173; in KMG: 253).

Sellars conceives of science as being, in part, a systematic and rigorous revision of the natural kind terms we apply to the world. The common-sense observation framework offers us an extensive and variegated set of natural kinds with which we can do a good job of describing and explaining phenomena in the world, but in science we develop a finer-grained, simpler, more elegant, more powerful and ultimately more extensive set of natural kinds that better enable us to describe, explain and predict the phenomena of the world. Recall Sellars's criterion of ontological commitment discussed in Chapter 4: existential quantification into a sentence with an empirical common noun. Postulational science certainly develops new thing-kind terms, for example, 'electron', 'neutrino' and 'gene', and, Sellars claims, we have good reason to believe that we encounter instances of these kinds, for we explain observation-level phenomena by *identifying* them with structures of theoretical entities. A good explanation justifies a belief in the existence of the theoretical entities referred to by the explanation.[13]

How good does a good explanation need to be? How impressed should one be with the meta-induction that since so many scientific theories have been shown to be false and have been replaced by other theories, we should believe that every scientific theory is, in fact, false and ultimately to be replaced by a further theory? The meta-induction is hardly a straightforwardly good argument. Self-correcting enterprises often proceed by a series of failed approaches to the goal, and the run of failures does not license the inference that success is impossible. Is there at least comparative improvement? Sellars thinks there is. It is reasonable to adopt a healthy scepticism towards the ultimate reality of any of the entities postulated by our *current* scientific theories, for it is clear that we are nowhere near a Peircean ideal science. But in so far as we have good theories even now, we have reason to believe in the entities they postulate, even if it is far from conclusive. As our theories become more inclusive and more powerful, those reasons strengthen. If there were, however, good reasons to believe that the goal of the scientific enterprise were somehow incoherent or clearly impossible, then Sellars would be in trouble.

If a good theoretical explanation justifies belief in the existence of the entities postulated by the theory, what should be said about the observable entities identified with systems of the theoretical entities? Sellars's official answer is that the entities of the manifest image are phenomenal in something like Kant's sense. But we need to investigate this aspect of his philosophy more closely.

First let us consider the textual basis for attributing to Sellars the Kant-like treatment of the observable as the phenomenal. The sentence preceding the already cited *scientia mensura* is a good place to start: "*Speaking as a philosopher*, I am quite prepared to say that the common sense world of physical objects in Space and Time is unreal – that is, that there are no such things" (EPM: §41; in SPR: 173; in KMG: 253). Consider this passage from Section V of "Philosophy and the Scientific Image of Man".

> Three lines of thought seemed to be open: (1) Manifest objects are identical with systems of imperceptible particles in that simple sense in which a forest is identical with a number of trees. (2) Manifest objects are what really exist; systems of imperceptible particles being 'abstract' or 'symbolic' ways of representing them.

(3) Manifest objects are 'appearances' to human minds of a reality which is constituted by systems of imperceptible particles.

(PSIM in SPR: 26)

It is clear that (3) is his favoured alternative. Perhaps most straightforward of all is this paragraph from *Science and Metaphysics*:

49. The thesis I wish to defend, but not ascribe to Kant, though it is very much a 'phenomenalism' in the Kantian (rather than Berkeleyian) sense, is that although the world we conceptually represent in experience exists only in actual and obtainable representings of it, we can say, from a transcendental point of view, not only that existence-in-itself accounts for this obtainability by virtue of having a certain analogy with the world we represent but also that in principle *we*, rather than God alone, can provide the cash. (SM: 49)

Finally, in "The Language of Theories" Sellars says:

On one classical interpretation, correspondence rules would appear in the material mode as statements to the effect that the same objects which have observational properties also have theoretical properties, thus identifying the denotation, but not the sense, of certain observational and theoretical expressions. On another classical interpretation, correspondence rules would appear in the material mode as asserting the coexistence of two sets of objects, one having observational properties, the other theoretical properties, thus identifying neither the denotation nor the sense of theoretical and observational expressions. According to the view I am proposing, correspondence rules would appear in the material mode as statements to the effect that the objects of the observational framework *do not really exist – there really are no such things*. They envisage the *abandonment* of a sense and its denotation. (LT: 52; in SPR: 126)

There is some tension in Sellars's position in this area. In "Theoretical Explanation" (1963) Sellars explains his position in terms of the standard view of theories. But he makes a further distinction between two forms of correspondence rules that relate observation-language predicates and theoretical predicates. *Substantive correspondence rules*:

correlate predicates in the theory with empirical predicates pertaining to the objects of the domain for which the theory is a theory, where the important thing about these empirical predicates is that they occur in empirical laws pertaining to these objects.                                         (TE: 71; in PP: 329–30)

The example he gives of such a rule is:

| Temperature of gas in region $R$ is such and such | $\leftrightarrow$ | Mean kinetic energy of molecules in region $R$ is such and such |
|---|---|---|

and he comments that "the primary point of the rule is not of [a] methodological character, but rather to permit a correlation of a theorem in the deductive system with an empirical law, thus the Boyle–Charles law" (TE: 72; in PP: 330).

*Methodological correspondence rules* are "[r]ules which correlate predicates in the theory with predicates which, though empirical, need not pertain to the domain of objects for which the theory is a theory. (They may pertain, for example, to an instrument, e.g. a spectroscope)" (TE: 71; in PP: 330). In the example:

| Spectroscope appropriately related to gas shows such and such lines | $\leftrightarrow$ | Atoms in region $R$ are in such and such a state of excitation |
|---|---|---|

These rules differ from the substantive rules: the substantive rules plausibly *identify* the two predicates (e.g. temperature and mean kinetic energy) whereas the methodological rules do not (no one would identify spectral lines with excitation states).

Sellars is quite clear that correspondence rules cannot be treated as definitions of theoretical expressions in terms of their observation-language expressions, for theoretical expressions have a semantic autonomy, a "surplus value", that cannot be captured in the observation language. Instead, Sellars proposes to turn the tables and treat substantive correspondence rules as proposals for redefinitions of observation vocabulary.

> Does it make sense to speak of turning empirical predicates – and in particular observation predicates – into definitional abbreviations of complex theoretical locutions? Could observation predicates be so treated while continuing to play their perceptual role as conditioned responses to the environment? I see no reason in principle why this should not be the case ...
>
> As I see it, then, substantive correspondence rules are anticipations of definitions which it would be inappropriate to implement in developing science, but the implementation of which in an ideal state of scientific knowledge would be the achieving of a unified

vision of the world in which the methodologically important dualism of observation and theoretical frameworks would be transcended, and the world of theory and the world of observation would be one.                                                        (TE: 77–8; in PP: 335)

Given his own definitions in this article, this would be a *reduction* of observable objects to systems of theoretical objects. This conflicts with his official doctrine elsewhere, for there is a difference between reducing observable objects to aggregates or systems of theoretical objects and treating them as *phenomenal appearances* of the real.[14]

The tension between the reductivism Sellars evinces in "Theoretical Explanation" and the Kantian phenomenalism of other works can be summarized this way: Sellars explicates the reduction relation as an identity relationship, and identity relationships are equivalence relationships, with all that entails, including symmetry and transitivity. But the appearance–reality relationship is supposed to be asymmetrical; it is not a form of identity. Sellars therefore cannot consistently characterize the relation between the ultimate scientific framework and the manifest image as both a reduction and a form of the relation between the phenomenal and the real.

Sellars emphasizes the Kantian phenomenality of manifest image objects particularly around issues concerning sensation and perception. He does not believe that sensible qualities such as the pink of a pink ice cube can be *identified* with any property of or relations between the microconstituents of the ice cube. Sellars accepts the idea that sensible qualities are not really "out there", external to the mind; a world without sentient organisms would be a world in which the reduction of the macro to the micro would be relatively straightforward.[15] But once sentient organisms are added into the mix, reduction is blocked. It is blocked, because *there are sensible qualities* and if they are not "out there", reducible to the properties and relations of the microconstituents of objects, neither can they be located "in here" – that is, in the brain – as properties or relations of what are fundamentally *the same* microconstituents. The coloured, sonorous, odorous macro-objects of the sensible world in which we sentient organisms live and have our being are *appearances* of an underlying reality that, unlike the Kantian thing-in-itself, is not eternally hidden from us, but can be disclosed in its reality through scientific investigation.[16]

Why sensible properties resist reduction and how they will have to be dealt with as science advances need to be looked at in the context of Sellars's views concerning sensation. These issues will be taken up in Chapter 8.

There is one more dimension to Sellars's treatment of the manifest as merely phenomenal. The objects of the manifest image do not *really* exist. Among those objects are persons, the very persons whose norm-laden scientific efforts reveal their non-existence. The world of the manifest image is infused with normativity, which evaporates under the scientific microscope. Science *envisages* abandoning the manifest image and its norm-laden objects, but it *cannot* in fact do so without undercutting itself. The manifest image is transcendentally ideal but empirically and practically real. The world in which we live and have our being is necessarily a world of sensible objects that we constantly evaluate with regard to their aiding or impeding our intentions. We are simply built that way. This manifest world is grounded in, but not identical to, the world science reveals to us. It is a *phenomenon bene fundata,* in Leibniz's phrase. Should we then give ourselves over to scientific truth and abandon the manifest image altogether? No, because in the end practical reason retains primacy over theoretical reason. No one was satisfied with Kant's conception of the relation between phenomena and things-in-themselves; Sellars retains it, with revisions. But is it any more acceptable than Kant's? I return to this question in Chapter 10.

# Induction

We have now discussed Sellars's interpretation of the *nature* of laws and theories, but a major topic remains: the *justification* of laws and theories. Laws and (empirical) theories are justified inductively, so we turn to Sellars's treatment of induction. His papers on this important issue are among his most baroque and opaque, so I shall spend some time outlining a context that makes intelligible the form his treatment takes.

Laws and theories are things we *decide upon* and *reason to.* Observation reports, however, "just happen": they are often wrung from us by our circumstances, as it were. Laws and theories are artfully constructed with a goal in mind. Sellars does not abandon his conviction that justification arguments are always higher-order arguments. To that extent, the justificational story about observation reports is similar to the justificational story about laws and theories, but the important difference is a very explicit emphasis on *practical argument* in Sellars's account of induction. A practical argument is directed at justifying a *doing,* in this particular case, *accepting* a certain proposition. Whereas observation reports have basically back-ward-looking justifications in terms of one's perceptual capacities and the skills and dispositions developed during language learning and other forms of education, the justificational story of laws and theories is forward-looking, emphasizing the goal-directedness of accepting law-like statements and theories.

Induction always involves going beyond one's evidence. Observation reports – the paradigm of particular knowledge – are not them-selves inductive knowledge, although they are an essential condition for inductive knowledge. Observation provides ground-level evidence for induction and is not itself an instance of induction. Accordingly, if I take out the coins in my pocket one by one, note that each is a penny, and then conclude that all the coins in my pocket are pennies, I have not reached an inductive conclusion, for I have not gone beyond my evidence at any point.

Induction is not deduction, and this has consequences for Sellars. First, good inductive reasoning is no guarantor of truth. The concept of probability is intrinsically tied up with inductive reasoning and, indeed, is one of the focal points of Sellars's discussion of induction, described further in the first subsection below. Secondly, Sellars rejects talk of an "inductive logic". One of his papers is titled "Are There Non-Deductive Logics?" (1970) and his answer is "No". One consequence of this view is that the probability calculus cannot by itself account for the nature of inductive justification. Ultimately, he believes that inductive arguments are deductive *practical* argu-ments, the outcome of which is our accepting a proposition. They are not arguments aimed directly at establishing the truth of a proposition.

## *Probability*

Sellars's concept of probability is, first of all, non-metric and therefore not the concept captured by the mathematical calculus of probability. Sellars intimates, though, that the other senses of 'probability', metrical or non-metrical, can be understood in terms of the conception he provides. Moreover, probability applies directly only to sentences or propositions.[17] The root use of 'probably' is as an adverbial modifier in the object language signalling that an argument of a certain kind is in the neighbourhood. Sellars offers the example:

When black clouds gather, it usually rains
Black clouds are gathering.
So (probably) it will shortly rain.

This seems like a sound argument, even though it is not deductively valid. Sellars points out

Notice that the conclusion does not say

It is probable that it will shortly rain

any more than the conclusion of 'old mortality' said

It is necessary that Socrates is mortal.

Just as the deductive conclusion *asserted* that Socrates is mortal, and *implied* (or *signified*) that the conclusion was necessary relatively to true premisses; so the conclusion of the present argument *asserts* that it will shortly rain, and *implies* that this conclusion is *probable* relatively to premisses which are true and which satisfy a further condition which can be expressed by saying that the premisses formulate all relevant knowledge.

(NDL: 85)

(I prefer 'signifies' to 'implies' here, because 'implies' already has enough work to do in logic.) The fact that the primary use of 'probably' is as an adverbial modifier does not preclude Sellars from forming explicit probability judgements: "it is probable that it will shortly rain". As always, he takes the that-clause, "that it will shortly rain", to be a kind of quotation (effectively equivalent to dot-quotation), so that such sentences are metalinguistic and inform us of the status of the dot-quoted sentence.

Sellars proposes that:

to say of a statement or proposition that it is probable is, in first approximation, to say that it is worthy of credence, that it is acceptable in the sense of being worthy of acceptance; that is, to put it in a way which points toward a finer grained analysis, it is to say that relevant things considered there is good reason to accept it. (IV: 198)

By stipulating that his conception of probability is pre-metrical, Sellars avoids such familiar problems as the lottery paradox. That he is not simply ignoring the problems remains unclear; at least, he never got around to them.[18]

## *Induction, practical argument and policies*

Sellars distinguishes the "proximate outcome", the "practical outcome" and the "terminal outcome" of first-order probability arguments.[19] He speaks of *outcomes* rather than *conclusions*, because, in his view, such arguments do not aim to establish truths as such.

> [A]lthough the whole point of a first order probability argument is to generate a terminal outcome, the relation between a terminal outcome and the premises of the argument is radically different from that which obtains between what we ordinarily call the conclusion of an argument and its premises. (IV: 199)

Since, in Sellars's view, inductive argument is fundamentally *practical*, the point is not to trace relationships among truths, but to change our beliefs and our inferential propensities in order to *improve* our interactions with the world, not just to make them more consistent (something deduction can contribute to). A *terminal outcome,* in Sellars's sense, is a state of accepting a proposition. Suppose we have a (good) probability argument, that is, an argument that ends "it is probable that *p*". Sellars calls this the *proximate outcome* of the argument. In his view, the job is not yet finished with this proximate outcome: the terminal outcome is achieved and the job is finished *only* when we actually accept that *p*.

> Roughly, in the context of probability, the assertion that-*p* is the *manifestation* of a state, the *acquisition of which* is authorized by the probability statement "it is probable that-*p*." And the probability statement *authorizes* this acquisition in the sense that it is equivalent in meaning to "all things considered, it is reasonable to accept that-*p*." (IV: 200)

The third outcome, the *practical outcome*, is called for, because there is a gap between the proximate outcome (namely, the conclusion "It is probable that *p*") and the terminal outcome (namely, the acceptance of *p*). There is another argument called for, the conclusion of which is simply "I shall accept that *p*".

> For if
>> it is probable that-*p*
> has anything like the sense of
>> relevant things considered, it is reasonable to accept that-*p*
> then it tells us that

there is a good argument which takes relevant things into account and has as its conclusion *I shall accept that-p*

that is to say, it points toward an argument which can be schematically represented as

. . . . . . . . . . . . . . . . . .

therefore, I shall accept that-*p*.                    (IV: 201)

Notice that there are now *two* arguments attached to probability claims. The "first-order probability argument" (which concludes "It is probable that *p*") stands to the practical argument (which concludes "I shall accept that *p*") "as meta-argument to object-argument" (IV: 201).

This means that Sellars takes the conclusion of the "first-order probability argument" ("It is probable that *p*") to be a claim that there is a good practical argument (concluding with the intention statement "I shall accept that *p*") available.[20] Ultimately, though, the result is a change in one's position with respect to *p*.

Let us look briefly at the arguments that generate the "practical outcome" "I shall accept *p*". In Sellars's view, sentences of the form "S shall do A" or "It shall be the case that *p*" express intentions. He treats 'shall', his intention indicator, like a modal operator, and recognizes both conditional intentions, such as

Shall(I do *A*, if *p*)

and *general* conditional intentions, such as

I shall do *A* whenever *X* obtains,

which he calls a *policy*. Sellars also specifies an inferential principle governing the 'shall' operator.

If (...) implies (___), then [Shall (...)] implies [shall (___)]

Further details can await the discussion of Sellars's theory of practical reasoning in Chapter 9.

Given these principles, note that practical arguments always terminate in an intention and must include intentions among their premises as well. So, a good argument that has as its conclusion "I shall accept that *p*", has to have at least one intention in the premises. In arguments concerning belief acceptance, this would be an intention to pursue certain epistemic goals. Sellars describes it this way (using 'probable$_M$' to indicate a specific "mode" of probability):

> The key point now emerges that the major premise of the first level probability argument, i.e., briefly,

> a proposition is probable$_M$ if it satisfies condition $C$

has the sense of

> there is a good argument of kind $M$ for accepting a proposition if it satisfies condition $C$

and, hence, since the conclusion of this argument is a practical one, the sense of

> there is a good argument of kind $M$ which has as its conclusion 'I shall accept a proposition, if it satisfies condition $C$'

In short, the major premise of the first order probability$_M$ argument tells us that the *complete* practical reasoning which culminates in

> I shall accept $h$

(where this acceptance is bound up with probability$_M$) has the form

> I shall bring about $E$
> (but bringing about $E$ implies accepting a proposition, if it satisfies condition $C$)
> so, I shall accept a proposition, if it satisfies condition $C$
> $h$ satisfies condition $C$
> so, I shall accept $h$.

Thus,

> $h$ is probable$_M$

where the subscript indicates a specific mode of probability, asserts the availability of a good argument for 'I shall accept $h$', the ultimate major of which is the intention to achieve a certain end, and the proximate major is the appropriate intention to follow a certain policy with respect to accepting propositions.

(IV: 207–8)

Obviously, we need to ask what can substitute for $C$ and $E$ in the above schema, the conditions under which, and the ends for which, we accept theories, laws and empirical statements. $E$ and $C$ will differ for each of the objects of acceptance; the goal in theory acceptance is not the same as the goal in accepting a particular empirical statement or in accepting a lawlike statement.

For theories, Sellars says that $C$ is the character of being "the simplest available framework which generates new testable lawlike statements, generates acceptable approximations of nomologically probable law-like statements and generates no falsified lawlike statements" (IV: 209).[21] It is less clear exactly what *E* is for theories. In "Induction as Vindication" (1964), Sellars seems to offer "being able to give non-trivial explanatory accounts of established laws" (IV: 210) as the end-in-view of accepting theories, but this still smacks of the layer-cake view. In "On Accepting First Principles" (1988), however, he suggests that (i) the *ultimate* end of theory acceptance is "the direct ability to produce adequate conceptual pictures of relevant parts of our environment" (OAFP: 450); and (ii) the *proximate* end is possessing the most powerful set of confirmed law-like statements.

In "Are There Non-deductive Logics?", however, Sellars raises the question, "can we remain satisfied with the idea that the reasonableness of accepting law-like statements, theories, singular statements, etc. is simply a function of an end one *happens* to have?" (NDL: 101). In other words, how can we generate the *categorical* prescription "I ought to accept *p*"? Sellars cites two relevant considerations. First, probability statements are *intersubjective*. There are intersubjective standards of reasonability; "it is probable that *p*" makes a claim on others' credence. Secondly, as we shall see in Chapter 9, Sellars thinks that categorical oughts are grounded in we-intentions shared by all rational beings.

> In the second place whenever a person acts on a probability, he regards the kind of action he decides to do as *reasonable* because he thinks that a substantial series of such actions in the kind of circumstances in which the contingency may or may not occur would probably maximize relevant values and utilities. But, as Peirce pointed out, we regard such actions as reasonable even when we know that we *as individuals* will not be in that kind of circumstance often enough to make this consideration relevant and, to put an extreme case, we regard such actions as reasonable *even when we know that we are about to die.* Peirce concludes, correctly, I think, that in thinking and acting in terms of probability, we are, in a certain sense, identifying ourselves with a continuing community.
>
> Both of these considerations suggest that the prime mover of the practical reasoning involving [*sic.*] in probabilistic thinking, indeed all logically oriented thinking, 'deductive' as well as 'inductive', 'practical' as well as 'theoretical', is not an idiosyncratic *wish* to promote truth, but the intention *as a member of a community* to promote the total welfare of that community.          (NDL: 102)

This may not achieve an absolutely categorical imperative, but it is as close as the pragmatist can get. Ultimately, truth is a necessary condition of optimizing the general welfare, and good theories are our means to the truth. This is not the equation of truth with "what works" often attributed to James, but it is a pragmatic justification of enquiry and its results generally.

I cannot here go into the variations through which Sellars adapts this view to justifying the acceptance of laws or particular empirical statements, but such details can be found in the articles cited. What is important to hold on to here is the centrality of explanation in knowledge. While it seems obvious that we develop and accept theories in order to explain, Sellars thinks that its contributing to our ability to explain is also crucial to our justifiably accepting singular propositions. As Joe Pitt states it: "In Sellars' version of explanationism we are justified in accepting a theory if it *explains,* a description if it *is explained,* and a rule of inference if it *helps to explain*".[22]

### The problem of induction

Since Hume, empirically minded philosophers have sought to justify induction. But Sellars cannot accept Hume's challenge, for he rejects its assumptions: "The inductive establishing of laws is misconceived if it is regarded as a process of supplementing observation sentences formulated in a language whose basic conceptual meanings are plucked from 'data' and immune to revision ('Hume's Principle')" (PHM in SPR: 293*n*.2).

Sellars has rejected the given, has tied meanings and concepts constitutively to material inferences, and has insisted that *any* language is a *whole* language, which means that it must afford its speakers the wherewithal not *just* to describe what is immediately present, but also *to explain,* and *to prescribe,* concerning not just what is present but also what is not: what is future, what is past, what is hoped for and what ought to be. The problem of induction, strictly and narrowly conceived, can therefore not get off the ground.

> Thus, there is no such thing as a problem of induction if one means by this a problem of how to justify the leap from the safe ground of the mere description of particular situations, to the problematical heights of asserting lawlike sentences and offering explanations. The sceptics' notion that any move beyond a language which

provides only for the tautologous transformation of observation statement is a 'venture of faith' is sheer nonsense.

(SRLG in SPR: 355)

This does not mean that there are no problems concerning induction, but it does mean that someone who thinks there is a special problem attending inductive procedures generally has already misunderstood the way in which inductive procedures are knit into the fabric of any conceptual framework.

Everyone would admit that the notion of a language which enables one to state matters of fact but does not permit argument, explanation, in short *reason-giving*, in accordance with the principles of *formal logic*, is a chimera. It is essential to the understanding of scientific reasoning to realize that the notion of a language which enables one to state empirical matters of fact but contains no material moves is equally chimerical. The classical 'fiction' of an inductive leap which takes its point of departure from an observation base undefiled by any notion as to how things hang together is not a fiction but an absurdity. The problem is not "Is it reasonable to include material moves in our language?" but rather "*Which* material moves is it reasonable to include?" (SRLG in SPR: 355)

Here are two complementary passages in which Sellars summarizes the strategy with which we should approach this latter question:

Instead of justifying nomologicals by an appeal to observation statements the predicates of which would have conceptual meaning independently of any commitment to laws, the problem is rather that of deciding *which* conceptual meaning our observation vocabulary is to have, our aim being so to manipulate the three basic components of a world picture: (*a*) observed objects and events, (*b*) unobserved objects and events, and (*c*) nomological connections, so as to achieve a world picture with a maximum of 'explanatory coherence'. In this reshuffle, no item is sacred.

(SRLG in SPR: 356)

The rationality of 'induction' is, rather, the rationality of adopting that framework of material rules of inference (meanings – even for observation predicates) and, within this framework, those (sketchy) statements of unobserved matters of fact (world picture) which together give maximum probability to our observation utterances *interpreted as sentences in the system.*

(P in SPR: 293*n*.2)

Some naturalists apparently hope that induction collapses into learning theory: that is, that we cannot ultimately distinguish between the norms by which we *should* change our beliefs and the processes by which we *do* change our beliefs, as revealed by psychological theory. In that case, the pigeon in the Skinner box, the mechanic in the garage and the scientist in the laboratory are doing essentially the same thing: induction. But certainly one result of the complex architecture Sellars uncovers in his analysis of induction is that the languageless pigeon cannot be put on a par with self-critical human beings.

# Chapter 7

# *Intentionality and the mental*

## The context for Sellars's philosophy of mind

### *'Mind' versus 'sensorium'*

Sellars's major impacts on twentieth-century philosophy have been in epistemology and philosophy of mind. As we turn to his philosophy of mind, there are some boundary issues that the reader should be aware of right from the start. How is the philosophy of mind delimited? In most post-Cartesian discussions, 'mind' covers both intentional and sensory states. Discussions of the "mind–body problem" focus indifferently on pains and thoughts. Sellars thinks this is a major mistake, for he recognizes *two* problems: the mind–body problem proper, which concerns the relation between intentional and bodily states, and the sensorium–body problem, which concerns the relation between sensory and bodily states. In Sellars's eyes, Kant's most important single lesson is that thoughts and sensations are different in kind, a lesson that too many philosophers still have not learned. *Mental* states, according to Sellars, are *intentional* states.[1] Thus, purely sensory states are not *mental* states at all, a result that seems to run counter to the (tutored) intuitions of many philosophers. In his view we also need to distinguish between *perceptual* states – which are intentional states, although mixed with a sensory and non-conceptual component – and *purely sensory* states. Still, given the long tradition of including the sensory in the mental, the philosophy of mind includes *de facto* the treatment of the sensory and, accordingly, Sellars frequently uses 'mind' to include the sensory. His theory of the sensory will be the focus of Chapter 8. In this chapter we shall focus on the intentional.

## *The received view of mind*

Sellars is a philosopher, not a psychologist; his *philosophical* interest in mind is a metalevel interest in understanding our *concepts* of mind, not an object-level interest in particular minds or even generalizations about minds. On his own understanding of concepts, this means examining how we *use* mentalistic terms. We use mentalistic or psychological terms constantly in describing, explaining, understanding, expressing and generally coping with the behaviour of others and ourselves. A philosophical theory of mind, therefore, needs to tell at least two stories: (i) how mentalistic descriptions and explanations work, and (ii) how we are able to employ them. There are several different philosophical theories available in the tradition, most prominently the Aristotelian and the Cartesian theories, but the Cartesian theory was the dominant tradition against which Sellars had to fight.[2]

The Cartesian story about the nature of our mentalistic attributions and our ability to use them deserves quick review. From Descartes on, the general structure of mental acts was presumed to be relational. Mental states consist of persons standing in some determinate relation (its 'form') to some *content.* The relational forms were limited in number: in the *Second Meditation,* Descartes famously lists doubting, understanding, affirming, denying, willing, abstaining from willing and being aware of images and sensations. In as much as the forms of mental acts are of limited variety, the incredible richness of our mental lives is accounted for by the rich variety of the *contents* to which the thinker is related. The status of such contents posed a constant problem in the Cartesian tradition, but the general idea seems to have been that there is somehow a domain of "natures" that can be realized *formally* in some substance (material or mental) or *objectively* in some mental act.[3] The nature *tree* is realized formally in those green leafy things outside my window; it is realized objectively (or has intentional inexistence) in my perceptions and thoughts of trees.

The Cartesian explanation of how we are able to *use* mentalistic descriptions seems simple. We enjoy direct and privileged access to our own mental states. Abstraction – the ability to isolate one aspect of experience and form an idea of it divorced from its experiential context – is a primitive mental power that can be employed to abstract psychological concepts from actual and self-intimating instances of psychological states. In this regard, our conceptions of the mental differ from our conceptions of the material world, which is present to us only indirectly via representations or ideas.[4] Since psychological concepts are abstracted directly from self-intimating instances, first-person application of such concepts is unproblematic: scepticism about the reality of the mental is senseless. Most Cartesians also accepted the transparency of the mental; if one is in a certain mental state, then one does (or at least can) know that fact directly. Our clear and distinct beliefs about our own states of mind are incorrigible; each of us can be certain about his or her own psychological states. Furthermore, this knowledge is primordial or foundational. From it we derive our knowledge of everything external to our minds. From the materials we have direct access to, we somehow construct and apply concepts of physical objects and events. More problematically, once we have psychological concepts and some knowledge of our own psychological states, we can apply psychological concepts to describe, explain, understand, interpret and generally cope with other people as well. This assumes that the observable behaviour of others is tied to their internal psychological states in the same ways and in the same kinds of patterns that connect our own psychological states and behaviour. The argument for that assumption is a weak induction by analogy, and this was a stumbling block for the picture as a whole, but the rest of the picture seemed so solid, so obvious, that most philosophers preferred trying to find some way to solve the associated "problem of other minds" rather than rethinking the whole picture.

The Cartesian story about minds and our knowledge of them is notoriously anti-naturalistic. Minds, with their somewhat mysterious abilities to relate to contents, to abstract ideas from experience, and to reason, are clearly very different from run-of-the-mill material objects. Especially notable is the privileged access we each have to our own minds, which is different in kind from our access to anything else. This is explained, in turn by the *ontological* difference between minds, thinking substances, and extramental, extended substances. That this ontological distinction fit in well with the dominant Christian worldview did not hurt its cause. The realm of "natures" or "thinkables", relation to which is definitive of mental states, also seems to be incompatible with sound naturalistic principles.

Sellars rethinks the whole picture. He denies that the simple relational model applies to mental states, and develops a different model of how mental attributions/descriptions work. He denies that we know our own mental states first and best, that such psychological knowledge and the concepts involved therein are simply *given*, and that the best way to fit the mental into the world is as a distinctive kind of substance. In order to make his case convincing, he develops a radical alternative to explain how we come to have and employ psychological concepts. His alternative, unlike Cartesianism, is compatible with the naturalistic, nominalistic and realistic principles that drive his philosophical work, without sacrificing an appreciation of the fine-grained structure of ordinary folk psychological discourse.

## An inadequate revolt

Sellars was not the only one willing to radically reconceive the mental. At the beginning of the twentieth century, the behaviourists broke decisively with the received view by refusing to privilege the deliverances of reflection or introspection. Psychology, they declared, had to become the science of behaviour, describing and explaining its subject matter (which they broadened to include animal behaviour) on the basis of intersubjectively available evidence, just like any other science. However, several confusions dogged the efforts of the behaviourists. The primary confusion was between behaviourism as a substantive, or better, *ontological* thesis and behaviourism as a *methodological* thesis. As a methodological thesis, behaviourism is the claim stated above: observational evidence in psychology must be, as in other sciences, intersubjectively available. Some behaviourists interpreted this as entailing that psychology must restrict itself to operating *only* with terms that either occur in intersubjectively available observation statements or can be strictly defined in such terms. Thus extended, behaviourism seems to motivate the ontological claim that the traditional conception of the mental as essentially private, internal and directly accessible must be empty or confused. How could we acquire concepts of the essentially inner and private via essentially outer public observations? The conclusion seems to be that there are no such things as mental states traditionally conceived; there are only intersubjectively available behaviours and states defined in terms of them. At best, claims about minds can be reformulated in purely behaviouristic terminology. This is the line most philosophical, analytical, or logical behaviourists (three designations for one position) took: psychological sentences can be analysed into complex sentences about our actual and possible behaviours.

Sellars identifies himself as a methodological behaviourist, for that applies to psychological knowledge a fundamental methodological precept of empirical knowledge generally. But he rejects analytical behaviourism for several reasons. First, he denies that our ordinary mentalistic talk can be analysed without loss into purely behavioural terms. He cites several reasons why analytic behaviourism is an unconvincing reconstruction of mentalistic language. At times, particularly in his earlier work, Sellars emphasizes the difficulty behaviouristic reconstructions have with capturing the *episodic* structure of the mental,[5] but this strand of his dissatisfaction with analytic behaviourism fades in his later work. Indeed, in later work he often stresses the fact that dispositions and propensities can change quickly enough to account for the episodic structure of our mental life.[6] Clearly, the most important problem with analytic behaviourism is that it offers no convincing reconstruction of the intentionality of the mental; ultimately it is trapped in circularity.[7] As Chisholm pointed out, attempts to analyse mentalistic discourse into behaviouristic language are either palpably inadequate, or they end up (perhaps surreptitiously) importing intentional language into the analysans.[8] The grammar of mentalistic discourse is sufficiently different from the grammar of behavioural description that no analytic reduction is possible.

Sellars also rejects analytic behaviourism because he takes the prospect of an empirical, scientific psychology seriously. Like any other empirical science, it must have the freedom to postulate for explanatory purposes unobservable constructs that are not definable in observation terms.

# The journey inside: the myth of Jones

## *The myth of Jones*

Given an appropriately sophisticated understanding of theory construction, Sellars thinks he can offer a reconstruction of the grammar and use of mentalistic discourse that shows it to be perfectly compatible with naturalism and nominalism without the absurdities of philosophical behaviourism. If his reconstruction works, then the Cartesian approach to psychological states is not the only game in town, however self-evident it may seem after hundreds of years of dominance.

To show that there is a non-Cartesian alternative that makes sense of mentalistic discourse and illuminates the nature and the status of our psychological concepts and attributions, Sellars famously tells us a story, a myth, as he calls it.[9] Let me recount this story as it originally appeared in "Empiricism and the Philosophy of Mind".

Understanding the dialectical situation of the myth of Jones is important to getting its point. In the first half of "Empiricism and the Philosophy of Mind", Sellars's attack on foundations has also been an attack on the givenness of first-person knowledge of one's mental or sensory states. He must then develop an alternative, non-Cartesian interpretation and explanation of psychological knowledge, especially the privacy and authority of first-person knowledge. He does not want to *deny* that our self-ascriptions of mental states have some special, first-person authority, nor that we have in some respectable sense privileged access to them. He also wants to show us that inter-subjective knowledge of others' mental states can be as firm as our knowledge of material objects.

At this point in the essay, Sellars believes he has given an adequate, non-Cartesian reconstruction of observational knowledge of public physical objects and events, a reconstruction that notably does not require that human beings have *private* or *privileged* knowledge of their own mental states. He needs to account for concepts and knowl-edge of one's own mental states and those of others in a way that respects methodological behaviourism yet explains privacy, first-person authority and intersubjectivity without falling back into Car-tesian conceptions of givenness.

Sellars's strategy is fairly direct, given the situation. He tells a myth about some protopeople who exemplify the dialectical situation we face: the "Ryleans" have an object language and exhibit sophisti-cated abilities to describe and explain the behaviour of public physi-cal objects, utilizing the subjunctive conditional and other sophisti-cated syntactic forms. They have concepts of dispositional properties and causation. But they have no conception (and therefore no knowl-edge) of their own mental states; they possess no *psychological* concepts. They do not think of themselves as having beliefs, hopes or feelings, although they can think of themselves as disposed to do various things. Could these Ryleans acquire concepts and knowledge of mental states (their own and others') as inner, private states to which they have privileged access?

Sellars's answer is *yes, if* they also have (i) semantical concepts that apply to their language, and (ii) the ability to theorize, that is, the ability to explain some set of phenomena by formulating the concep-tion of a new domain, not otherwise perceptible, modelled on one's conception of an already familiar and more or less well-comprehended domain, and identifying the explananda with the items in this new domain of unobservables. In order to explain the Ryleans' abilities to engage in silent but highly intelligent behaviour and to be subject to certain kinds of illusions, the mythical character Jones constructs a theory, formulating a new conception of an inner domain consisting of *two* kinds of internal states.[10] One kind of state (thought) is attributed properties that are modelled on the semantic properties of speech acts. Such states have meanings, entailments, truth-values and so on. The other kind of state (sense impression) is attributed properties that are modelled on the perceptible properties of physical objects. Such states can be *in some sense* blue or red, sharp or flat, bitter or sweet.

In *Science and Metaphysics*, Jones is described as developing in the first part of his theory:

> the hypothesis that people's propensities to think-out-loud,[11] now this, now that, change during periods of silence as they would have changed if they had, during the interval, been engaged in a steady stream of thinkings-out-loud of various kinds, because they are the subjects of imperceptible episodes which are:
>
> (*a*)  analogous to thinkings-out-loud;
> (*b*)  culminate, in candid speech, in thinkings-out-loud of the kind to which they are specifically analogous;
> (*c*)  are correlated with the verbal propensities which, when actualized, are actualized in such thinkings-out-loud;
> (*d*)  occur, that is, not only when one is silent but in candid speech, as the initial stage of a process which comes 'into the open', so to speak, as overt speech (or as sub-vocal speech), but which can occur without this culmination, and does so when we acquire the ability to keep our thoughts to ourselves.
>
> (SM VI §23: 159)

Once he has developed the theory and taught others how to use it, though, "It is but a short step to the use of this language in self-description ... [I]t now turns out – need it have? – that Dick can be trained to give reasonably reliable self-descriptions, using the language of the theory, without having to observe his overt behaviour" (EPM: §59, in SPR: 189; in KMG: 269). Thus are born the notions of privileged access and privacy.

If one accepts the possibility of Sellars's myth, then the Cartesian story is not the only one in town. There is an account of our psychological concepts that is both methodologically and ontologically compatible with empirically and naturalistically respectable science and that requires no given. Sellars's attack on the given is complete: he has not only shown us the problems with the given, he has shown us how to do without it.

## Understanding the myth I: some methodological points

One thing to be clear about from the outset is what some commentators on Sellars have not recognized: whereas *Jones's* theory is about our behaviour and mental states, *Sellars's* theory is about the nature and status of our *concepts* of mental states. Jones was the first psychologist; Sellars is a philosopher. Sellars admittedly assumes that Jones's theory is a good one, and in that sense (provisionally, as always in science) endorses it. But Jones is not Sellars, for Jones does not share the latter's metaconceptual interests.

Sellars offers us a theory, a philosophical theory, and it is part of his overall view that theories are usually constructed using *models*. A model is a domain of which one presumes to have an understanding, and which one proposes to be in some way analogous to the domain one is currently trying to understand. Interestingly, in his metaconceptual enquiry, Sellars uses theoretical concepts (theoretical language) as his model for the domain of mentalistic concepts (psychological language) that we are trying to understand. He presumes that after twenty or thirty years of philosophy of science, this is now familiar and well-understood territory.

Furthermore, when we use models in theory formation the analogy is always limited, and the terms of a theory can acquire "surplus value" from their use in their new context, which entails that they become independent of the model and can proceed to develop in their own way in confrontation with experience. To say that the analogy is limited is to say that the analogy is always accompanied, more or less explicitly, by a commentary that specifies which aspects of the model domain are denied to the domain theorized and which aspects of the model domain are attributed to the domain theorized.

Overt verbal behaviour provides the model *Jones* uses to formulate *his* theory of human behaviour. The introduction of theoretical concepts in science provides the model *Sellars* uses to formulate *his* theory of psychological concepts. Jones does not think that there are sounds or wagging tongues in one's head when one is thinking; he does think that there are inner episodes that possess properties like the semantic properties of the utterances that would express them.

Sellars does not think that psychological concepts *are* theoretical concepts, for there are disanalogies between psychological and theoretical concepts, most notably in two dimensions already mentioned:[12] psychological concepts are directly applicable in immediate, introspective reports, whereas purely theoretical concepts are applicable only via inference; and psychological concepts were not originally developed and adopted via a process of explicit theory formation.[13]

How does the myth of Jones get us beyond behaviourism? It does not move beyond methodological behaviourism, of course. But it differs from substantive and from analytic behaviourism because it is incompatible with the claim that talk about the newly postulated domain of inner episodes can be reduced or analysed into a purely behavioural language. Behaviourism had at least two kinds of motivations: the methodological motivation of justifying a scientific approach to human behaviour, and the ontological motivation of demonstrating the compatibility of the mental with a monistic materialism, dispensing with dualism. Methodologically, the mentalistic discourse introduced by Jones is as scientifically respectable as one could want. Behaviourists hamstring themselves if they limit themselves to terms strictly definable in the observation vocabulary; a better appreciation of the actual methods of theory construction in science removes this artificial limitation. New terms can be creative extensions of our language. Also, if concepts of inner, subjective episodes arise in the course of methodologically rigorous theory construction, there is no reason to think that such episodes must belong to some immaterial or otherwise non-natural domain. Notice, however, that the Jones story does not *force* us to construe the postulated inner episodes as specifically material, and it certainly does not tell us how such episodes might be embodied in any specific form of material reality.

## Understanding the myth II: language and thought

Jones's theory is that intelligent behaviour is caused by inner episodes that are analogous to overt utterances, and Sellars endorses this view. Language plays an absolutely indispensable role in the myth of Jones, but it is a complex role that has not always been properly understood. This section examines the role of language and its relation to thought.

The received view of the thought–language relation goes something like this (massively oversimplified for expository purposes). Thoughts owe their identity principally to the relations they bear to their contents (thinkables existing either in a Platonistic realm of abstracta or conceptualistically via their inexistence in the thought itself). Utterances owe their identity to the thoughts they express (in the causal sense of 'express').[14] Language is a highly convenient, but in principle dispensable, phenomenon: a person could think perfectly well without it and even know that she is thinking, since our thoughts are directly accessible and immediately knowable. Thought is, therefore, causally, conceptually and epistemically prior to language. Without language, all we would lack is the ability to communicate our thoughts to others.

In Sellars's view, the relation between thought and language is far more complex than this. In fact, his views on the relation seemed to have changed a bit over the years, evolving generally in the direction of greater complexity and sophistication.

## *Preliminary excursus: languages and metalanguages*

A short digression here is necessary. In the myth of Jones, one of the preconditions claimed to be essential for the Ryleans to be able to add psychological concepts to their framework is that they possess semantic concepts that apply to their language. That is, the Ryleans must have both a language and a metalanguage for it, even though they have no psychological concepts. Sellars's whole approach makes sense only if the analysis of the semantic properties of linguistic expressions contains no *essential* reference to thoughts or intentional states: that is, if possessing a metalanguage does not presuppose possession of "the framework of mental acts". As he states in "Inference and Meaning" (1953):

> The argument presumes that the meta*linguistic* vocabulary in which we talk about linguistic episodes can be analysed in terms which do not presuppose the framework of mental acts; in particular that
>
> "..." means p
>
> is not to be analysed as
>
> "..." expresses t and t is about p
>
> where t is a thought.                                          (ITM: 522)

This is the central point in the Sellars–Chisholm correspondence, for Chisholm thinks that any analysis of semantic language will import, either openly or surreptitiously, reference to intentional states. Suppose, for instance, that the only sensible approach to understanding the concept of linguistic meaning were Gricean, a theory that analyses the meaning of one's utterances in terms of one's intentions to create beliefs in others and their corresponding recognition of those intentions.[15] Then the Ryleans could have a semantic metalanguage only if they also possessed the framework of mental acts and intentional states. If Grice's theory of meaning were the only possible story, the myth of Jones would be incoherent.

Other alternatives are also incompatible with the myth. Consider an analysis of semantic concepts in terms of relations between expressions and propositions, properties and other such abstracta. The Ryleans would apparently have to have conceptions of abstracta, if they are to have a semantic metalanguage. However, is it plausible that people could have (i) concepts of abstracta, such as propositions and properties, (ii) concepts of relations between linguistic expressions and such abstracta, yet have no (iii) psychological concepts (which, one assumes, would then be analysed in terms of relations between people or their states and abstracta)? The Rylean myth, although coherent on such a view, is surely highly implausible. After all, the relation between a linguistic token and some abstractum (the "expression" relation in the logical sense) seems mysterious; Cartesians usually take it to be mediated by a *mind*. Minds somehow have the ability to relate directly to abstracta (contents); the linguistic tokens they produce can then relate to the abstracta indirectly through the thoughts of the minds that produce them. Linguistic meaning is causally and conceptually derivative from the intentionality of mind.

Sellars rejects both of these views of semantics. He offers a significant alternative: the terms of a syntactical and semantical metalanguage classify expressions functionally. Suppose that the Ryleans, including Jones, in fact possess a correct understanding of semantics. What are the relevant functions of linguistic expressions? We tend to think that the functions of utterances include communicating our thoughts, changing the beliefs of our interlocutors, informing others of our intentions and so on. Clearly, the Ryleans cannot think of the functions of their speech acts in these terms. But they can recognize language-entry functions ('That is red' is an appropriate response to something red), language-exit functions (If one says, 'I'm going now', one should then, other things being equal, leave), and intralinguistic or inferential functions (if one says something of the form 'If $p$, then $q$' and something of the form $p$, then one may also say something of the form *q*). The Ryleans can classify utterance types by behaviourally specified function.

Sellars is convinced that a Rylean metalanguage is possible. The Chisholmian squirms, convinced that somewhere or other reference to the mental has to sneak back in. For instance, 'I'm going now' ought to be followed by one's leaving only if it is said with the intent of describing one's action-to-come. We often say it with the intent of hurrying someone up. Sellars characterizes the notion of a Rylean "thinking-out-loud" by reference to *candid* and *spontaneous* utterance; could the Ryleans distinguish between candid, sincere utterances and guarded, deceitful or insincere utterances? Does a covert reference to belief sneak in here? As Chisholm responded to Sellars: "If the people of your myth were to give just a little bit of thought to the semantical statements they make, wouldn't they then see that these semantical statements entail statements about the thoughts of the people whose language is being discussed?" (ITM: 537).

We cannot and should not assume that the Ryleans have *our* concepts. By hypothesis they do not have our psychological concepts to begin with, and (especially given Sellars's rather holistic approach to meaning and intentionality) this lack will have broad implications for other concepts as well. Plausibly, *our* metalinguistic terms involve psychological concepts; but Sellars does not claim that the Ryleans have *our* metalinguistic concepts. His claim is that the Ryleans possess legitimate metalinguistic concepts that, while not our *current* metalinguistic concepts, are their possible predecessors. Objecting to the Ryleans because their metalinguistic concepts are not ours misses the point. We could point to linguistic phenomena that the Ryleans could not understand well, but their metalinguistic concepts are *predecessors* of ours in part because they are not as *good,* do not explain as many of the relevant phenomena, as our current concepts. The Ryleans will be susceptible to systematic errors in their metalinguistic descriptions and explanations because their metalinguistic concepts are less sophisticated than ours. Indeed, the Rylean metalinguistic concepts will be mere approximations of our own, giving good results only under narrow conditions and otherwise susceptible to error. How do we decide whether their behaviouristic metalinguistic concepts are legitimate, coherent, possible predecessors of our own more sophisticated concepts? Surely, the standard rules for philosophical thought experiments hold here. One can propose one's fiction as one wants, and it is up to anyone who objects to demonstrate why the proposal is incoherent, unsound or otherwise unacceptable.

Pending a clear roadblock to Sellars's proposal, we should accept the possibility of the Ryleans and their behaviouristic metalanguage.[16]

Could there be a language without metalinguistic (syntactic, semantic and even pragmatic) terms? One's initial temptation may be to answer "Why not?", but Sellars would probably claim that a symbol system that contains no such terms is not yet a fully fledged language. It could not be taught explicitly to or by its own users, for they would have no way to express the proprieties of formation and usage that make it a normative, rule-governed system. (Admittedly, though, we do not in this sense *teach* our children their first language.) More importantly, from Sellars's point of view, without metalinguistic concepts the speakers of such a language would be unable to formulate any of the rules of their language. *None* of their activity would be rule-following in the strict sense. But then it is unclear that their activity is *rule*-governed rather than *pattern*-governed. Sellars thinks ought-to-be's imply ought-to-do's, so beings utterly unable to recognize linguistic ought-to-do's cannot be said to be respecting linguistic ought-to-be's.[17] The users of a representational system can engage in its linguistic practices *knowingly* only if they have metalinguistic concepts. Sellars consistently requires that fully fledged normative practices must be capable of being done knowingly (and equally that they must not *always* be actions). If language is a rule-governed system, then its users must also possess its metalanguage.

## Language and thought, again

Jones posits inner episodes, thoughts, that are unlike speech episodes in that no sounds or inscriptions are involved, but that do have properties like the semantic properties of speech episodes. Thus, the thought that skiing is fun has some kind of compositional structure that enables us to identify a subject of the judgement and a predicate attributed to it. Furthermore, it is, like the utterance "skiing is fun", true and participates in various logical relations, for example, entailments and incompatibilities. Sellars sometimes describes these internal episodes as being in "Mentalese", which would seem to name "the language of thought."[18] But there are dangers here. One common misunderstanding is to identify Jonesian thoughts with verbal imagery, the stream of imagined words that often populates one's consciousness but leaves no external sign. Verbal imagery may be a common upshot of thought, but Jones's theory does not identify verbal imagery and thought. Sellars makes this clear in Part XI of "Empiricism and the Philosophy of Mind":

> Now the classical tradition claimed that there is a family of episodes, neither overt verbal behavior nor verbal imagery, which are *thoughts*, and that both overt verbal behavior and verbal imagery owe their meaningfulness to the fact that they stand to these *thoughts* in the unique relation of "expressing" them.
>
> (EPM: §47, in SPR: 177; in KMG: 257)

But, Sellars goes on to explain, things are muddied by the tendency to assimilate thoughts and sensory states, so the distinction between thoughts and imagery gets lost. Still:

> If we purge the classical tradition of these confusions, it becomes the idea that to each of us belongs a stream of episodes, not themselves immediate experiences [that is, sensory experiences], to which we have privileged, but by no means either invariable or infallible, access. These episodes can occur without being "expressed" by overt verbal behavior, though verbal behavior is – in an important sense – their natural fruition. Again, we can "hear ourselves think," but the verbal imagery which enables us to do this is no more the thinking itself than is the overt verbal behavior by which it is expressed and communicated to others. It is a mistake to suppose that we must be having verbal imagery – indeed, any imagery – when we "know what we are thinking" – in short, to suppose that "privileged access" must be construed on a perceptual or quasi-perceptual model.
>
> (EPM: §47, in SPR: 177–8; in KMG: 257–8)

This "revised classical analysis of our common sense conception of thoughts" (EPM: §47, in SPR: 178; in KMG: 258) is Sellars's position in "Empiricism and the Philosophy of Mind" and throughout his career.[19]

Dale Jacquette succumbs to another danger when he claims that "whether it is the nature of thought always to be packaged in language is the very problem dividing Chisholm and Sellars".[20] Jones and Sellars are committed to Mentalese being *like* a language in important ways, but not to its *being* a language *strictu sensu*. When he is being careful, indeed, Sellars does not *identify* the semantic properties of speech episodes with the properties assigned to intentional states. In *Science and Metaphysics* (VI §§25–43: 160–67), he is careful to distinguish the sense of the terms that apply to overt utterances from the sense of the analogical terms Jones creates to apply to inner episodes, even showing how a more generic set of senses can be generated that would apply to both linguistic and mental acts.

Still, Sellars gives his readers many reasons to believe that he thinks thinking must itself be a linguistic affair. Most prominent among them is a passage from "Empiricism and the Philosophy of Mind" (§29), in which Sellars advocates a position he calls:

> psychological nominalism, according to which *all* awareness of *sorts, resemblances, facts*, etc., in short, all awareness of abstract entities – indeed, all awareness even of particulars – is a linguistic affair. According to it, not even the awareness of such sorts, resemblances, and facts as pertain to so-called immediate experience is presupposed by the process of acquiring the use of a language.               (EPM: §29, in SPR: 160; in KMG: 240)

This is not the only passage. In "Autobiographical Reflections", Sellars recalls how difficult he found it, in the 1930s, to unite the act–content conception of mental acts with a naturalistic approach to mind, and remarks that he did not begin to resolve these difficulties until ten years later, in the mid-1940s, when "I began to *equate* thought with language" (AR: 286).

Whether thought is essentially linguistic is important for understanding the status, both epistemic and ethical, of languageless beings such as animals and babies. Language is something we learn in a social context, not something we are born with, in Sellars's view, so beings that do not or cannot learn a public language are entirely languageless.

Yet there are also notable passages in which Sellars disavows the claim that all thought is linguistic. Two stand out in particular and merit careful consideration. The earlier is in "The Structure of Knowledge":

> For if one ties thinking too closely to language, the acquisition of linguistic skills by children becomes puzzling in ways which generate talk about 'innate grammatical theories'.
> 33. Not all "organized behavior" is built on linguistic structures. The most that can be claimed is that what might be called "conceptual thinking" is essentially tied to language, and that, for obvious reasons, the central or core concept of what thinking is pertains to conceptual thinking, Thus, our common-sense understanding of what sub-conceptual thinking – e.g., that of babies and animals – consists in, involves viewing them as engaged in "rudimentary"

forms of conceptual thinking. We interpret their behavior using conceptual thinking as a model but qualify this model in *ad hoc* and unsystematic ways which really amount to the introduction of a new notion which is nevertheless labeled 'thinking'. Such analogical extensions of concepts, when supported by evidence, are by no means illegitimate. Indeed, it is essential to science. It is only when the negative analogies are overlooked that the danger of serious confusion and misunderstanding arises.

34. One must also take into account the sensibilities not only of animal lovers but of artists: painters, musicians, and the like. These are, of course, "thinking beings." But do they "think" in the course of their distinctive creative activity?

35. One is tempted to say that the musician not only thinks *about* sound, but also "in sound". Thinking about sound, it might be admitted, can be construed on a linguistic model – as "inner speech" using the vocabulary of auditory qualities and relations. Indeed much of the thinking that a composer does is conceptual thinking about the relationships of sound patterns, and since the notion of conceptual thinking as analogous to language leaves open the question of how *precise* the analogy is, it is surely not too far-fetched to take a linguistic approach to this aspect of the composer's activity.

36. But is there not a more intimate relationship between composition (and other forms of musicianship) and sound: the aspect I referred to above as "thinking in sound"? And is not this aspect also a mode of *thought*? Is not a performer a "thinking being" even while he performs? The "linguistic model" begins to look far too narrow and specialized to capture the nature of thinking, even at the strictly human level – let alone the sense in which animals think.                    (SK I §§32–6: 303–4)

In the long run, the role of the imagination in thought will have to be addressed, for both visual perception and imagination are "in a sense most difficult to analyze, a *thinking in color* about colored objects" (SK I §37: 305). This passage is allusive and illusive. The idea that the core of our concept of thinking is explicitly *conceptual thinking*, which we extend in unsystematic ways to describe and explain sublinguistic beings and episodes was a long-term conviction of Sellars's. There is a clear statement in "Intentionality and the Mental" (1957):

Not only do the subtle adjustments which animals make to their environment tempt us to say that they do what they do because they *believe* this, *desire* that, *expect* such and such, etc.; we are able to *explain* their behavior by ascribing to them these beliefs, desires, expectations, etc. *But,* and this is a key point, we invariably find ourselves *qualifying* these explanations in terms which would amount, in the case of a human subject, to the admission that he wasn't *really* thinking, believing, desiring, etc. For in the explanation of animal behavior the mentalistic framework is used as a *model* or *analogy* which is modified and restricted to fit the phenomena to be explained. (ITM: 527)

On his own principles, if this analogical extension of the concepts of the framework of conceptual thinking to subconceptual thought can be made systematic and given empirical support (and it makes sense to see the development of the cognitive sciences subsequent to "Intentionality and the Mental" as precisely such an effort), there will be ample reason to attribute thoughts\* to animals, but thoughts\* will not be identical to thoughts, just as, for example, the spin property of electrons is not identical to the spin property of tops, even though in some sense it is modelled on it.[21] Sellars moves in this direction in his later article "Mental Events" (1981), discussed below.

It seems clear that the activity of the musician, painter or vivid daydreamer resembles linguistic activity at least to the extent that there are conventional proprieties governing the formation and transformation of the sounds, colours, or images involved. Sellars would probably hold that the manipulation of sounds, smells, colours and so on, could count as non-linguistic "trains of thought" if, but only if, the manipulator has a language in the strict sense. Having a language is crucial to rule-following, which makes possible taking up other non-linguistic activities into the "logical space of reasons". Once language makes it possible to formulate and then follow rules, rules of criticism enable us to subject non-actions and non-agents to rule-based judgement and assessment. All kinds of human activities are thereby subject to justification, subject to treatment as items in the "logical space of reasons", and appropriately seen as expressive of, even forms of, human thought. Sellars does *not* believe that thought is always packaged in language, even if language is a necessary condition of thought.

The second place where Sellars explicitly rejects an equation of thought and language is the opening lines of "Mental Events", a late essay in which he considers at length what to say about representational systems generally, the genus of which linguistic systems are species.

1. I find that I am often construed as holding that mental events in the sense of thoughts, as contrasted with aches and pains, are

linguistic events. This is a misunderstanding. What I have held is that the members of a certain class of linguistic events are thoughts. The misunderstanding is simply a case of illicit conversion, the move from 'All *A* is *B*' to 'All *B* is *A*'. (MEV: 325)

He means that while thinkings-out-loud, our candid and spontaneous utterances, *are* linguistic events *and* thoughts, he has never committed himself to the notion that all thinkings are linguistic events.

The characterization of psychological nominalism quoted above from "Empiricism and the Philosophy of Mind" seems to force us to identify thought and language, but there is evidence even in "Empiricism and the Philosophy of Mind" that Sellars did not intend to go so far.

Now, the friendly use I have been making of the phrase "psychological nominalism" may suggest that I am about to *equate* concepts with words, and thinking, in so far as it is episodic, with verbal episodes. I must now hasten to say that I shall do nothing of the sort, or, at least, that if I *do* do *something* of the sort, the view I shall shortly be developing is only in a relatively Pickwickian sense an equation of thinking with the use of language. I wish to emphasize, therefore, that as I am using the term, the primary connotation of "psychological nominalism" is the denial that there is any awareness of logical space prior to, or independent of, the acquisition of a language.
(EPM: §31, in SPR: 162; in KMG: 241)

In *this* quote, Sellars is claiming only that language is a necessary condition of thought and "awareness of logical space". Is *all* awareness "awareness of logical space"?

In "Empiricism and the Philosophy of Mind" Sellars does not have available adequate resources to grant that there is good reason and plenty of evidence for attributing propositional attitudes to infra-linguals while drawing a significant distinction between them and fully fledged, language-using persons. For in "Empiricism and the Philosophy of Mind", Sellars essentially equates the *linguistic* with the *propositional*. Saying that animals "think", but they don't *really* think, or that "think" is equivocal when applied to persons and animals is unsatisfactory unless backed up with far more argument than Sellars gives in "Empiricism and the Philosophy of Mind".

Sellars understood the problem and "Mental Events" is designed to alleviate the pressure.

17. Now, of course, animals, e.g. our useful friend the white rat,

also have representational systems. They do not, however, have languages. Do they think? Have they mental events? Are they perhaps fraught with intentionality? Do they refer and characterize? (MEV: 328)

The distinctions developed in "Mental Events" enable Sellars sensibly to attribute to animals and other sublinguistic beings propositional attitudes or internal representational states such as those regularly posited by cognitive scientists, without granting infralinguals the full range of human conception.

He introduces a *new* distinction between *propositional form* and *logical form*: "To have propositional form, a basic representational state must represent an object and represent it as of a certain character" (MEV: 336). Both referring and characterizing are, of course, functional roles played by items in a system that interacts with the world in ways that utilize such items as representations to modulate its activity. Referring and characterizing are by no means restricted to *linguistic* entities, however, nor need these distinct roles be played by distinct items. A mark on a map, for instance, can both refer to a city and characterize it as located in a certain place, as of a certain size.[22] Sellars analyses the structure of atomic representational or propositional states in terms of counterpart properties, as seen in Chapter 4. Sellars now claims that "Propositional form is more primitive than logical form" (MEV: 336).

Those representational systems, the items in which have *logical* and not just *propositional* form, contain logical words or symbols; they are *logic-using* systems. Logical expressions enable a system to formulate complex truth-functional compounds and generalizations. Logical expressions, as Brandom has so clearly brought out, enable the connections among representations to become explicit within the system. Representational systems that lack logical operators can nonetheless "ape reason" by possessing dispositions to change their representational states in ways that parallel the inferential transitions made by a fully fledged reasoner acting on general principles. Yet without the logical connectives and quantifiers, a representational system cannot formulate or explicitly obey conditional principles (If $C$, then D) or generalizations (All $C$ are $D$; Whenever $C$, do $D$), although the system could have dispositions to represent $D$ if (or whenever) it represents $C$ as the case. Consider the two inferences:

| | |
|---|---|
| Smoke here | Smoke here |
| (So) Fire nearby | Wherever there's smoke, there's fire nearby |
| | (So) Fire nearby |

Sellars calls the first a "Humean inference", the second an "Aristotelian inference".[23] (In other places with other concerns, he would have called these "material" and "formal-logical" inferences, respectively.) Of course, Aristotelian representational systems can – indeed, *must* – *also* often infer in the Humean mode. In Aristotelian systems, however, principles of inference can be thematized in ways that are closed off to pure Humean systems. The most significant consequence of this is that the Humean representational system cannot formulate the notion of a *rule*. Without a conception of a rule, there is no rule-following, and without rule-following somewhere, there are no rules anywhere, even rules of criticism. Thus, the distinction between Aristotelian and Humean representational systems is the important one for Sellars.[24]

> 78. In order to carve nature at the joints, then, it would seem clear that the place where the cut is to be made is neither at the distinction between RSs [representational systems] which do and those which do not involve the subject–predicate distinction, nor between propositional and non-propositional RSs.
> 79. Where, then, does it lie? The answer is straightforward and should not surprise. The crucial distinction is between *logic-using* RSs and RSs which do not *use* logic, though their operations are described by *mentioning* logical operations.          (MEV: 340)

Sellars now has no problem attributing internal states with propositional form to animals and other sublingual beings. Later Sellars claims that animals have propositional attitudes. More radically, he can also break the connection between language and awareness that seemed so strong in "Empiricism and the Philosophy of Mind".

> 57. Such representational systems (RS) or cognitive map-makers, can be brought about by natural selection and transmitted genetically, as in the case of bees. Undoubtedly a primitive RS is also an innate endowment of human beings. The concept of innate abilities to be aware *of* something *as* something, and hence of pre-linguistic awarenesses is perfectly intelligible.          (MEV: 336)

The first description of psychological nominalism from "Empiricism and the Philosophy of Mind" insisted that *all* awareness is a linguistic affair, but this is rejected in Sellars's later work. The second characterization of psychological nominalism from "Empiricism and the Philosophy of Mind" ties together language and "awareness of logical space". In the context of "Empiricism and the Philosophy of Mind", the temptation is to think that *all* awareness is, somehow or other, an awareness of logical space. But our encounter with "Mental Events" shows that the phrase "awareness of logical space" is ambiguous, for the Aristotelian representational system, capable of formulating rules and principles, can have an awareness of logical space in a richer sense than a Humean representational system, which can manoeuvre within a logical space that it cannot be aware of *as such.*

Ultimately, then, Sellars believes that only Aristotelian systems can be thinkers in the fully fledged sense. Given the reflexivity requirement that attaches to real knowers and real languages, being an Aristotelian representational system is only a necessary and not yet sufficient condition for being a fully fledged thinker, for Aristotelian systems need not be reflexive in the requisite sense.

What are the consequences of this for the relation between language and thought? Jones proposes that there is a language-like system of representational states within intelligent beings like people. As we now understand (but Jones probably did not), 'representational system' is a genus with many different species, and Jones is proposing that there is a species of that genus with some particular and specifiable characteristics internal to us and involved in the aetiology of our behaviour. Because Jones takes *language* as his model, he effectively ascribes to humans a logic-using system capable of reflexive self-representation. A proper theory of meaning as functional classification makes it relatively straightforward to extend the semantic categories applied, *strictu sensu,* to language tokens to the items of the newly posited representational system. Sellarsian dot-quotes are not just interlinguistic: they are applied more broadly across representational systems. ·Not· is a common noun that applies not only to any item of any (overt, natural) language that functions in a relevantly similar way to the illustrated word (the English word 'not'), but to any item in any relevantly similar representational system (not necessarily a language in the strict sense) that is relevantly similar in function. Since semantics is functional, the material realization of the item performing the function is relatively indifferent, and can as well be an internal state as an overt utterance. The fundamental point is that thinking need only be language-*like.* Developmentally, we embody a complex series of increasingly sophisticated representational systems that eventually enable us to share the intersubjective representational system that is language.

# Privacy, privileged access, first-person authority and other minds

Sellars needs to be able to explain both the structure of mentalistic talk and how we are *able to use* mentalistic language. This latter task includes being able to account not just for our possession of mentalistic concepts, but our ability to apply them successfully. I have two things in mind here: (i) first-person attributions of mental states have a special status not accorded to second- and third-person attributions; and (ii) second- and third-person attributions are sometimes made with great confidence.

I take the special treatment of first-person attributions to be a *fact*, in the sense that we do it and that we are right to do it. Depending on what aspect one is concerned with, the terms 'privacy', 'privileged access' and 'first-person authority' have all been used to describe or label the phenomenon.[25] The *fact* of special status for first-person mentalistic descriptions and attributions is beyond question: its exact nature, scope, strength and explanation are matters of great dispute.

Similarly, I take it to be a fact that we assume that other human beings have minds, and that we are right to do so. We also often know what others are thinking or feeling, sometimes with great assurance, often quite defeasibly. The exact nature, scope, strength and explanation of our knowledge of other minds are also matters of great dispute. Sellars needs to account for these phenomena, as does any philosopher of mind.

According to the Cartesian, we acquire the basic elements of first-person knowledge, our concepts of mind and mental states, by abstraction from instances directly available to us. Moreover, the traditional Cartesian account affords first-person (or self-)knowledge the strongest possible epistemic status: certainty, incorrigibility, even infallibility. It attributes universal scope to such knowledge, in the sense that nothing in the mind is thought to be beyond the reach of introspection. And it explains the special status of first-person knowledge by a neat metaphysical story: we are each simple, self-contained substances who have causally and epistemically direct access to our own states, and thus know them immediately as they are. Any other thing we know, we know *indirectly* through its effects on our senses and our abilities to use the evidence of our senses. The epistemic distinctiveness of first-person knowledge is a reflection of its metaphysical immediacy. Latter-day Cartesians have often weakened the epistemic status accorded basic self-knowledge or restricted its scope in some ways

(Freud cannot simply be ignored), and many have sought to hold on to some version of the Cartesian epistemology of self-knowledge while rejecting its metaphysical dualism.

However, the Cartesians cannot easily shake the problem of other minds; such knowledge, according to the Cartesians, has a totally different basis from our knowledge of our own minds. Furthermore, in the Cartesian picture, the minds and mental states of others are at a double remove from us. We can know them only indirectly through their effects on material objects, which, in turn, we know indirectly through their effects on our senses.

Sellars has shown us a different way to think about psychological *concepts*, but it is time to think about our psychological *knowledge*, both our self-knowledge and our knowledge of other minds. In the case of self-knowledge, the challenge he faces seems particularly steep, for the directness and surety of first-person mentalistic claims seem antithetical to the idea that our concepts and our knowledge of mind are theory-like. Return to the myth of Jones with these questions in mind; perhaps unsurprisingly, we find the text frustratingly brief:

> [O]nce our fictitious ancestor, Jones, has developed the theory that overt verbal behavior is the expression of thoughts, and taught his compatriots to make use of the theory in interpreting each other's behaviour, it is but a short step to the use of this language in self-description. Thus, when Tom, watching Dick, has behavioral evidence which warrants the use of the sentence (in the language of the theory) 'Dick is thinking "p"' (or 'Dick is thinking that p'), Dick, using the same behavioral evidence, can say, in the language of the theory, 'I am thinking "p"' (or 'I am thinking that p.') And it now turns out – need it have? – that Dick can be trained to give reasonably reliable self-descriptions, using the language of the theory, without having to observe his overt behavior. Jones brings this about, roughly by applauding utterances by Dick of 'I am thinking that p' when the behavioral evidence strongly supports the theoretical statement 'Dick is thinking that p'; and by frowning on utterances of 'I am thinking that p', when the evidence does not support this theoretical statement. Our ancestors begin to speak of the privileged access each of us has to his own thoughts. *What began as a language with a purely theoretical use has gained a reporting role.*          (EPM: §59; in SPR: 188–9; in KMG: 269)

Jones's protégées first apply psychological concepts to others in a strictly theoretical manner. That is, they observe the non-psychologically characterized behaviour of others. They then infer, using Jones's theory, the presence of certain psychological states. They apply Jones's theory to themselves on exactly the same basis. Later, Sellars tells us, they come to be able to make *direct reports* of their own states.

There is so much Sellars does *not* tell us. How do those first-person reports get made? Since sensory mechanisms are not involved in first-person reports, what mechanisms, if any, *are* involved? Nor does Sellars tell us anything further about the second- or third-person cases. Can Jones's protégées also be trained to report immediately on the psychological states of others? This is important, because being able to *report* on something, in Sellars's view, removes it from the realm of the theoretical *strictu sensu*. If we make first-, second- and third-person mentalistic *reports*, then in neither the first-, second- nor third-person cases are we literally *applying a theory* when we attribute mental states. If Sellars held that psychological concepts must be applied by the inferential means common to theoretical concepts, his theory of mind could not account for privacy, privileged access or our assurance that others have minds.

Sellars thinks that anything we can immediately and knowingly report is as good as observable, but we do not normally consider self-reports as expressions of *observations*. (Imagine the fit Ryle would throw, and properly so, at the idea that I *observe* my mental states!) In normal usage, 'observation' seems tied to the use of our five senses, and self-reports of our mental states do not employ the five senses as intermediaries (although sensory states may be the *object* of such reports). Sellars's story does help us understand the temptation to assimilate our mentalistic self-reports to sensory observation reports and introspection to perception: the justificational structures are, indeed, very similar, even though the causal mechanisms involved differ in important respects.[26]

Although Sellars says nothing about the second- and third-person cases, it is plausible that Jones's disciples learn to apply his new mentalistic vocabulary *to others* directly and non-inferentially at least some of the time. They learn to make *observation reports* about the mental states of others. To the Cartesian, this is a blasphemous idea: we have and can have no immediate access to the mental states of others. Certainly, we often must *figure out* what other people are thinking or feeling. But, at least phenomenologically, we sometimes *see* another's anger or happiness. There is no Sellarsian reason against saying that, in the proper conditions, I can be both a reliable and a knowing meter of an admittedly limited range of the mental states of others.[27] Perhaps the fact that there are significant limits on my ability to report non-inferentially on the mental states of others (e.g. I may be able to do so only for a very limited range of people – my family and good friends or maybe the members of my cultural community – and/or for only a very limited range of mental states – principally stronger emotions – and under fairly stringent conditions) discouraged Sellars from mentioning this possibility. In at least one case, however, it is clear that we can observe another's thoughts: when we observe their candid verbal behaviour.

> Thus, at the primary level, instead of analyzing the intentionality or aboutness of verbal behavior in terms of its expressing or being used to express classically conceived thoughts or beliefs, we should recognize that this verbal behavior *is already thinking in its own right,* and its intentionality or aboutness is simply the appropriateness of classifying it in terms which relate to the linguistic behavior of the group to which one belongs. (LTC: 116–17)

That Sellars acknowledges our ability to report directly on the mental states of others is an indication of how far Sellars's position moves us from the traditional problem of other minds, and it emphasizes the important point that in Sellars's theory, psychological vocabulary is univocal across first- and third-person application.

Sellars says more about the first-person case: "And it now turns out – need it have? – that Dick can be trained to give reasonably reliable self-descriptions, using the vocabulary of the theory, without having to observe his overt behaviour" (EPM: §59, in SPR: 189; in KMG: 269). The parenthetical "need it have?" is important, for it raises the question of the *necessity* of privileged access.[28] In one important sense, that question is already settled by Sellars's myth. Some within the Cartesian tradition think that privileged accessibility is a defining characteristic of the mental. But, in Sellars's view, his myth:

> helps us understand that concepts pertaining to such inner episodes as thoughts are primarily and essentially *inter-subjective*, as inter-subjective as the concept of a positron, and that the reporting role of these concepts – the fact that each of us has a privileged access to his thoughts – constitutes a dimension of the use of these concepts which is *built on* and *presupposes* this intersubjective status. My myth has shown that the fact that language is essentially an *intersubjective* achievement, and is learned in intersubjective contexts ... is compatible with the

"privacy" of "inner episodes." It also makes clear that this privacy is not an "absolute privacy." For if it recognizes that these concepts have a reporting use in which one is not drawing inferences from behavioural evidence, it nevertheless insists that the fact that overt behaviour *is* evidence for these episodes *is built into the very logic of these concepts*, just as the fact that the observable behaviour of gases is evidence for molecular episodes is built into the very logic of molecule talk.

(EPM: §59; in SPR: 189; in KMG: 269–70)

Given Sellars's views, the exact extent of our privilege – how much of our thinking is directly knowable with what degree of certainty – is ultimately an empirical matter that depends in part on our mechanisms for thought detection.

One possibility being explored by a significant set of developmental psychologists is that the mechanisms we utilize to detect and attribute thoughts in ourselves and others operate as a kind of tacit theory application.[29] Overstating it a bit, these psychologists treat each child as a Jones who develops a (tacit) "theory of mind" to account for the behaviour of others. Phenomenologically, it seems clear that our competence in folk psychology is not a matter of applying a theory in any explicit way, but the notion of a *tacit* theory that we can apply without being conscious of it as a theory, or of the process as a theory-application process, has shown itself to have some value. So it seems worth exploring this possibility empirically.

Does Sellars think that our actual, empirical competence at psychology is best accounted for as the application of an implicit theory? As noted earlier, Sellars is (and knows himself to be) a philosopher and not a psychologist. Jones is intended to be a myth, not the everyday reality of the human condition. The developmental story behind our psychological competence is outside Sellars's purview as a philosopher. The myth of Jones would not explain how children can come to acquire psychological expertise by four or five, well before they would be capable of mastering an explicit Jonesian theory. Nor is Sellars interested in the empirical details of the cognitive processing story beyond the commitments contained in Jones's theory that *something, somehow* like overt language is going on in us when we think. The latter-day theory-theory (as it is called) is a creative extension of Sellars's proposal that, although consistent and coherent with his original proposal, is not already contained or intended therein. The theory-theory is subject to empirical, not philosophical, confirmation and refutation. Should the theory-theory prove not to be the best available empirical explanation, Sellars's original suggestion remains untouched, for the theory-theory goes beyond anything Sellars himself claimed.[30]

The theory-theorists have been opposed by the simulation theorists, who maintain that we recognize the psychological states of others by using our own psychological mechanisms ("off-line", as it were) to perform a kind of simulation of the other.[31] By simulating being in the other's situation, we can hypothesize what psychological state the other is in. Simulation theorists have at times attacked Sellars, hoping to discredit the supposed father of the theory-theory and thereby his progeny.[32] But this attack seems misplaced. Sellars is hardly an empirical theory-theorist, and there are some aspects of his approach that are congenial to simulationists. One aspect of simulationism Sellars would not be sympathetic to is the apparent assumption that we have prior and independent access to our own psychological states.[33] That smacks of a return to the inside-out Cartesian view that we have primitive, privileged access to our own psychological states independently of any other knowledge we may have.

In Sellars's view, because many important relationships among our intentional states are mirrored in corresponding relationships between the speech acts that would express them, language learning creates a competence that can also be recruited to perform psychological work, especially when combined with an understanding of and competence in social interaction.

When we attribute intentional states to people, we are *classifying* their states. Consider a standard propositional attitude attribution, for example,

Ralph believes that it is raining.

This functions much like a piece of indirect discourse such as

Ralph asserts that it is raining.

Because I am an accomplished speaker and interpreter of English, I may be able to say many things about the proper use of the phrase, but could not finally articulate all the "rules" at work in my know-how concerning even this simple phrase. However, I can employ my *linguistic* know-how to generate *psychological* insight, for my knowledge of the appropriate situations for asserting that, denying that, apologizing for or praying that it is raining can be utilized to recognize appropriate situations for believing, disbelieving, regretting and hoping that it is raining, and the consequences thereof. Similarly, my knowledge of the material inferences from 'It is raining' to 'The ground is wet' or 'Open the umbrella' enables me to recognize that if Ralph believes it is raining, he will probably believe that the ground is wet and regret having forgotten his umbrella. In what is close to a fell swoop, Jones acquires a rich nomenclature of internal states, which we can perfectly well call a classificatory theory of mental states.[34]

This classificatory theory classifies items by what we might call normalized causal powers. The belief that something is red will normally and appropriately tend to give rise to a belief that it is coloured. So causal connection among psychological states is presumed throughout, but nowhere made fully explicit and articulate. In particular, it does not commit anyone to any particular set of causal generalizations.

Jones and his protégées, while still in the awkward early stages of mastering his theory, can reason as follows:

Ralph is in a state that he would candidly express by asserting that *p*, so Ralph believes that *p*.

Ralph is also in a state that he would candidly express by asserting that *if p, then q,* so Ralph believes that *if p, then q.*

So, *ceteris paribus*, it is likely that Ralph believes that *q* (although I have no direct behavioural evidence of that).

Jones's reasoning here is perfectly good and familiar to us all. Notice that it is not explicitly a form of causal reasoning, however much it presupposes underlying causal connections. Jones and company get the connection between these states of mind for free via their semantic characterization. They (and we) can assume that there are causal connections among our internal states that enable those internal states to relate to each other in ways that conform to their semantic characterization, but how those causal connections work, what kinds of mechanisms instantiate them, how they might develop and how they might break down, are left untouched. The "internal structures" recognized in Jonesian psychology are almost completely parasitic on the structure of the language Jones and company speak.

Our attributions of psychological states rests on a kind of pretheoretic know-how, but it is not knowing how to invoke our own psychology (which would have to be known to us in a different way) in order to model another's. Rather, they rest on knowing how language and social situations work "from the inside". This knowledge can then be recruited to make sense out of both our own and others' behaviour without having to take a detour through externalization in an explicit theory of psychology.

# A philosophy of mind

The Sellarsian mind is naturalistic, but not reductively so. The concepts we use to understand each other – where 'understanding' is, in fact, not just a matter of describing, predicting and explaining another's behaviour, but also includes such things as assessing that behaviour, sympathizing (or not) with it, cultivating it and coming to mutual agreements concerning it – are concepts of internal states that are not, in general, observable, but are conceptually tied via evidential relations to intersubjectively available behaviours. The rich, articulated structure of the intentional states we attribute to human beings (ourselves and others) is modelled on the rich, articulated structure of language and its relations to the world and other pieces of language. In particular, the concept of intentionality, of the *content* of our states, is modelled on the notion of the meaning of an utterance. In Sellars's functional-role conception of semantics, the content of our thoughts is to be understood in terms of a functional role played by a token of an internal representational system. The internal representational system operating in human beings must be sufficiently analogous to language to contain logical particles and permit the formulation of metarepresentations, but beyond these fairly obvious formal requirements, it is a matter of empirical investigation to establish its nature. Sellars has no doubt that we are naturally endowed with an incredibly potent internal representational system as matter of evolutionary development. Unfolding the full power of this representational system, however, requires cultivation in an intersubjective linguistic arena.

A representational system that does not contain logical particles or metarepresentations is essentially simpler than one that does. Its representations are normative; the mapping function between the world and tokens of the system is not purely *de facto*, as evidenced by the fact that things can "go wrong". But such representational systems are subject only to *external* correction. *We,* the external observer, can describe the internal state of such an animal representation system as, for example, *representing a fly*, but that is to classify that internal state by a likeness to a kind of internal state we might be in. Such animal representational systems and their states are essentially thinner than human representational systems and states, for the normativity of the animal representational system is not, to use a Hegelian turn of phrase, *for itself.*

In human representational systems the normativity of the representational has emerged from the in itself and become for itself, to continue the Hegelese. Human representational systems, using the logical particles, can formulate general principles, and since they can metarepresent, can formulate general principles concerning representations. We can not only represent the world (accurately or inaccurately), we can worry about the accuracy of our and others' representations of the world. We can also worry whether the representations of others agree with our representations, and whether we want them to be accurate or to agree with ours.

According to Sellars, the metarepresentational concepts of syntax, semantics, or intentionality are not reducible to or eliminable in favour of purely physicalistic or purely behaviouristic concepts. Not only do they pick out a level of uniformity in the world that would not be salient without the introduction of a new level of concept not strictly definable in physicalistic or behaviouristic terms, but also they are involved in a form of speech or thought that has different aims and concerns from the physical or strictly behavioural. There is no purely physicalistic, behaviouristic or empirical description that is equivalent to an attribution of either a meaning or a thought.

Sellars says many times that language is prior to thought in the *ordo cognoscendi*, but thought is prior to language in the *ordo essendi*. This claim, however, is multivalent, for the relations between thought and language are complex. By claiming that thought is prior in the order of being, Sellars means both that (1a) the innate, internal representational system of normal humans is a causal prerequisite for their acquisition of a particular set of natural languages; and (1b) individual linguistic episodes are the causal result and expression of internal thought episodes. That language is prior to thought in the order of knowing means both that (2a) it is by coming to participate in the linguistic life of a community that we unfold the full power of our natural, internal representational systems, because (2b) it is by learning a language that we are able to develop the logical and metarepresentational capacities otherwise dormant in our native representational systems, the capacities that (i) extend the scope of our representations to the general and the abstract and (ii) enable the internalization of the constitutive norms of the practice, thus subjecting it to our partial control. Furthermore, (2c) overt linguistic episodes provide the basis on which we (generically and individually) are able to develop conceptions of intentionally rich internal episodes in ourselves and others.[35]

Sellars's philosophy of mind is thoroughly naturalistic in the sense that it at no point invokes abstracta, immaterial substances or supernatural beings or powers in its explanation of the nature and the capacities of the human mind. But it is not reductivist: we cannot and never shall be able to replace the intentionalistic concepts of mentality with the descriptive concepts of neurophysiology or any other lower level of scientific description and explanation. On the other hand, there is a sense in which Sellars is willing to let us identify neurophysiological states with thoughts, namely, the same sense in which we are willing to identify utterances with patterns of sound or inscriptions.[36]

Some think that it must be possible to dispense with the language of intentionality in favour of the language of neurophysiology.[37] This move seems to reap extra support from Sellars's brand of scientific realism, for the concepts of intentionality are clearly manifest-image concepts. Sellars claims that the manifest image is only phenomenally real, in more or less Kant's sense, and that science is the measure of what is. Does that mean that mentalistic language is bound to be replaced by some more scientific idiom? The eliminative materialist cannot hope for support from Sellars. As we have seen, our common-sense view of the world is not a *theory*, according to Sellars, and thus is not subject to replacement the way theories are. Secondly, Sellars grants the ascendency of science in matters of describing and explaining, but there is so much more that we do with language, especially mentalistic language. Particularly important in this regard would be activities of intersubjective deliberation such as negotiating, planning, disagreeing, validating or confirming and speculating. Nor should we neglect other forms of activity such as imagining, narrating, apologizing, promising and so on. Creative human activity of all kinds is, for Sellars, constituted by the linguistic *cum* mentalistic framework that makes it possible. Mentalistic language is tied to all of these activities; it is tied to our humanity itself. The root of it is this: mentalistic language is the language of rational agency. Could science, a paradigmatically rational activity, convince us rationally to abandon our self-image as rational creatures?[38]

Sellars's dictum that attributing knowledge to someone is locating that person's state "in the logical space of reasons, of justifying and being able to justify what one says" (EPM §36, in SPR: 169, in KMG 248) has become well known of late. But it is essential to see that the dictum does not apply only to *knowledge* attributions. The attribution of *any* mental state presupposes that the subject is sensitive to the norms of reason and concerned with the proprieties governing behaviour and interaction. By attributing a content to a mental state, we locate it in a richly articulated set of connections to the world, both perceptual and behavioural, and connections to other such states, both formal and material. This *is* the logical space of reasons, and justification is as relevant to what one *does* as what one *says*. The things that have minds are those that occupy and move around in that space, things for whom justification of action as well as belief is a problem.

# Chapter 8

# *Sensory consciousness*

Sellars's treatment of sensory consciousness is a culminating episode in his philosophy: many different lines of his thought come together in a position that is unique to him, both bold and puzzling. I shall begin with two myths to introduce the issues and then try to clarify Sellars's commitments and his arguments by analysing several significant passages from Sellars's later works.

## The sensible qualities: the mythical history

Sellars used to tell the story of the sensorium–body problem in his classes. Hints and even some pieces of the story show up in some of his essays, but it appears nowhere as a cohesive narrative. The story is not an *argument* for his treatment of the sensible qualities, but it sets up a motivating context for it, like his other myths. Like the story of the "original image" in "Philosophy and the Scientific Image of Man" (1962), in which *everything* is thought of as a person, and out of which the manifest image develops, the mythical part of the sensorium–body problem has an unclear relationship to the myth of Jones. Furthermore, after the beginning, the story is not mythological; it is a portrayal of the actual history of our concepts of the sensible qualities, as Sellars sees it.

It begins with the "pre-pre-Socratics", at the very dawn of human beings as thinking beings. (These pre-pre-Socratics are pre-Jonesian, I believe; they have not yet achieved the conception of sense impressions.) These pre-pre-Socratics perceive red things, sweet things, and such like. Unsophisticated as they are, however, in their language the terms for the proper sensibles, for example, 'red', 'blue', 'sweet' and 'sour', do not have the grammar of adjectives, but that of mass terms, like *stuffs*.[1] When a pre-pre-Socratic says "There is a blue triangle" or "There is a rectangle of red", it should be read like "There is a titanium triangle" or "There is a rectangle of mud". The blue triangle is, in their view, not a triangle of some stuff that has the property blue, but the blue is the very stuff of the triangle.[2] (The *common* sensibles, particularly the geometric properties of things, are thought of as structural–relational properties, forms that have proper-sensible stuffs as their contents.[3]) The things we think of as sugar cubes would be cubically shaped mixtures of white and sweet, and Sellars's famous pink ice cube would be a mix of pink and coolth. The pre-pre-Socratics are terrifically naive: the most superficial and easily detectable classifications are taken to reach to the very essence of things.

However, the notion that colours, tastes, smells, sounds and feels are the very substance of the objects that confront us in the world cannot hold up. Organizing one's world around the properly sensible characteristics of things just does not do a very good job of helping one explain, understand, or predict the behaviour of things. Red things are not always good to eat, nor blue things bad; some red things rot, others do not. Apples are red or green on the outside, but white where it counts. We just do not get very good empirical generalizations if we classify things solely on the basis of the sensibles.

This seems so obvious that it can be difficult to take seriously Sellars's suggestion that our most primitive concepts of objects take them to be composed of sensible stuff, reifying the proper sensibles as the very *content of the world,* its very *substance.* But the reader should take this suggestion seriously. Here is a way to think of this "weird" idea: Sellars believes that the proper (and for that matter, the common) sensibles have a privileged position in *any* conceptual scheme. They are, because of the way we are built, the front line in the confrontation between the causal realm and the conceptual realm.

Now, truculent philosophers will want to construe this to be (aha!) an admission on Sellars's part (at last) that there is a given, namely, the sensibles. But, of course, it is not a givenness that conflicts with Sellars's epistemology. A "confrontation between the causal and the conceptual" has to happen *somewhere,* but does not entail an objectionable *given* because the point of confrontation is not fixed; one's confrontation with the causal realm can insert one into the conceptual realm at any number of different points, depending on one's conceptual framework, sensory capacities, trained responses, perceptual set, interests and so on. There is no principled difference in the structure of the justificational story of our immediate conceptual responses to the world, regardless of the conceptual sophistication of the concepts used. Still, there is something special about perceptions involving only the proper and common sensibles: they are both conceptually minimal and causally most proximate.[4] That is, we can expect every humanly usable conceptual framework to contain concept-families that classify the immediate and minimal sensory responses of the human knower to the world. Ultimately, in Sellars's view, this is a matter of the causal constitution of the input systems to the cognitive system of the knower. Such perceptions are not *givens* in the invidious sense, for, although the structure of the immediate and minimal sensory response of the knower to the world turns out to be a matter of the causal constitution of the input systems of the knower, the immediate and minimal sensory response need not be treated *as* (or appear to the knower *as*) characterizing the causal constitution of the input systems of the knower.

In fact, Sellars is essentially telling us, our overwhelmingly realistic proclivities make it a hard-won achievement of the intellect to realize that our minimal reporting vocabulary actually has more to do with our own structure than the structure of the world outside us. Our initial reflex is to assume that our most basic reporting vocabulary limns the most basic structures in the world we report on.[5] Mythologically expressed, our reflex is to interpret the proper sensibles as the very stuff of the world.[6]

Now back to our story. Given a categorial framework that treats 'red', 'sweet' and 'cold' as substantives, the pre-pre-Socratics are not well-positioned to deal with the world. They develop new ways of categorizing things that do not rely solely on what is directly sensible; the dispositional properties and capacities of things become crucially important. They develop complex concepts that mix occurrent, sensible qualities and dispositional properties: concepts of *wood, flesh* and *bread*, where these concepts collect not only different groups of proper sensibles but different non-occurrent genetic and dispositional properties and capacities in logically complex combinations (wood comes from trees, can burn, (usually) floats, splits more easily along the grain than across it). They can now distinguish in principle between the thing and its properties.[7] The material inferences and generalizations of this framework do a much better job of explaining, predicting and guiding our action. The development of these more robust thing-kind terms is a fascinating topic, but what is important for us is that the proper sensibles are not *rejected,* but *transposed.* The post-pre-pre-

Socratics (are these the familiar pre-Socratics?) do not *discard* 'red', 'blue', 'sweet', as later theorists discarded 'phlogiston'; they *transpose* them categorially from substantives to adjectives. New terms are introduced, slightly different in use (and therefore sense) from the old substantives 'red', 'blue' and so on, but very closely analogous to them in terms of the relationships of similarity and difference they involve. Colours and smells are now taken to be occurrent properties of material objects.

Presumably, at this point Jones comes along and introduces the concept of internal and private sense impressions that have properties analogous to the sensible properties of physical objects. So we turn to the second myth.

# The myth of Jones, part II

## *Introducing sense impressions*

When we last left our hero, Jones, he had postulated unobservable, internal states to help explain why and how people do intelligent, reasonable things even when they are silent: they are reason*able*, he says, because they are *reasoning*, although not reasoning-out-loud. They harbour an internal process that is like reasoning-out-loud and contains elements analogous to the elements of reasonings-out-loud, sentences, inferences and so on.

Jones thereby invents the notion of human psychology. But Jones has not thereby exhausted the field. Besides explaining the remarkable fact that our behaviour is often both silent and reasonable, a theory of human behaviour must also be able to explain other aspects of our behaviour, and that includes the glitches. False beliefs are sometimes the result of bad reasoning, but not always. After all, not all beliefs are the result of reasoning; we acquire many beliefs non-inferentially.

We can assume that the (pre-Jones) Ryleans distinguish between observation reports – a verbal episode that purports to be a direct, descriptive response to the situation it describes – and other speech acts. Given Jones's theory of thoughts, they can develop a conception of perceptions, the inner analogue of reports. Perceptions are thinkings: they have conceptual content, (purported) reference, and are correct or incorrect. But perceivings are not *just* thinkings. Further-more, the theory of thoughts itself has nothing to say about the process of non-inferential belief acquisition and especially nothing to say about how that process can go wrong. Jones realizes, therefore, that he needs *another* theory to explain such things.

Why is it that, at times, people will report that there is a red rectangle over there, when the thing over there is a white trapezoid or when there is nothing over there at all? Sometimes, of course, they may be lying or play-acting, but sometimes they are sincere and obviously so. How do we explain this? The problem is not exclusively a third-person problem; each of us has had the experience of sincerely reporting or forming a perceptual belief that turned out to be quite wrong, and in our own cases it is easier to disqualify play-acting or lying as explanatory hypotheses. The issues stand out most clearly in cases of perceptual error but, of course, we cannot have a theory of perceptual error *alone*. The theory has to tell us both what happens when things go right and what happens when things go wrong.

Jones could just say that such cases are flashes of brute irrationality, cases where people just say or think something without reason or cause. But that is not an explanation so much as a resignation from the task of explanation. The alternative is to postulate that something explains what is in common between cases in which

- one sees a red rectangle over there;
- the object over there looks to be red and rectangular to one;
- there looks to one to be a red and rectangular object over there.

Although the environs of the perceiver may have little in common in these three cases, Jones posits inner episodes within the perceiver that are all of a kind, the impression-of-a-red-rectangle kind, to which the perceiver is conceptually responding in each of these episodes. Jones thereby invents the theory of sense impressions.

As in his previous effort, Jones has a *model* for these new posits, namely, the very objects that, if everything were going well in standard conditions, would be the objects perceived.[8] According to the theory, when one sees a red and rectangular object, or it looks to one as if there's a red and rectangular object before one, there is something (somehow) *like* a red rectangle inside one. Sellars stresses that it is the analogue of an object that the theory posits, not an analogue of a *seeing* of a object; that would assimilate impressions to thoughts (since seeings are a kind of thinking).

Sellars also stresses that these episodes are *states of the perceiver*, not objects or particulars in their own right. While *perceivings* are clearly conceptual episodes, the new states Jones posits are *not* conceptual episodes, for they are conceived of as *causing* perceptual episodes, not as themselves perceptions. Also, there is a temptation to think that, if the things impressions are modelled on are particulars (red rectangles, green spheres, etc.), then impressions are also particulars. But that would be wrong. If a theory T posits the existence of a hitherto unknown kind of entity, $t_k$, modelled on a familiar kind of entity, $m_k$, there have to be *some* characteristics of $t_k$ that are claimed to be like characteristics of $m_k$, but *ontological category* need not be one of those. This is an important point for Sellars, for his account of the correct treatment of the sensory depends heavily on such transcategorial analogies.[9]

Some examples of transcategorial analogies demonstrate that this is, indeed, a phenomenon that has not been concocted just to draw certain conclusions about sense impressions. Consider computer models. Although in a computer model of the weather, such characteristics as temperature and wind speed, which are arguably *states* of the atmosphere, are modelled by *states* of the computer system, and are thus not transcategorial, this will not be the case for all computer models. In a computer model of an automobile accident or in a computer-based racing game, for instance, the cars (particulars) are modelled by complex states of the computer, a transcategorial analogy. Another example, not involved with digital models, is the wave interpretation of quantum particles. The waves familiar to us from the beach and the bathtub are processes in some stuff or medium, but the probability waves of quantum theory are not *in* any stuff or medium. What is "waving" is the probability of finding a particle, or the square of that probability, or something; in any case, the analogy is transcategorial.

### The problem of the intrinsic character of sense impressions

The other point Sellars is particularly intent on making in "Empiricism and the Philosophy of Mind" (§61) is that the analogical predicates Jones introduces to characterize the entities or states he has postulated are properly thought of as giving an *intrinsic* characterization of those entities or states. This is a marked contrast to *thoughts,* for thoughts are explicitly given a functional characterization, and a functional characterization is entirely *relational* and therefore not *intrinsic*. But things are different with sense impressions. That an impression is *of a red rectangle* is not supposed to be a merely relational characterization of the impression; it is supposed to get at its very nature.

Frankly, the argument(s) given in "Empiricism and the Philosophy of Mind" to support this are murky at best. Sellars argues, for instance, that characterizing an impression as *of a red triangle* is characterizing it "by something more than a *definite description*, such as 'entity of *the kind which* has as its standard cause looking at a red and triangular physical object in such and such circumstances'" (EPM: §61, in SPR: 192; in KMG: 272). This is because the predicates of a theory are not shorthand for definite descriptions given in terms of observation predicates; as we might say it today, the observation language description may fix the reference, but does not determine the meaning of the theoretical predicate. That is determined by its use in the theory and in observations (should it acquire a reporting role). But this is no less true of the terms of Jones's theory of thoughts, so it does not give us reason to think that sense impressions are more intrinsically characterized than thoughts.

In another remark that might offer some support for his claim, Sellars points out that the objects that sense impressions are modelled on have intrinsic properties, and it is these properties that the analogy exploits.[10] But he rejects the idea that sense impressions should therefore be taken to have those properties, "the familiar properties of physical objects and processes" (EPM: §61, in SPR: 192; in KMG: 273). Sellars does not draw the conclusion that since their models are objects purportedly known by their intrinsic properties, sense impressions must also be entities known by their intrinsic properties. In fact, he points out that all we have is an *analogy* between the properties of the model entities and the properties of sense impressions, which analogy is principally a matter of the relational structure of the two property fields.

This works against the idea that the properties Jones attributes to sense impressions are intrinsic to them, so Sellars considers the opposing position that, since Jones attributes to his fellow human beings a set of states that "stand to one another in a system of ways of resembling and differing which is structurally similar to the ways in which the colors and shapes of visible objects resemble and differ", our concept of these states can only be "purely formal" (i.e. relational), "which can acquire a 'content' only by means of 'ostensive definition'" (EPM: §61, in SPR: 193; in KMG: 273). This is rejected out of hand as falling back into the myth of the given: sense impressions are as capable of intrinsic characterization as any theoretical entity. The critique of ostensive definition in the earlier part of "Empiricism and the Philosophy of Mind" prevents us from assuming that the intrinsic–extrinsic distinction maps onto the acquaintance–description distinction (or the content/scheme distinction). But again this is not a positive reason for thinking that sense impressions are intrinsically characterized whereas thoughts are not.

Last, Sellars considers how Jonesian impressions might relate to further developments in the scientific image. He rejects any straightforward identification of Jonesian impressions with neurophysiological states, warning us against mixing: "the framework of *molar* behaviour theory with the framework of the *micro*-theory of physical objects. The proper question is, rather, 'What would correspond in a *micro*-theory of sentient organisms to *molar* concepts pertaining to impressions?'" (EPM: §61, in SPR: 193–4; in KMG: 274). In such a microtheory of sentient organisms there might, indeed, be particulars like sense data (although neither "found" by analysis nor capable of functioning as an epistemic given) that are the objects immediately responded to when something appears to us. These objects would be (literally) internal to the perceiver and would provide the ultimate ontological home of the perceptible qualities of the physical objects of the common-sense framework. But this is speculation, not argument.

Sellars is clearly very concerned here with finding a place in the overall scheme of things for sensible qualities as sensed (raw feels, qualia, phenomenal properties – call them what you will), but we cannot say that his discussion in "Empiricism and the Philosophy of Mind" is successful. He spent significant time over the next 25 years trying to state and argue for his position more clearly. There are, however, a few more things to say about the Jonesian myth before turning to Sellars's subsequent attempts to clarify the ontology of sense impressions.

### Sense impression reports

Jones teaches his theory to his fellows. The available evidence people using the theory can employ now includes not just overt behaviour, but introspectable appearings. ("These two lines *look* different in length, but I measured them carefully, twice.") As with the theory of thoughts, people come to use the theory of sense impressions in direct reports. They can non-inferentially report, for example, "I have a sense impression of a red triangle" in just those situations where the theory would attribute such an impression to them. These situations, of course, include cases in which they are, indeed, *seeing* a red triangular before them, cases in which the triangle before them merely appears red, and cases in which there is no triangle, red or otherwise, and they are dreaming, hallucinating or entertaining an eidetic image of a red triangle.

Sellars is silent concerning *third-person* reports of sense impressions. There is no barrier in principle to such a report: sometimes can we not just *see* another's pain? We occasionally express it by saying, "That must hurt", where the 'must' indeed expresses the fact that we are drawing a conclusion, but is there good reason (without Cartesian assumptions) to believe that *all* second- or third-person attributions of sense impressions must be inferential?

This example points to another potential trap for Sellars's story. Sensations of red triangles and sensations of blue spheres are introduced by analogy to red triangles and blue spheres, but we cannot say the same thing about sensations of *pain*. Pains are not inner replicas of any physical objects; nor are they replicas of their typical causes, wounds or nerve stimulation. Sellars has to tell a different story about pain attributions. It might go as follows. We can, for example, feel heat. Some sensations of heat are pleasant, some are painful, nor need there be universal agreement about the threshold of pain. Pleasure and pain could, therefore, be functional, extrinsic, characteristics of sensations that are dependent in some way on their intrinsic characteristics.[11]

In any case, Sellars thinks his story helps us understand how our concepts of sense impressions can be:

> primarily and essentially *inter-subjective,* without being resolvable into overt behavioural symptoms, and that the reporting role of these concepts, their role in introspection, the fact that each of us has a privileged access to his impressions, constitutes a dimension of these concepts which is *built on* and *presupposes* their role in intersubjective discourse. It also makes clear why the "privacy" of these episodes is not the "absolute privacy" of the traditional puzzles. For, as in the case of thoughts, the fact that overt behaviour is evidence for these episodes is built into the very logic of these concepts. (EPM: §62, in SPR: 195; in KMG: 275)

## Accommodating the sensory: from the manifest to the scientific image

Sellars's writings from the 1950s are full of hints and allusions concerning the nature and status of sensations.[12] In the 1960s, he began more systematically addressing the issues. "Phenomenalism", written in 1959 but not published until 1963, goes further than "Empiricism and the Philosophy of Mind", but it is in "Philosophy and the Scientific Image of Man" that Sellars first presented a sketchy but relatively complete treatment of sensibility. 'Complete' here does not mean detailed and clearly articulated, but the overall shape of his theory is present. 'Complete' here also does not mean finished and unchanging: Sellars made adjustments in later years, adjustments that he thought conserved his central views, but that others have seen as abandoning central pillars of his thought.

For Sellars, solving the sensorium–body problem requires figuring out how the sensory aspect of experience would be dealt with in an ideally adequate scientific treatment of perception. Of course, the sensory aspect of experience is not a new phenomenon, like, say, superconductivity, discovered in the course of scientific exploration. We possess already a sophisticated and subtle framework for dealing with the sensory. An adequate scientific treatment of the sensory will have to be a *successor* to the framework already in hand. That entails that our current framework acts as a constraint on the ultimate scientific theory, for if such a theory developed without regard or ties to our current framework, it could be justly accused of simply changing the subject, and not explaining the sensory aspect of experience at all. Therefore, correct analysis of the manifest image treatment of the sensory is essential to understanding what future developments might be possible. This analysis was begun in "Empiricism and the Philosophy of Mind", but needs development in at least two dimensions. First, Sellars provides a more detailed analysis of the ontological commitments of the manifest image concerning sensible characteristics like colours, sounds and odours. After a discussion of why Sellars thinks that the key to the sensory (unlike the key to thinking) lies with future science, this analysis is the topic in the second section below. Secondly, Sellars refines his account of introducing theoretical entities, distinguishing two different modes of it, only one of which, he argues, applies to sense impressions. This is the topic of the third section.

The scientific theory that respects what we already know about the sensory well enough to be a legitimate *successor* to our current conceptions of the sensory, Sellars argues, will have to give the sensory special treatment, adding to the stock of primitive entities sufficient for explaining and describing non-living things, another set of primitives, just as fundamentally physical, but required only in descriptions and explanations of sentient things.

## Science, thoughts and sensations

Notice that considerations pertaining to the development of a thoroughgoing scientific image of man in the world played no large role in Sellars's philosophy of mind *strictu sensu*, that is, his theory of intentionality. Mentalistic language and mentalistic concepts won't be displaced as science progresses because the mentalistic framework we operate within is, at least in principle, adequate to its central purposes. Empirical research in cognitive psychology can still improve our understanding of the mind in manifold ways; the new explanatory–descriptive vocabulary that science develops will offer tremendous opportunity for refinement. But beyond a great deal of empirical refinement and fascinating new detail, a wholesale categorial revision is not in store. We can expect fascinating discoveries about how the functionally classified items attributed in mentalistic discourse are embodied in the physical world, but not a categorial revision of mentalistic discourse itself. It could be the case that the pursuit of science (especially psychology) could *cause* us to cease thinking of ourselves as rational agents and truth-seekers, but science couldn't coherently *reason* us into believing that we are not rational agents and truth-seekers.[13] So science seems committed to leaving the basic structure of intentionality intact.

But this reasoning does not apply to sense impressions and the theory of sensibility, in Sellars's view. The outlines of an adequate theory of intentionality are already in hand;[14] the outlines of an adequate theory of sensibility are yet to be achieved. In fact, he thinks he can show that the manifest image conception of sensibility is currently *inadequate in its own terms* – it forces upon us questions that it cannot, even in principle, adequately resolve. It is not just that we need to *refine* our conception of sensibility; it is in need of fundamental, categorial revision. Sellars thinks it is part of the philosopher's job not only to point out the puzzles in the dominant manifest image conception of sensibility that, correctly interpreted, indicate the inadequacy of that conception; it is also part of the job to speculate on how the puzzles might get resolved.

## The manifest phenomena

We begin by reviewing some basic distinctions that Sellars portrays as arising from a sound phenomenology of perception. These distinctions form the backbone of our conception of the sensory, so they will have to be preserved in any acceptable successor image.[15] Since they concern the phenomenology of perception, these distinctions constrain the nature of sensation, but do not directly address the ontology of the sensory itself.

Sellars focuses on visual perception: *seeing*. (Remember, Sellars regards seeing as an *achievement*; one can see only what is there to be seen. 'Seeing' something that is not there is not a seeing, *strictu sensu*, but an ostensible seeing.) The first distinction is between propositional seeing (seeing *that* something is the case) and objectual seeing (seeing something). Objectual seeing has sometimes been construed as a kind of pre- or non-conceptual relation, often called 'acquaintance', but Sellars does not intend any such thing by his distinction. Since, for him, seeing is always conceptual, and concepts are, as Kant put it, "predicates of possible judgments",[16] objectual seeing is tied to propositional seeing. In Sellars's treatment, objectual seeings provide potential subjects of propositional seeings, but also have slightly different criteria of success from their propositional counterparts.[17]

We sometimes express our perceptual experiences in sentences with complex demonstrative subjects, for example, "This brick with a red and rectangular facing surface is larger than that one". In such a sentence, the subject term represents what we (perceptually) take there to be; the predicate expresses what we take it to be or take it as. There is a temptation to think of such a sentence as having the deep structure "This is a brick and it has a red and rectangular facing surface and it is larger than that one". This would leave us with a bare 'this' as the subject of the perceptual judgement, as what is 'taken'. Sellars thinks that this move leads to serious confusion; bare particulars are ontological nonsense, and demonstratives always have some categorial context, even if it is merely implicit. Effectively, Sellars holds that perceptual takings always have some conceptual content; we always take a *this-such*.

Sellars also distinguishes between *what* we see and what we see *of* it. I see, for instance, the brick. But I see *of* it its facing surface. I also see *of* it its redness. These last two, however, are *not* the same in form. Seeing of the brick its facing surface is still fundamentally objectual in structure, for the facing surface of the brick is an object, a particular, in a way in which the redness of the brick is not. The facing surface of the brick is a dependent particular, a constituent part of the brick (although not an actual part of brick in the sense of something easily or already divided from the remainder of the brick).[18] In the manifest image, the redness of the brick, however, is a *property* of the brick, not a constituent *part* of the brick. We have to respect this difference in the categorial grammar of surfaces and colours, even if we can see of objects both their facing surfaces and their surface colours.

While we can see *of* something both properties and parts, there are restrictions on what we can see *of* objects. We can see of objects their facing sides, their colours and shapes. But can one see of the pink ice cube its iciness? We do not think of iciness as a particularly visual characteristic, for one thing; for another, iciness seems essentially to be dispositional and causal, and it would be surprising if a property with essential ties to possibilities could be *fully* present in a single perceptual experience. We can surely see *that* the cube is ice; we can see it *to be* a cube of ice; we can also see it *as* a cube of pink ice. There seems to be no particular limit to what we can see things *as*; *seeings that* and *seeings to be* are (as achievement terms) limited only by the facts. But what we can see *of* things is limited to occurrent properties and parts fully present to our sensory capacities.

The point of these distinctions finally comes into focus when Sellars points out that the content evidently present in perceivings *as* and perceivings *that* is well accounted for as *conceptual* content. Seeing the cube as ice is very like seeing it while believing in its iciness. Since perceptions are thinkings, and very like believings, it makes sense that some of the content of a perception is present in the mode of being thought of or believed in. But not everything in a perception is present in this way. "We see not only *that* the ice cube is pink, and see it *as* pink, we see *the very pinkness* of the object; also *its very shape* – though from a certain point of view" (SSOP §25: 88). What we see *of* the ice cube is present to us in a different way from that in which the (merely) conceptual content of our experience is present to us. What we need now is:

> an analysis of the sense in which we see of the pink ice cube its very pinkness. Here, I believe, sheer phenomenology or conceptual analysis takes us *part* of the way, but finally lets us down. How far does it take us? Only to the point of assuring us that
> *Something, somehow* a cube of pink in physical space is present in the perception other than as merely *believed in*.
> (SSOP §26: 89)[19]

This claim forms a kind of *datum* for Sellars. It is not that he thinks it has some kind of intuitive authority or is simply self-evident, in the sense that its epistemic authority is *independent* of other claims. But it is intuitively recognized by one who is at home in the manifest image in the sense that it seems to be a framework principle of the image. It is the kind of thing philosophy leads one to say in the course of clarifying and making explicit the otherwise unreflective structure of our conceptual framework. Philosophers can and have disagreed with it but, in Sellars's view, that is a sign of misunderstanding something about the structure of the manifest image.

Jones got us this far in his postulation of sense impressions: *something, somehow* a cube of pink in physical space is present in the perception other than as merely *believed in*. The trick is now to fill in the blanks: what kind of something that is in what kind of way a cube of pink, and how can it be present in a perception in some way different from being believed in? This programme of enquiry has been pursued for thousands of years, and there are many attempts to fill these blanks: sense-datum theories and adverbial analyses of sensing are two to which Sellars devoted some attention.[20] Early on, he defended the idea that sense-datum theories contain important metaphysical insights into sensory phenomena, despite significant epistemological errors. Later, he defended the adverbial analysis of sensation as best representing the commitments of the manifest image. But he did not think the difference between the theories terribly significant, in that clever theoreticians could take the fundamental vocabulary of either theory and, by invoking the proper insights at the right time, generate what would be, essentially, notational variants of a correct view.[21]

However, there are limits to what philosophical analysis can reveal. Sellars thinks his predecessors committed the mistake of assuming that it is the job of philosophical analysis alone to specify the nature of sensations. Analysis of the manifest image conception of sensation gets us only to the threshold. The manifest image does not possess the resources to resolve the problems. We shall need science to take the matter further.

There is, in Sellars's view, a complementary mistake as well, namely, assuming that what is revealed by careful philosophical analysis of the manifest image conception of sensory experience is dispensable, and we can disregard its lessons in order to shove perception into whatever Procrustean bed fits the science of the day.

## *Theoretical entities: relocation versus postulation* **de novo**

### *A revision of "Empiricism and the Philosophy of Mind"?*
Sellars's attempts to justify special treatment for sense impressions in "Empiricism and the Philosophy of Mind" were not very successful.

Consider now one of his last major pieces, "Foundations for a Metaphysics of Pure Process" (the Carus Lectures), principally devoted to restating and defending his treatment of sensation. In Part III of Lecture III ("Is Consciousness Physical?"), Sellars rejects what we have to say has been the standard interpretation of "Empiricism and the Philosophy of Mind" concerning sense impressions. Since the standard interpretation is not unfounded in the text, either most people missed something important in "Empiricism and the Philosophy of Mind" or Sellars has revised his theory in some important ways. Sellars begins the relevant passage by restating the standard interpretation of his view.

> 36. When one comes to think, as we eventually must, of sense impressions as theoretical constructs, it is tempting to follow a familiar paradigm and to think of the theory as introducing a new domain of entities, e.g., sensations of volumes of pink, as microphysics introduces a new domain of entities, e.g., molecules.
> 37. One would think of the theory as inventing predicates to be satisfied by these postulated entities and formulating principles to describe their behavior, as kinetic theory invents predicates and formulates principles pertaining to molecules.     (FMPP III: 72)

Comparisons between Jones's theories and molecular theory abound in "Empiricism and the Philosophy of Mind"; Sellars could certainly be describing his own proposal in "Empiricism and the Philosophy of Mind".

> 38. If one follows this paradigm, of course, one will be disposed to acknowledge that these predicates and principles are not invented out of whole cloth. One will stress the role of models and analogies in theoretical concept formation.
> 39. One would, therefore, be disposed to think of the pinkness of a pink sensation as *analogous* to the pinkness of a manifest pink ice cube, as the elasticity of a molecule is *analogous* to the elasticity of a tennis ball.     (FMPP III: 72)

Again, this captures succinctly what is proposed in the text of "Empiricism and the Philosophy of Mind".

> 40. One would, however, grant that in the last analysis the ascription of attributes and behaviors to sense impressions, like the ascription of attributes and behaviors to molecules, is to be justified solely in terms of the explanatory power of supposing there to be such items.     (FMPP III: 72)

This, too, although less clearly addressed in "Empiricism and the Philosophy of Mind", seems to be its doctrine. But in the late 1970s, Sellars now sees a danger.

41. Thus, one who is captured by the paradigm could easily be led to grant that the postulated analogies would be justified only to the extent that they contribute to the explanatory power of the theory, and to allow that *in principle* sense impressions need no more have attributes interestingly analogous to those of manifest objects, than micro-physical particles need have attributes interestingly analogous to those of middle-sized things.

42. Or, to put the same point in a less extreme form – but one which is directly relevant to the history of the problem – might not this philosopher be led to admit that certain complex *physicalistic* attributes (roughly, attributes definable in terms of "primary qualitites") might be both interestingly analogous to the perceptible features of manifest objects and, when ascribed to sense impressions, satisfy the requirement for explanatory power? And also led to allow that the demand for a *nonphysicalistic* attribute to play these roles might be just another example of "pictorial thinking"? (FMPP III: 72–3)

This is hardly clear, but there seem to be two points. First, the model used in postulating sense impressions is only a *guide*. The entities postulated could turn out to be vastly different from their models. Secondly, all that seems needed are some entities or structures at the physicalist level that maintain a formal analogy with the proper sensibles. Thus, Sellars is acknowledging a common criticism of his position: surely there is *some* set of physical states or properties of persons that is sufficiently analogous to the structure of colour space to play the role of sensations of colour without having to run to entities radically different in kind from those already countenanced.

But Sellars rejects this tack.

43. The possibility of such a challenge should make it clear that while there is much good sense in the above strategy for dealing with sense impressions, it is not quite on target.

In the following paragraphs, we are at least given a hint where to find an argument to back this claim up.

44. And it is not difficult to see what has gone wrong. For the argument of the first lecture should have made it clear[22] that the theory of sense impressions does not *introduce,* for example,

cubical volumes of pink. It reinterprets the *categorial status* of the cubical volumes of pink of which we are perceptually aware. Conceived in the manifest image as, in standard cases, *constituents* of physical objects and in abnormal cases, as somehow 'unreal' or 'illusory', they are *recategorized* as sensory states of the perceiver and assigned various explanatory roles in the theory of perception.

45. To make this point, one refers to them by the use of the *category neutral* (i.e., in scholastic terminology, *transcendental*) expression 'entity'.

46. Obviously there are volumes of pink. No inventory of what there is can meaningfully deny that fact. What is at stake is their status and function in the scheme of things.

47. The pinkness of a pink sensation is 'analogous' to the pinkness of a manifest pink ice cube, not by being a *different quality* which is in some respect analogous to pinkness (as the quality a Martian experiences in certain magnetic fields might be analogous to pink with respect to its place in a quality space), but by being the same 'content' in a different categorical 'form'. (FMPP III: 73)

Two things are notable: (i) Sellars's emphasis on the connection between explanation and justification, and (ii) his distinction between two different ways of introducing theoretical entities.

## Explanation and the sensory

When Sellars describes the rejected interpretation of sense impressions, he emphasizes that the sole justification for such a move is "the explanatory power of supposing there to be such items". Since Sellars is an explanationist – one for whom justification and explanatory power are inextricably linked – the extra emphasis here seems odd. Belief in postulated entities and their properties is justified, because accepting them permits the best explanation of the observable phenomena. Notice, though, that this presupposes the rational theory–choice procedures of science. In the manifest image, these are not universally applicable. Perhaps Sellars is suggesting that something different is going on with statements and beliefs about particular cases of sensible characteristics: their justification is not exhausted by their being a conclusion in an inference to the best explanation of observable phenomena.

After all, for sense impressions, the observable phenomena are not distinct from the observations of them; we seek to understand the very seemings themselves, the being of the phenomenal. One's justified belief in an observation report is grounded in its being the spontaneous response of a well-trained speaker. Normally, when something goes (or might go) wrong, and one's unedited belief is (possibly) erroneous, we fall back to a claim about how things seem. These claims are not infallible, but because they make a purposefully minimal claim, they are strongly justified.

P1: I just thought-out-loud 'Lo! Here is a red apple'.

P2: (I'm not sure no countervailing conditions obtain).

C1: Nevertheless, there is excellent reason to believe that something, somehow a red sphere in space was just present to me, even if no red apple or object of any kind is before me.

C2: Nevertheless, there is excellent reason to believe that I just had a sensation of a red spherical shape in space, or that I just sensed red-spherically.

These inferences are like those Sellars believes justifies our acceptance of normal observation reports, but, because the content of the conclusion has been pared down to a minimum, they are actually stronger inferences than the inference justifying the acceptance of a standard observation report.[23] This increase in the strength of the inference is bought at a price, of course: C1 explicitly abstracts away from all categorial commitment, leaving us with only the category-neutral quantifier 'something somehow'. Still, it is important to note that C1 is *not* empty of all content. Its content, however, rests entirely in the predicative phrase 'red sphere in space'. C2 goes a bit further than C1, in that a protocategorization of the something-somehow-a-red-sphere-in-space is proposed. It is a protocategorization, because the manifest image is not (and in Sellars's view cannot become) determinate about the relation of sensations (or manners of sensing) to the coloured, shaped objects of the manifest image, including the persons who have them.

Once categorially determinate commitments are abstracted from, what is left in the claim that something-somehow-a-red-sphere-in-space is present to one? Only the commitment that the logical spaces of colours and shapes are applicable to something somehow immediately related to one? Sellars might therefore have in mind that in understanding and explaining appearances themselves, a point is reached where one cannot use entities with some *other* characteristics in the explanations; the best we can do is properly to locate within our overall explanatory/conceptual scheme the indispensable characteristics – the logical spaces of the sensibles – reported in epistemically minimal (least committal) states. This seems to be what Sellars is getting at when he writes:

> Now it is not the logical spaces of occurrent perceptible qualities and relations which generate the demand for scientific explanation, but rather the logical space of the powers and dispositions of physical objects and processes. Here one must be careful, for there is clearly a sense in which the latter space is an off-shoot of the former. Roughly, it is not such facts, expounded in a "phenomenology" of sensible qualities and relations, as that to be orange is to be between red and yellow in color, which demand scientific explanation, as it is such nomological facts as that black objects sink further into snow that [*sic.*] white objects when the sun is shining.
>
> (IAMB in PP: 387)

Could Sellars be putting *anything* outside the realm of scientific enquiry? Not any *natural* fact. So this passage should be read as follows. There is a logical space of colour. It need not have any particular structure *a priori*, for example, it need not come pre-articulated into seven basic colours (e.g. Roy G. Biv) rather than five, nor need hue, saturation and brightness be understood *a priori* to be the dimensions of the colour solid. It is articulated, however we *learn* to articulate it. Thus orange's being between red and yellow in colour demands no scientific explanation, for that is determined by phenomenologico-conceptual analysis. In other words, orange's being between red and yellow in colour is not a natural or causal fact. What makes objects orange, or makes us see orange when we look at them *is* a natural, causal fact and demands scientific explanation. Ultimately, then, what is at issue is just what aspect of or domain in the causal nexus of the world the logical space of colour really articulates or applies to.

To many this will sound like a return to the given, but a given must be epistemically independent, and nothing here entails that beliefs about the characteristics of sensa or sense impressions would be epistemically independent of other beliefs. The structure of justification remains anti-foundational, and the question of which concepts to apply to which objects remains empirical.

*Introducing theoretical entities*
In the Carus Lectures Sellars says that, although he earlier exploited an analogy between the introduction of microphysical particles in statistical thermodynamics and Jones's "introduction" of sense impressions in the psychology of perception, there is an important

disanalogy between the cases. In the case of statistical thermodynamics, phenomenological heat theory was already available and contained a number of well-supported empirical generalizations, the relative accuracy of which requires explanation in a successor theory. The new entities introduced in statistical thermodynamics do not themselves have a temperature or a pressure (and if they have a volume, it does not become relevant until the theory gets fairly sophisticated).[24] The theory then shows how these macroproperties of gases and liquids can be explained. So in the statistical thermodynamics case, new entities are introduced as having a very different fundamental structure from the phenomena to be explained, and the theory succeeds because it is able to reconstruct the structures we already knew.

But that is not how the postulation of sense impressions works. Sellars does not postulate entities with a different kind of fundamental structure and show how to use them to reconstruct the generalizations about colours and shapes that we already command. Rather, the logical spaces of colours and shapes (specified by the material rules of inference or true generalizations governing the manifest terms), are *not* reconstructed on a new and different basis, but imported and applied to a categorially different set of entities. The difference between the two domains is *only* categorial. There is still an advance: it permits a uniform treatment of *seeing a red rectangle* and *its seeming to one that a red rectangle is before one,* whereas before the sense-impression inference there was always a problem with understanding how false observation reports are possible. The move is still theory-like and still a postulation of new entities, but it is, in a way, less radical than the moves made by the corpuscularians or those who proposed statistical thermodynamics, because Sellars does *not* propose a reduction of colours, replacing one set of properties with a set of a fundamentally different basic structure. Statistical thermodynamics *reduces* heat and pressure. Sellars proposes *transposing* colour and sound.

*Excursus on reduction*
Consider for a moment Sellars's conception of reduction. He says that:

> if an object is *in a strict sense* a system of objects, then every property of the object must consist in the fact that its constituents have such and such qualities and stand in such and such relations or, roughly,
>
> > every property of a system of objects consists of properties of, and relations between, its constituents. (PSIM in SPR: 27)[25]

This principle of reducibility requires interpretation.[26] First, it is a principle of *object* reduction. If an object has a property that does *not* consist of properties of and relations between its constituents, then that thing is *not* strictly a system of objects, and cannot be reduced (at least within that framework).[27] It is a basic object in that framework. Nowadays, spatial composition looms large in our thinking; it is tempting to think that anything extended must be reducible to its constituents. But this is not a general principle of the manifest image, according to Sellars. An object can, given Sellars's principle, be complex and have constituents, yet be irreducible because not all of its properties consist in facts about its constituents' qualities and relations.[28] Persons are such basic objects in the manifest image.[29]

Manifest objects certainly *can* be reducible in Sellars's sense: a ladder is an arrangement of rails and rungs; a regiment is an organization of soldiers. In fact, Sellars's principle of reducibility does not directly authorize the claim that *colour* is irreducible, for colour is not an object. According to Sellars:

> I have already stressed that physical objects as construed in the Manifest Image are colored in what Cornman calls the "naive realist" sense. In this context I used my principle of reducibility to argue that whatever manifest objects may be *correlated with*, they cannot literally *consist of* micro-physical particles, or be literally identical with wholes consisting of micro-physical particles. For, given this principle, a whole consisting of micro-physical particles can be colored (in the naive realist sense) only if these particles are themselves colored (in the naive realist sense) which, ... "doesn't make sense".                                (SSIS: 412)

Sellars's principle directly authorizes the claim that manifest physical objects could not be reducible to systems of scientific objects, *given* that colour is not a reducible predicate in the scientific image; it forces us to demarcate the manifest and scientific frameworks, and it forces us to worry about property reduction.

Sellars's principle of reducibility is not, but rather presupposes, a criterion of *property* reduction.[30] The reason manifest physical objects cannot be reduced to systems of microphysical objects is that they have proper sensible properties that supposedly cannot be reduced to properties of systems of microparticles.

Sellars addresses what it is for a property to *consist of* other properties and relations in "The Identity Approach to the Mind–Body Problem". There are really two problems: *intra*-theoretic property reduction and *inter*-theoretic property reduction. Here first is the inter-theoretic case. In a nutshell, Sellars's analysis of inter-theoretic property reduction is that it is *prospective identification*. The obstacle to property reduction between theories, given Sellars's overall views, is that properties are expressed by predicates, and predicates are terms with a certain functional role in a language. Different theories develop their own special, independent languages. So Sellars has to ask: "How can the predicates of current chemical theory, which have no definitional tie to micro-physical primitives, have the same use as any predicates of future micro-physical theory which will have such a tie?" (IAMB in PP: 383). The answer has to be that the predicates of the current theory to be reduced cannot be identified with the predicates of the reducing theory. They can, however, both be predecessors of concepts in an encompassing theory in which there is an appropriate definitional relation between the two levels. "The universals which will be expressed at $T'$ by the predicates of a more adequate theory of chemical processes are identical with the universals which would be expressed at $T'$ by the predicates of a more adequate micro-physical theory" (IAMB in PP: 383).

Traditionally, reducing the proper sensibles to some scientific predicates has been dismissed because "raw feel predicates, at least in their first-person use, are as *untheoretical* as predicates can be" (IAMB in PP: 384). But that response is not open to Sellars, since he construes raw-feel predicates as theoretical: "if both raw-feel and brain-state predicates are theoretical predicates, can we not conceive of a reduction of raw-feel theory to brain-state theory?" (IAMB in PP: 385).

But Sellars demurs, for there is another alternative: "instead of the primitive predicates of one theory ending up as *defined* predicates in the unified theory – which is the chemistry–physics case – these primitive predicates may end up as *primitive* predicates in the unified theory" (IAMB in PP: 385). They would be *primitive* predicates because they would no more be *definable* in the unified successor theory than they are now. There is no *definition* of 'red' or 'blue' in the manifest image; "ostensive definitions" certainly do not count. In Sellars's view there are always primitive predicates in any framework that are undefined, but not meaningless. Their meanings are determined by the role they play in language-entry, language-exit and intralinguistic transitions. But we may not be able to *say* what that is, nor have other simple equivalent phrases.

Sellars's criterion for intra-theoretic property reduction is simply definability in terms of the reducing properties of some successor framework.

> [T]he to-be-discovered sense-impression universals would be no more complex than the sense-impression universals expressed by current sense-impression predicates; they would have a different categorial framework, and be logically related to (but *not* complexes of) universals expressed by other primitive predicates in the to-be-achieved unified sense-impression, brain-state theory. The logical space of sense-impressions would, so to speak, have been transposed into a new key and located in a new context. It would not, however, have become internally more complex in the way in which the logical space of chemical properties becomes internally more complex by virtue of their identification with micro-physical properties. (IAMB in PP: 385–6)

In other words, 'red' would, in the ultimate Peircean image, no more be definable in terms of the other primitives of the language than it is now in the manifest image. Sellars still owes an argument, to be examined in the next section, why this non-reductive alternative is preferable.

Sellars thinks that in order to unite sense-impression theory and brain-state theory as sketched here, it will have to be the case that brain-state theory or neurophysiology possesses an important level of autonomy. We cannot assume that Peircean neurophysiology:

> is of necessity a theory the scientific objects of which, nerves, are reducible, along with their properties, to systems of micro-physical particles in a sense which implies that all the predicates of an ideal brain theory would be definable in terms of micro-physical primitives none of which apply *exclusively* to micro-physical systems which are the theoretical counterparts of brains. (IAMB in PP: 386)

This difficult sentence expresses a constant theme in Sellars's work: the set of primitives necessary to the ideal scientific description and explanation of non-living objects in the world will not be adequate to describe and explain the phenomenon of sentience. In order to explain sentience, some new primitives will be necessary, terms that apply only in the context of those systems of objects that correspond in the scientific image to the things called sentient organisms in the manifest image. In the terminology developed originally in "The Concept of Emergence" (1956), co-authored with Paul Meehl, there will be a set of physical$_1$ primitives not included in the physical$_2$ vocabulary adequate to explain non-living objects and phenomena.[31]

"The Concept of Emergence" is an answer to an argument of Stephen Pepper's, originally published in 1926, that any emergent property has to be epiphenomenal and that therefore there is really no point to emergentism.[32] Very briefly, Sellars and Meehl argue that a generalization that is well confirmed in a certain range of conditions might need modification by the addition of further variables in order to be extended to cover a further range of conditions.[33] Furthermore, they argue, even if these newly added variables are themselves ultimately functions of the variables used in the original, restricted generalization, there is a good sense to the claim that the new variables "make a difference" and are thus not epiphenomenal. The purpose of "The Concept of Emergence" is purely negative; it is intended to show only that Pepper's argument is not generally valid, although it allows that there may be forms of emergentism that fall to Pepper's argument.[34]

"The Concept of Emergence" intends to keep open a possibility that Sellars then argues must be taken seriously, namely, that a proper explanation of sentience will introduce new entities that are not called for in the explanation of the behaviour of non-sentient objects. Given Sellars's treatment of laws, as seen in Chapter 6, it is clear that he has no objection to the notion that some well-confirmable, subjunctive-supporting generalizations become salient only at a certain "level of integration". We need to add as a kind of codicil to Chapter 6 that, while Sellars rejects the idea that there is a basic observation vocabulary, the meaning of which is fully determined either innately or by "ostensive definition", he does not run to the opposite extreme. The vocabulary of the sensibles is basic in a very real sense, for it relates to the fundamental sensory capacities of humans. It is, in that regard, empirically conditioned. But, in view of its role in the acquisition of empirical knowledge, there is no reason to think that further empirical investigation will radically change its basic structure. The logical space defined by the vocabulary of the sensibles will not change significantly as science progresses. But our categorization of that vocabulary, our conception of the subjects to which those predicates properly apply, is up to further scientific investigation to reveal.

### The grain argument (at last)

What convinces Sellars that we cannot identify either manifest physical objects (which have colours "in the naive realist sense") nor sentient beings with systems of scientific objects like those we currently acknowledge? The basic argument that colours and the other proper sensibles will have to receive special ontological treatment in an ultimately satisfactory scientific theory has been dubbed the "grain argument", and it is quite controversial. It is widely agreed that there are two stages (or maybe even two arguments) that fall under the rubric. The first stage concludes that colours (and odours, etc.) are not really properties of physical objects *per se*. Historically, the further conclusion was drawn that therefore colours, odours and so on are really only modifications of the mind. The second stage concludes that the proper sensibles also cannot be modifications of the brain *qua* system of micro-particles. That seems to leave us with a stark choice: either the proper sensibles are (modifications of) immaterial or non-physical things, or they are so totally illusory that *nothing* in the world explains them, or we have to provide for them in the scientific picture of the world, for example, recognize in the ultimate scientific image basic particulars to which the sensible predicates directly apply.

Beyond this, there is not much agreement about the grain argument. Most of Sellars's commentators assume it is a very complex and opaque argument; William Lycan remarks that his attempt to reconstruct the argument has reached fifty-five steps, "but so far I have only hit the high spots".[35] But Sellars does not seem to have regarded it as either complicated or opaque (a fact Lycan also notes). My approach here is fairly deflationary, but if it kindles the reader's interest, the discussions by Lycan, Muilenberg and Richardson, Hooker, and Cornman are well worth studying.[36]

The grain argument requires things to have a grain; that is, it assumes a Democritean–mechanistic framework. It has no force against Aristotelianism, for instance, so its force began to be felt significantly first in the seventeenth century, when the first stage of the argument became a fixture in philosophical circles.

In seventeenth-century corpuscularianism, the corpuscles were imperceptible and characterized only by their *mechanical* properties: mass, shape, motion and so on. They retain a *tie* to the sensible, however, since spatial and temporal properties are *common* sensibles. Most important, the behaviour of material objects seemed to be solely a function of their mechanical properties; other properties either played no explanatory role or seemed to be reducible to the basic mechanical properties.

Thus the *proper* sensibles no longer seemed to fit into the world "out there". None of the significant new empirical laws being discovered seemed to use such properties essentially.[37] The rise of mechanism allowed one to think that the proper sensibles *could be* dispensed with in the explanation of the behaviour of material objects. Why then *actually* dispense with them? The first stage of the grain argument seems to have been the primary motivation: The proper sensibles do not seem to be reducible to mechanical properties.

Why not? The mechanists thought of material objects as *systems of imperceptible objects*. Does the mere fact that the proper sensibles are perceptible entail that they could not be properties of systems of imperceptibles? Clearly not: shape is perceptible, but systems of imperceptibles have shape. Indeed, the imperceptibles themselves have shape; their imperceptibility is not a matter of lacking all perceptible properties.[38] Furthermore, "There is no trouble about systems having properties which its parts do not have *if these properties are a matter of the parts having such and such qualities and being related in such and such ways*" (PSIM in SPR: 26).

But the proper sensibles do not fit into this picture of how the properties of material macro-objects are related to the properties and relations of micro-objects.

> It does not seem plausible to say that for a system of particles to be a pink ice cube is for them to have such and such imperceptible qualities, and to be so related to one another as to make up an approximate cube. *Pink* does not seem to be made up of imperceptible qualities in the way in which being a ladder is made up of being cylindrical (the rungs), rectangular (the frame), wooden, etc. The manifest ice cube presents itself to us as something which is pink through and through, as a pink continuum, all the regions of which, however small, are pink. It presents itself to us as *ultimately homogeneous*; and an ice cube variegated in colour is, though not homogeneous in its specific colour, 'ultimately homogeneous', in the sense to which I am calling attention, with respect to the generic trait of being coloured.          (PSIM in SPR: 26)

Two immediate remarks: Sellars is *not* concerned here with the dispositional, causal property of being able to cause a sensation of pink in normal perceivers; he is concerned with occurrent cases of pink itself. A system of non-coloured objects could have the property of causing normal perceivers to have sense impressions of pink, but then that system is not itself pink in the primary sense (consider the Land Effect). Secondly, surfaces can appear uniformly pink or aquamarine, but turn out to have patterns of red and white or blue and green covering them.

Such cases do not counter Sellars's claim that coloured expanses present themselves to us as everywhere coloured. Sellars thinks, however, that it is built into our conception and our sensory experience of colour that we can make no sense of the idea that coloured expanses could be composed of entirely uncoloured expanses, the colour of the whole expanse arising only in and through the relations among its uncoloured parts.[39] That, however, would have to be the case if the atomists were right, and we held on to the idea that colour is a basic, occurrent property of material objects.

In the seventeenth century, no one was willing to eliminate colours and smells from the world altogether. Somehow or other, there *is* colour. Whereas the pre-modern world blithely accepted the notion that the proper sensibles had two modes of existence, actuality in material objects and being-for-sense in our sensorium, the moderns now deny that what there really is in the material world can be coloured or odorous or tasty in the strict, occurrent (or as Sellars used to say, "aesthetically interesting") sense. Colours, tastes and odours, strictly speaking, exist *only* in the mind: structures of corpuscles in space can have only the dispositional powers to awaken occurrent episodes of colours, tastes and odours in our minds. "It was concluded that manifest physical objects are 'appearances' *to human perceivers* of systems of imperceptible particles" (PSIM in SPR: 27). Colours are now thought of as solely modifications of the mind and not (that is, *not possibly*) modifications of material things. What happened is not a *rejection* or *abandonment* of the concepts of colour, taste and odour, but a categorial transposition.

This is, in Sellars's view, one (although only one) of the sources of Cartesian dualism. For once the reality of the proper sensibles can be only *in* the mind or as modifications of the mind:

> ... there would remain the following argument:
>
> We have pulled perceptible qualities out of the physical environment and put them into sensations. If we now say that all there really is to sensation is a complex interaction of cerebral particles, then we have taken them out of our world picture altogether. We will have made it unintelligible how things could even *appear* to be coloured. (PSIM: 30)

If structures of physical microparticles cannot *really* be coloured, and colours *really* exist *in* or as modifications of the mind, then minds cannot be structures of physical microparticles. Thus dualism accepts the first step of the second stage of the grain argument, and proposes a radical solution: colours are modifications of immaterial objects.

Sellars rejects the dualism, but the problem it addresses is well taken. Because colour is non-composite, it is not reducible to properties or relations of uncoloured objects. If colours are non-composite, and sensations are the true home of colours, then either sensations must also be non-composite, and thus cannot be composite states of material brains, or there is some non-composite or primitive ingredient in sensation states that accounts for the presence of colour.[40]

This argument turns on the claim that colour is non-composite. Ultimately, this comes down to a claim that even in the ultimate, Peircean framework, colours (or odours, etc.) will not be *defined* predicates, for they will not be identified with any structure of more fundamental entities. It is easy to believe that colour words are undefined predicates in ordinary language and thus in the manifest image. In Sellars's own view, however, scientific progress consists partially in developing finer-grained languages in which previously undefined common-sense terms can now take a place as defined predicates. 'Water', 'heat' and 'inheritable trait' are examples. Why not 'red'? The fact that 'red' does not occur in the laws of physics or chemistry is part of the answer. 'Red' and its successor will be needed only to explain how sentient beings behave in the world, and in particular, their linguistic behaviour, especially their use of 'red'. Given this explanandum, the facts (i) that 'red' is an undefined primitive in ordinary language, (ii) that it is part of our normal reporting or observation vocabulary, (iii) that it is tied to the fundamental structures of our sensory capacities, and (iv) that it is epistemically minimal make it hard to imagine that any significantly complex defined term in a neurophysiological theory will be recognized as its appropriate scientific successor. So Sellars thinks we shall have to hold on to the term as a primitive. There is some plausibility to this, but it is surely not a *compelling* argument. Is it all Sellars has to give us?

In science, at least as it has progressed so far, we are presented with a picture in which the world is treated as ever more discrete in its basic structure. Quantum physics even flirts with treating space and time as having a discrete fundamental structure. Sellars notes the relationship between his problem of the homogeneity of the pink ice cube and Eddington's problem of the "two tables".[41] The Sellarsian treatment of Eddington's problem is fairly straightforward: the *real* table is the table science tells us about, a blooming, buzzing confusion of imperceptible particles zooming about amid vast spaces. The manifest table, a dense, substantial and solid three-dimensional object with a surface that is smooth and continuous and everywhere coloured, is an *appearance* to us. But Sellars balks at applying this treatment to sensations themselves: if sensations are blooming, buzzing confusions of imperceptible particles zooming about amid vast empty spaces inside one's cranium, then what is to be made of the continuous, everywhere-coloured expanses that are the appearances of things? Since sensations *explain* appearances, sensations cannot themselves *be* appearances, on pain of circularity or regress.

*Reuniting colours and shapes*
Sellars wants to make still one more move concerning the constraints our current conception of the sensory puts on an adequate successor to the manifest image: colour and shape are seamlessly joined in experience. This was a major problem for the early moderns.[42] Primary and secondary qualities were commonly distinguished in the seventeenth century. The proper sensibles characterize only our mental acts, strictly speaking, though most of us wrongly assume they also characterize material objects. The primary qualities, for example, shape and motion, however, seem to be in a different situation. First, they are sensible. They are also used in mechanical explanations and apply to material objects. How can a property such as shape properly characterize *both* material objects in space and ideas or impressions in the mind? Since one of the defining characteristics of the mind is that it is unextended, mental acts cannot have shape proper. One attempt to answer this question says that, strictly speaking, the primary qualities characterize material objects, the sensible ideas we have of shape and motion merely *resemble* the properties of the material objects. This was not a very convincing resolution. (Is perceived triangularity merely triangularity-likeness, or do we perceive the very triangularity of the object?) But the difficulties become all the more intractable once it is pointed out that colours always have extension in our visual field, and they usually have shapes: red squares, green oblongs, pink cubes, etc. In our experience, colour and extension are joined *seamlessly,* even with a kind of *necessity.* But given the way the Cartesians have arranged things, the *really* extended things cannot be *really* coloured, and the *really* coloured things cannot be *really* extended. Something has gone wrong. Sellars requires a treatment of the ontology of sensory qualities that avoids this problem.

This is one reason (among many) that Sellars finds Kant so amenable: he also believes that there is a kind of "inner space-time" whose structure mimics physical space-time to a large degree, so that it can serve as a "counterpart representation" of space-time. Call this internal arena "space$_i$-time$_i$." Sensations, then can be literally spatial$_i$ and temporal$_i$. When we see a red box next to a green line, it is typically the case that we shall be in a state of having a red box$_i$ sensation next$_i$ to a green line$_i$ sensation. Phenomenal shape and colour have been reunited, because they are both present in sensory experience *other than as believed in*.

## Mistaking sensations

Reunifying the common and the proper sensibles in experience is a plus, but there is at least one odd consequence of Sellars's position: sensations are, in one sense, the "ultimate" referents of our perceptual takings. One of Sellars's teachers, H. A. Prichard,[43] had argued for this position earlier in the century, and Sellars returned to it in the mid-1970s, although a bit tentatively. Consider an incorrect perceptual taking: suppose, for instance, the content of the taking is "This dangerous black bear rearing before me ..." and there is no such bear in front of you, but only a bush. In the last section of "Some Reflections on Perceptual Consciousness" (1975), Sellars argues that when a perceptual taking fails, we generally do not say that no reference was made by the perception. After all, providing referents for judgement is one of perception's functions. We "preserve the reference" of the taking by saying that the subject took the bush to be a bear. We thereby preserve the notion that there is *something* the perception is about. What if there is nothing before the subject that we can say was mistaken for a bear? Of course, one popular response is to say that if there is nothing over there in space for the subject to be referring to, we have to admit no reference is made at all. After all, in qualifying the perceptual claim, moving to ever more cautious, less committal expressions of our experience (a form, by the way, of phenomenological reduction), we seem to remain committed to something's being over there in space facing me. "And it is surely a categorial feature of sensations that they are *not* over there facing me" (SRPC §57: 184). But perhaps the phenomenological reduction does not need to remain committed to space, particularly after an internal analogue of space has been postulated.

> [I]f we take seriously the idea that the thinning out of perceptual commitment which is implied by phenomenological reduction ends not with
>
> This cube of pink over there facing me edgewise ...
>
> but rather with

This *somehow* (a cube of pink over there facing me edgewise)
...

then the way would be open to save the reference by construing it
to be the sensation, for the sensation is indeed that in the experience which is *somehow* a cube of pink over there facing one
edgewise.                                              (SRPC §59: 184)

Sellars immediately adds the caveats that (i) there is no entailment
that the perceiver conceptualizes her sensation *as* a sensation, and (ii)
the 'somehow' could be 'straightforwardly', that is, this still allows the
referent of the experience to be pink cubes in physical space facing
their perceivers. The sensation is only the *last ditch* referent.

Just a bit later, in "Sensa or Sensings" (1982, but originally written
in 1976), Sellars strengthens the claim fairly significantly. There,
Sellars suggests that what we (ostensibly) see *of* an object, that which
is present in the experience other than as merely believed in, is, in fact,
a reference of the experience.

> 93. I, therefore, suggest that even when a visual taking is concep-
> tually rich, as in the example of
>
> *This red brick with a red and rectangular facing side* ...
>
> it includes as a proper part
>
> *this red and rectangular facing side*
>
> and it is the referent of *this* conceptual 'this' which is taken to be
> the red and rectangular facing side of a physical object, thus
> constituting an awareness of the referent of 'this' *as* the red and
> rectangular facing side of a physical object, in this case a brick.
> ... If this is correct, then, when there appears to *P* to be a physi-
> cal object with a red and rectangular facing surface:
>
> (a) There is a *sensum* or *objectless sensing* which is an ˢ(red
> rectangle) or an ˢ(red rectangle)ing;
> (b) *P* is aware of (conceptually refers to) this *sensum* or *sensing*;
> (c) *P* mistakes this *sensum* or *sensing* to be the red and rectangu-
> lar facing surface of a physical object.
>
> (SSOP §§93–4: 110–11)[44]

Sellars thus claims that our perceptual lives are riddled with mistakes, for we project the direct and immediate objects of our sensory
awareness into physical space and onto systems of scientific objects.[45]
Presumably, were we to abandon the manifest image conception of
physical objects as coloured, odorous entities, we would cease to fall

prone to such error, although it is unclear that we could ever fully overcome the proclivity towards realism that Sellars finds innate in us.
The idea that our perceptual experiences are always *about* something – in a non-intentional sense of 'about' – seems welcome. But the
idea that we almost always mistake the object sensed seems to some
difficult to reconcile with the overall realism Sellars attributes to the
manifest image. If he's right, people who deny the existence of sensations are committing a deep *conceptual* error, not merely a *factual*
error, for our every perceptual report presupposes the presence of
sensations as referents of the last resort.

This section has been tortuous. It is a mistake, I think, to believe
that the entire weight of Sellars's claims rests on the grain argument,
although it is an important part of his argument. As I see it, he
offers us:

1. a phenomenologico-linguistic analysis of (the language of)
   perceptual experience that reveals the indispensability of the
   vocabulary of the proper and common sensibles in any framework
   that includes a conception of a perceiving cognitive subject;[46]
2. an argument that the proper sensibles are not reducible, that is,
   that the vocabulary of the proper sensibles is not definable in any
   vocabulary we currently project to be adequate to the scientific
   explanation of the behaviour of mere physical objects (the grain
   argument);
3. (a) a distinction between two ways of postulating theoretical
       entities:
       (i)  as only partially analogous to and otherwise independent
            of their models or
       (ii) as a *transposition* into a new category of the original
            models; and
   (b) an argument that sensations are a transposition of the
       sensibles, not a *de novo* new kind of entity;
4. an argument that the common sensibles as such cannot be given
   a drastically different treatment in a drastically different ontological category from the proper sensibles; and
5. a suggestion that our use of the proper and common sensibles
   presupposes the presence of an actual referent as the bearer of
   those qualities.

Sellars thinks that we will find ourselves forced, as enquiry into the
physiology of perception proceeds, to postulate a domain of entities, to

be found only in the context of sentient beings, that allow us to preserve the logical space of the sensibles.[47] Sellars believes that these entities, sensa, raw feels or qualia, will be items in an ideal scientific theory adequate to the physical$_1$ phenomena; they will not show up in any theory that would be restricted to physical$_2$ phenomena. Some regard Sellars as anti-materialist (e.g. Cornman and Lycan); others declare him not only a materialist, but the strongest kind, an eliminative materialist (e.g. Margolis and Churchland). The truth is that Sellars does not easily fit the standard classification of positions on the mind–body problem. He does not believe that examining the physics of non-living things will ever lead us to an adequate understanding of sentient things, so if materialism cannot draw any ontologically important distinctions between persons and (mere) material objects, Sellars is anti-materialist. But Sellars also believes that a systematically pursued science will expand its categories to include sensa or qualia, so if materialism is the belief that all causal phenomena will eventually fall prey to scientific explanation, then Sellars is a materialist. But does the claim that Peircean physics will have to *expand* to handle sensory phenomena by *preserving* the logical space of the proper sensibles within physics make Sellars an *eliminative* materialist?

## The sensible qualities: a final metaphysical home?

Sellars offers a putative history of the sensibles with the following stages:

1. The sensibles (both common and proper) are the exhaustive form and content of reality, the very substance of the world.
2. The sensibles are modifications of the causally complex substances that constitute the world.
3. The sensibles are modifications of the causally complex substances that constitute the world, but also possess a subsidiary and analogous being-for-mind that explains our ability to apprehend them directly (and sometimes mistakenly).
4. (a) The common sensibles are formal modifications of the causally complex microsubstances and the systems they compose that constitute the (material) world, but also possess a subsidiary and analogous being-for-mind that explains our ability to apprehend them directly (and sometimes mistakenly).

(b) The proper sensibles are formal modifications of the mind and are not modifications of or present in material reality.

Sellars thinks the manifest image is a stage 3 framework. In stage 4 the process of revising the manifest image in the face of scientific discovery has begun, but is nowhere near finished. Stage 4 is clearly unsatisfactory for several reasons. First, phenomenologically, dividing the primary and the secondary qualities ontologically is at best implausible. Secondly, excluding the proper sensibles from the material realm poses a serious problem: what *is* the manner of their being?

## Metaphysics and the unity of a person

The standard responses at stage 4 to these problems, substance dualism, reductive materialism and epiphenomenalism, are treated in the Carus Lectures as responses to the problem of the unity of a person.[48] Effectively, Sellars sees stage 4 as confronted with the following problem:

(i) The proper sensibles are neither reducible to nor eliminable in favour of micro-entities of the lowest physical level that possess no such properties (the grain argument).
(ii) The proper sensibles have a causal role in the behaviour of sentient organisms.
(iii) All causation is, ultimately, at or strictly dependent on the lowest level of physical causation.

Dualism clearly denies (iii), requiring metaphysically distinct mental substances and causation, and splitting a person irretrievably into a team of the physical and the non-physical. Truly reductive materialism unifies the person, but at the cost of rejecting (i) and abandoning the logical spaces of the sensible properties.[49] Epiphenomenalism fragments a person into a causally active part (that is not as such an experiencer) and an experience that is causally inert. Since Sellars accepts the Platonic (and pragmatic) dictum that to be is to have power, epiphenomenalism is, in his eyes, an attempt to have one's cake and eat it too.[50] It both asserts the existence of experience and denies experience the most essential hallmark of existence.

Sellars objects to *any* position that would deprive the sensory of causal efficacy, any position that fits:[51]

The diagram can be differently interpreted: $\phi$ and $\psi$ can be states of different substances or different kinds of states of a substance. The arrows can also differ: assuming the horizontal arrow $\Rightarrow$ is always physical causation, the vertical arrow $\uparrow$ can represent mere correlation, a special form of causation or even, in reductive materialism, some logical or semantic relation (e.g. theoretical identification). Sellars objects to any position the form of which can be captured in this diagram.

According to Sellars, these difficulties derive principally from assuming the sufficiency of "explanation in terms of mechanistic variables in the case of objects in the inorganic realm" (FMPP III §101: 83). As long as we assume that all things are governed by the mechanical principles adequate to explain the inorganic, the sensory will remain a mystery.

> 104. That the proper sensibles – e.g., shades of color – could function alongside of mechanistic variables in psycho-physical laws in such a way that the mechanical variables by themselves did not constitute a closed system with respect to necessary and sufficient conditions (as they do for Epiphenomenalism) made no more scientific sense, given the paradigms of the day, than would a Compatiblist attempt to involve the proper sensibles in the laws of motion. (FMPP III §104: 83)

The sufficiency of the mechanical has been a (background) assumption in much philosophical reflection since the seventeenth century. But Sellars sees no good reason to accept such a constricted view of the nature of the causal. The problem of providing an adequate place for the sensory drives us beyond mechanical paradigms. Sellars therefore, joins the dualists in rejecting (iii), but denies that this requires a dualism of substances. It does require a dualism of properties, but, remember, he doesn't believe in the independent reality of properties as abstracta either. Unlike substance dualism, his position does not entail a breakdown in the fundamental physical laws. For, remember, in "The Concept of Emergence", Sellars argues that the need to postulate different laws that govern in special contexts need not entail a denial of the universal, fundamental laws of the inorganic realm. Sellars offers the ontology of absolute processes as a way to escape

237

mechanistic paradigms that generate systematically unsatisfactory metaphysics.

## Absolute processes

*Absolute* processes contrast with *object-bound* processes. Object-bound processes (he also speaks of object-bound events) are anchored to some (set of) object(s), the normal case in the manifest image, for in the manifest image, on Sellars's analysis, the basic entities are *things* and *persons*. This means that, according to Sellars, events are *not* basic entities in the manifest image; events are changes in things or persons and are thus dependent entities. Sellars does not say much about the relationship between events and processes, but I assume that an object-bound process is an ordered set of events.[52] Water freezes, Achilles runs, a bird sings, a choir sings, a country votes; all are object-bound processes.

But Sellars also notes the availability in our language of verbs that take "dummy subjects". His examples include

'It rains', 'It thunders', 'It lightnings'        (FMPP II §48: 47)

There may be some object-bound paraphrases of these sentences, but Sellars argues that such paraphrases are at best hard to find, and these subjectless sentences in the language offer an opportunity philosophers can exploit. Sellars invokes Broad's notion of "absolute processes", "which might also be called subjectless (or objectless) events. These are processes, the occurrence of which is, in the first instance, expressed by sentences ... which either do not have logical subjects or which have dummy logical subjects" (FMPP II §50: 48).[53] We must distinguish between a good *paraphrase* of such sentences in terms of changing things and a good *explanation* in terms of changing things. Talk of electrons jumping gaps may *explain* the truth of statements about lightning, but it is certainly no *paraphrase* of them. If there is no adequate object-bound paraphrase of some absolute-process sentences of the manifest image, then absolute processes exist in the manifest image. And, since, unlike object-bound events or processes, they have no subject on which they depend, they must be non-dependent, that is, *basic* particulars in the framework. *Are* there absolute processes in the manifest image? Sellars remains uncommitted; he's really interested in whether there might be some way and some point to taking them as basic particulars in a scientific framework that would ultimately replace the manifest image. Sentences with dummy subjects might offer us a model for the analogical construction of new forms of thought that could prove useful as science and metaphysics advance. Absolute processes, as Sellars sees them, can have intrinsic characters. For instance, consider a buzz. (Although Sellars starts with lightning and thunder as examples, he ultimately follows Broad in using sounds as his example.) Does 'buzz' primarily characterize a certain kind of activity that things (such as bees) can engage in "in a way which is conceptually independent of the intrinsic character of the process produced by the buzzing" (FMPP II §63: 50)? He finds that suggestion implausible and suggests that we call a certain kind of activity that bees or doorbells engage in 'buzzing' because it produces a characteristic kind of sound, a 'buzzing' in a different, although clearly related sense.

65. This line of thought suggests that what is primary in the various senses of the verb 'to buzz' is the concept of the intrinsic character of a certain kind of process which can be *identified* in terms of its typical causes. The verb 'to buzz', then, would have a sense in which processes of that intrinsic kind would be buzzings, even when they were not being brought about by one of these typical causes.                                          (FMPP II: 50)

A tinnitus sufferer hears a buzzing, even if there is nothing around buzzing. Furthermore, the buzzing heard is a buzzing in the *primary* sense; the buzzing of the bee is a buzzing in a derivative sense, as healthy food is healthy in a derivative sense.

Absolute processes are susceptible to change. A buzzing can get louder or softer; its timbre can change. They can also come to be and cease to be, and they do so *absolutely*, in the sense that there is no enduring subject in which they come to be or cease to be. We have to worry about individuation and identification of absolute processes, and Sellars suggests that relevant considerations include continuity, spatial location and causality, although these need not be exhaustive.

If absolute processes have intrinsic characters, are changeable and capable of absolute comings- and ceasings-to-be, they could be the kind of thing Sellars needs as sensa.

Sellars's efforts here begin to come into focus when he then invokes the ontological framework of logical atomism, in which a domain of basic, non-composite objects is postulated, all other objects being construed as wholes consisting of basic objects as their parts. In Sellars's view, though, this framework is not to be taken as *fact,* but as

a regulative ideal that helps us regiment our examples and our categories.[54] There are two important points here. First, he emphasizes that:

> the *subjunctive* dimension of the conditional properties of the
> objects of the manifest image would be correlated with lawlike
> truths involving patterns of basic objects, thus
>> If there *were* to be a pattern, $P_i$, at s, t there *would* be a
>> pattern, $P_j$, at s', t'. (FMPP II §88: 54)

There might be subjunctive or conditional connections between basic
objects in such a framework, but there would be no potentialities *in*
basic objects. That is, "*basic* objects would not have *basic* properties of
the form 'If x were $\phi$, x would be $\psi$'" (FMPP II §89: 55). They would
themselves be pure occurrents.

Secondly, if one develops a framework along logical atomist lines,
it need not be construed as an *analysis* of the manifest image, even if
this was the original intent of the logical atomists. It could be a successor image, a new framework for thinking about the world "justified by
a concilience of metaphysical considerations" (FMPP II §96: 55).

If we take the idea of a process ontology seriously, then "[w]e suddenly see that the world we have been constructing is one in which
every basic state of affairs is expressed by the use of verbs and
adverbs" (FMPP II §102: 56). This would be "a truly heracleitean
ontology ... There are no *objects*. The world is an ongoing tissue of
goings on" (FMPP II §103: 57). In such a framework, the objects of the
manifest image and their object-bound processes would be patterns of
absolute processes. There would be laws concerning the co-occurrence
(both positive and negative) of absolute processes, but no laws concerning any kind of internal structure or development of the isolated
processes. Internally, they would be purely and occurrently *qualitative*; everything structural or formal is now *external* to them.

Interestingly, this returns us to some remarks Sellars *fils* makes
about the treatment Sellars *père* gives consciousness. Roy Wood
Sellars thought that science could not, ultimately, deal with consciousness, because science can postulate *structure*, but not *quality*. Wilfrid
asks his father:

> But why not? Why could not concepts of sensible redness, etc., be
> introduced into a theory of the visual cortex as concepts of certain
> qualitative features of neurophysiological events which play
> specific roles in the functioning of the visual system centers, and
> in the discriminative behavior of the larger system which is the
> organism as a whole?

Notice that after expressing his [Roy Wood Sellars's] "considered opinion" that "physical science ... must ignore consciousness altogether" he goes on to write "... all it can say is that the content of being must be *such as* to have the structure and behavior deciphered." But is this not to admit that the qualitative dimension of the brain state can be determinately characterized in terms of its explanatory role in the theory of the functioning sensory cortex?

(DKMB: 287)

Many of Wilfrid's critics have wondered why a functional specification of sensory states in terms of their role in determining the behaviour of the whole organism is not adequate, for, they think, some complex neural state could play that role, allowing us to reduce sensations to neural states. Sellars, in effect, agrees that in the final analysis determinate characterizations always are functions of roles in a framework. But he requires that a term that determinately characterizes a qualitative feature of experience, such as red, has to preserve the logic of colour space, which entails that it applies in the strict sense only to something non-composite. He does not believe that any of the microstructures we are currently familiar with can fulfil this requirement. But, if we were to move to a framework of absolute processes, they could exhibit the requisite homogeneity or non-compositeness. The idea seems to be that the qualitative is essentially contrasted with the structural, and thus the truly irreducibly qualitative must be unstructured. If we can locate a bottom level, below which further analysis cannot penetrate, we have reached the ultimate being of the qualitative. That will be the ultimate location of the sensible qualities. Sellars thinks that the notion of an absolute process, itself a pure occurrent without internal structure, but tied to other such processes in regular patterns, may afford us a workable idea of such an unanalysable bottom level.

Sellars believes that other scientific realists who have considered the sensory have thought of the central nervous system as consisting of objects and object-bound processes: "as a result they have been taking a form of ontological epiphenomenalism for granted" (FMPP III §117: 85). Thus the classical epiphenomenalist structure has been lurking in the back of their minds:

$$\psi_i \qquad \psi_j \qquad\qquad \psi_1$$
$$\uparrow \qquad \uparrow \qquad\qquad \uparrow$$
$$\phi_i \Rightarrow \phi_j \Rightarrow \phi_k \Rightarrow \phi_1$$

119. But if they were to accept (programmatically, of course) an ontology of absolute process, they would immediately be freed from this last refuge of metaphysical dualism. If the particles of microphysics are patterns of actual and counterfactual $\phi_2$-ings, then the categorial (indeed, transcendental) dualism which gives aid and comfort to epiphenomenalism simply *vanishes*.[55]

120. And once this picture has gone, they would be in a position to realize that the idea that basic 'psycho-physical' laws have an epiphenomenalist form is a speculative scientific hypotheses [*sic*.] which largely rests on metaphysical considerations of the kinds we have been exploring.

121. Psycho-physical theory, to the extent that it is well confirmed, does, indeed, entail that uniformities pertaining to the occurrence of σ-ings specify that they occur in the context of $\phi_2$-ings which belong to patterns of absolute processes which constitute specific kinds of neuro-physiologic process.

122. What it does *not* require is that these $\phi_2$-ings be nomologically autonomous.

123. Nor does it require that neuro-physiological objects which have $\phi_2$-ings as constituents, have *only* $\phi_2$-ings as constituents. σ-ings could in a legitimate sense be constituents of neurophysiological objects  (FMPP III §§119–23: 86).[56]

Sellars's appeal to absolute processes is somewhat like the neutral monist's appeal to sense data. In the view of the neutral monist, sense data are neither mental nor physical. The yawning gap between the mental and the physical that the dualists could not seem to overcome is, in the eyes of the neutral monist, itself an *artifact* of the logical constructions that generate physical versus mental objects.

But the analogy to neutral monism is weak. In Sellars's view, absolute processes afford a category of entities (we can call them 'objects' only with extreme care) of which objects, both mechanical, non-living, non-sentient objects and persons, are patterns. Sellarsian absolute processes, however, are clearly entirely *physical* and not at all mental (intentional); they are physical₁, involved in the causal nexus of space-time. Physical₂ objects, whatever science tells us they are – structures of atoms and molecules, or leptons and baryons – would be patterns of absolute processes. Persons or sentient organisms would also be patterns of absolute processes, but they would differ from physical₂ objects by including certain absolute processes, σ-ings, that occur only in certain highly complex contexts, that is, highly complex patterns of the absolute processes that constitute physical$_2$ objects. These σ-ings are sensa, qualia or raw feels, and would be the ultimate home of the sensible qualities. Our sensory awareness is, when it comes right down to it, a direct and immediate awareness of the intrinsic characteristics of such absolute processes, although most certainly not an awareness of them *as* intrinsic characteristics of absolute processes.[57]

Sellars proclaims that his view opens the road to a real "bundle theory of persons", where the "bundle" would include both σ-ings and $\phi_2$-ings (FMPP III §125: 87). This seems to me overstated, for the connotations of "bundle" are that such things are unstructured. But persons are, for Sellars, highly organized systems of scientific entities.[58] However, we cannot give cold, hard cash to support the claim that persons are highly organized, complex systems until we know what it is they are systems of. Sellars thinks that we have good reason to believe that persons could not be systems of the kind of scientific objects we currently acknowledge. An important *part* of the problem of the unity of persons is solved by finding the right kind of ingredients. That's what he's hoping absolute processes are.

What Sellars thinks a stage 5 theory – a Peircean theory – of the sensibles would look like can now be stated: the proper sensibles are relocated as intrinsic characters of absolute processes, and the common sensibles as adverbial modifications of those characters. Such absolute processes, however, occur only in the context of the highly complex patterns of absolute processes that we identify in the manifest image as sentient organisms.

Sellars's conjectures concerning sensa and absolute processes are bold and revisionary. They compare, for instance, to Penrose's speculations that solving the puzzle of consciousness requires a theory of quantum gravity and the microtubules in the neurons. To ask for *compelling* arguments seems a bit out of place; it is not supposed to be *a priori*, demonstrable philosophical argumentation. It is supposed to be a projection of a possible satisfactory solution to a complex problem, a projection that has to be responsible to empirical developments. I worry that it seems like a solution in part because we do not grasp the notion of an absolute process well enough to be able to see where the problems lie. Others should engage these texts on their own and decide whether Sellars on absolute process is profoundly insightful, merely idiosyncratic or somewhere in between.

## In conclusion

Many are sceptical about the grain argument and the argument that we systematically mistake sensations for physical objects. The notion of absolute processes is intriguing yet puzzling. But there are solid achievements in Sellars's treatment of the sensory that should be taken to heart. Some of these achievements are negative, in the sense that he diagnoses real problems with other positions. His recognition of the historical malleability of our concepts makes his diagnoses both more complex and more powerful than usual. His critiques of reductive materialism, although we have not had the space to treat them in detail, are subtle and powerful, as is his treatment of dualism. But there are also positive results that I think he defends well and that belong in any sound philosophy of mind:

- There is a distinction in kind between the intentional and the sensory. These two categories within the broader notion of the mental speak to different phenomena and play different roles, so it is important to keep the distinction strong.
- Because they are distinct in kind, the intentional and the sensory require different accounts. Some of the apparent difficulty of the mind–body problem arises from the attempt to find one account for both the intentional and the sensory.
- The sensory plays a causal role in perception and is crucial for an explanation of the occurrence of merely ostensible perceptions.
- The sensory is non-cognitive: being in a particular sensory state entails neither knowledge nor awareness of any particular kind.
- The proper and common sensibles require special treatment among perceptible qualities.
- The relations between the proper and common sensibles must be preserved; the two sets of properties ought not to be given disjoint ontological locations or treatments.
- The unity of the person and the seamlessness of experience must be respected.

Let me close this chapter, however, with a question. The most contentious parts of Sellars's theory of the sensory seem to rest on the idea that postulating theoretical entities by categorial transposition is really a different mode of entity-postulation than is normal in theoretical science. Are there any fairly clear cases of this mode of entity-postulation in the history of science? This is a question for historians of science. A positive answer, however, would strengthen the idea that Sellars is on to something interesting at this crucial juncture of his argument.

# Chapter 9

# *Practical reason*

Almost thirty years ago, W. David Solomon lamented the neglect of Sellars's ethical writings.[1] The situation has not changed in the interim. With a few exceptions, Sellars's essays in ethical theory are as daunting as his most technical work in metaphysics, highly abstract and compact in the statement of the problems considered and the solutions proposed, and bristling with formalisms. This may explain the neglect of his ethical work, but it cannot justify it. Sellars stands out from his contemporaries Quine and Davidson by his significant body of writings on ethics. Since a great deal in his "system" rides on the nature of the normative, a well-worked-out treatment of actions and oughts is crucial to the overall completeness of his philosophical vision.

In moral theory, as in so many areas of philosophy, Sellars thinks that rationalism (generally called 'intuitionism' in ethics) best captured the "grammar" of ethical concepts, but "contaminated it with platonizing factualism".[2] Classical empiricism rejects the platonizing, but attempts to inappropriately (that is, reductively) naturalize ethical concepts instead, either in a theory of moral sentiments or in psychologistic consequentialism. The naturalizing impulse should not mislead us into a reductive account of ethical concepts.

Sellars takes the idea of *practical reason* absolutely seriously. At the time Sellars was forming his ethical views, that idea was very much in doubt. Emotivism divorced reason and practice almost absolutely, and the intuitionist opposition that insisted on a link between reason and practice, such as that of Prichard, offered "not even the beginning of a satisfactory analysis ... which would account for the fact that moral thinking differs from, but resembles, other forms of thinking by relating both to the fundamental categories of an adequate philosophy of mind" (IIO: 161). The way to fit ethics into a naturalistic framework is to offer just such an analysis, a theory that shows how ethical thoughts can be *thoughts* – with intentional content, inferential relations, and subject to intersubjective standards of consistency and truth – while also being *practical* – not merely fact-stating but action-involving or -motivating. And, of course, this analysis needs to fit into a generally adequate philosophy of mind.

We have not really finished with Sellars's philosophy of mind, for we have not looked closely yet at Sellars's theory of action. Action theory is the general account of the connection between thinking and acting; it clarifies the action–behaviour distinction, the notions of intention, volition, acting on impulse versus acting for reasons and so on. It is philosophy of mind, but it is also continuous with ethical theory, in Sellars's view, for ethical theory is devoted to an account of the principles by which some actions can be singled out as universally and intersubjectively incumbent on agents.

That pretty much dictates the course of this chapter. We begin with an examination of Sellars's general theory of action and then focus in on his account of ethics.

## Intentions, volitions and actions

The basic distinction between (mere) behaviour and action is that actions are behaviours caused by *volitions*. Volitions are a proper subset of intentions, so actions are intentional behaviours. Intentions form the general category of practical, that is, action-guiding thoughts. Volitions are intentions that have ripened into effect. It is essential to intentions and volitions that they are tied to action, in Sellars's view. Someone who regularly and (apparently) sincerely said things of the form

I shall now do *A*

but only rarely, or never followed them with the appropriate action (doing *A* or trying to do A) would thereby show that he does not have command of our practical concepts and is not yet an intending, willing agent.[3]

Just as the notion of a language-entry transition underlies Sellars's theory of observation and empirical knowledge, the notion of a language-exit transition underlies his discussion of action and practical reason. The paradigmatic language-exit transition (e.g. an utterance of "I'm going to raise my hand *now*" immediately conjoined with a raising of one's hand) is the expression of one's *volition*. Volitions are internal, mental states that, like observation reports, have a split personality: on the one hand, they have an intentional content and therefore inferential relations to other intentional states; on the other hand, they are items in the causal nexus – a volition to raise one's hand will, *ceteris paribus*, cause the raising of one's hand. Neither perceptual takings nor volitions can be singled out solely in virtue of their linguistic form. That a certain thought is a perception or a volition is not solely a matter of its internal structure or its intentional content; it is also a matter of its place in the causal interaction of the thinker with the world. If we concoct the notion of one's "action vocabulary", where that consists of terms for those actions one can "just do" without having to do them by doing some other action (Sellars calls these "minimal actions" (FD: 157)), the parallels between observation statements and expressions of intention become clear. Observation reports are thoughts in one's observation vocabulary that are brought about directly by one's sensory situation without inferential mediation. Volitions are thoughts in one's "action vocabulary" that directly bring about actions. For most of us, raising one's hand is something one can "just do" in this sense. If we do it by contracting various muscles a certain amount and in a certain order, we do rarely, if ever, intend these muscle-contractions as such. Most of us, in fact, could not contract these muscles intentionally except by, for example, raising our hand. The set of actions one can "just do" is no more fixed than the set of things or situations one can "just see".

Sellars reserves the word "shall" to mark the expression of intentions and volitions, and we will keep this formal convention; "will" then indicates the standard indicative future. Ordinary language is, of course, far more flexible concerning the forms in which intentions are expressed.

There are several different distinctions in this neighbourhood to be wary of. There is, for Sellars, an important distinction between *expressing* an intention and *ascribing* (even *self-ascribing*) an intention, similar to the distinction between *expressing* a belief in, for example, a candid thinking-out-loud, and *ascribing* a belief. Thus, I can formulate the intention, perhaps as a candid intending-out-loud,

I shall leave the office in ten minutes.

But this is not the same as my thinking-out-loud

I intend to leave the office in ten minutes,

which ascribes to me an intention, and does not *express* it directly, but only by way of implication. Compare, for instance, my thinking-out-loud

Ralph intends to leave the office in five minutes,

which clearly ascribes an intention to Ralph and has no particular implications concerning my own actions, with my intending-out-loud

Ralph shall leave the office in five minutes.

This latter, given Sellars's linguistic conventions, expresses *my* intention that Ralph leave in five minutes and commits me to doing such things as will bring it about that Ralph leaves in five minutes, such as telling him to go or even helping him get ready to leave. *Expressions* of intention are in this sense *always first-personal* in their very form, committing the subject (*ceteris paribus*) to action, if available.

There is also a difference between my intending something or expressing the intention to do something and my *predicting* that I will do it. I could think-out-loud

I will leave the office in ten minutes

not as an expression of intention, but simply as a prediction, because I know that my embezzlement scheme has been discovered and the police are about to take me away. Of course, if I *intend* to leave the office in ten minutes, I shall also *predict* (again, *ceteris paribus*) that I will leave the office in ten minutes. But the strength of my prediction need not match the strength of my intention, if, for instance, I know that there are difficult obstacles in my way and appreciate the real possibility of failure, or if I know that new information might come to light that would change my mind, my intentions. *Expressing* an intention is thus very different from *describing* an intention or *predicting* a future action.

However, in Sellars's view, the content of an intention need not be restricted to actions I am in a position to undertake. I can intend that some state of affairs obtain. For such intentions Sellars uses the form

It shall be the case that $p$.[4]

Such "shall be"s are less directly related to one's actions, but they must have implications for action under some (possible) conditions to be significant intentions. Every "shall be" implies some "shall"s. Therefore, as one thinks about complex states of affairs one would like to see realized, one can *reason* one's way into an intention which will eventually (*ceteris paribus*) ripen into a volition.[5] I can intend that the Hubble telescope have a long life, even though I am in no position to do anything about it directly. But, of course, if my congressman were for some reason to ask me about NASA funding, that intention would have consequences for my actions.

In Sellars's model of our conative selves, expressions of intention, unlike descriptions of intentions or attributions of intentions, are neither true nor false. Still, they have success conditions that provide nearby relatives we can consider as their semantic value: realized and unrealized. My intention to do $A$ is realized if I do $A$, otherwise it is unrealized. It seems intuitively correct to say that two intentions, let's say my intention to do $A$ and my intention to do $B$, are *inconsistent* iff $A$ and $B$ cannot be jointly realized.

We must also distinguish between what is implied by an intention and what is implied by the fact that a person *has* the intention. Whatever is implied by the intention that the Hubble telescope have a long life, it is clear that the implications of someone on the development team at NASA *having* that intention are different from the implications of me, a non-rocket-scientist philosopher-type at a distant university, *having* that intention.

As Sellars notes, "Intentions, like beliefs pertaining to particular matters of fact, involve an apperceptive framework of orientation in a spatio-temporal world" (TA: 110). As one's location in space and time changes, updates are made in the content of one's beliefs and intentions. Under normal circumstances and barring a change of heart, then, the intention to leave the office in ten minutes will naturally ripen in stages into the intention

I shall leave the office *now*.

And this intention *is* the volition to leave the office and will typically result in my leaving the office.

The notion of volitions has been criticized for several reasons in the tradition. Some have accused it of incoherence, because if actions are behaviours caused by volitions, then (it is claimed) each volition presupposes some prior volition, which generates a regress. Sellars is quite clear, however, that volitions, although mental acts in the sense of *actualities*, are *not* actions. We do not and cannot will to will directly, although we can certainly engage in actions intended to cultivate or discourage propensities to have some volitions rather than others. Some philosophers have been troubled by the fact that volitions have a place in both the intentional and the causal orders. Some argued that since there is a logical connection between the volition to do *A* and doing *A*, there could not be a causal connection. Sellars saw before Davidson that reasons can be causes. Again, some have argued that if volitions cause actions, then all our behaviour is caused, determinism is unavoidable, and freedom impossible. Sellars has a sophisticated response to the hard determinists that, unfortunately, we do not have time to investigate (creating one of the major gaps in this overview of Sellars's philosophy).[6] We shall have to make do with pointing out that a volition's causing a behaviour is not the same as a volition's causing a person to do an action. Furthermore, having a volition to do *A* is not itself a form of being *compelled* to do *A*.

Although volitions stand at the crux in action, intentions are really the fundamental category for practical reason, for practical *reasoning* essentially involves relations between and movement among intentions. Practical reasoning starts from our intentions, takes account of our beliefs and eventuates in volitions and therefore actions.

Before we delve into Sellars's extensive investigations of the logic of intentions, it is worth spending a moment reflecting on the broader point of this exercise. Sellars investigates the logic of intention expressions because he takes it that such expressions provide us with a *model* of intentions and their relations. His choice of intentions as the primary form of practical thought is a calculated choice. Ultimately, he claims that moral judgements are a subset of intentions, and this claim does double duty for him. On the one hand, it responds to those who have difficulty understanding how moral judgements can be intrinsically tied to action. If we assimilate moral judgements to run-of-the-mill descriptive, factual claims – if "You ought to support your children" states a fact, just as "You sought to support your children" – there can be no satisfactory answer to the question of how moral judgements are tied to action. By choosing intentions as the fundamental formal category of moral judgements, Sellars commits himself to a form of motivational internalism: to accept a moral judgement is to have an intention, which is to be moved to act accordingly.

On the other hand, Sellars's claim that moral judgements are really a certain kind of intention is also a complex response to common forms of non-cognitivism. Early non-cognitivism emphasized the connection between moral 'judgement' – we might better call it 'moral attitudinizing' as far the emotivists are concerned – and action, but at the cost of removing moral 'judgement' from the conceptual realm. Then moral judgements are neither true nor false; more importantly, there are no valid patterns of inference in which moral judgements play a role. This amounts to a rejection of practical reason itself. But there *are* valid forms of practical reasoning, Sellars maintains, and therefore moral judgements are clearly in the conceptual realm.[7] The inferences the emotivists were most concerned to reject were inferences that moved from an attribution to an object or event of some (set of) empirical property(ies) to the attribution of some moral or normative property, and Sellars agrees that no such inference, in fact, is valid. But Sellars, who was not alone in this response, points to inferences such as:

Jones ought to do *A* and *B*
So, Jones ought to do *A*.

There are valid inferences in which our moral or normative vocabulary occurs essentially, and this needs to be taken account of. Sellars's analysis of truth as 'semantic assertibility' even allows him to attribute truth to moral judgements, even though they do not play a fact-stating role.[8]

R. M. Hare objected to emotivism for much the same reasons and proposed to retain the action-guiding aspect of moral judgement while reinserting moral judgements in the conceptual, inferential realm by treating moral judgements as imperatives or commands and constructing a logic of imperatival inference. Sellars is very sympathetic to Hare's efforts and his examples, but ultimately rejects the attempt to assimilate moral judgements to imperatives or commands. One reason is that a command is a speech act with specific preconditions, including certain principles of obligation-production. An imperative is binding only if the person issuing it has the appropriate authority to issue it. That is, commands presuppose 'oughts' in a way that precludes them from serving non-circularly in an analysis of 'ought'.

One might, however, distinguish between a command and a simpler imperative, something like the instructions for assembling a toy or baking a cake. One can tell someone what to do without its being a command. But Sellars rejects this weaker form of imperativism as well. Essentially, his objection is that speech acts such as commanding or even telling to do are the wrong kinds of things to occur in arguments, the wrong kinds of thing to enter into a logic.

> Promising, telling to, telling that, and telling of are all public performances which require an audience. Reasoning is something which can go on *in foro interno*; and if it goes on out loud, it is the sort of thing which is overheard ... It makes sense to suppose that

an expressed reasoning could have occurred without being expressed; and if so, there cannot be such things as expressed reasonings the premises or conclusions of which are promisings, tellings to, or tellings that. In particular, there is no such thing as imperative inference. (IIOR: 170–71)

Hare chose the wrong model to explicate the status of moral judgement. Sellars offers expressions of intention as the correct model. There is a logic of intentions that Sellars constructs with care and in detail. Thus, Sellars can explain why moral judgement is necessarily action-guiding while also conceptual and subject to standards of consistency and coherence, just like any other form of judgement.

## The logic of intentions

Besides the published articles in which he goes into this topic in some depth, there are also some lengthy exchanges with Hector-Neri Castañeda and Bruce Aune, where these matters are a central focus.[9] We can give only a superficial overview here.

Following Sellars's convention, we shall regiment the intention I might express as "I'm going to have the chocolate mousse for dessert" as:

Shall [I will have the chocolate mousse for dessert].[10]

Intentions that others do things will be regimented in the same way, always with the understanding that they express the intention of the thinker or speaker, not the agent of the action. Thus "He's going to pay for his crimes" becomes

Shall be [he will pay for his crimes].[11]

The principle governing the logic of intentions (PLI), in Sellars's view, is

PLI: 'Shall $(A)$' implies 'Shall $(B)$' iff '$A$' implies '$B$'.

In some places Sellars says that there is also a principle to the effect that no expression of intention can be derived from anything other than an expression of intention, but that actually falls out of PLI as stated.[12] This, of course, entails that no (set of) purely descriptive expression(s) implies any intention; the fact–value gap remains in place. The implication relation in question here is to be construed as a metalinguistic inference licence, along the lines we have discussed in earlier chapters. It follows from PLI that implication relations among intentions ride piggyback on implication relations (which can be logical or material, in Sellars's view) among the indicatives stating their content. The distinction between an intention and someone's having an intention is relevant here. Someone need not *have* all the intentions implied by the intentions he or she does have. The intention to eat a healthy diet may imply (in virtue of the principles of good nutrition) the intention to eat a diet low in saturated fats, but I can certainly have the former intention without having the latter. However, if I have the former intention without also having the latter, I am subject to criticism on logical grounds.[13]

This is already enough to generate valid practical arguments.

> All basic practical reasoning pertaining to intentions can be reconstructed as a sequence of shall-statements, each of which follows from that which precedes it in accordance with the above principle [PLI] or, more accurately, since this principle belongs to the third level of practical discourse, in accordance with a second-level principle which accords with it. Thus, according to this principle,
>
> > 'Shall [P and Q]' implies 'shall [P]'
>
> follows from
>
> > 'P and Q' implies 'P'
>
> and hence the following piece of first-level practical reasoning
>
> > Shall [P and Q]
> > Therefore, shall [P]
>
> is valid.                                            (SM: 180)

There is a contentious aspect to Sellars's logic of intentions that we now need to mention. As he states it, "The implications between intentions which arise from implications pertaining to matters-of-fact concern only the *content* of intentions and not their status *as intentions*" (ORAV: 86). The force of this is that logical words, such as 'not', 'and' and even 'if … then' can occur inside the scope of a 'shall' operator, but not outside it.

> Thus, in our idiolect, we have
>
> > I shall do $A$                    It shall be the case that-$p$
> > I shall *not* do $A$             It shall *not* be the case that-$p$
>
> but *not*
>
> > I *not*-shall do $A$
> > It *not*-shall be the case that-$p$.                    (ORAV: 86)

If we play this out, we get the following results:

| *Well-formed* | *Ill-formed* |
|---|---|
| Shall [I not do *A*] | Not shall [I do *A*] |
| Shall be [*p or q*] | Shall be [*p*] or shall be [*q*] |
| Shall [If *p*, then I do *A*] | If *p*, then shall [I do *A*] |
| Shall be [*for all x,* if *x* is a future danger, then I will escape *x*] | *For all x*, shall be [if *x* is a future danger, then I will escape *x*] |

We can be tricked into thinking that the ill-formed expressions make sense, because there is something nearby, namely *ascriptions* of intentions, that do allow external logical operators. I can deny that I intend to do something, but that is a reflective or higher-order description of my mental state and *not* a base-level *expression* of that mental state. One's intentions are expressed in two ways: verbally through intendings-out-loud and non-verbally in the actions they cause once they have ripened into volitions. But there is no verbal expression of a lack of intention, just as there is no verbal expression of an absence of thought.

Sellars identifies another way we could be misled into thinking that there are logical complexes of intentions as well as logically complex intentions. He contrasts the punctuated *text*

My children *shall* have a good education.
I have already begun to put money aside.

with the conjunctive statement

My children *shall* have a good education *and* I have already begun to put money aside.

The latter looks alright, but it is misleading, according to Sellars, because it violates the rule that logical connectives occur only *inside* intention statements, even when the connection is to a non-intention. Of course, in standard sentential logic, we have the rule of conjunction introduction (CI), which tells us that a text in which two sentences are asserted implies their conjunction, that is:

CI: '*P*' and '*Q*' imply '*P* and *Q*'.

Given PLI, this yields

CIS: 'Shall [*P*]' and 'Shall [*Q*]' imply 'Shall [*P* and *Q*]',

which is fairly unproblematic. But Sellars introduces one further

*Wilfrid Sellars*

principle here that tells us how unintended or given states of affairs can be taken into account in our practical reasonings. He calls it "So-be-it".

So-Be-It: "Shall be [φ]" and "*p*" imply "Shall be [φ and *p*]" where 'φ' is a formula which may or may not be logically complex.

(ORAV: 88)

Thus, in Sellars's view, our beliefs about how the world is are taken up *into* the scope of our intentions and reasoned with. The interested reader can follow some examples of how this works in "On Reasoning about Values" (1980) (ORAV: 89–91). Sellars's summary, however, puts the picture succinctly:

94. Thus CI together with So-be-it, takes our separate purposes and relevant beliefs and puts them together into encompassing alternatives:

1. Shall be [I do *A* at *t*, which means that ...]?
2. Shall be [I do *B* at *t*, which means that ...]?
3. Shall be [I do *C* at *t*, which means that ...]?

The successive steps are

(a) elaboration by CI and So-be-it, and the drawing of implications
(b) choice, e.g. (2), or, continuing indecision
(c) simplification. Shall be [I do *B* at *t*]
(d) intention to act. Shall [I do *B* at *t*]

which, when time *t* comes (and I do not change my mind), generates a doing (or an attempt to do) *B*.

95. This picture is one according to which practical reasoning is essentially the process of elaborating alternative scenarios for a choice.

(ORAV: 91)

As he also points out, the elaboration of these alternatives is rational, but there's also a question about whether the choice itself is rational, above and beyond being tacked on to a process of rationally elaborating alternatives. That (finally) raises the question of morality.

## Intentions and relative reasonableness

What we have so far certainly allows us to judge some combinations of intentions as inconsistent and, in that straightforward sense,

256

unreasonable. We can also construct a notion of *relative reasonableness*. Given an intention to do *A*, some intention to do *B* can be reasonable, if doing *B* is, let's say, a necessary condition of doing *A*. This does *not* mean, of course, that doing *B* is reasonable, period. Still, we can introduce a first form of 'ought' – although not yet the *moral* 'ought' – on this basis. We can now reconstruct assertions of the form

If S wants *A*, then she ought to do *B*.

The very first thing to notice about such assertions, though, is that if we also know that

S wants *A*

it would still be a mistake to conclude outright

S ought to do *B*.

In Sellars's example, from

If Jones wants to poison his aunt quickly, then he ought to give her prussic acid

and

Jones wants to poison his aunt quickly

there is at best something fishy about concluding

Jones ought to give his aunt prussic acid

because it is also incumbent on Jones's advisors to tell him he really ought not to give his aunt prussic acid.

We can sum up the apparent moral of our discussion to date by saying that although the 'ought' of

If X wants A, he ought to do B

looks as though it concerned the propriety of *doing B* on a certain hypothesis, it actually concerns the logical propriety or impropriety of certain complex valuings. To offer advice of the form

If you want A you ought to do B

is not to offer *substantive* advice as does

You ought to do X

It is to give *logical* advice. (OMP: 8)[14]

Notice that, given the way Sellars has set up the logic of intentions, there is a conceptual pressure built into the very logic of practical reasoning to take into account all relevant facts and purposes. A large part of practical reasoning consists, as we have seen, in elaborating alternative scenarios among which we then choose. The more fully elaborated the alternatives are, the more reasonable the ultimate choice, it would seem. This, then, seems to point in the direction of an ideal: if we could really get to a position in which *all* things were considered, the choice we would then make, the intention we would then adopt, would not owe its reasonableness to derivation from any particular intention we have, for it would include and subsume them all. Should we say that it is *un*reasonable? Should we say that it is non-relatively or absolutely reasonable?

There is a tradition stretching back at least to Plato that we each possess an overarching or most general intention that informs all our action and is something like "I shall live a satisfying life". Of course, we do not all agree about what constitutes a satisfying life, even all things considered, but it isn't assumed that there is one and only one life (or life-style, if you will) that all would find satisfying. Sellars does believe, however, that there is a strong strand in this tradition that endorses the ideas that (i) there is an objective answer to the question of what would be, for a given person, a satisfying life all things considered; and (ii) as a matter of psychological necessity, we all have the intention to lead a satisfying life.

Indeed, there is something very odd about lacking (much less rejecting) the intention to lead a satisfying life, all things considered. Is this a matter of violating some law or principle of psychology? Is it odd only because it is an impossibility, something we simply *cannot* do? In that case, it certainly wouldn't follow that the intention to have a satisfying life *is* reasonable. Perhaps though, Sellars seems to suggest, the reasonableness of the desire for a satisfying life all things considered is ultimately tied to the fact that *all* things are supposedly considered. After all, if the chosen alternative really does take everything into account, there is no danger of hidden contradictions with other intentions coming to light; there seems to be no danger of incoherence. At very least, there seems to be no *reason* the agent would have to reject a choice made *all things considered*.

We need not accept the idea that it is psychologically impossible to wish for a less than satisfying life, and we need not think, with Plato, that a justification of morality must ultimately appeal to our egoistic impulses to gain hold on our actual motivational structure. For we need not appeal to such "facts" to explain the oddness of the idea of someone rejecting a satisfying life, all things considered. That oddness can be accounted for, in Sellars's view, by the logical pressures to sum up or conjoin our various intentions into one coherent mass.

We have just, essentially, reconstructed the outlines of rational egoism. The 'oughts' of rational egoism are not yet moral 'oughts', despite the attempts of Plato (and others) to show that morality could be justified from the rational egoist's point of view. However important Plato's insights are, we need to push further to understand morality. One attempt to get beyond the narrow intentions of enlightened self-interest to the universality and intersubjectivity characteristic of moral oughts is to opt for a different, more general goal. Perhaps the difference between the 'ought' of rational egoism and the 'ought' of morality is that morality intends not the individual happiness of the agent, but the welfare of agents (or organisms) generally. When the rational egoist considers all things, he considers them all in relation to himself; maybe, the suggestion runs, morality consists of those intentions that arise when all things are considered in relation to the general welfare. This would give rise to a system that looks a lot like utilitarianism or other forms of universalistic consequentialism (depending on how the details get filled in).

Sellars argues that making this move is not sufficient to recover the moral ought. There seem to be two principal complaints. First, this form of universal benevolence predicates morality on a particular (however general) goal, namely, a desire or intention to maximize the general welfare. This leaves a number of subproblems in its wake: what are we to say to someone who simply does not have that goal? The moral 'ought' seems to be categorical and unqualified, that is, inherently independent of one's particular desires. Secondly, it is easy to picture a moral agent confronted with two coherent but potentially conflicting subsystems of intentions:

| | |
|---|---|
| If I want (*ceteris paribus*) to be happy, I ought to pursue such and such policies. | If I want (*ceteris paribus*) to promote the general welfare, I ought to pursue such and such other policies. |

In such a case, Sellars complains, it is not clear how to resolve these into one embracing and coherent system.

> We feel that moral *'ought'* is *in principle* embracing and unequivocal, i.e. that if we had ideal knowledge, what we ought to do would be uniquely determined ... If we recognize a duality of basic valuings, the moral pattern seems closer, but the uniqueness disappears. (OMP: 13)

# Categorically reasonable intentions

In order to capture the distinctively moral 'ought', Sellars turns, not surprisingly, to Kant, for "if anyone has captured its essence it is surely Kant" (SM VII §86: 208). Kant emphasizes the universality of moral judgements, a universality that is multi-dimensional. In Kant's view, moral judgements apply to everyone, in all circumstances, and are objectively acceptable to all. Sellars wants to show how to isolate a set of intentions with such characteristics. That will conclude his reconstruction of morality.

First, Sellars follows Kant in distinguishing between the *hypothetical* and the *conditional*. Hypothetical imperatives, of course, depend upon the possession of some want or desire. Sellars understands this in terms of the relative reasonableness of some intentions.[15] The question posed in the attempt to reconstruct the moral 'ought' is whether there are any *categorically* reasonable intentions. But it is a mistake to think that the 'categorical' in "categorical imperative" is a term of *grammar*, and simply distinguishes a class of sentences that are non-conditional in structure. Although there may be highly abstract imperatives that hold good in *every* circumstance (e.g. perhaps, respect persons!), morality cannot consist solely of such imperatives, for the activities that constitute respecting persons seem variable, depending on the circumstances. If we are to be able actually to apply or carry out the categorical injunctions of morality, they must, in fact, have a conditional structure:

If in circumstances $C$, do $A$.

This differs from a hypothetical imperative in that the agent's own desires are not considered part of the circumstances of an action.[16] What is important here is that the specific desires or intentions of the agent regarding C are irrelevant to the reasonableness of this conditional intention.

We are thus led to the idea that

I ought to do $A$, if I am in $C$

is equivalent to

"I shall do $A$, if I am in $C$" is categorically reasonable.

(SM VII §97: 211)

We must explain how such a conditional intention can be categorically reasonable.

The first-person 'ought', though, is still far from the universal ideal Kant put before us. Is there a way to bridge the gap that remains? Sellars takes it that "the hypothetical imperative which comes closest to capturing the moral point of view is that of impartial benevolence" (SM VII §100: 212). He seems to mean by this that "the actions it prescribes coincide with the prescriptions of morality" (SM VII §100: 212).[17] So consider the hypothetical imperative

If $S$ wants to maximize the general welfare, $S$ ought to do $A_i$ if $S$ is in $C_i$.

This tells us, transposed into his language of intentions, that

"I shall maximize the general welfare" implies (for $S$) "I shall do $A_i$ if I am in $C_i$".

In turn, this tells us that "I shall do $A_i$, if I am in $C_i$" is reasonable relative to the intention "I shall maximize the general welfare". If this latter intention were itself categorically reasonable, so would be the conditional intention "I shall do $A_i$, if I am in $C_i$". What can we say about the intention to maximize the general welfare? "It is a worthy intention, one that we should encourage people to have – though not, as Kant emphasizes, at the expense of the sense of duty. Yet it does not seem to have any feature which calls for the predicate 'intrinsically and categorically reasonable'" (SM VII §106: 214). But this egocentric hypothetical imperative, relying as it does on the impersonal material implication between maximizing the general welfare, being in circumstances $C_i$ and doing $A_i$, can be generalized, yielding the general practical implication:

For all values of '$x$', 'it shall be the case that $x$ maximize the general welfare' implies (for each rational being) 'it shall be the case that $x$ does $A_i$ if $x$ is in $C_i$'.

This practical implication authorizes each person to reason, not only about himself or herself, but about people generally. We can, therefore, recover one aspect of the universality of moral judgements, namely, the universality of *content,* via this reconstruction of moral reasoning. But it is still not close to a full moral ought, for the personal desires of each agent to maximize the general welfare still play a crucial role.

The big hurdle to be overcome here is not so much the universality of moral judgements but their *intersubjectivity,* according to Sellars, a kind of universality in *form* rather than content. For what are we to say if Tom has the intention "It shall be the case that Dick maximizes the general welfare" and Dick thinks, in contrast, that "It shall not be the case that Dick maximizes the general welfare"? These two intentions are clearly opposed, but we cannot say that they *contradict* each other, for the irreducible egocentricity of intentions entails that they differ enough in content not to contradict each other directly.

> Two people can affirm the same proposition in a strong sense of 'same'. But as far as the intentions we have so far considered are concerned, intentions can at best be parallel. They are irreducibly egocentric, even when this egocentricity is latent as in
>
> > Tom: it shall be the case that the war ends
> > Dick: it shall be the case that the war ends
>
> This dialogue provides an excellent example of 'agreement in attitude'. But if the depth form of these statements is
>
> > Tom: (*Ceteris paribus*) I (Tom) shall do what I can to end the war
> > Dick: (*Ceteris paribus*) I (Dick) shall do what I can to end the war
>
> the agreement in attitude is not an identity of intention.
>
> (SM VII §116: 217)

Until we can apply the notions of identity and contradiction to intentions intersubjectively and not merely within each person's intention-set, the notion of truth is not really appropriate to them (and in particular to the moral judgements that express the subset of intentions we are worried about) either. Sellars thinks this problem can be overcome, for there are intentions that are shareable, not just in their non-egocentric content (such as "It shall be the case that the war ends"), but in their *form* as well, namely, intentions in the first-person *plural*: *we*-intentions.

## Our intentions

Tom and Dick can share the intention "We shall do what we can to end the war". When they do, their intentions are identical in a stronger sense than the two egocentric intentions "I (respectively Tom or Dick) shall do what I can to end the war". Now, since "I" is always one of "us", the we-intention implies an egocentric intention. But, Sellars argues, that does not render the we-intention redundant or otiose. Talk about an egocentric intention, in practical contexts, implies a certain kind of motivational structure. If Dick has derived his intention to do what he can to end the war from the fact that *we* have that intention (because we intend that our country not waste resources on hopeless and unnecessary conflicts) and he is one of *us*, there is a palpable difference from, say, his having the egocentric intention because he would like to save his own skin by avoiding military service. This can, indeed, show up in the intention:

> Shall [I (Dick), *because* I am one of us, do what I can to end the war].

Even so, the we-intentions discussed so far are refracted through individual I-centred intentions when applied in action. Sellars asks whether there is any way in which an intention can be not only *we*-referential, but *action* we-referential.[18] His answer, as we might anticipate, is *yes*.

> We-referential action intentions imply intentions to act on the part of individuals, not simply by virtue of the general principle which relates "Shall be" to "Shall I do," but *directly* by virtue of the relation between "Shall *anybody* do" and "Shall *I* do."
>
> ... if a person *has* the intention
>
> > Shall [I do *A*]
>
> and has it *because* it is implied by the intention
>
> > Shall [any of us do *A*]
>
> which he also *has*, we can say that Jones intends to do A *sub specie* "one of us," and flag our representation of his intention with a subscript "we," thus,
>
> > Jones intends "Shall$_{we}$ [I do *A*]". (ORAV: 99)

The intersubjective form of a we-intention does not conflict with its being subjectively action-guiding.

As I mentioned in note 14, Sellars reconstructs the notion of *valuing* as well as that of a moral judgement, taking the optative "Would that *P*" as the canonical expression of such an act or attitude.[19] We can value things from different points of view, however, and the optative allows us to make this explicit.

> I would that American students had an easier time affording college

is not the same valuing as

We would that American students had an easier time affording college.

These are valuings from two different points of view. The first is commonly given a default egocentric reading: it expresses my personal values (although we can now recognize that another, non-egocentric reading of it is possible, if the context makes it clear, for instance, that I take my own values in this case to be grounded in morality itself and not mere personal preference). The "we" form, however, clearly and immediately raises the question: who is "we"? And there is no univocal answer here. It could be "we educators", "we Democrats" or "we citizens", among other choices.

Before turning to the proper identification of the moral *us*, let us return to the search for categorically reasonable intentions. One candidate was the rational egoist's overriding intention

Shall [I will lead a satisfying life, all things considered].

It is a candidate for being categorically reasonable because, if all things are really considered, there are really no competing reasons that would clash with it, at least from the personal point of view. Since it seems necessary that agents have a personal point of view, prudential considerations are at least always in play (even if one thinks they can be overridden by other considerations). Sellars calls this general prudential intention a *formal* intention, for left to itself it is just the (empty) form of prudential reasons and in reality has to be spelled out or filled in with details of one's circumstances. If this formal intention is intrinsically reasonable, given the structure of our practical lives, then the intentions which are implied by it are also categorically reasonable.

The moral philosopher is confronted with the question:
Is there an intrinsically (and hence categorically) reasonable formal intention which is the regulative principle of the moral point of view? (ORAV: 100)

The suggestion that

It shall$_{we}$ be the case that our welfare is maximized

is such an intention unites themes from Plato as well as from Mill and the utilitarians. Furthermore, Sellars says, this intention:

does seem to have an authority which is more than a mere matter of its being generally accepted. It is a conceptual fact that people constitute a community, a *we*, by virtue of thinking of each other as *one of us*, and by willing the common good *not* under the species of benevolence – but by willing it as one of us, or from a moral point of view. (SM VII §132: 222)

By accepting this intention as the fundamental or constitutive intention underlying morality, Sellars brings his reconstruction of the basic logic of moral judgements to a close, for he has shown us how to isolate a set of intentions with the requisite universality:

(a) in their content
    ... if any of us is in $C_i$ he do $A_i$
(b) in their subjective form (their logical intersubjectivity)
    We would that ...
(c) in their objectivity (in that there is, in principle, a decision procedure with respect to specific ethical statements).
(SM VII §133: 222).[20]

Sellars can, in other words, reconstruct Kant's metaphysic of morals.[21]

His statement in "'Ought' and Moral Principles" is particularly intelligible:

... the question

    What ought I to do in these circumstances (from the moral point of view)?

is at heart the question

    What would we that I do in these circumstances?

and to answer the question is to answer the question

    What would we that any of us do in these circumstances?

and this again

    On what valuings of the form "we would that any of us did such and such in these circumstances" would we agree if we had ideal knowledge?

and this again

    What practices would we agree to be conducive to our common good – if we had Ideal Knowledge? (OMP: 17)

But we are not yet finished, for we have to return to the important question concerning the scope of morality's "we".

There are two points to be made immediately. First, the moral "we" has no explicit membership rider: it is not "we educators", "we Democrats" or even "we human beings". But there might be an *implicit* membership rider that a philosopher could make explicit; for example, Kant believed that membership in the moral "we" included all and only rational beings. Secondly, just as we can distinguish between what an agent *thinks* her circumstances are and what is it *reasonable* for her to think her circumstances are, we can distinguish between the community an agent operating in the framework of this constitutive moral intention actually *thinks of as us* and those that it is *reasonable* for the agent to think of as *us*, all things considered. So we need not accept a *de facto* identification with one's co-religionists, one's racial group, or even one's species as holding special weight. Sellars believes that the logical pressures built into the structure of practical reason that continually invite, perhaps even force, one to take *all* relevant considerations into account push us towards taking "us" to include every being with whom we can share intentions. If this is right, then the moral "we" does include all rational beings, as Kant maintained.

If this line of reasoning vindicates Kant's view of the scope of the moral "we", it does so only *formally*. That is, we can see logical pressures operating in practical reason that would make thinking of all rational beings as *us* a regulative ideal built into practical reason. But in order to make this community a reality, all rational beings would have to share the intersubjective intention

It shall$_{we}$ be the case that each of us rational beings so acts as to promote our welfare.

Again, we can point out that an individual can have an intention of such intersubjective form, even if no one in fact shares it with her. So it is possible for one to think of oneself as a member of a community, even though no such community in fact exists.

The reality of the moral community of rational beings could be established, Sellars claims, if we could justify the following claims:

(a)  To think of oneself as rational being is (implicitly) to think of oneself as subject to epistemic oughts binding on rational beings generally

(b)  The intersubjective intention to promote *epistemic* welfare implies the intersubjective intention to promote welfare *sans phrase*.                    (SM VII §144: 225).[22]

If these are both true, then the moral community is real, even if only implicitly so. However, while Sellars thinks the first of these claims is "not implausible" (SM VII §145: 226), the second "despite Peirce's

valiant efforts, remains problematic, and without it the argument for
the reality of an *ethical* community consisting of all rational beings,
the major premise of which is the 'fact of reason', remains incomplete"
(SM VII §145: 226).

Perhaps a fully inclusive moral community will remain ever a regulative ideal rather than a grounded reality. In effect, Sellars cannot
claim that there is an *argument* to show that the moral point of view
is more reasonable than (and therefore overrides) the self-interested
point of view. We do *care* and are *raised to care* about the well-being
of at least some of our fellow beings. We are always subject to the logical pressures that push us towards an ever more inclusive "we". But,
absent psychological pathology, we also experience a psychological
pressure to care about others. Furthermore, in Sellars's view, the
commitment to the well-being of others

> is a commitment deeper than any commitment to abstract princi-
> ple. It is this commitment to the well-being of our fellow man
> which stands to the justification of moral principles as the purpose
> of acquiring the ability to explain and predict stands to the justi-
> fication of scientific theories.          (SE in PP: 411)

The ability to care about others, he also points out, is itself necessary
to a full life.

Community membership plays a linchpin role for Sellars. It is a necessary condition of the possibility of moral judgement. To shift to a more
Kantian mode of expression, it is also the transcendental condition of
meaning, and of fully articulate thought, as it is the transcendental
condition of morality. This is because it is the transcendental condition
of normativity. Our commitment to shared epistemic and practical
goals and values constitutes us as the value-laden beings we are.

We have only sketched Sellars's ethics. He is very concerned with
the *structure* of ethical reasoning, and has much less to say about the
applied content of ethics, but in both dimensions questions are left
that cry out for answers. What are the existence conditions for a we-
intention? What, exactly, is the relation between we-intentions and I-
intentions? *We* might intend that each of us tell the truth unless some
significant harm would result; exactly what does that entail for *my*
intentions, if I am one of us? Sellars argues that the we-intention to
promote our welfare is categorically reasonable, but seems to assume
that what would, indeed, promote our welfare would be unproblematic, if only we had complete information. It seems harder today to
accept without further argument the idea that disagreement about

fundamental choices would vanish in the face of ideal knowledge. Still, Sellars's ethical writings constitute a significant attempt to construct a coherent view that unites the Kantian, the Hegelian, and the Utilitarian; the internalist and the externalist; the rationalist and the naturalist strains of modern ethical theory.

## Chapter 10

# *The necessity of the normative*

## Real and ideal, empirical and transcendental

Sellars often characterized his project as a Kantian response to the dominant empiricism of his day. The comparison with Kant is illuminating, but it can also be a trap, masking some important features of Sellars's philosophy. It invites one to assimilate Sellars's distinction between the manifest and scientific images to Kant's distinction between the phenomenal and noumenal realms, for instance, which Sellars himself at times encourages. While there is *something* to the analogy, it requires a commentary. The most obvious disanalogy between the manifest–scientific image distinction and Kant's phenomenal–noumenal distinction is that Kant's noumenal realm is *in principle* beyond our ken. As a latter-day Critical Realist, Sellars rejects the idea that reality is *in principle* beyond our knowledge. In Sellars's view, the dogged pursuit of science is *in principle* capable of revealing reality as it is in itself. Achieving knowledge of the intrinsic nature of things may well be indefinitely far off in a Peircean culmination of enquiry, but the scientific image is not an unknowable noumenon. The world targeted by the scientific and the manifest images is one and the same, even if the particular objects in the scientific image and the manifest image differ significantly.

For Sellars, both the manifest framework and the scientific framework are transcendentally ideal and empirically real, although, again, we need commentary to keep these claims from being terribly misleading. For Kant, remember, something is transcendentally ideal if, as a ground of *a priori* knowledge, it is mind-dependent; it is empirically real if, as an object of sensible or empirical knowledge, it is mind-independent. Both of Sellars's frameworks are transcendentally ideal because both frameworks are, ultimately, human constructs, and the structural features of these representations of reality will inevitably reflect features or artifacts of *our* cognitive capacities. As we saw in Chapter 3, Sellars believes that any conceptual framework will determine some synthetic *a priori* truths, because every conceptual framework, *necessarily*, includes valid forms of material inference. But synthetic *a priori* truths are framework-relative; there is no set of absolute or framework-independent synthetic *a priori* truths. The structure of our conceptual framework, which is responsible for our *a priori* knowledge and which we often take to reflect the structural articulation of reality itself, is in fact mind-dependent to a significant degree.

There is nonetheless an important difference in the status of the scientific and manifest images, according to Sellars. The *objects* of the manifest image are transcendentally ideal, whereas the *objects* of the (culminating) scientific image are transcendentally *real*.[1] Thus there is an apparent paradox: the *objects* of the scientific image are real, even though the framework is ideal. The paradox is only apparent, however, and quickly dissolves when one takes two crucial facts into account. (i) The resources of the (culminating) scientific image allow its users to construct arbitrarily accurate *pictures* of arbitrarily delimited realms of reality. Sellars is committed to the belief that progress in the sciences converges on a univocal *picture* (in his technical sense) of the world. At the object level, therefore, Peircean science "carves nature at its joints". The objects of the world *really are* as they are depicted by Peircean science, for Peircean science gives us an intrinsic characterization of the objects of the world. (ii) Science cannot be identified with the picture of the world it produces. The scientific image of the world cannot be identified merely with the *pictures* Peircean science produces, for the scientific framework necessarily contains methods for *generating* such pictures, and methods for generating the methods for generating such pictures, and these require material inferences. The generative and methodological mechanisms of the scientific framework will be transcendentally ideal, because they will be tuned to our capacities and mind-dependent. The pictures generated, though, will have a *natural* relation to the realm pictured; the "representation relation" between picture and realm pictured will not be an *intentional* relation. Since the picture–pictured relation is not intentional, it is, at least arguably, not mind-dependent in the requisite sense. (Notice that the pictures generated by Peircean science will be just that: pictures. There is, for example, no representation in them of causality as such, just which objects are where, when. Causal laws are, for Sellars, part of the generative mechanism of science, not object-level representations of reality.)

The manifest image, in contrast, does not "carve nature at its joints"; it cannot construct arbitrarily accurate maps or pictures of the world. At any number of levels, its methods and techniques are too coarse to accurately reflect the world; it gets some things wrong, sometimes *very wrong*. The objects and laws of the manifest image only approximate the actual, verified patterns of interaction discovered by science. The objects conceived of by the manifest image are not to be found outside that framework. So not only is the generative or inferential framework of the manifest image transcendentally ideal (like every inferential or generative framework), its *objects* are also transcendentally ideal.

The *objects* of the manifest image are, however, *empirically real*, in the sense that they are subject to observation and are known empirically. There *is* empirically verifiable truth and falsehood with respect to the manifest framework. In the Sellarsian dispensation, however, it makes sense to say that the objects of the scientific image are *empirically more real* than the objects of the manifest image, or at least that they have a much stronger claim to empirical reality than those of the manifest image. Sellars believes that the manifest framework makes it possible to ask questions that cannot be answered within the confines of the manifest framework. The scientific framework, however, has been deliberately constructed to offer determinate answers to such questions and in general to withstand much more stringent empirical tests than the manifest image could bear. Peircean science will be able to answer all the scientific questions it stimulates.

## Practical reality

While these are interesting points of comparison between Kant and Sellars and show the influence of Peirce, the most interesting points and the true depth of Sellars's pragmatism appear when we push further and realize that the world of the manifest image is *practically real*, whereas the world of the scientific image is not. Ultimately, the objects of the scientific image are *practically ideal*. Neither Kant nor Sellars uses this notion of the practically real, but it is a revealing concept to add to their arsenals. The real and the true are obviously deeply related. You will recall that for Sellars 'truth' is a generic concept, roughly equivalent to ideal semantic assertibility. This way of thinking about truth let him make sense of the notion of moral or practical truths, even if practical judgrments are modelled, not on declarative sentences, but expressions of intention. We can now exploit this architecture to construct a conception of the *practically real*. A framework or object is practically real iff there are *categorical prescriptive truths* with respect to that framework or object. A framework is practically real iff there are within the framework intentions that are warrantedly assertible, that is, intersubjectively reasonable and universally applicable. A practically real framework is one in which there are objective rules.

From the point of view of practical reality, there is an asymmetry between the manifest and the scientific images that Sellars never bothered to point out, but that needs to be thought through. The scientific image has a claim to greater empirical reality than the manifest image because it is empirically more determinate, more complete and better supported. The manifest image has a claim to greater practical reality than the scientific image, and whatever practical reality the objects of the scientific image have, it is strictly derivative from the prior practical reality of the objects of the manifest image.

The manifest image has greater practical reality than the scientific image for the same kind of reason it has lesser empirical reality. The manifest image raises empirical questions it is not in a position to answer, but the scientific image is. The opposite is true in matters of practice: the scientific image raises practical questions it is not in a position to answer. One might think that the scientific image or framework is simply devoid of practical claims, because it aims only at description and explanation. But the scientific framework must also contain methods and canons, and these consist in part of prescriptive claims. There are ways experiments ought to be done and ways they ought not to be done; ways data ought to be interpreted and ways it should never be interpreted. There are inferences one may make and inferences one is forbidden to make. Every conceptual framework necessarily has a prescriptive or normative dimension. Indeed, conceptual frameworks are *essentially* and *principally* normative in their being, for a conceptual framework is *constituted* by the valid inferences, both formal and material, and by the proprieties of response and behaviour that are licensed by it. Thus, the scientific framework itself is practically real, for there are objectively true prescriptions or rules with respect to it.

The prescriptive dimension of a scientific framework, however, is neither complete nor comprehensive. Scientists do not, as such, deal with questions about when scientific investigation is worthwhile or how the knowledge science generates is best used. Scientific activity has to occur within and answer to a broader set of societal norms and social goals. As noted in Chapter 9, Sellars acknowledges that the intention that underlies science, the intersubjective intention to promote our epistemic welfare, has at best a *problematic connection* to the broader intersubjective intention to promote our welfare unconditionally (SM VII §145: 226). In the face of practical questions and problems that over-reach the competence of science, we have to leave the scientific frame-work, strictly so-called, and return to the manifest image.

It does not seem possible to *guarantee* answers to such questions even in the manifest image, but by Sellars's own account of moral deliberation, there remains a hope that in the long run, with ever-increasing (scientific) knowledge of the consequences of our actions and their *de facto* effect on our welfare, we could in our moral delibera-tions converge on a set of mutually satisfactory choices. It may not be *clear* that the manifest image contains the resources to answer all the normative questions it makes possible, but it is clear that the scientific image does *not*. In this regard, therefore, the manifest image retains priority, *practical priority,* over the scientific.

The *objects* of the scientific image will have practical reality in so far as their concepts enter into true prescriptive claims and valid practical inferences. There is no barrier to their doing so. The objects of the scientific image can be as involved in our actions, both as means and as ends, as we let them be. The practical reality of scientific objects, *as such,* however, is extrinsic to them. Their practical reality is not intrinsic to them, for it is not, for instance, tied in to their iden-tity and individuation conditions. Normatively identified properties do not make scientific objects what they are. The identity and individuation conditions of a scientific object should be resolutely non-normative, purely factual.[2] Any normative or prescriptive dimension to them is a mind-dependent addition, so the objects of the scientific image are practically ideal.

That is not the case with objects of the manifest image. The vocabu-lary of the manifest image is richly laden with normative valences. It can be difficult at times to find a truly norm-neutral description of a state of affairs or an object in the manifest image. For instance, arti-facts, common objects of the manifest world, are generally identified by reference to a function that they are intended to perform and which serves as a standard against which to assess them. Even natural objects can become laden with normative baggage, such as the dogwood tree, which in Christian mythology has a special meaning because Jesus was supposedly crucified on a cross of dogwood. In the ancient and medieval worlds, it was taken for granted that natural objects had some deeper symbolic, moral significance derived from complex relations to a larger world-order. The idea that such "properties" of things are subjective attachments, excrescences to be purged from a purified, value-free conception of nature, is a latter-day notion, inspired by an arguably inappropriate urge to remake the manifest image in the image of the scientific image.

Sellars does not always convey the richness of practical discourse to his readers. In his discussion of Feyerabend in "Scientific Realism or Irenic Instrumentalism" (1965), Sellars explicitly commits himself to the following propositions:

(α) Micro-physical entities do not have the second class existence of mere "conceptual devices."

(β) The framework of common sense is radically false – i.e. there are *really* no such things as the physical objects and processes of the common sense framework.[3]

(γ) Propositions (α) (β) are to be clarified in terms of the concept of its being reasonable *at some stage* to abandon the framework of common sense and use only the framework of theoretical science, suitably enriched by the dimension of practical discourse.[4]  (SRI: 189, in PP: 354)

One way to take this is to say that in the Peircean millenium, we shall let science do *all* the describing and explaining, and the presence of practical discourse in our language need amount to nothing more than the presence of the intention operator 'shall'. The contents of our intentions, our beliefs and our desires, will all be formulated solely in the language science has developed.

Ultimately, though, Sellars cannot mean that. The footnote to (γ) is crucial. It acknowledges that, at the very least, artifacts have a practical dimension that cannot be reconstructed in the vocabulary of science alone, because practicality is already built into the artifact itself. How would a Peircean formulate the intention to get a hammer (for however wonderful the Peircean world might be, things will still need building or fixing)? No straightforwardly and purely physical description of a complex object will be equivalent to 'hammer'. For a hammer is "a hand tool consisting of a solid head set crosswise on a handle and used for pounding" (*Merriam-Webster's Eleventh Collegiate Dictionary*). Any attempt to capture that in the language of microphysics alone would be at best wildly disjunctive, and even so, it would be inaccurate. A hammer is not just something with which it is possible to pound; stones are not hammers, nor are hatchets. It is not merely an empirical generalization that hammers are used for pounding. Hammers are *to be used* for pounding. There is an ought-to-be sitting in the background that is at home in a set of institutional practices constituted by still more ought-to-be's and their related ought-to-do's. Hammers, furthermore, are *hand tools,* which again conveys norms about their uses. If, then, Peircean Jones asks Smith to bring him a hammer, will he have to formulate a complex description in the vocabulary of physics-cum-intentions that reconstructs more precisely and adequately the idea of a hammer? That just seems silly. Why not just retain the notion of a hammer?

When Sellars talks of abandoning the framework of common sense, he cannot really mean that we will cease talking of hammers, of shoes and ships and sealing wax, of cabbages and kings. If we ceased using such terminology, we would just have to re-invent it all over again in our new language. However wonderful the language of Peircean science is, however many more questions it permits us to ask and answer, it would be foolish to think that it would replace wholesale the language of artifacts and useful objects. Peircean is aimed at enabling the construction of arbitrarily fine-grained pictures of the world, but such pictures serve our purposes only under certain circumstances.

These reflections, though, just scratch the surface. Even though artifacts carry along with them implicit reference to functions, to social institutions and practices, and thereby to systems of norms, they are all capable of value-free description as physical objects. That is, we can both distinguish the role-player and the role played, the function embodied and the embodiment of the function, and accept their convergence, even their (token) identity in the particular objects. That is why we are willing to *identify* the artifact with its physical presence. After all, in the final wash, the normativity implicit in artifacts is *imposed* on them by us from the outside.

## Persons as basic practical realities

I now want to argue that there are some *basic* objects of the manifest image for which a value-free description, at least within the manifest image, is impossible: persons. In the manifest image, the normativity implicit in persons is not imposed from the outside and artifactual, but, in a crucial sense, is natural and intrinsic. Persons, in the manifest image, grow normativity as naturally as bees find honey. In the manifest image, the practical reality of persons is unassailable and foundational.

I have said little about Sellars's speculation in "Philosophy and the Scientific Image of Man" that the most primordial image, the "original image", was one in which *everything* is treated as a person, in which *person* is *the* fundamental category of being. The manifest image, Sellars speculates, developed out of this original image by noting that most entities lack the full set of capacities persons are endowed with. The concept of a mere thing, then, is originally the concept of a truncated person or person *manqué*. In this sense *person* remains the primordial category of the manifest image. Persons, however, are intrinsically normative beings in several dimensions. First, they possess *intrinsic* value; objects have value *for* them. As Kant said, as the source of all values, persons have absolute value. Secondly, their states and behaviours have value. They have pleasures and pains, virtues and vices, and undertake actions that are good or bad, justified or unjustified. Persons simply cannot be thought apart from the norms, proprieties, demands and permissions in which they are embedded and that constitute them as persons. Apart from persons, practical reality itself is nothing, less even than a dream.

And yet, says Sellars, science is the measure of what is that it is and what is not that it is not. His naturalism favours empirical reality, for a world of empirical objects but without persons is easily conceived, whereas a world of persons without empirical objects is nonsense. Persons are, empirically, dependent objects, complexes of the objects science posits. But they are, practically, basic and irreducible, constituted by the norms they make possible. This is the fundamental and ineluctable dualism that still sits at the heart of Sellars's philosophy.

> To think of a featherless biped as a person is to think of it as a being with which one is bound up in a network of rights and duties. From this point of view, the irreducibility of the personal is the irreducibility of the 'ought' to the 'is'. But even more basic than this (though ultimately, as we shall see, the two points coincide), is the fact that to think of a featherless biped as a person is to construe its behaviour in terms of actual or potential membership in an embracing group each member of which thinks of itself as a member of the group. (PSIM: 39)

Ontologically, science tells us what is really real, and thus Sellars has been accused of being an eliminative materialist, for persons will show up in the pictures produced by science as complex objects reducible to patterns or complexes of scientific objects. That is, persons *per se* simply do not show up in the pictures produced by science. But notice that science cannot eliminate or rationally force us to abandon the concept of personhood, for, even if persons do not show up in the pictures science produces, both science itself and the pictures it produces are the products of persons. It is persons who inhabit the logical space of reasons and can use or apply the methods and canons of science to produce a picture of reality. Science is something people do.

I do not see any coherent way for Sellars to deny the reality of persons, but there is reality and there is reality. Persons are *practically real,* and they are practically real because they make themselves such. Practical reality is a matter of the truth of prescriptive and normative claims, and that, in turn, is a matter of recognized, intersubjectively held, intersubjectively applicable, shared intentions. The existentialist turns of phrase Sellars uses at the beginning of "Philosophy and the Scientific Image of Man" to describe the emergence of human (self-)consciousness are not a fluke or joke on his part.[5] Humanity's self-recognition as humanity is the *fons et origo* of humanity. It is in this context that Sellars's reflexivity requirement falls into place as absolutely central to his entire philosophy. This requirement appeared in Chapter 2 as a requirement for mastery of a language, in Chapter 5 as the epistemic reflexivity requirement on epistemic subjects, and in Chapter 7 as a general requirement on fully fledged participants in rule-governed practices.

Is the idea that persons are practically real, although not fundamental ontological realities, just a sorry band-aid, an inadequate bow to the undeniable fact that we exist as thinking things? What are we to make of the claim that we, as persons, are not *really,* that is, *empirically,* real? The discussion of artifacts above is relevant, for although people are not artifacts, the category of persons and their attendant properties, such as having intentional states, bear some analogies with artifacts.

Beliefs and intentions are certainly not artifacts, for they are not generally the product of intentional design and construction. In Sellars's theory of intentionality, however, they are functional states. Intentional-state attributions, in Sellars's view, always presuppose the (linguistic) intentionality of the attributor, for the attributor characterizes the attributee's state by classifying it as of a kind with a linguistic or intentional content available in the attributor's background language. Implicitly, then, every such attribution also presupposes that the subject of the intentional state participates in a complex, intersubjective linguistic community within which the individual states of individual subjects can be assigned roles similar to those available to the attributor in her linguistic community. This is no mere accident, in Sellars's view. One might think that it is just *attributions* of intentional states that presuppose such relational structures, and that this is a quirk of the epistemology of such states; "in themselves" they are quite independent of such functional roles. Sellars holds, in contrast, that this functionality is all there is to their intentionality. Like the artifacts we discussed earlier, intentional states have built into their very concept a background of rule-governed practices and institutions against which they emerge.

Does this mean that attributions of intentional states lack truth-values or that there really is no "fact of the matter" about what people think and desire? Does Sellars's treatment of persons and intentionality demote them to subjective illusions like ghosts or poltergeists? No. It does mean that persons and intentional states are phenomena available only to a certain point of view, the point of view of a self-conscious, rational, logic-using agent who is a member of a community that is, individually and collectively, engaged in pursuing various ends in a world it did not make. The fact that the interpretation of others and their intentional states is rarely, if ever, a clear-cut and determinate matter, and ultimately rests on one's own inarticulate mastery of the shared practices and linguistic system of one's community does not preclude the *objectivity* of claims about the existence of other people or what they are thinking or desiring. Claims about the intentional states of others are subject to objective corroboration, for the claim that S is in a state that functions similarly to the state we would express candidly by saying that *p* is a claim for which there is objective evidence. That there is a great deal of vagueness and indeterminacy in such matters is not incompatible with objectivity.

Part of what Sellars intends to convey by denying persons and intentional states full-blooded ontological reality is that they do not show up in the point-of-viewless *pictures* created by fundamental science. They are perspectival phenomena, and Sellars seems to want to reserve the honorific "really real" for aperspectival phenomena available to the "view from nowhere". Being perspectival, however, is not the same as being subjective. There are perspectival phenomena that are nonetheless objective, because there is intersubjectively available evidence concerning them and rules governing their behaviour.

If one occupies the perspective of a self-conscious, rational, logic-using agent who is a member of a community that is, individually and collectively, engaged in pursuing various ends in a world it did not make, then it is objectively true that there are people around one who believe and desire, people with whom one shares a language and some intentions, with whom one can (and must) negotiate in the course of one's life.

> [T]he conceptual framework of persons is the framework in which we think of one another as sharing the community intentions which provide the ambience of principles and standards (above all, those which make meaningful discourse and rationality itself possible) within which we live our own individual lives. A person can almost be defined as a being that has intentions. Thus the conceptual framework of persons is not something that needs to be *reconciled with* the scientific image, but rather something to be *joined* to it. (PSIM: 40)

## A synoptic vision

Joining the dimension of practical discourse with the language of science will have to result in a very richly articulated language indeed. The dimension of practical discourse is not exhausted by the addition of the "shall" operator to our language, for the language of practical discourse must be practically useful. We shall come to observe the world in scientific terms. Science may offer instruments, even prostheses, to improve and supplement our basic, biologically determined capacities; perhaps we shall even be able to augment those biologically determined capacities by genetic engineering, but at any point there will always be some basic, minimal observational capacities and a corresponding vocabulary, some minimal set of basic actions and a corresponding vocabulary, and those will, to a very large degree, determine the way it makes sense for us to parse the world into the objects we deal with and care about.

For most of the objects we are concerned with, there will be no intelligible definitions in pure scientific language unladen with any reference to norms and practices. The things we deal with on a daily basis we relate to as they fit into our cultural practices and our

Wilfrid Sellars

individual goals. (Does this sound Heideggerean?) I see no reason in Sellars to believe that that would change as we approach the Peircean millenium. We would clearly be better equipped to handle breakdowns in our coarse-grained conceptions and to fill in gaps left indeterminate by the subtly functionalized language of daily life, but I see no reason to believe that we would cease to have a complex language of daily life that would perforce differ significantly from the precision and complexity of scientific language itself.

Also, in order to reach the Peircean framework, we shall have to have had and be conscious of having social interactions that are not only rule-governed, but striving towards an intersubjectively accepted ideal of knowledge. Whether this would also require broad agreement or achievement on other fronts, such as human welfare, is not clear. But would it make sense that, as we approach closer and closer to the Peircean framework, we would also be less and less inclined to see ourselves as agents engaged in rule-governed social practices that we believe will bring us ever closer to our common goals?

In the scientific millenium, are we likely to cease needing or wanting food, clothing, entertainment? Shall we not still need shelter, employment, supportive friendships and love? Shall we not need to cultivate virtue and abjure vice? Shall we not have to act in the face of uncertainty and noisy data, seek guidance in difficult times, and offer succour to the unfortunate? If achieving Peircean science removes such concerns and such concepts from us, then Peircean science will not be achieved by persons. Such concerns require us to have concepts of kinds that will not always coincide with the concepts of natural kinds that advanced science will develop. Enriching the language of science with the dimension of practical discourse will have to include a normatively grounded scheme of classification in order to be practical, or we must assume that science itself offers the most practical and efficient scheme of classification, even for such tasks as deciding how to design one's domicile, how to win the heart of a loved one, or what is the best way to spend a hot day in August. Much of the texture of the manifest image, I believe, will have to remain or be duplicated in the framework of the Peircean millenium, for as vastly as the human condition will have changed, it will still be the human condition.

We have survived despite widespread ignorance of the empirical reality of things, because the practical reality of things is sufficient to keep us alive and our societies relatively functional. As we gain ever better knowledge, through science, of the empirical reality of things, the practical reality of things will never become irrelevant. Sellars hopes that we would continually adjust the practical reality within which we live and have our being to the empirical reality of things as we gain more and more knowledge. But we could never abandon practical reality without, in fact, abandoning reality altogether.

As practice is adjusted to the scientific image, what will be abandoned is the residue of magical or mythological thinking that persists in the manifest image. Magical thinking is a belief in empirically ungrounded forms of causal influence, for example, the belief that names have a particular kind of power over what is named. In Sellars's view, even the causal powers of our mental states must ultimately be given an empirical grounding, although such objects will not be *defined* in those strictly empirical terms. There is still much magical thinking in the untutored common imagination. In a Peircean world, we shall not only have dispensed with the obviously superstitious beliefs in astrology or numerology, but God would be realized to be our creation and not our creator; supposedly transcendent values delivered by revelation and held without regard for their human consequences would be revealed as mystification and false consciousness. For instance, we shall not expect biology alone nor transcendent revelation to determine the boundaries of our moral community. The abortion debate would be transformed into a search for the practices and principles that maximally respect the general nature of personhood and the particulars of human welfare. Dogmatic insistence that human values or goals require certain public policies without regard for empirical evidence connecting those policies with the achievement of those goals would be revealed as mere demagoguery. We would have to face squarely our relative triviality in an overwhelming universe without transcendent meaning or purpose.

Yet spirituality and the sense of transcendent value need not die or be rejected. For Sellars writes that the "only frame of mind which is the living source of moral commitment is what Josiah Royce called Loyalty, and what Christians call Love (Charity). *This is a commitment deeper than any commitment to abstract principle*" (OMP: 18). This commitment to the well-being of our fellows, *agape*, takes us outside the all too narrow confines of our daily concerns and opens more than adequate room for spirituality, although of a distinctly humanistic form.

Sellars has been criticized (for example, by McDowell) for scientism: an uncritical faith in science as itself the final answer. This criticism is unjustified, if the accommodation of practical discourse in the language of the Peircean scientific framework takes the form argued for here. If the language of science cannot afford us a practically useful reconstruction of the concept of a person – and I do not see how, alone, it can – then the Peircean framework will have to preserve the logic of personhood as it has evolved in the manifest image. To do otherwise would be to undercut the very rationale that led us to the threshold of the Peircean millenium. This seems to me a much stronger argument for the preservation of these manifest-image concepts, in fact, than Sellars gave us for the preservation of the logic of the proper sensibles by the postulation of sensa. Sellars's scientific realism is not a repudiation of morality or of the primacy of human values. Values are real in the only way appropriate to them; they are *practically real*. To ask for more is to begin to creep back into the magic forms of thought that humanity has struggled for so long to escape.

# Notes

## Chapter 1. Sellars's philosophical enterprise

1. H. Feigl and W. Sellars (eds), *Readings in Philosophical Analysis* (New York: Appleton-Century-Crofts, 1949) and W. Sellars and J. Hospers (eds), *Readings in Ethical Theory* (New York: Appleton-Century-Crofts, 1952).

2. Consider the opening lines of *Science and Metaphysics*: "The history of philosophy is the *lingua franca* which makes communication between philosophers, at least of different points of view, possible. Philosophy without the history of philosophy, if not empty or blind, is at least dumb" (SM: 1).

3. "Physical Realism" (1955) and "The Double-Knowledge Approach to the Mindy–Body Problem" (1971). Sellars remarks in "Autobiographical Reflections" (1975) that in his late teens he began a philosophical dialogue with his father that lasted the rest of his life (AR: 280).

4. For an overview of Oxford Realism, see Mathieu Marion, "Oxford Realism: Knowledge and Perception I", *British Journal for the History of Philosophy* 8(2) (2000), 299–328 and "Oxford Realism: Knowledge and Perception II", *British Journal for the History of Philosophy* 8(3) (2000), 485–519.

5. Sellars provides for what he calls the "original image", which is primitive in the sense that it takes the central category of the manifest image – personhood – and applies it universally, seeing *everything*, for example, trees, rivers and mountains as well as men and women, as ways of being a person. Under the pressure of experience and reflection, and by gradual stages, we have ceased to apply to "mere" things the predicate-families and explanatory strategies paradigmatic of persons, and developed other predicate-families and explanatory strategies.

6. Famously, in "Empiricism and the Philosophy of Mind" (1956) Sellars treats psychological states as if they are very like theoretical entities postulated to help us explain human behaviour. The mythical community of Ryleans Sellars posits in "Empiricism and the Philosophy of Mind", note, would not count as a community of *persons* yet, precisely because it is a community the members of which have not yet come to be aware of themselves as humans-in-the-world. The acquisition of psychological concepts is itself a necessary episode in that story. One might conclude that the manifest image, which surely includes concepts of psychological states at its very core, can itself be seen as a step along the road to a fully scientific image made possible only by the move definitive of the scientific image.

7. There is some tension between the historical myths of "Empiricism and the Philosophy of Mind" and "Philosophy and the Scientific Image of Man" (1962). The Ryleans in "Empiricism and the Philosophy of Mind" are supposed to have a usable and recognizable (to us) conceptual framework for dealing with public physical objects and events to which they add, in order to account for the behavioural peculiarities of some objects (i.e. persons), concepts of inner, subjective, psychological states. But in the picture Sellars draws in "Philosophy and the Scientific Image of Man" (published six years after "Empiricism and the Philosophy of Mind"), the "original image" with which persons apparently begin their history is one in which *everything* is treated as a person, and the notion of a mere physical object or event has yet to be developed. But the thing to remember is that these are both *myths* that play expository roles for Sellars. For a fascinating treatment of the role of myth in "Empiricism and the Philosophy of Mind", see Rebecca Kukla, "Myth, Memory and Misrecognition in Sellars' 'Empiricism and the Philosophy of Mind'", *Philosophical Studies* **101** (2000), 161–211.

8. For instance:

one can certainly admit that the tie between 'red' and red physical objects – which tie makes it possible for 'red' to mean the quality red – is causally mediated by sensations of red without being committed to the mistaken idea that it is 'really' sensations of red, rather than red physical objects, which are the primary denotation of the word 'red'.
(EPM: §29, in SPR: 161; in KMG: 240)

or

and if, as is often done, 'red' as predicable of physical objects is tacitly shifted from the category of *primitive* descriptive predicates (where it properly belongs) to the category of *defined* descriptive predicates by being given the sense of 'power to cause normal observers to have impressions of red', then the very stuffing has been knocked out of the framework of physical objects, leaving not enough to permit the formulation of the very laws which are implied by the existence of these powers, and which are presupposed by the micro-theory which might be invoked to explain them.
(PHM in SPR: 98)

Or most explicitly:

Thus, consider, to use a favorite example of mine, a pink ice cube. Many are tempted to *identify* its pinkness with a causal property, the property of causing normal observers in standard conditions to have sensations pink, indeed, of a pink cube. Now there may be a place for some such move when the scientific revolution is taken into account. But it is a *revisionary* proposal, and it is, in my opinion, a sheer mistake to think of it a correct analysis of the common-sense notions of color which function in 'basic' perceptual experiences.
(SK I §25: 302)

9. Rudolph Carnap, *The Logical Syntax of Language*, A. Smeaton, Countess von Zeppelin (trans.) (London: Routledge & Kegan Paul, 1937), 277–333. Carnap distinguished between an object language, the terms of which refer to items in the world, and its metalanguage, the terms of which refer to items in the object language. For formal languages, this distinction can be quite striking: for instance, logicians usually use either set-theory or some natural language like English as the metalanguage when discussing the language of propositional logic. But in natural languages, the distinction is not at all clearly marked: we can use English to talk about English. Carnap believed that many of the assertions made by metaphysicians can be made sense of as what he

called "material mode" formulations of formal, that is, syntactical assertions that really belong to the metalanguage. Such material mode sentences appear to be about items in the world by using a vocabulary that masks the fact that they are (really) in the metalanguage and are about the object language, not things in the world. Here are some examples from Part V of Carnap's *The Logical Syntax of Language:*

| *Material mode sentence* | *Formal mode sentence* |
|---|---|
| The moon is a *thing*; five is not a thing, but a *number*. | 'Moon' is a thing-word; 'five' is not a thing-word, but a number-word. |
| A *thing* is a complex of sense-data. | Every sentence in which a thing-designation occurs is equipollent to a class of sentences in which no thing-designations but sense-data designations occur. |
| *Time* is continuous. | The real-number expressions are used as time-coordinates. |

## Chapter 2. Sellars's philosophy of language

1. Richard Rorty, *The Linguistic Turn* (Chicago, IL: University of Chicago Press, 1967).
2. See the opening sections of both "Pure Pragmatics and Epistemology" (1947) and "Epistemology and the New Way of Words" (1947) and Section IV of "Realism and the New Way of Words" (1948).
3. This is a way of pointing to the performance–competence distinction familiar from Chomsky.
4. See PPE: 182.
5. Charles W. Morris "Foundations of the Theory of Signs", in *International Encyclopedia of Unified Science*, vol. 1(2), O. Neurath (ed.), (Chicago, IL: University of Chicago Press, 1938), reprinted (Chicago, IL: University of Chicago Press, 1970–71).
6. It is not essential to languages as such that they be about the world in which they are used. We can easily invent and use a language adequate to describe some extremely simple hypothetical world: say, a world that contains only two qualitatively identical spheres rotating around each other. But it is not a language that is (or could be) used in that world, for in the world it is about there is nothing that can use a language at all. This language is used in *our* world, while being about the hypothetical two-sphere world.
7. Is this because Davidson and Dummett inherited Quine's distrust of meanings and therefore meaning statements? Sellars's analysis of meaning claims is intended to show, *inter alia*, that there is no reason to consider them intrinsically suspect.
8. See Janet Dean Fodor, *Semantics: Theories of Meaning in Generative Grammar* (Cambridge, MA: Harvard University Press, 1980) and F. R. Palmer, *Semantics*, 2nd edn (Cambridge: Cambridge University Press, 1981).
9. See MFC: 430.
10. Sentences containing distributive singular terms are not syntactically distinguished from sentences containing regular singular terms. There are contexts in which the sentences I offer as examples containing distributive singular terms are properly interpreted as containing regular singular terms. So contextual or pragmatic factors must be involved in determining whether a singular term is to be read distributively or not. While Sellars

avails himself of distributive singular terms, he does not offer any detailed analysis of them, nor am I aware of any other detailed analysis of such usage. See his discussion of them (AE in PP: 232–4). Sellars mentions C. H. Langford, "The Institutional Use of *The*", *Philosophy and Phenomenological Research* **10**(1) (September 1949), 115–20, although he claims to have developed his views about distributive singular terms independently of Langford's paper. But see also John Wisdom's discussion in "Logical Constructions (I)", *Mind* **40** (April 1931), 189–93.

11. There is an important underlying point: knowing the meaning of an expression is ultimately, in Sellars's view, a form of know-how. Knowing that '*rot*' and 'red' play the same roles in German and English, respectively, does not entail knowing what that role is and therefore how to use these terms appropriately within the relevant linguistic communities.

12. Notoriously, Quine was so worried about being committed to meanings as entities that he rejected the very idea of a theory of meaning. Davidson is also worried about meanings as entities, but attempts to save us from commitment to such things by requiring that a theory of meaning for a language always be formulable in an extensional metalanguage. Given that simple predication itself does not commit us to predicative entities, Sellars's interpretation of meaning claims avoids any commitment to meanings as entities, and puts no artificial requirement of extensionality on the metalanguage. Sellars's arguments that predication does not commit us to predicative entities will be examined in Chapter 4.

13. This triad appears throughout Sellars's essays (e.g. LRB: 310; SRLG in SPR: 327–31; SM IV §61: 114; MFC: 423–4; NAO: 67, 69). Sellars nowhere claims it is exhaustive.

14. To my knowledge, in his discussions of these "moves" or "transitions", Sellars never directly addresses how they apply to intersubjective linguistic interaction. Suppose a teacher begins her class by saying, "Name the first transfinite cardinal" and Johnny responds "$\aleph_0$". Is the teacher's initial question a language-entry transition? It is not a perceptual and/or introspective response to the world, but an extension of the conversation of the previous class. Are both of these utterances language-entry transitions, because each person enters the language game independently, or has the teacher's question essentially put them both (or the whole class) into the language game?

15. "Not all roles are conceptual roles, i.e. roles that contribute to the conceptual character of a linguistic expression. Thus, 'Hélas!' and 'Ach weh!' play much the same role in French and German, respectively, as 'alas!' in English, but we should scarcely say that 'Ach weh!' expresses a concept. It seems to me that the distinguishing feature of conceptual roles is their relation to inference" (TC: 203).

16. Merely having some intrasystemic moves does not automatically raise a representational system to the level of a language. A sophisticated thermostat may represent not just the actual and the intended temperatures of the room, but also the time of day and day of the week, so that the representation of the intended temperature depends on the representations of the time of day and day of the week. We might even say that there is a programming language for the thermostat, but that is a metaphorical use of 'language'.

17. Robert Brandom, *Making it Explicit: Reasoning, Representing, and Discursive Commitment* (Cambridge, MA: Harvard University Press, 1994). See especially pages 97–107 on this topic.

18. Of course, '__ is true' requires a propositional subject. For non-propositional subjects there is the closely related expression 'is true of', for example, "Triangularity is true of the gable window".

19. "I conclude that Wittgenstein was right in claiming that *reference* is not a matter-of-factual relation, although the fact that a term refers entails that it stands in certain matter-of-factual relations. That it stands, at least contingently, in such and such matter-of-factual relations to objects in the world is known by knowing its *reference*. Those in which it *necessarily* stands can only be determined by tracing out the implications of its *sense*, that is, what it stands for" (TTC: §41, in KTM: 335).

20. The lone quotation mark at the end of (2) was probably supposed to be mated with a (missing) quotation mark before 'describe', preserving parallelism with the form of (3) and (4).

    Sellars calls this "an attempt to give an informal or intuitive account of how referring expressions function in first-level matter-of-factual discourse". He further notes that condition "(2), by speaking of propositions as 'describing the spatio-temporal location of objects with respect to each other', is of a piece with explaining the job of '*a*' to be that of referring to *a*. 'Describe', like 'refer', does not stand for a specific linguistic job, but rather a job classification. Thus the job in question must ultimately be put in terms of uniformities pertaining to the use of spatio-temporal predicates. Similar considerations apply to (3) and (4)" (SM V §31: 126).

21. Let us apply Sellars's explanation of language–world relations to expressions such as 'Pegasus' or 'hobbit'. These expressions belong to the 'natural' order, in the sense that there are manifold tokens of them that actually occur in discourse. But, notably, these terms do not occur in observation reports, nor in the assertions of empirically grounded, first-order theories about the world. Instead, the language-entry transitions that involve 'Pegasus' or 'hobbit' will tend to be *metalinguistic*, in the sense that they are responses to other occurrences of 'Pegasus' or 'hobbit' in something written or spoken. Indeed, occurrences of 'Pegasus' or 'hobbit' in purported observation reports will be generally ruled inappropriate or erroneous, because these terms are marked as *without* spatiotemporal import, because they occur in contexts that abstract from the strict, unitary spatiotemporal framework of empirical reality, that is, mythological or fictional contexts (cf. LRB: 302–3).

22. This is certainly not the right way to phrase such a rule. We certainly do not have an *obligation* to call Venice 'Venice'. The further refinements necessary are indifferent to the purposes at hand.

23. These first two are the alternatives Sellars attempts to steer between in one of his early articles, "Language, Rules and Behavior" (1949).

24. See EPM: §34, in SPR: 167; in KMG: 246.

25. See, for instance, LRB: 290, 301; SRLG in SPR: 323–4. Sellars clearly rejects this alternative, calling it a "sham" solution to the problem at hand (SRLG in SPR: 324).

26. See, for instance, SM: 76, 157, 175; LTC: 95–7.

27. Sellars offers only the schematic "(Other things being equal) one ought to say such and such, if in *C*" (LTC: 97). Fairly clear examples might be instructions on the proper forms of address in the face of various personages. But, of course, virtually any linguistic rule can be cast in the form of an ought-to-do. "In a declarative sentence, always put the verb in second position" is a valid rule of German, and many non-native German speakers obey the rule as a rule of action. But native German speakers (and the well-practised non-

native speakers) do not *obey* the rule in the sense used above, although they *observe* or *conform* to the rule in their speech patterns.

28. LTC: 96.

29. The basic idea of Tarski's theory is that there is a fundamental *satisfaction* relation that holds between expressions and things. The truth property for a language can be inductively defined for all sentences of the language on the basis of the satisfaction relation. Such a definition would validate all sentences of the form "'*p*' is true ≡ *p*": the so-called "T-sentences".

30. This does not entail that there is no later, improved version of the language at time $t_{n+m}$, according to which the sentence that satisfies all the rules at $t_n$ no longer does so and is no longer considered ideal.

31. It is a pity, but we just don't have time for the details here. See SM V §§65–78: 139–43.

32. C. S. Peirce, *Collected Papers*, 8 vols, C. Hartshorne & P. Weiss (eds) (Cambridge, MA: Belknap Press, 1960), 5.407.

33. Rosenberg makes two criticisms of it in *One World and Our Knowledge of It* (Dordrecht: D. Reidel, 1980). The first is that Sellars appears to make picturing a criterion of correctness for conceptual schemes, and it cannot play that role. The second is that Sellars could not make good sense of a picturing relation between the elements of a theoretical representational system and what they represent. In his latest work, Rosenberg revisits the question and now maintains that there is a viable interpretation of Sellars's text on which his position on picturing is not subject to these criticisms (see "Sellarsian Picturing", unpublished). I think the interpretation given by Rosenberg in this paper is consonant with the interpretation I give here, although his is worked out in much greater detail.

34. I have in mind here people such as Ruth Millikan (a Sellars student) (*Language, Thought, and Other Biological Categories* (Cambridge, MA: MIT Press, 1984); *White Queen Psychology and Other Essays for Alice* (Cambridge, MA: MIT Press, 1993)), David Papineau and Fred Dretske.

35. It would be fascinating to investigate in detail the relations between Sellars's conceptions of picturing and maps and the theories of content and cognition of the teleosemanticists or those using information theory as their base.

36. "76. Nor need ideal matter-of-factual truth be conceived of as one complete picture existing in simultaneous splendour. The Peirceish method of projection must enable picturings (by observation and inference) of *any* part, but this does not require a single picturing of *all* parts" (SM V §72: 142). In the next paragraph, Sellars disavows as well the idea that speakers of Peirceish must be able to picture arbitrary pieces of distant times. A theory's ability to construct a detailed picture will depend on the evidence available.

## Chapter 3. Categories, the *a priori*, and transcendental philosophy

1. *Metaphysics* VII 1028a10.

2. *Phaedrus* 266b.

3. See TTC in KTM: 323.

4. For instance, there is nothing in Kant's list of categories that reflects the "logical form" of propositional attitude statements. Teleological judgements also appear to have a logical form that cannot be squeezed into the Procrustean bed of Kant's categories. Hegel explicitly recognizes such categories and many (too many?) more.

5. Here is a possible example. For most of our history the "logic" of particle-talk

and the "logic" of wave-talk seemed mutually incompatible. An object could be a particle or a wave, but not both. Moreover, this seemed an *a priori* matter, precisely because the logics of the different kinds differed so markedly. But quantum theory seems to demand that we abandon this *a priori* prejudice. *Particle* and *wave* may not be fully categorial in stature, absolutely highest kinds (although they seem relatively basic object-kinds), but it does not seem beyond the scope of imagination that other developments in science could occasion even more radical revisions in the way we speak.

6. "Is There a Synthetic *A Priori?*" (1956). Quine's essay is "Two Dogmas of Empiricism", *The Philosophical Review* **60**(1) (January 1951): 20–43, reprinted in *From a Logical Point of View: 9 Logico-Philosophical Essays*, 20–46 (Cambridge, MA: Harvard University Press, 1953).

7. That is, truth in virtue of the meanings of the terms involved.

8. Donald Davidson, "On the Very Idea of a Conceptual Scheme", *Proceedings and Addresses of the American Philosophical Association* **47** (1974), 5–20, reprinted in *Inquiries into Truth and Interpretation*, 183–98 (Oxford: Oxford University Press, 1984).

9. From an interview with Davidson published in *The Dualist* **7** (2000): 60.

## Chapter 4. Sellars's nominalism

1. Sellars is certainly not committed to reconstructing *everything* the most rabid Platonist asserts in such a way as to render it true. Platonists, in Sellars's view, have a fine appreciation of the structure of our linguistic-conceptual framework – but there is no reason to think that they are always right about it.

2. Both Sellars's intent and his method can be glimpsed in this footnote from the relatively early "Aristotelian Philosophies of Mind" (1949): "The solution of the problems of universals consists exactly in showing that the following statements are all true: (1) Universals exist. (2) Thoughts mean universals. (3) It is nonsense to speak of any psychological relationship between thought and universals. The solution involves *first* a making explicit of the ambiguities of the term 'existence,' and *second* a distinction between 'meaning' as a term belonging to the framework of logical analysis and criticism, and 'meaning' as a descriptive term in empirical psychology relating to habits of response to and manipulation of linguistic symbols. The classical conception of mind as apprehending universals and meanings is based on a confusion of the logical with the psychological frame of reference. To deny that universals 'exist' *when speaking in the framework of logical analysis* (logical nominalism) is as mistaken as to assert that universals 'exist' *when speaking in the framework of the psychological description of thought* (ontological realism or Platonism)" (APM: n.11).

3. W. V. O. Quine, "On What There Is", *Review of Metaphysics* **2**(5) (September 1948), 21–38, reprinted in *From a Logical Point of View: 9 Logico-Philosophical Essays*, 1–19 (Cambridge, MA: Harvard University Press, 1953), 15.

4. Sellars's first comprehensive statement of his approach to the proper understanding of the place of quantification in ontology was in "Grammar and Existence: A Preface to Ontology" (1960) but it left little mark on the field. He returned to this issue at greater length in *Naturalism and Ontology* (1980). The only real change in his position between the two is the addition in NAO of the first argument I canvass below, that is, that the Quinean standard for ontological commitment is ultimately incompatible with a robust naturalism.

5. The reference in a *universally* quantified sentence *seems to be*, however,

determinate. Such sentences refer to everything, so there is no difficulty saying *which* things are being referred to. But the universal and the existential quantifier are interdefinable: $(\exists x)Fx \equiv \sim(\forall x)\sim Fx$. Is the reference of the existential quantifier therefore really determinate? Or is the apparently determinate reference of the universal quantifier not, in fact, so clearly determinate after all? Perhaps there is a distinction between the determinate and the sweepingly inclusive, just as there is a difference between a knife and an atomic bomb, although both can kill determinate people.

6. In his discussion of these issues, Sellars falls back into a use of 'reference' that treats it as the basic word–world relation. As seen in Chapter 2, this is not his own construal of reference, which he treats as a form of metalinguistic functional classification. I take it that this discrepancy is neither a matter of change nor of confusion on his part, but rather a function of a desire to engage with the dialectic as it then stood in the discipline. I concede to this in my exposition a bit reluctantly, because otherwise trying to negotiate the differences in terminology itself becomes a significant complication unsuited to this survey of his views.

7. Notice that we never finally dispense with the quantifier: we explicate the semantic value of the object-language quantifier by using a quantifier in the metalanguage as well. So there is never any question of a reductive definition of the quantifiers. This is also the case in a Tarski-style treatment of the existential quantifier.

8. The adequacy of a substitutional interpretation of the quantifier is difficult and controversial. Sellars never defends the substitutional interpretation at length or in depth. Significant progress towards a Sellarsian treatment of substitutional quantification has been made by Mark Lance in "Quantification, Substitution, and Conceptual Content", *Noûs* **30**(4) (1996), 481–507.

9. From Sellars's footnote in "Grammar and Existence" dealing with this possibility:

> it would be a serious mistake to suppose that all common nouns pertaining to physical objects are built from adjectives and the category word 'thing' in accordance with the formula
>
> (17)   S is an N $=_{Df}$ (S is a thing) and S is $A_1 \ldots A_n$
>
> (Where 'N' is a common noun and the 'A$_1$'s adjectives). To suppose that 'thing' is the sole *primitive* common name is (a) to overlook the fact that the category word 'thing' has a use only because there are statements of the form 'S is an N'; (b) to expose onself to all the classical puzzles about *substrata*. (This point is elaborated in my "Substance and Form in Aristotle: an Exploration" in *The Journal of Philosophy*, **54** (1957), 688–99)
>
> (GE in SPR: 253–4)

10. The variables of quantification are a lot like pronouns, and using pronouns in such constructions seems to finesse the problem:

> There is a man such that he is tall
> There is an otter such that it is swimming.

But it really only postpones it. For pronouns inherit their grammatical type from their antecedents.

11. P. T. Geach and the position he sketches in "On What There Is", *Proceedings of the Aristotelian Society*, supplementary volume **25** (1951), 125–36, is the principal target in "Grammar and Existence" (1960). In *Naturalism and Ontology* (1980) Sellars adds Dummett as a target as well, although without referring to any particular work(s) by Dummett.

12. The diagram reproduced as Figure 1 appears in TTP.

13. Not that this move has not been elaborated with sophistication and subtlety. Sellars singles out Gustav Bergmann as particularly skilful in this regard.

14. Sellars names it after the Jumblies, mentioned in an eponymous poem by Edward Lear. The last four lines of each stanza are
    Far and few, far and few,
    Are the lands where the Jumblies live;
    Their heads are green, and their hands are blue,
    And they went to sea in a sieve.

15. For a more complete schema for translating between Jumblese and standard predicate calculus notation, see NS in SPR: 233–5.

16. Notice, it determines not the relation in which $a$ and $b$ stand, but the relation in which 'a' and 'b' stand.

17. See NAO III §6: 42 and III §69: 60.

18. Quine has pointed out that names can also be dispensed with. We can exchange, for example, 'Pegasus' for 'the pegasizer'. Sellars would clearly complain that Quine's move, which makes quantification the sole mechanism of reference, falls to the first argument I rehearsed against the quantification criterion of ontological commitment. It makes the indeterminate reference of the quantifier more primitive than any form of determinate reference, and this seems incompatible with a respectable naturalism.

19. See TTP: 320. The relation Sellars labels 'LR' ("linguistic representative"), I interpret as being, in fact, the picturing relation he mentions in other works.

20. "Classes as Abstract Entities and the Russell Paradox" (1963). This is a companion piece to "Abstract Entities" (1963), which was his first systematic statement and defence of his nominalism.

21. There is a careful, indeed, painstaking attempt to outline a Sellarsian theory of mathematics. See Jeffrey Sicha, *A Metaphysics of Elementary Mathematics* (Amherst, MA: University of Massachusetts Press, 1974).

22. I have adapted the Pears-McGuiness translation here for greater fidelity to the original German, which reads "Mein Grundgedanke ist, daß die 'logischen Konstanten' nicht vertreten."

23. Robert Brandom's work on the expressive function of logical terms is inspired by Sellars and works it out in great detail many of its implications. See Brandom, *Making it Explicit*.

24. Needless to say, there are many, many details to Sellars's account of 'ought' that are being glossed over wholesale here. This will be made good in Chapter 9.

## Chapter 5. Knowledge and the given

1. Certainly Sellars's first successful piece of writing, "Realism and the New Way of Words" (1948), is one such piece. So are "Language, Rules and Behaviour" (1949) and "Being and Being Known" (1960), to name others.

2. Firth's original is "Coherence, Certainty, and Epistemic Priority", *The Journal of Philosophy* **66** (October 1964), 545–57. Sellars's responses to it are: (i) the Appendix to "Lecture I: Perception" in "The Structure of Knowledge" (SK: 313–16); (ii) "Givenness and Explanatory Coherence" (1973); (iii) "More on Givenness and Explanatory Coherence" (1979); (iv) "The Lever of Archimedes" in "Foundations for a Metaphysics of Pure Process" (1981) (FMPP I: 3–36). Each new response is longer and more complex than the preceding one.
    Another valuable source is *The Metaphysics of Epistemology* (1989). This book is edited by Pedro Amaral, based on Sellars's course on the theory of

knowledge at the University of Pittsburgh in the mid-1970s. This book is far less dense than Sellars's official professional lectures. It probably cannot be cited in matters of detail as an authoritative source, but it is well worth reading and gives the reader insight into Sellars's thought processes.

3. See Sellars's comments at the beginning of the Carus Lectures:

> 3. In lectures given some twenty years ago, I explored various forms taken by what I called the "myth" of the given. As the years have passed I have had, of course, second and third thoughts on this matter. The views I expressed are so central to my way of thinking that if they were to fall apart the result would be a shambles. Fortunately for my peace of mind – if nothing else – these afterthoughts invariably turned out to be variations on the original theme.
>
> 4. Yet I have become increasingly aware that as first presented the argument was not without flaws. Relevant distinctions were either not drawn at all, or drawn poorly. Some formulations were at the very least misleading, and, in general, the scope of the concept of the given was ill-defined. (FMPP I §§3–4: 3)

Unfortunately, Sellars makes no effort in these lectures to make either explicit or precise what he considered to be the "flaws" in his earlier presentations.

4. Sellars usually begins a treatment of epistemology by thinking through issues of perception: "Empiricism and the Philosophy of Mind" opens with a critique of sense-datum theories, *Science and Metaphysics* with a discussion of Kant's conception of intuition, "The Structure of Knowledge" with a lecture on perception, and "Foundations for a Metaphysics of Pure Process" with (yet another) response to Firth's defence of the given in perception. The metaphysics of perception is then thoroughly intertwined with the epistemics of perception throughout Sellars's discussions. I want to leave extensive discussion of the metaphysics of perception until later, so that it will stand out more clearly in contrast to his metaphysics of the mental. I have to beg the reader's indulgence: I shall occasionally simply postpone important questions until Chapter 8.

5. Sellars's epistemology has often been mischaracterized in the literature. For a review of some of the common errors, see the Introduction, to W. deVries and T. Triplett, *Knowledge, Mind, and the Given: Reading Wilfrid Sellars's "Empiricism and the Philosophy of Mind"* (Indianapolis, IN: Hackett, 2000), xxi–xxxii.

6. See ME: 165–228.

7. This is an oversimplification. Some foundationalists hold that what is epistemically basic is subpropositional, perhaps even subconceptual. Nonetheless, if it is to play the role of *basic* knowledge, it must be able to transmit justification to propositions or propositional states.

8. This is also, and for similar reasons, an oversimplification. Classical coherentists also did not always think of the relations that constituted coherence as relations among *propositions* or *judgements*. As long as an Aristotelian logic of terms or the new way of ideas was dominant, in fact, the primary tendency was to think of these relations as obtaining between concepts or ideas.

9. Many coherentists have made the difficulty of finding certainty or a broad enough base of certainty the keystone to their criticism of foundationalism. Some reference works wrongly attribute such an argument to Sellars (e.g. A. H. Goldman's article on the given, "The Given", in *A Companion to Epistemol-*

*ogy,* J. Dancy and E. Sosa (eds), 159–61 (Oxford: Blackwell, 1992)). In fact, I know of no passage in Sellars where he makes such an argument. Sellars was a thoroughgoing fallibilist, but there is simply no indication that he believed that fallibilism itself threatens foundationalism.

10. For further discussion of this characterization of the given, see KMG: xvi ff. Sellars recognizes the wide variation among candidates for the given: "Many things have been said to be 'given': sense contents, material objects, universals, propositions, real connections, first principles, even givenness itself" (EPM: §1, in SPR: 127; in KMG: 205). Sellars's own characterizations of the "myth of the given" include: EPM: §26, in SPR: 157 (in KMG: 236); EPM: §30, in SPR: 161–2 (in KMG: 240–41); EPM: §32, in SPR: 164 (in KMG: 243–4); EPM: §43, in SPR: 174 (in KMG: 254); FMPP I §§44–5: 11–12.

11. For more detailed analysis of Sellars's examination in "Empiricism and the Philosophy of Mind" of various forms of the given, see deVries and Triplett, *Knowledge, Mind, and the Given.*

12. Russell used this notion often. See "On Denoting", *Mind* 14 (1905): 479–93. See also "Knowledge by Acquaintance and Knowledge by Description", *Proceedings of the Aristotelian Society* 11 (1910): 108–28 and *The Problems of Philosophy*, (London: Williams and Norgate, 1912).

13. See EPM: §§3–4, in SPR: 128–30; in KMG: 206–8.

14. Propositional knowledge itself depends (causally) on the know-how we manifest in making material inferences. Know-how itself cannot be reduced to propositional knowledge for Sellars; indeed, it is presupposed (in the form of our inferential capacities) by all *knowledge that.* (This is the pragmatist strain in Sellars.)

15. For an example, look at Carnap's treatment in the *Aufbau.*

16. "What the phenomenalist obviously wants are generalizations which will serve the same purpose as the familiar principles about what people generally experience in various kinds of circumstances, but which will not lead to circularity or vicious regress when put to phenomenalistic use ... The best he can *get,* however, are essentially autobiographical uniformities in which the antecedents, however complex, are the actual sense content counterparts of the presence to *this* perceiver of *these individual things* ... Once it is granted that the framework of physical things is not reducible to that of actual and conditional sense contents, and, in effect, this is the burden of our argument to date, we see that the very selection of the complex patterns of actual sense contents in our past experiences which are to serve as the antecedents of the generalizations in question presuppose our common sense knowledge of ourselves as perceivers, of the specific physical environment in which we do our perceiving and of the general principles which correlate the occurrence of sensations with bodily and environmental conditions ... Thus, the very principles in terms of which the uniformities are selected carry with them the knowledge that these uniformities are *dependent* uniformities *which will continue only as long as these particular objects constitute one's environment,* and hence preclude the credibility of the generalization in sense content terms which abstract consideration might lead us to think of as instantially confirmed by the past uniformities" (PHM in SPR: 83–4).
One can think of this argument as parallel in many ways to Chisholm's argument that the language of intentionality cannot be reconstructed out of (or reduced to) purely behaviouristic language.

17. The claim is not that knowledge of *every* fact of the form "*X* seems *F* to *S*" is in principle independent of knowledge about how things *are.* For instance,

knowledge of the fact that the thing in the box appears to me to be a miniature nuclear resonance spectrometer surely presupposes a good deal of knowledge about non-appearances.

18. A similar analysis is offered by Anthony Quinton roughly simultaneously in "The Problem of Perception", *Mind* **64** (1955): 28–51. Quinton uses his analysis to argue for a realistic construal of perception talk, as does Sellars, but does not make the further move to criticize foundationalism.

19. (EL) is the least risky assertion, but that does not make it the *best* report of one's situation, for not only do we want to avoid error, but we want as much of the truth as we can get.

20. Of course, we do not use the idioms of looking and appearing only in observational contexts. But even in other contexts, for example, "It looks as if Congress will reauthorize the education act" or "John appears to have positioned himself well for the promotion", the idioms function to express one's level of confidence.

21. For a discussion and defence of this notion of an experience "containing" a propositional claim, see John McDowell, "Having the World in View: Sellars, Kant, and Intentionality", *Journal of Philosophy* **95**: 431–91, esp. Lecture I, Part III: 437–41.

22. Daniel Bonevac, "Sellars vs. the Given", *Philosophy and Phenomenological Research* **64**(1) (January 2002): 1–30, esp. 6.

23. *Ibid.*, 7.

24. *Ibid.*, 4–5. Bonevac does not make clear what he takes to be the relationship between logical and epistemic priority, particularly where the logical priority is founded in something as basic as compositionality. If the meaning of 'looks red' "is a function of the meanings of 'looks' and 'red'", and "All one needs to establish that *being* is logically prior to *looking* is an appeal to compositionality" (*ibid.*), then why is the following line of thought unsound? In order to understand 'looks red', one must understand 'looks' and 'red', and understanding 'red' is understanding *being red*. But understanding *being red* entails being able knowledgeably to apply the concept *red* in appropriate circumstances. Being able knowledgeably to apply the concept *red* in appropriate circumstances includes instances of knowing that something is red. So, in fact, *being red* is epistemically prior to *looking red*. The appearance theorist could escape this argument if she holds that 'red' applies primarily to experiences, and not to physical objects. But then we encounter all those difficulties with the intersubjectivity of language and concepts that were so dismaying in the mid-twentieth century.

25. Sellars has in mind Roderick Chisholm's position in the first edition of his *Theory of Knowledge* (Englewood Cliffs, NJ: Prentice-Hall, 1966). That explains why this argument does not make an appearance in "Empiricism and the Philosophy of Mind".

26. Firth, "Coherence, Certainty, and Epistemic Priority", 547.

27. He takes Firth to task for this in "The Structure of Knowledge": "Firth is clearly confusing the proper sense of 'looks', in which it contrasts with 'is seen to be', with the contrived sense ... in which 'looks red' contrasts with 'is red' and means something like 'causes a red item in my visual experience'" (SK I Appendix §6: 315).

28. Firth, "Coherence, Certainty, and Epistemic Priority", 547.

29. *Ibid.* Firth's full claim here is that "In fact, at this stage the child says 'red' just in those circumstances in which we, as adults, could truthfully say "looks red to me now," so that it would not be unreasonable to assert that the child is

using 'red' to express a primitive form of the concept "looks red" (*ibid.*). In "The Structure of Knowledge" Sellars rebuts this by constructing a parallel argument: "in fact, at this stage the child says 'red' just in those circumstances in which we, as adults, could truthfully say 'electromagnetic waves of wave length λ are striking his retina', so that it would not be unreasonable to assert that the child is using 'red' to express a primitive form of the concept 'electromagnetic waves of wave length λ striking a retina'" (SK I Appendix §8: 316).

30. Firth, "Coherence, Certainty, and Epistemic Priority", 548.
31. For instance, William Lycan, *Consciousness* (Cambridge, MA: MIT Press, 1987), Ch. 8.
32. I have followed the text of "Scientific Realism or Irenic Instrumentalism" (1965) in the Boston Studies volume; the text in *Philosophical Perspectives* (1967) has some obvious misprints.
33. Gary Gutting, "Philosophy of Science", in *The Synoptic Vision: Essays on the Philosophy of Wilfrid Sellars*, C. F. Delaney *et al.* (Notre Dame, IN: University of Notre Dame Press, 1977): 73–104.
34. *Ibid.*, 86.
35. Epistemic independence of what? Whatever functions as the smallest non-derivative epistemically efficacious units must be independent of any other such units. If one holds that the whole is the given, then no (proper) justification can cite less than the whole, whatever the whole is.
36. Sellars goes on to say in the same paragraph that "A report can be correct as being an instance of a general mode of behaviour which, in a given linguistic community, it is reasonable to sanction and support" (EPM: §35, in SPR: 167; in KMG: 247).
37. Several critics of Sellars pick up on this theme and argue, *contra* Sellars, that, while Sellars's critique of the given is effective against internalist forms of foundationalism, it leaves externalist foundationalism untouched. See Robert G. Meyers, "Sellars' Rejection of Foundations", *Philosophical Studies* **39** (1981): 61–78; Jack C. Lyons, "Externalism and the Sellarsian Dilemma" http://comp.uark.edu/%7Ejclyons/papers/ESD.PDF (accessed June 2005).
38. I cannot find where in the preceding lecture Sellars thinks he has made the point he claims we have already seen. Once again, we are left at a crucial juncture without an argument for the epistemic reflexivity requirement. The point itself is clearly parallel to the epistemic reflexivity requirement on concept possession discussed above.
39. In *Knowledge, Mind, and the Given*, deVries and Triplett label the requirement that an observer know that his observation reports are reliable the "level ascent requirement", following a usage stemming, as I recall, from Alston. I now prefer the term "epistemic reflexivity requirement" because it is more descriptive and because reflexivity requirements turn out to be common in Sellarsian thought: there are reflexivity requirements on concept possession, observation knowledge, language use and agency.
40. W. Alston, "What's Wrong with Immediate Knowledge?", in *Epistemic Justitification*, 57–78 (Ithaca, NY: Cornell University Press, 1989), 66.
41. We do recognize non-propositional reasons: "My children are the reason I'm working double shifts", "My wife is the reason I dress up for class". But, as with cases of objectual knowledge, these seem to serve as a kind of shorthand for more complex propositional reasons.
42. For instance, see R. Brandom, "Study Guide to 'Empiricism and the Philosophy of Mind'", in W. Sellars, *Empiricism and the Philosophy of Mind*, 119–81 (Cambridge, MA: Harvard University Press, 1997), 159.

43. For a more detailed working out of the argument, calling on Sellars's analysis of presupposition in "Presupposing" (1954), see KMG: 95–9.
44. Had Sellars had the sloganizing talent of Quine, perhaps he would have pointed out that to ERR is human.
45. SK I §§32–8: 303–5. We think of the activities of animals and infants as like ours. To explain and describe their activities, we then form analogous concepts, on the model of those that apply to adult human psychologies:

    Thus, our common-sense understanding of what sub-conceptual thinking – e.g., that of babies and animals – consists in, involves viewing them as engaged in 'rudimentary' forms of conceptual thinking. We interpret their behavior using conceptual thinking as a model but qualify this model in *ad hoc* and unsystematic ways which really amount to the introduction of a new notion which is nevertheless labeled 'thinking'. (SK I §33: 304)

46. See Triplett and deVries, "Sellars's Principle of Observation Knowledge" (unpublished) for a more extensive examination of the evidence and how Sellars ought to treat it. See also deVries, "Sellars, Animals, and Thought", www.ditext.com/devries/sellanim.html (accessed June 2005).
47. See, for instance W. Alston, "What's Wrong with Immediate Knowledge?" in *Epistemic Justification*, 57–78 (Ithaca, NY: Cornell University Press, 1989), and Meyers, "Sellars's Rejection of Foundations".
48. [Sellars's note (added 1963)] My thought was that one can have direct (non-inferential) knowledge of a past fact which one did not or even (as in the case envisaged) could not conceptualize at the time it was present (EPM: §37n, in SPR: 169; in KMG: 249).
49. E. Sosa, "Mythology of the Given", *History of Philosophy Quarterly* **14** (1997): 275–86; E. Fales, *A Defense of the Given* (Lanham, MD: Rowman & Littlefield, 1996).
50. E. Sosa, "Mythology of the Given", 281.
51. Note that when Sellars talks of non-inferential beliefs, he is referring to their aetiology, not the source of their justification. Foundationalists believe that beliefs can be non-inferentially justified as well as non-inferentially acquired.
52. Firth, "Coherence, Certainty, and Epistemic Priority", 549–50. My bracketed insertion reflects Sellars's interpretation of Firth's "real" intent.
53. *Ibid.*, 554.
54. Page numbers in citations of "More on Givenness and Explanatory Coherence" are from Jonathan Dancy (ed.), *Perceptual Knowledge*. Oxford Readings in Philosophy, 177–91 (Oxford: Oxford University Press, 1988).
55. These are Sellarsian adaptations of principles from the first edition of Chisholm's *Theory of Knowledge*. Firth has implied that PE is the *only* ultimately non-inferential warrant-increasing property, but then it seems the MJ3 and MJ4 would not be basic. Lewis did, however, accord initial warrant to memory claims. So Sellars seems to have reason to supplement Firth's principal implicit principle MJ1 with MJ3 and MJ4.

## Chapter 6. Science and reality: induction, laws, theories and the real

1. Sellars recognizes that even contingent generalizations such as "all the coins in my pocket are pennies" support "subjunctive identicals": "if something (or this thing) were identical to one of the coins in my pocket, it would be a penny". But he does not think subjunctive identicals are of great interest philosophically.

2. Notice that under some conditions we would be willing to treat "All the coins in *S*'s pocket are pennies" as lawlike. If we know that *S* has a powerful phobia about permitting non-cuprous material into his pockets, then we might accept an inference from "*X* is a coin in *S*'s pocket" to "*X* is a penny". We would then accept the subjunctive "If *x* were a coin in *S*'s pocket, *x* would be a penny" (which is stronger than the subjunctive identical "If *x* were identical to a coin in *S*'s pocket, *x* would be a penny"), because we know there is a reliable connection between coming to be in *S*'s pocket and being made of copper.

3. For his official treatment of this problem, see "Conceptual Change" (1973).

4. For an overview of the vicissitudes of the standard view up to the mid-1970s see Frederick Suppe's Introduction and Afterword in *The Structure of Scientific Theories* 2nd edition (Champaign, IL: University of Illinois Press, 1977). He calls it the "received view". For statements of the view, see R. B. Braithwaite *Scientific Explanation* (Cambridge: Cambridge University Press, 1953); R. Carnap, "Theories as Partially Interpreted Formal Systems", in *Readings in the Philosophy of Science*, B. A. Brody and R. E. Grandy (eds), 5–11 (Englewood Cliffs, NJ: Prentice Hall, 1989) and originally published in Carnap's *Foundations of Logic and Mathematics* (Chicago, IL: University of Chicago Press, 1939); P. Duhem, *Aim and Structure of Physical Theory* (New York: Atheneum 1954); C. Hempel, *Aspects of Scientific Explanation* (New York: Free Press, 1965), Chs 4 and 8, and *Philosophy of Natural Science* (Englewood Cliffs, NJ; Prentice-Hall, 1966), Ch. 6; and E. Nagel, *The Structure of Science: Problems in the Logic of Scientific Explanation* (New York: Harcourt, Brace & World, 1961), Chs 5 and 6.

5. For instance: "I shall assume, at least to begin with, that *something* like the standard modern account of this type of theory is correct. And in view of the distinguished names associated with this account, it would be most surprising if it were not close to the truth" (LT: §3, in SPR: 106). But, in fact, Sellars revises virtually everything about the standard account to some degree.

6. Some instances: the last paragraph of "Philosophy and the Scientific Image of Man", where he speaks of joining "the conceptual framework of persons" to the scientific image (PSIM in SPR: 40); PHM: §7, in SPR: 95ff., where Sellars is worried about the relations between "the framework of sense impressions and the framework of physical objects." See also SRLG: *passim*.

7. This is a consistent theme in Sellars's earliest papers (PPE, ENWW, RNWW, CIL). He argues that we must think of our language as schematic for an *ideal* language that would provide a place for everything and everything in its place: essentially, not just a *framework*, but a whole world-story.

8. It is important to see that to say that we did not *acquire* a framework by reasoning to it does *not* entail that it is not reasonable to retain or maintain it, once we have it.

9. See Hempel, *Aspects of Scientific Explanation*, 179. See also Marc Lange, "Salience, Supervenience, and Layer Cakes in Sellars's Scientific Realism, McDowell's Moral Realism, and the Philosophy of Mind", *Philosophical Studies* **101** (2000): 213–51.

10. The notion of explanation (and in particular explanatory coherence) is so central to Sellars's views, both ontological and epistemological, that he has been called an "explanationist". Sadly, he never details what makes an explanation an explanation or what different forms explanation (and explanatory coherence) can take.

11. This is dispensability *in principle*. In practice, computational simplicity and other pragmatic factors may keep the empirical generalization alive and in use.

12. Sellars does not think that the observation–theory line is *absolutely* malleable. There is a minimal set of observation terms, the proper and common sensibles, that do have a special status, although it is not that of a given. He does not believe that we could discard the vocabulary of the proper sensibles, but we can relocate that vocabulary, under the pressure of theory, in a new category. See, for instance, SRT: 316–18. More on this in Chapter 8.

13. Unfortunately, I must skim over some very important questions about scientific realism here. Sellars has been one of its most sophisticated and vocal defenders, both against the earlier forms of instrumentalism, as found in Nagel, and the more recent constructive empiricism of van Fraassen, with whom Sellars had important exchanges. (Van Fraassen was a student of Sellars at Pittsburgh.) See van Fraassen, "Wilfrid Sellars and Scientific Realism", *Dialogue* 14 (1975): 606–16, "On the Radical Incompleteness of the Manifest Image (Comments on Sellars)", in *PSA 1976, Volume II*, F. Suppe and P. Asquith (eds), 335–43 (East Lansing, MI: Philosophy of Science Association, 1977) and *The Scientific Image* (Oxford: Clarendon Press, 1980). I treat this lightly here, because there is an excellent and very intelligible dialogue tracing out the Sellars–van Fraassen debate in Gary Gutting's "Realism vs. Constructive Empiricism", *Monist* **65** (1982), 336–49.

14. Interestingly, "Theoretical Explanation" (1963) is a later publication than "The Language of Theories" (1961), although publication order need not reflect order of composition. "Theoretical Explanation" stands in tension with what are clearly some of Sellars's long-standing commitments. I can only assume he had specific concerns and goals for "Theoretical Explanation" that he did not want to complicate with the more radical picture he really believed.

15. I say *relatively* straightforward because if intentionality is possible without sensibility, accommodations would have to be made for the functional descriptions of intentional items. The reduction would be token-wise, not type-wise. Is intentionality possible without sensibility?

16. See, for instance, the final two paragraphs of "The Language of Theories", for example:

> would not the abandonment of the framework of physical things mean the abandonment of the *qualitative* aspects of the world? ... To this *specific* question, of course, the answer is yes. But it would be a mistake to generalize and infer that *in general* the replacement of observation terms by theoretical constructs must "leave something out".

(LT: 53–4; in SPR: 126).

17. Nomological probability concerns lawlike generalizations, and the probability of theories concerns the complex proposition that conjoins the definitions, axioms and postulates.

18. See Joseph Pitt, *Pictures, Images and Conceptual Change: An Analysis of Wilfrid Sellars' Philosophy of Science* (Dordrecht: D. Reidel, 1981), 76.

19. A probability argument, in his sense, is simply an argument that a certain statement is probable.

20. Pitt argues that Sellars's conception of probability is incoherent (Pitt, *Pictures, Images and Conceptual Change*). Sellars admits that what he calls first-order probability statements are "incomplete" in the sense that, while they terminate in the claim that there is good reason, all things considered, to accept a certain proposition, they do not, in fact, allow one to actually construct the practical argument they claim to exist. Sellars discusses what he calls *second-order* probability statements (of the form "it is probable that-$p$ in relation to $e$ . $R_L$(that-$p$, $e$)"), in which the logical relation between the total

evidence and the hypothesis in question is made explicit and which therefore do permit one to reconstruct the argument for accepting the hypothesis. Pitt then complains that

> To claim that a statement is probable is to claim there are good reasons for accepting it. Since for first order probability arguments there are no good reasons available for accepting their conclusions we seem compelled [*sic.*] to conclude that they must not be probability arguments. (*ibid.*: 63)

But, as far as I can tell, Pitt has neglected to distinguish between the first-order probability *statement* "it is probable that-*p*", which Sellars admits is incomplete, and a first-order probability *argument*. A first-order probability argument concludes with a first-order probability statement, and while the *statement* does not *contain* the reasons that support it, if it is indeed the outcome of a good piece of probability reasoning, we know that there *are* reasons and that they are somehow *available*.

21. At OAFP: 449, Sellars, apparently believing he is quoting himself, repeats this almost verbatim, but substitutes "empirically confirmed" for "nomologically probable". Is the difference significant?

22. Pitt, *Pictures, Images and Conceptual Change*, 15.

## Chapter 7. Intentionality and the mental

1. See, for instance SSMB: 46; even more to the point is MEV §7: 326.

2. See, for example, APM, BBK and BD.

3. "The classical theory takes there to be an intersubjective domain (the exact ontological status of which it usually does not attempt to specify) of what might be called *thinkables*. There is, for example, the thinkable that $2 + 2 = 4$. When a person thinks that $2 + 2 = 4$, he or she is in some way directly related to the thinkable" (BLM: 8). See also KPT: Ch. 4.

4. Not everyone believed in this direct, non-representational access to our own thoughts (e.g. Leibniz's doctrine of apperception, which was appropriated by Kant).

5. The episodic, in this sense, must be something purely *occurrent,* as opposed to the "iffiness" of dispositions. See EPM §§45–6, and especially ITM: 521–2.

6. See, for example, BLM: 9. For a late-middle-period consideration of the episodicity of the mental, see SK II §§48–55: 327–9.

7. See, for example, EPM: §46, in SPR: 177; in KMG: 257.

8. Chisholm put forward this argument in several places, but the most relevant here is "Sentences about Believing", which originally appeared in the *Proceedings of the Aristotelian Society* **56** (1955–56): 125–48, and was reprinted as part of the published correspondence with Sellars (ITM: 510–20).

9. Sellars does not *need* to propose his take on psychological discourse via a myth. In "The Structure of Knowledge", for instance, he does so without the narrative trappings. But Jones and the Ryleans appear both in "Empiricism and the Philosophy of Mind" and in *Science and Metaphysics*.

10. For more detailed discussion of what Jones's theories allow him to explain see deVries and Triplett, *Knowledge, Mind, and the Given*, 142–4 and 159–64.

11. "Think-out-loud" is the term the Ryleans use for candid speech and is, for them, an unanalysable whole that holds no implications about a contrast class of thinkings that would not be out loud.

12. Some text to support the claim that Sellars does not present psychological concepts as straightforwardly theoretical: "I am going to argue that the distinction between theoretical and observational discourse is involved in the

logic of concepts pertaining to inner episodes. I say 'involved in' for it would be paradoxical and, indeed, incorrect, to say that these concepts *are* theoretical concepts" (EPM: §51; in SPR: 183; in KMG: 263).

13. Thus, ultimately, it is important for Sellars that the story is a *myth*. For one of his principle reasons for objecting to treating folk psychology as *really* a theory is that it is a framework we did not choose to adopt but were caused to develop, and in that way it is quite different from a theory in the strict sense. Since folk psychology is thus part of our evolutionary heritage and identity, it is not optional in the way that Newton's theory is and cannot be abandoned in the same way. Sellars has to believe that ultimately we cannot tell a true story about the *rational* adoption of the framework of intentionality, although this does not entail that we cannot tell a true story about the rational *retention* of the framework of intentionality once we have it. The framework constitutive of rationality could hardly itself be adopted via a reasoning process. For a fascinating exploration of the Jones myth that emphasizes its mythic aspects, see Kukla, "Myth, Memory and Misrecognition".

14. "Here it is essential to note that the term 'express', indeed the phrase 'express a thought', is radically ambiguous. In one sense, to say of an utterance that it expresses a thought is to say, roughly, that a thought episode *causes* the utterance. But there is another and radically different sense in which an utterance can be said to express a thought. This is the sense in which the utterance expresses a proposition (i.e., a thought in Frege's sense (*Gedanke*)—an 'abstract entity' rather than a mental episode). Let me distinguish between these two senses of 'express' and the 'causal' and the 'logical'. ...". (NI in PP: 308–9)

15. H. P. Grice, "Meaning", *The Philosophical Review* **66**(3) (July 1957), 377–88; "Utterer's Meaning and Intention", *The Philosophical Review* **78**(2) (April 1969), 147–77.

16. There are powerful challenges in the literature to the coherence of the Ryleans. The most significant of these challenges come from Ausonio Marras in a number of works: "Introduction", in *Intentionality, Mind, and Language*, A. Marras (ed.), 3–27 (Champaign, IL: University of Illinois Press, 1972); "Correspondence between Wilfrid Sellars and Ausonio Marras" (1972–1976), www.ditext.com/sellars/csm.html (accessed June 2005); "On Sellars' Linguistic Theory of Conceptual Activity", *Canadian Journal of Philosophy* **2** (1973), 471–83; "Reply to Sellars", *Canadian Journal of Philosophy* **2** (1973), 495–501; "Sellars on Thought and Language", *Noûs* **7** (1973), 152–63; "Sellars' Behaviourism: A Reply to Fred Wilson", *Philosophical Studies* **30** (1976), 413–18; "The Behaviourist Foundation of Sellar's Semantics", *Dialogue* (Canada) **16** (1977): 664–75; and "Rules, Meaning and Behavior", in *The Philosophy of Wilfrid Sellars: Queries and Extensions*, J. C. Pitt (ed.), 163–87 (Dordrecht: D. Reidel, 1978). Regretfully, there is not enough time or space here to deal with Marras's objections in detail.

17. See, for example, SM: 76; LTC: 95–7.

18. He uses this term, for instance, in "The Structure of Knowledge".

19. In his "revised classical account" of thoughts, it is actually permissible to identify some verbal imagery with thoughts, although this does not come out clearly in these passages from "Empiricism and the Philosophy of Mind". That is, in the sense that Sellars is willing to say that candid, spontaneous utterances *are* thoughts, he would also be willing to say that verbal imagery that does not get externalized in verbal behaviour, is thinking.

20. D. Jacquette, *Philosophy of Mind* (Englewood Cliffs, NJ: Prentice Hall, 1994), 104.
21. See the discussion in Jay Garfield, *Belief in Psychology* (Cambridge, MA: MIT Press, 1988).
22. "But, of course, the map is a parasitical RS [representational system]. It depends for its mappishness on its use by human RSs" (MEV: 337).
23. Although he refers to Aristotle in characterizing logic-using representational systems, Sellars's distinctions seem clearly intended also to evoke a Kantian conception of rationality. "Everything in nature works in accordance with laws. Only a rational being has the power to act *in accordance with his idea* of laws –that is, in accordance with principles ..." (Kant, *Groundwork of the Metaphysics of Morals*, H. J. Paton (trans.) (New York: Barnes and Noble, 1967), 412).
24. There is an interesting symmetry here. At the beginning of his writing career in the 1940s and 1950s Sellars spent a fair amount of time emphasizing the importance of the notion of a material inference. It was, for him, the important *liaison* between the notion of a behavioural uniformity and a reason-guided action. In "Mental Events", near the end of his writing career, things had changed enough in the philosophical arena that he felt it necessary to return to the notion in order to emphasize the *gap* between mere behavioural uniformity and reason-guided action.
25. All of these terms are dangerous. For instance, William Alston (1971) "Varieties of Privileged Access", *American Philosophical Quarterly* 8 (1971), 223–41, lists over a dozen varieties of privileged access.
26. For further discussion of a Sellarsian view of introspection, see Jay L. Garfield, "The Myth of Jones and the Mirror of Nature: Reflections on Introspection", *Philosophy and Phenomenological Research* **50** (1989): 1–26.
27. As Jay Garfield points out (personal communication), there is good reason to believe that our expression of and abilities to perceive emotions and other mental states evolved as mechanisms to facilitate social interaction. It is very natural to treat emotion-detection mechanisms as perceptual, because they are fast, mandatory, domain specific and so on. And sometimes we do not know what we are thinking, but others around us do.
28. But Sellars's "need it have?" is also frustrating, for it raises important questions without even hinting at an answer. Could there be a linguistic community in which there is a robust psychological vocabulary in use, but in which first-person reports using that vocabulary have no special status?
29. Here is a selection of such work, emphasizing those works with "theory of mind" in the very title: J. Astington, "What is Theoretical about the Child's Theory of Mind?: A Vygotskyan View of its Development," in *Lev Vygotsky: Critical Assessments: Future Directions, vol. IV*, P. Lloyd & C. Fernyhough (eds), 401–18 (New York: Routledge, 1996); S. Baron-Cohen, "Evolution of a Theory of Mind", in *Evolution of the Hominid Mind*, M. Corballis and S. Lea (eds), 261–77 (Oxford: Oxford University Press, 1999) and "Theory of Mind and Autism: A Fifteen Year Review", in *Understanding Other Minds,* S. Baron-Cohen *et al.* (eds), 3–20 (Oxford: Oxford University Press, 2000); P. Carruthers and P. Smith, *Theories of Theories of Mind* (Cambridge: Cambridge University Press, 1996); P. Mitchell, *Introduction to Theory of Mind: Children, Autism, and Apes* (Oxford: Oxford University Press, 1997); J. Perner, T. Ruffman and S. Leekam, "Theory of Mind is Contagious: You Catch it from your Sibs", *Child Development* **65** (1994): 1224–34; D. Premack and G. Woodruff, "Does the Chimpanzee have a Theory of Mind?", *The Behavioral*

*and Brain Sciences* **4** (1978): 515–26; H. M. Wellman, *The Child's Theory of Mind* (Cambridge, MA: MIT Press, 1990).

30. Indeed, the hard-core theory-theory, in light of current research, faces an uphill battle as an empirical theory:

It requires an implausible degree of inductive and hypothesis-testing competence in three- and four-year-olds, an implausible universal, uniform and rather selective fixation on the mind as a domain of study, and fails to explain why [theory of mind] would be selectively impaired in those like high-functioning autistics who are nonetheless theoretically competent in other domains (that is, it doesn't account for the false picture/false belief performance dissociation).

(J. L. Garfield, C. C. Peterson and T. Perry, "Social Cognition, Language Acquisition and The Development of the Theory of Mind", *Mind & Language* **16** (2001), 526).

This article provides a good survey of the field and, moreover, puts it into a generally Sellarsian context. It is highly recommended.

31. Some examples of this literature: A. Goldman, "Interpretation Psychologized", *Mind and Language* **4** (1989), 161–85 and "The Psychology of Folk Psychology", *The Behavioral and Brain Sciences* **16** (1993), 15–28; R. M. Gordon, "Folk Psychology as Simulation", *Mind and Language* **1** (1986), 158–71 and "Sympathy, Simulation, and the Impartial Spectator", *Ethics* **105** (1995), 727–42; R. M. Gordon and J. Barker, "Autism and the 'Theory of Mind' Debate", in *Philosophical Psychopathology: A Book of Readings*, G. Graham and L. Stephens (eds), 163–81 (Cambridge, MA: MIT Press, 1994); P. Harris, *Children and Emotion* (Oxford: Blackwell, 1989); J. Heal, "Replication and Functionalism", in *Language, Mind, and Logic*, J. Butterfield (ed.), 135–50 (Cambridge: Cambridge University Press, 1986); Carruthers and Smith, *Theories of Theories of Mind*; M. Davies and T. Stone (eds) *Folk Psychology: The Theory of Mind Debate* (Oxford: Blackwell, 1995) and *Mental Simulation: Evaluations and Applications* (Oxford: Blackwell Publishers, 1995).

32. See R. M. Gordon, "Sellars's Ryleans Revisited", *Protosociology* **14** (2000), 102–14.

33. Gordon works hard to avoid this commitment, but it is clearly evident in Goldman's work, cited above.

34. It seems worth calling it a 'theory' because it contains a wealth of implications about relations among the states we attribute to people with this nomenclature. We can therefore use it to generate new knowledge not otherwise available.

35. (2a) could, however, also be construed as a dimension in which language is ontologically prior to thought, for the behaviour we engage in prior to language acquisition cannot, in the strict Sellarsian view, be called *thinking*, except projectively in so far as it presages and allows us to acquire language.

36. This is a form of token-identity, but not type-identity. See, for instance, PSIM in SPR: 34.

37. For instance, Paul Churchland, "Eliminative Materialism and the Propositional Attitudes", *Journal of Philosophy* **78** (1981): 67–90.

38. Since Sellars takes there to be two distinct problems, a mind–body problem and a sensorium–body problem, he has to face accusations of being an eliminativist twice, for the story he tells about the relation between mind (that is, intentional states) and body is different from the story he tells about the relation between sensorium and body. We return to this issue in Chapter 8.

## Chapter 8. Sensory consciousness

1. Cf. FMPP I §46: 12.
2. FMPP I §§46–62: 12–15; III §29: 70.
3. In "The Double-Knowledge Approach to the Mind–Body Problem", Sellars attributes to his father the notion that there are two kinds of attributes, "attributes pertaining to *qualitative content*, and attributes pertaining to structure" (DKMB: 280). "External" knowledge (including all inductive knowledge that is not directly introspective) is restricted to the structural, according to Sellars *père*, but being must have content, not just structure. Sellars *père*, in contrast to Whitehead, does not restrict qualitative content to feelings, "But though the content of the world is not restricted to feeling, sensation, and the like, it is only in our acquaintance with the latter that we encounter qualitative content. Not only is this the only place where we *encounter* it, it is the only source of *determinate concepts of content*" (DKMB: 281). Now, it is not clear just how many of the details of his father's approach Sellars *fils* is willing to accept, but he does endorse his father's interpretation of consciousness as "fundamentally correct" (DKMB: 284). The idea that our experience cannot be merely structural in its characteristics, but must involve qualitative content, seems clearly operative in the thinking of Sellars *fils*.
4. What's important here in preserving Sellars's rejection of the given is that neither conceptual minimality nor causal proximity entails epistemic independence: even knowing that one is appeared to redly requires command of "the logical space of reasons".
5. "We have a natural tendency to take volumes and surfaces of color which are not, in point of fact, constituents of physical objects, to be exactly that" (FMPP III §35: 71).
6. This also throws light on Sellars's long-standing dialogue with Firth. Firth claims that our most basic reporting concepts will be concepts of kinds of *experience*. Sellars insists that that is wrong: our most basic reporting concepts, the ones in the most direct contact with reality, are concepts of *objects*, for the fundamental grammar of any usable human framework is realistic, and the reflective conception of an experience is a higher-level, posterior acquisition.
7. Again, the Hegelian echoes are striking. In Sellars's view the "science of consciousness" indeed requires a phenomenology (and not just in the Husserlian sense).
8. Sellars actually misstates this in "Empiricism and the Philosophy of Mind", for he writes there that "the model is the idea of a domain of 'inner replicas'" (EPM: §61, in SPR: 191; in KMG: 271). Sellars says that in developing his theory of thoughts, Jones used overt verbal behaviour itself as the model, not a domain of "inner speakings" (see EPM: §56, in SPR: 186; in KMG: 266). "Inner speech" (or at least inner-speech-like episodes) is what the theory posits, not what it takes as the model. So to keep things parallel, since Jones's new theory posits inner replicas of perceptible objects, we should say that perceptible objects are themselves the model.
9. The points made in the last couple of paragraphs are also reiterated by Sellars (PHM: 93).
10. Two points: (i) Jones thinks that, for example, red is a property of physical objects, not a mind-dependent secondary quality; and (ii) the treatment of impressions contrasts with the treatment of thoughts. Thoughts are modelled on verbal episodes. Verbal episodes may have intrinsic properties (e.g. a certain volume and timbre), but such intrinsic properties are totally discounted

in the analogy. All that matters are (some of) the relational properties of the episodes.

11. Pain is mentioned briefly in his discussion of and argument for an adverbial construal of sensing in the manifest image (MP: 230–35, in KTM: 291–5). I do not recall specific passages where Sellars gives a detailed treatment of pain or pleasure, but he was aware of the difficulties it created for his early modern forebears. See, for instance, BD: Sections III and VI. Here's a problem for my suggestion in the text: toothaches are not like burns. The pain that accompanies a burn is easily thought of as a painful sensation of heat: the 'of heat' specifies the intrinsic characteristic of the sensation (since one can get a sensation of heat from handling dry ice, which is very cold), and the 'painful' tells us something about the organic function of this state. Low-intensity sensations of heat are often pleasant, welcomed and sought after. High-intensity sensations of heat are usually painful, unwelcome and avoided. But toothaches do not seem to have a "carrier sensation"; there is no "tooth sensation" that gets painful at a certain intensity or character. I have never heard anyone remark on a "tooth pleasure", that is, a particularly pleasant feeling in one's teeth; *any* feeling in a tooth seems to be a bad thing (or should I switch dentists?). If some pains are "pure", and not painful versions of some "carrier sensation", then such pure pains pose a problem for this approach to sense impressions. Worse, it seems fine to say that we sense the very painfulness of our pains; that's the whole point of pains. Given Sellars's treatment of qualities (such as $Q$), the very $Q$ness of which is present to us, it would seem difficult to treat painfulness as a merely functional characteristic of first-order sensory states. See also Jay Rosenberg, "Perception and Inner Sense: A Problem about Direct Awareness," *Philosophical Studies* **101** (2000): 143–60.

12. "A Semantical Solution of the Mind–Body Problem" (1953) makes it clear that intentionality requires a different treatment from sensibility, and that sensory consciousness "is not a *mental* fact" (SSMB: 76). But the treatment of sensibility there is very cursory. "The Concept of Emergence", published simultaneously with "Empiricism and the Philosophy of Mind", is clearly concerned with the issue of sensation, but does not treat it directly in great detail. In "The Concept of Emergence", Sellars is trying to keep an emergentist solution to the sensorium–body question on the table, but says little about what it is supposed to be.

13. For further discussion, see Garfield, *Belief in Psychology*.

14. Although the *outlines* of an adequate theory of intentionality are in hand, it is not yet common coin. There are still many faulty theories of intentionality advocated by philosophers as diverse as Carnap, Chisholm, Ryle and Bergmann, or, more recently, Fodor, Lewis, Stalnaker and Dretske (just to stay in the analytic tradition). That there are numerous faulty interpretations of intentionality does not show that there is something wrong with the manifest image conception of intentionality generally. As long as there is one good interpretation of intentionality, the conception is safe.

15. Although he makes these distinctions in several places, the text of "Sensa or Sensings" is the primary guide here. Very similar distinctions are made in "Some Reflections on Perceptual Consciousness", written about the same time (mid-1970s). See also MEV: 26–8.

16. *Critique of Pure Reason*, A69/B94.

17. So, for instance, he points out that one can see *that* there is a jet flying overhead without seeing the jet, because what one sees is the growing contrail (MEV: 26).

18. One of the reasons Sellars likes his pink ice cube so much is that it is transparent; one doesn't see of it only its facing surface, but its entire volume. This enables Sellars to avoid getting sidetracked on the ontology of surfaces.

19. For a parallel argument using slightly different terminology but coming to the same conclusion, see SK I Pt. VII: 305–10. See also FMPP I §§88–98: 20–22.

20. Implicit here is also a rejection of intentionalism in the treatment of sensation and a reaffirmation of his Kantian distinction between sense and conception. An intentionalistic or representationalistic treatment of sensation has again become popular since Sellars was writing. It is a pity we cannot see how Sellars would have reacted to this most recent revival of a position he thought we had finally moved beyond.

21. Thus, he expresses his ultimate conclusions in "Sensa or Sensings" in terms of both *sensa* and *objectless sensings*, having shown how to convert between the vocabularies. Similarly, in "The Stucture of Knowledge", (I Pt. VIII), he expresses a preference for the adverbial approach, but does not reject the sense-datum approach. It is a pity there is not time or space to examine in detail Sellars's contributions to the adverbial theory of sensation.

22. There is a footnote in the original here referring the reader to section IV of the first lecture.

23. Still, the conclusions of these inferences are neither infallible nor incorrigible. To the extent that they are tensed, memory could be playing tricks; even if we forget the tenses, one might be hypnotized, or there might be a glitch in the mechanisms by which one formulates sentences or beliefs in response to sensory stimulation.

24. Recall the discussion of the van der Waals equation in Chapter 6.

25. It is assumed in this characterization that only the intrinsic or non-relational properties of the object are in question.

26. For a different (although equivalent) take on object reduction, see SK I §18: 300. Sellars admits in his 1971 response to Cornman that he has not given a direct defence of his principle of reducibility; as far as I can tell, he never did give one in print. "A defense of this principle would take one to the very heart of the philosophy of logic, relating, as it does, the functional calculus to the calculus of individuals. I have as yet published no such defense, but have simply stated that I find the principle in accordance with my logical intuitions" (SSIS: 393). See James Cornman, "Sellars, Scientific Realism, and Sensa," *The Review of Metaphysics* **23** (1970): 417–51.

27. "When it is said that some wholes have attributes which do not consist in their parts having such and such qualities and standing in such and such relations, it is, in effect, being denied that all conjunctive individuals are reducible" (SK I §19: 300).

28. There's one more complication here. Sellars argues in a couple of papers (LCP; P) that (i) ultimately basic particulars can have only a single, simple intrinsic quality. So something like persons, who have multiple intrinsic properties, cannot be satisfactory ultimate basic particulars. Here is yet another way in which the manifest image is necessarily unsatisfactory. He also argues that (ii) adjectival predication applied to complex particulars ought, in the last analysis, to be construed as assigning basic particulars with that characteristic to be constituents of the complex object in question. The consequences of this (Anaxagorean) part of his system, which he doesn't return to or extend after 1952, have not been dealt with here. This is a lacuna in my treatment of Sellars's metaphysics. See also Jay Rosenberg "The Place of Color in the

Scheme of Things: A Roadmap to Sellars' Carus Lectures", *The Monist* **65** (1982), 315–35, esp. 322.

29. It helps to think "Aristotelianly" here. A human being consists of flesh and blood, bone and so on. But the properly human property of rationality does not consist in an arrangement of flesh, blood and bone. The rational soul needs a particular material, but cannot be reduced to that material. See PHM: 99–100. The analytic, atomistic paradigm typical of the modern era and evident in corpuscularian mechanism encourages the idea that all spatial objects are, strictly speaking, systems of (micro)objects. So in the seventeenth century it seemed essential to preserving the basicness of persons that they be identified with extentionless souls.

30. In his critique of Sellars's views, Cornman tries several different formulations of the principle of reducibility, in one of which he substitutes the notion of reducibility for Sellars's "consists of". Sellars notes this substitution in his response to Cornman, and remarks that "This enables him to mobilize the fact that philosophers of science have given a variety of accounts of the 'reduction' of one scientific framework to another. My principle, however, concerns the *internal* structure of conceptual frameworks, and belongs, properly speaking, to logic or general ontology, rather than to the philosophy of science" (SSIS: 411). But this does not mean that the conception of reduction is totally inappropriate here, for Sellars elsewhere makes it clear that there is a perfectly respectable conception of *intra*framework reducibility. This is, indeed, the topic of The Structure of Knowledge (I Pt. III: 297–300), although the topic there is the reduction of individuals, not properties.

31. The distinction is characterized there as follows:
    Physical$_1$: an event or entity is *physical$_1$* if it belongs in the space-time network.
    Physical$_2$: an event or entity is *physical$_2$* if it is definable in terms of theoretical primitives adequate to describe completely the actual states though not necessarily the potentialities of the universe before the appearance of life. (CE: 252)
    Judging from the use made of the distinction, what is important for the *physical$_2$* is really the appearance of *sentience*, not life itself. But there's some indication that Sellars and Meehl thought that the development of evolved structures in the world was sufficient to force the introduction of new non-physical$_1$ primitives in an ideally complete science: see the mention of protoplasm (CE: 247). Indeed, there's even question about whether colours and feels are emergent in just the way they sketch.

32. Stephen C. Pepper, "Emergence", *Journal of Philosophy* **23** (1926), 241–5.

33. Sellars and Meehl, following Pepper, state their argument in terms of functions on a state-space. Having a well-confirmed generalization that is a function of four variables, schematically $f_1(q, r, s, t) = 0$, is not inconsistent with there being another function, $f_2(q, r, s, t) = 0$, where $f_1 \neq f_2$, if $f_1$ and $f_2$ cover different regions of the four-space. Now suppose that there is a further function $E(q, r, s, t, a, b)$ that holds more generally, covering both regions of the four-space, but apparently extending the four-space by the addition of new variables. What should we say if we then discover that the variables $a$ and $b$ are themselves functions on $(q, r, s, t)$, say $a = g(q, r)$ and $b = h(s, t)$? Then there will be a function $f_3(q, r, s, t) = 0$ that holds in both regions of the four-space. while the emergentist must indeed admit that if $f_3$ and $f_1$ are equivalent, then $a$ and $b$ make no difference, it is open to him to say that the difference made by $a$ and $b$ is just the fact that f$_1$(qrst), which holds in regions of

qrst-space which are unaccompanied by $a$ and $b$, is not equivalent to the function which holds of these variables for regions in which they are accompanied by a and/or b.

(CE: 248; *sic.*, Sellars and Meehl are not consistent in their italicizing in this passage).

The basic thrust of the argument is to keep open the sense of saying that different laws operate in inorganic and organic contexts, even if, ultimately, there is one set of laws that operates everywhere in space-time.

34. For instance, Sellars and Meehl say at one point that their argument does not support employing the notion of 'supervenience':

But while the notion of different regions in the fourspace $qrst$ exhibiting different functional relationships is mathematically unexceptionable, is it emergence? Here the first thing to note is that the notion, as such, involves no "supervenience." For (a) no emergent variables have been introduced; $f_1$ and $f_2$ being functions of the same four variables; and (b) it is not being claimed that there are 'piggy-back' regularities. When a situation exhibits a constellation of values of $q$, $r$, $s$, and $t$ falling within $\text{region}_1$ of the fourspace, it is not exhibiting a constellation falling within $\text{region}_2$, and vice versa. When a situation conforms to $f_2$, it is not conforming to $f_1$, and vice versa. Thus, to the extent that 'emergence' connotes the simultaneous presence in a single situation of two or more levels, the notion we have been analyzing is not, as such, a matter of emergence. (CE: 246–7)

But we cannot take this as a general disavowal of the notion. This disclaimer occurs relatively early in their argument. After they have, later, introduced the function $E(q, r, s, t, a, b)$ [= $f_3(q, r, s, t)$], where the variables $a$ and $b$ have been introduced to extend the reach of the original generalization $f_1(q, r, s, t) = 0$ into a new region of the state-space, 'supervenience' does seem appropriate. New variables have been introduced, and, since $a = g(q, r)$ and $b = h(s, t)$, there are "'piggy-back' regularities" as I would understand the term.

35. W. Lycan, *Consciousness* (Cambridge, MA: MIT Press, 1987), 145.

36. *Ibid.*, 93–111; C. A. Hooker, "Sellars' Argument for the Inevitability of the Secondary Qualities", *Philosophical Studies* **32** (1977), 335–48; G. Muilenberg and Robert C. Richardson, "Sellars and Sense Impressions", *Erkenntnis* **17** (1982), 171–212; James Cornman, *Materialism and Sensations* (New Haven, CT: Yale University Press, 1971).

37. There are, of course, perfectly respectable empirical generalizations involving the proper sensibles: black objects tend to warm up more quickly in sunlight than white objects; eating food that smells putrescent tends to make one sick. These are more-or-less common sense and common knowledge, and did not seem to hold out the promise of radically new, mathematically exact and indefinitely refinable laws and theories.

38. This is true of the imperceptibles posited in most seventeenth-century scientific theories and their immediate successors. But I am oversimplifying, for it was a topic of much debate. Berkeley thought nothing could be like any idea but another idea, so, since sensory ideas can have shape, non-ideas could not.

39. Some readers are sure to retort that this is perfectly conceivable: for instance, the rainbow of colours of an oil slick or a bubble. We do not think of the bubble as having coloured parts that change in their relative location to each other, thereby producing the ever-changing pattern of colours that we see. (Well, at least adults do not.) We now recognize, for instance, the difference between

pigmental colour and 'structural' colour, colour that is generated by interference among the light rays refracted or reflected by the surface structure of an object. The colours of bubbles and oil slicks are structural in this sense; butterfly wings exhibit both kinds of colour. But notice how much sophisticated theory has gone into this distinction. (Apparently, the notion of structural colour can be traced back to Robert Boyle, Newton's contemporary, and was first explained well by Thomas Young in the early nineteenth century as an interference effect.) So really, we have here a case of significant invasion of the manifest image by developing science, and it was precisely such facts as that things that were intrinsically uncoloured (or all of one colour) could appear to have colour(s) (or different colours) that led Boyle's contemporaries to believe that the colours themselves must be in the mind, not out there in the material objects. I recommend http://newton.ex.ac.uk/research/emag/ butterflies/ (accessed June 2005) for information on structural colour in biology.

The Land Effect is another and different case of apparent colour. Again, the conclusion from investigating it tends to be that the colours are really "in the mind".

The compulsion to infer from such phenomena as structural colour and the Land effect the idea that colours are "really" in the mind reinforces Sellars's claim that we do not think of colours as possibly composed of the uncoloured. If we cannot find really coloured objects to compose the coloured expanse, we displace the colour into a realm where its "composition" seems unproblematic.

40. Stated this way, Sellars's argument can be accused of a fallacy of ambiguity: he is switching between a reading of 'non-composite' as *continuous and homogenous* and 'non-composite' as *primitive and undefined.* This would be forgivable if *continuous and homogenous* were the "material mode" equivalent of *primitive and undefined,* but it is not.

41. Eddington's classic discussion occurs in the introduction to his Gifford Lectures of 1927: A. S. Eddington, *The Nature of the Physical World* (New York: Macmillan, 1928), ix–xvii.

42. See "Berkeley and Descartes" (1977), where this problem is a centrepiece of the discussion; see also "Kant's Transcendental Idealism" (1976).

43. H. A. Prichard, "Perception", in *Knowledge and Perception: Essays and Lectures,* 52–68 (Oxford: Oxford University Press, 1950).

44. The superscript 's' marks the predicate as a common noun applicable to sensory states and formed by analogy to its unmarked version.

45. This is clearly a change in Sellars's thinking. Consider the following from "Phenomenalism" (1963, but written in 1959):

> It is, indeed, true, from the standpoint of this sophisticated framework that when a person sees that a physical object is red and triangular on the facing side, part of what is "really" going on is that a red and triangular sensum exists where certain micro-theoretically construed cortical processes are going on; but it would be a mixing of frameworks to say, with some philosophers, that people "mistake sensa for physical objects", or "take sensa to be *out there*". For these latter ways of putting it suggest that sensa belong to the conceptual framework in terms of which people experience the world. (PHM: 103)

Sellars's new position is, in effect, that sensa are implied by the conceptual framework in terms of which people experience the world, although not many philosophers have been able to see this implication.

46. … if one thinks of "sense impressions" or "raw feels" as theoretical con-

structs introduced for the purpose of explaining "discriminative behavior" such as is found in white rats, then there is no reason to suppose that the postulated states might not be identified with neural states and conceived of as reducible along the lines described previously. It is therefore crucial to my thesis to emphasize that sense impressions or raw feels are common sense theoretical constructs introduced to explain the occurrence *not* of white rat type discriminative behavior, but rather of perceptual propositional attitudes, and are therefore bound up with the explanation of why human language contains families of predicates having the logical properties of words for perceptible qualities and relations.
(IAMB in PP: 387)

47.     Thus I accept the identity theory only in its weak form according to which raw feels or sense impressions are states of core persons, and according to which, therefore, the logical space of raw feels will reappear transposed but unreduced in a theoretical framework adequate to the job of explaining what core persons can do. In my opinion, such a theory is not yet even on the horizon.               (IAMB in PP: 386)

48. In "Foundations for a Metaphysics of Pure Process", Sellars claims that reductive materialism is, "*at this stage of dialectic* ... absurd" (FMPP III §80: 79). The reason he gives is that we are not being offered "a recategorization of the original entity, an unproblematic cube of pink, but a recategorization of a supposedly *postulated* entity, a sense impression of a cube of pink". He also says the mistake made is "pinpointed in paragraphs 40–42", which is quoted above.

But Sellars also maintains that there is another thesis often confused with reductive materialism, namely, that "the only *objects* involved are atoms in the void" (FMPP III §82: 70). Spelled out, however, this position is emergent or wholistic materialism.

49. Sellars distinguishes between real reductive materialism and a thesis often confused with it: "This thesis is not, so to speak, that all states of a person – including sensings – are complex motions of atoms in the void, but rather the thesis that the only *objects* involved are atoms in the void" (FMPP III §§79–84: 79). Real reductive materialism accepts Sellars's principle of reduction, and thus holds that the sensory states of persons are also reducible to the states and relations of their constituents. If one holds that the only *objects* involved in a sensory state are "atoms in the void", but that the sensory state is not just a matter of the states and relations of its constituents, one is espousing emergent or wholistic materialism.

50. See FMPP III §126: 87. Sellars's reference is to *Sophist* 248C.

51. See FMPP III §96: 82, §§109–10: 84.

52. For more discussion of this, see Johanna Seibt, *Properties as Processes: A Synoptic Study of Wilfrid Sellars' Nominalism* (Atascadero, CA: Ridgeview Publishing, 1990), 254–70. Seibt's book is very helpful on many topics. Those more inclined to formalisms will especially appreciate her approach in contrast to mine.

53. Broad's discussion of absolute processes occurs in *An Examination of McTaggart's Philosophy,* vol. 1 (Cambridge: Cambridge University Press, 1933), 142–66.

54. See Section V of FMPP II: 53–5.

55. In these passages from "Foundations for a Metaphysics of Pure Process", "$\phi_2$-ings" stands for processes that are physical$_2$, that is, that are expressed by predicates adequate for the description of non-living things and processes.

"σ-ing" stands for a sensum, for example, a "redding".

56. I have reproduced so much of the text here because there is a serious printing error in the printed version, which corrupts §121 and omits §122 almost entirely. I have corrected the text by consulting the mimeographed typescripts Sellars gave to his students at Pittsburgh.

57. Sellars's picture here invites speculation that all absolute processes are ultimately qualitative. Why, then, are we aware of only a very restricted range of the absolute processes that constitute us, namely, those that embody the sensibles?

58. See, for instance, MP: 252, in KTM: 307.

## Chapter 9. Practical reason

1. W. David Solomon, "Ethical Theory", in *The Synoptic Vision: Essays on the Philosophy of Wilfrid Sellars*, C. F. Delaney *et al.* (Notre Dame, IN: University of Notre Dame Press, 1977), 149.

2. This quote comes from "Epistemology and the New Way of Words", and is applied to metaphysical and epistemological predicates, but it would be just as applicable to moral predicates, in Sellars's view. Compare the following from his "Autobiographical Reflections" concerning his time as a student at Oriel College, Oxford:

> Of a piece with this development was my growing sympathy for deontological intuitionism in ethics, particularly in the less metaphysically structured form which I found in the writings and lectures of H. A. Prichard. It struck me as far more adequate to the complexities of moral thinking than Moore's ever so clear and distinct Ideal Utilitarianism. I was conscious, however, of being an intuitionist in a Pickwickian sense. As I put it to myself at the time, Prichard's insights would somehow have to be cashed out in naturalistic terms.
>
> When emotivism appeared on the scene, it struck me as wrongheaded in its early insistence on the pseudo-conceptual character of ethical terms, propositions, and reasonings. And yet I also felt, from the start, that it had located one of the missing ingredients of the solution. Somehow intuitionism and emotivism would have to be *aufgehoben* into a naturalistic framework which recognized ethical concepts as genuine concepts and found a place for intersubjectivity and truth. (AR: 284–5)

3. See, for example, SM: 177; TA: 109; ORAV: 84.

4. In *Science and Metaphysics*, Sellars says that "shall" operates on action verbs, as opposed to "shall be the case", which operates on statements. But, in fact, he treats them both as sentential operators. Hector-Neri Castañeda generates a number of problems for Sellars's approach in *Science and Metaphysics* in his "Some Reflections on Wilfrid Sellars' Theory of Intentions", in *Action, Knowledge and Reality: Critical Studies in Honor of Wilfrid Sellars*, H.-N. Castañeda (ed.), 31–5 (Indianapolis, IN: Bobbs-Merrill, 1976). These get corrected in "On Reasoning About Values" (1980). There Sellars introduces instead a way of marking within the content of a "shall be" intention those factors that are taken to be "up to the agent" and those factors that are not, but are treated as givens of the circumstances. What is "up to me" includes performances in my "action vocabulary" and the foreseeable consequences thereof.

5. Sellars says explicitly that "every intention must have at least one 'up-to-me' constituent" (ORAV: 89). But as far as I can see, there is nothing wrong with an intention so removed from my sphere of direct action that the "up-to-me"

element is essentially negligible or present only in extremely unusual and highly unlikely circumstances.

6. For Sellars's treatment of the freedom–determinism dialectic see "Fatalism and Determinism" (1966) and "Reply to Donagan" (1975). The typescript of a revised version of "Fatalism and Determinism" was also circulated.

7. As we have seen, Sellars equates conceptuality with inferential potency. As he expresses it in "Science and Ethics" (1967), "The criterion I propose is that a word stands for a concept when there are good arguments in which it is essentially involved" (SE: 408).

8. There is an interesting complication here. Sellars does not think an ordinary expression of intention, say, "I'm going to have the raspberry tart for dessert" is either true or false. We assess such utterances in terms of realized–unrealized, reasonable–unreasonable. Moral judgements are expressions of intention, but, because of their universality and intersubjectivity, the vocabulary of 'true' and 'false' is appropriate to them.

9. See Bruce Aune, "Sellars on Practical Reason," in *Action, Knowledge and Reality*, H.-N. Castañeda (ed.), 1–26; *Reason and Action* (Dordrecht, Reidel, 1977); and "Sellars on Practical Inference", in *The Philosophy of Wilfrid Sellars: Queries and Extensions*, J. C. Pitt (ed.), 19–24; H.-N. Castañeda, "Some Reflections on Wilfrid Sellars' Theory of Intentions"; "Intending and the Logic of Intentions: Reply to Wilfrid Sellars", in *Agent, Language and the Structure of the World: Essays Presented to Hector-Neri Castañeda, With His Replies*, J. E. Tomberlin (ed.), 195–221 (Indianapolis, IN: Hackett, 1983); and CPCI. Sellars's correspondences with Castañeda and Aune are available on the website "Problems from Wilfrid Sellars", www.ditext.com/sellars/correspd.html (accessed June 2005).

10. An absolutely complete treatment would use dot-quotes to show that the points are not language specific. But not even Sellars gets that technical.

11. The original sentence can be used either to make a prediction or to express an intention. Although the surface grammar may be the same in each case, their logical form differs significantly in Sellars's estimation.

12. For example, TA: 110.

13. See ORAV: 85. But, clearly, we need still further distinctions. We would not criticize Thomas Jefferson as irrational in some way because he intended to eat a healthy diet but did not also have the intention to eat a diet low in saturated fats. Jefferson did not and could not (at the time) have had the concept of a saturated fat.

14. This quotation is from "'Ought' and Moral Principles", an unpublished typescript dated "Pittsburgh, February 14, 1966". The bibliography in *Kant and Pre-Kantian Themes* (2002) lists it as a predecessor of "Science and Ethics" (1967), but I doubt that. Although "Science and Ethics"was first published in *Philosophical Perspectives* in 1967, the acknowledgments there list it as having been given as a talk in 1960. "'Ought' and Moral Principles" shares its last two paragraphs with "Science and Ethics", but very little else. It includes a discussion of Jones and the Academy that directly prefigures the discussion in *Science and Metaphysics* (1968) (SM: 190ff.). In "'Ought' and Moral Principles," Sellars uses the notion of a *valuing* (expressed by an optative such as "Would that John's grant application be funded") instead of that of an intention as his basic element, probably because it was aimed at a non-professional audience. But there is no significant change in his position.

15. Thus the reasonableness invoked by a hypothetical imperative is the reasonableness of a conclusion intention relative to the premise intention in a

(possible) piece of practical reasoning. It does not commit itself concerning the reasonableness of either the premise intention or the conclusion intention *per se* (SM VII §91: 209).

16. This oversimplifies. There can be complex situations in which the facts of one's desires indeed need to be considered among the circumstances of one's actions. People trying to break a habit or addiction need to consider those desires and their strength. Putting themselves into situations where temptation would be almost impossible to overcome would be unreasonable.

17. Does he mean this literally: that the actions commanded by universal benevolence are an exact extensional equivalence for the actions commanded by morality? But even if the two set of actions were extensionally equivalent, it would not mean that universal benevolence is a proper *analysis* of morality.

18. See ORAV: 97. An *action* we-referential intention would be one, I take it, that itself can become a volition, that is, a "shall" and not merely a "shall be" intention.

19. It is important to distinguish the *expression* of a valuing from the *ascription* of a valuing. To my expressing a valuing "I would that my students had an easier time affording college" corresponds the *ascription* of the valuing to me: "DeVries values, from a personal point of view, that his students had an easier time affording college".

20. In "'Ought' and Moral Principles", Sellars repeats this in less technical language:
    (a) in their *content*
    ... that if *any* of us is in C he do A
    (b) in their subjective form
    *we would* that...
    (c) in their acceptance, i.e. in the fact that all *agree* in so valuing.
    (OMP: 16)

21. See SM: 222–3 for his argument defending this claim.

22. One can recognize here the outlines of a programme attempted not just by Peirce, but by Habermas in his "discourse ethics".

## Chapter 10. The necessity of the normative

1. This reveals a potentially dangerous ambiguity in Sellars's "image" metaphor. In speaking of what is in an image of the world, we can be referring simply to the *objects depicted* or we can be referring to the *manner of depiction*.

2. Of course, the *concept* of a scientific object is involved in normative proprieties, rules and so on. It is a concept. But the scientific *object* itself should be specifiable in purely descriptive, non-normative terms.

3. Sellars's note here: "This does not, of course, mean that there are no tables or elephants, but rather that tables and elephants as conceived by common sense do not really exist, i.e. that these concepts are *in principle* to be replaced by a counterpart built on a theoretical foundation. For an explication of what is meant by 'really exist' in this context, see 'Empiricism and the Philosophy of Mind,' 39ff."

4. Sellars's note here: "This aspect of the situation, which is not stressed by Feyerabend, is illustrated by the practical dimension of such common sense concepts as that of what it is to be a hammer."

5. The manifest image:
    is, first, the framework in terms of which man came to be aware of himself as man-in-the-world. It is the framework in terms of which, to use an existentialist turn of phrase, man first encountered himself – which is, of

course, when he came to be man. For it is no merely incidental feature of man that he has a conception of himself as man-in-the-world, just as it is obvious, on reflection, that "if man has a radically different conception of himself he would be a radically different kind of man".     (PSIM: 6)

# Bibliography

## The philosophical works of Wilfrid Sellars, in chronological order

1934. "Substance, Change and Event". MA thesis, State University of New York at Buffalo.

1947. "Pure Pragmatics and Epistemology". *Philosophy of Science* 14: 181–202. [Reprinted in PPPW.]

1947. "Epistemology and the New Way of Words". *Journal of Philosophy* 44: 645–60. [Reprinted in PPPW.]

1948. "Realism and the New Way of Words". *Philosophy and Phenomenological Research* 8: 601–34. [Reprinted in *Readings in Philosophical Analysis*, H. Feigl & W. Sellars (eds) (New York: Appleton-Century-Crofts, 1949) and in PPPW.]

1948. "Concepts as Involving Laws and Inconceivable without Them". *Philosophy of Science* 15: 287–315. [Reprinted in PPPW.]

1948–49. "Review of Ernest Cassirer, 'Language and Myth'". *Philosophy and Phenomenological Research* 9: 326–9.

1949. "Aristotelian Philosophies of Mind". In *Philosophy for the Future, The Quest of Modern Materialism*, R. Wood Sellars, V. J. McGill & M. Farber (eds), 544–70. New York: Macmillan. [Reprinted in KPT.]

1949. "Language, Rules and Behavior". In *John Dewey: Philosopher of Science and Freedom*, S. Hook (ed.), 289–315. New York: Dial Press. [Reprinted in PPPW.]

1949. "On the Logic of Complex Particulars". *Mind* 58: 306–38. [Reprinted in PPPW.]

1949. "Acquaintance and Description Again". *Journal of Philosophy* 46: 496–505.

1949. *Readings in Philosophical Analysis*, H. Feigl & W. Sellars (eds). New York: Appleton-Century-Crofts.

1950. "The Identity of Linguistic Expressions and the Paradox of Analysis". *Philosophical Studies* 1: 24–31.

1950. "Quotation Marks, Sentences, and Propositions". *Philosophy and Phenomenological Research* 10: 515–25. [Reprinted in PPPW.]

1950. "Gestalt Qualities and the Paradox of Analysis". *Philosophical Studies* 1: 92–4.

1950. "Review of Arthur Pap, Elements of Analytic Philosophy". *Philosophy and Phenomenological Research* 11: 104–9.

1951. "Obligation and Motivation". *Philosophical Studies* 2: 21–5.

1951. "Review of C. West Churchman and Russell L. Ackoff, *Methods of Inquiry: An Introduction to Philosophy and Scientific Method*". *Philosophy and Phenomenological Research* 12: 149–50.

1952. *Readings in Ethical Theory*, W. Sellars & J. Hospers (eds). New York: Appleton-Century-Crofts.

1952. "Obligation and Motivation". In *Readings in Ethical Theory*, W. Sellars & J. Hospers (eds), 511–17. New York: Appleton-Century-Crofts. [A revised and expanded version of OM.]

1952. "Comments on Mr. Hempel's Theses". *Review of Metaphysics* **5**: 623–5.
1952. "Mind, Meaning, and Behavior". *Philosophical Studies* **3**: 83–95.
1952. "Particulars". *Philosophy and Phenomenological Research* **13**: 184–99. [Reprinted in SPR.]
1953. "Is There a Synthetic A Priori?". *Philosophical Studies* **20**: 121–38. [Reprinted in a revised form in *American Philosophers at Work*, S. Hook (ed.), 135–59 (New York: Criterion Books, 1956). Reprinted in SPR.]
1953. "A Semantical Solution of the Mind–Body Problem". *Methodos* **5**: 45–82. [Reprinted in PPPW.]
1953. "Inference and Meaning". *Mind* **62**: 313–38. [Reprinted in PPPW.]
1954. "Presupposing". *The Philosophical Review* **63**: 197–215.
1954. "Some Reflections on Language Games". *Philosophical Studies* **21**: 204–28. [Reprinted in SPR.]
1954. "A Note on Popper's Argument for Dualism". *Analysis* **15**: 23–4.
1955. "Physical Realism". *Philosophy and Phenomenological Research* **15**: 13–32. [Reprinted in PP and PPME.]
1955. "Putnam on Synonymity and Belief". *Analysis* **15**: 117–20.
1955. "Vlastos and 'The Third Man'". *The Philosophical Review* **64**: 405–37. [Reprinted in PP and PPHP.]
1956. "Imperatives, Intentions, and the Logic of 'Ought'". *Methodos* **8**: 228–68.
1956. "The Concept of Emergence" (with Paul Meehl). In *Minnesota Studies in the Philosophy of Science*, vol. I, H. Feigl & M. Scriven (eds), 239–52. Minneapolis, MN: University of Minnesota Press.
1956. "Empiricism and the Philosophy of Mind". In *Minnesota Studies in the Philosophy of Science*, vol. I, H. Feigl & M. Scriven (eds), 253–329. Minneapolis, MN: University of Minnesota Press. [Originally presented at the University of London Special Lectures in Philosophy for 1956 as "The Myth of the Given: Three Lectures on Empiricism and the Philosophy of Mind"). Reprinted in SPR with additional footnotes. Published separately as *Empiricism and the Philosophy of Mind: with an Introduction by Richard Rorty and a Study Guide by Robert Brandom*, R. Brandom (ed.) (Cambridge, MA: Harvard University Press, 1997). Also reprinted in W. deVries & T. Triplett, *Knowledge, Mind, and the Given: A Reading of Sellars' "Empiricism and the Philosophy of Mind"*. (Indianapolis, IN: Hackett, 2000).]
1957. "Logical Subjects and Physical Objects". *Philosophy and Phenomenological Research* **17** (1957): 458–72.
1957. "Counterfactuals, Dispositions, and the Causal Modalities". In *Minnesota Studies in the Philosophy of Science*, vol. II, H. Feigl, M. Scriven & G. Maxwell (eds), 225–308. Minneapolis, MN: University of Minnesota Press.
1957. "Intentionality and the Mental". A symposium by correspondence with Roderick Chisholm. In *Minnesota Studies in the Philosophy of Science*, vol. II, H. Feigl, M. Scriven & G. Maxwell (eds), 507–39. Minneapolis, MN: University of Minnesota Press.
1957. "Substance and Form in Aristotle". *Journal of Philosophy* **54**: 688–99. [Reprinted in PP and PPHP.]
1960. "Grammar and Existence: A Preface to Ontology". *Mind* **69**: 499–533. [Reprinted in SPR.]
1960. "Being and Being Known". *Proceedings of the American Catholic Philosophical Association* (1960), 28–49. [Reprinted in SPR.]
1961. "The Language of Theories". In *Current Issues in the Philosophy of Science*, H. Feigl & G. Maxwell (eds), 57–77. London: Holt, Rinehart and Winston. [Reprinted in SPR.]
1961. "Comments on Maxwell's 'Meaning Postulates in Scientific Theories'". In *Current Issues in the Philosophy of Science*, H. Feigl & G. Maxwell (eds), 183–92. London: Holt, Rinehart and Winston.
1962. "Time and the World Order". In *Minnesota Studies in the Philosophy of Science*, vol. III, H. Feigl, & G. Maxwell (eds), 527–616. Minneapolis, MN: University of Minnesota Press.
1962. "Philosophy and the Scientific Image of Man". In *Frontiers of Science and Philosophy*, R. Colodny (ed.), 35–78. Pittsburgh, PA: University of Pittsburgh Press. [Reprinted in SPR.]
1962. "Naming and Saying". *Philosophy of Science* **29**: 7–26. [Reprinted in SPR.]
1962. "Truth and Correspondence". *Journal of Philosophy* **59**: 29–56. [Reprinted in SPR.]
1963. "Imperatives, Intentions, and the Logic of 'Ought'". In *Morality and the Language of Conduct*, H.-N. Castañeda & G. Nakhnikian (eds), 159–214. Detroit, MI: Wayne State University Press. [A radically revised and enlarged version of IIO.]

1963. "Empiricism and Abstract Entities". In *The Philosophy of Rudolf Carnap*, P. A. Schilpp (ed.), 431–68. La Salle, IL: Open Court. [Reprinted in EPH.]

1963. "Raw Materials, Subjects and Substrata". In *The Concept of Matter*, E. McMullin (ed.), 259–72, 276–80. Notre Dame, IL: University of Notre Dame Press (remarks by Sellars on pages 55–7, 100–101 and 245–7). [Reprinted in PP and PPHP.]

1963. "Comments on McMullin's 'Matter as a Principle'". In *The Concept of Matter*, E. McMullin (ed.), 209–13. Notre Dame, IL: University of Notre Dame Press.

1963. "Abstract Entities". *Review of Metaphysics* 16: 627–71. [Reprinted in PP and PPME.]

1963. "Classes as Abstract Entities and the Russell Paradox". *Review of Metaphysics* 17: 67–90. [Reprinted in PP and PPME.]

1963. "Theoretical Explanation". *Philosophy of Science: The Delaware Seminar* II, 61–78. New York: John Wiley. [Reprinted in PPME and in EPH.]

1963. *Science, Perception and Reality*. London: Routledge & Kegan Paul. [Reissued (Atascadero, CA: Ridgeview Publishing, 1991). Includes items P, ITSA, SRLG, EPM, GE, BBK, LT, PSIM, TC, PHM.]

1963. "Phenomenalism". In *Science, Perception and Reality*, 60–105. London: Routledge & Kegan Paul.

1964. "The Paradox of Analysis: A Neo-Fregean Approach". *Analysis*, supp. vol. 24: 84–98. [Reprinted in PP and PPME.]

1964. "Induction as Vindication". *Philosophical Studies* 31: 197–231. [Reprinted in EPH.]

1964. "Notes on Intentionality". *Journal of Philosophy* 61: 655–65. [Reprinted in PPME.]

1965. "The Identity Approach to the Mind-Body Problem". *Review of Metaphysics* 18: 430–51. [Reprinted in PPME.]

1965. "Meditations Leibnitziennes". *American Philosophical Quarterly* 2: 105–18. [Reprinted in PPHP.]

1965. "Scientific Realism or Irenic Instrumentalism: A Critique of Nagel and Feyerabend on Theoretical Explanation". *Boston Studies in the Philosophy of Science*, vol. 2, R. Cohen & M. Wartofsky (eds), 171–204. Dordrecht: D. Reidel. [Reprinted in PPME.]

1966. "The Intentional Realism of Everett Hall". *The Southern Journal of Philosophy* 4 (special issue *Commonsense Realism: Critical Essays on the Philosophy of Everett W. Hall*, E. M. Adams (ed.)): 103–15. [Reprinted in PPME.]

1966. "Thought and Action". In *Freedom and Determinism*, K. Lehrer (ed.), 105–39. New York: Random House.

1966. "Fatalism and Determinism". In *Freedom and Determinism*, K. Lehrer (ed.), 141–74. New York: Random House.

1966. "The Refutation of Phenomenalism: Prolegomena to a Defense of Scientific Realism". In *Mind, Matter, and Method: Essays in Philosophy of Science in Honor of Herbert Feigl*, P. K. Feyerabend & G. Maxwell (eds), 198–214. Minneapolis, MN: University of Minnesota Press.

1966. "'Ought' and Moral Principles". Unpublished typescript dated "Pittsburgh, February 14".

1967. *Philosophical Perspectives*. Springfield, IL: Charles C. Thomas. [Reprinted in two volumes (Atascadero, CA: Ridgeview Publishing, 1977). Includes SC, VTM, AMI, SFA, RMSS, ML, PR, IRH, AE, CAE, PANF, NI, TE, SRI, IAMB, SE.]

1967. "Aristotle's Metaphysics: An Interpretation". See *Philosophical Perspectives* (1967).

1967. "The Soul as Craftsman". See *Philosophical Perspectives* (1967).

1967. "Science and Ethics". See *Philosophical Perspectives* (1967).

1967. "Vlastos and 'The Third Man': a Rejoinder". See *Philosophical Perspectives* (1967).

1967. "Phenomenalism". In *Intentionality, Minds and Perception*, H.-N. Castañeda (ed.), 215–74. Detroit, MI: Wayne State University Press. [An abbreviated version of essay PHM.]

1967. *Science and Metaphysics: Variations on Kantian Themes*, The John Locke Lectures for 1965–66. London: Routledge & Kegan Paul. [Reissued (Atascadero, CA: Ridgeview Publishing, 1992).]

1967. "Reply to Aune". In *Intentionality, Minds and Perception*, H.-N. Castañeda (ed.), 286–300. Detroit, MI: Wayne State University Press.

1967. *Form and Content in Ethical Theory*, The Lindley Lecture for 1967. Department of Philosophy, University of Kansas.

1967. "Some Remarks on Kant's Theory of Experience". *Journal of Philosophy* 64: 633–47. [Reprinted in EPH.]

1967. "Some Reflections on Thoughts and Things". *Noûs* 1: 97–121. [Reprinted as Chapter III of SM.]

1967. "Reflections on Contrary to Duty Imperatives". *Noûs* 1: 303–44.

1967. "Kant's Views on Sensibility and Understanding". *Monist* **51**: 463–91. [Reprinted as Chapter I of SM.]
1969. "Metaphysics and the Concept of a Person". In *The Logical Way of Doing Things*, K. Lambert (ed.), 219–52. New Haven, CT: Yale University Press. [Reprinted in EPH.]
1969. "Some Problems about Belief". In *Philosophical Logic*, J. W. Davis, D. T. Hockney & W. K. Wilson (eds), 46–65. Dordrecht: D. Reidel. [Reprinted in *Words and Objections: Essays on the Work of W. V. Quine*, D. Davidson & J. Hintikka (eds), 186–205 (Dordrecht: D. Reidel, 1969) and in EPH.
1969. "Language as Thought and as Communication". *Philosophy and Phenomenological Research* **29**: 506–27.
1970. "Belief and the Expression of Belief". In *Language, Belief, and Metaphysics*, H. E. Kiefer & M. K. Munitz (eds), 146–58. Albany, NY: SUNY Press.
1970. "Are There Non-deductive Logics?" In *Essays in Honor of Carl G. Hempel*, N. Rescher *et al.* (eds), 83–103. Dordrecht: D. Reidel. [Reprinted in EPH.]
1970. "On Knowing the Better and Doing the Worse". *International Philosophical Quarterly* **10**: 5–19. [Reprinted in EPH.]
1970. "Ontology, the A Priori and Kant", Part One: Introduction (Part Two is KTE). See *Kant's Transcendental Metaphysics* (2002).
1970. "Towards a Theory of the Categories". *Experience and Theory*, L. Foster & J. W. Swanson (eds), 55–78. Amherst, MA: University of Massachusetts Press.
1971. "Science, Sense Impressions, and Sensa: A Reply to Cornman". *Review of Metaphysics* **25**: 391–447.
1971. "The Double-Knowledge Approach to the Mind-Body Problem". *The New Scholasticism* **45**: 269–89.
1972. "...this I or he or it (the thing) which thinks". Presidential address 1970, American Philosophical Association (Eastern Division). *Proceedings of the American Philosophical Association* **44**: 5–31. [Reprinted in EPH.]
1973. "Actions and Events". *Noûs* **7**: 179–202.
1973. "Reason and the Art of Living in Plato". In *Phenomenology and Natural Existence: Essays in Honor of Marvin Farber*, D. Riepe (ed.), 353–77. Albany, NY: SUNY Press. [Reprinted in EPH.]
1973. "Reply to Marras". *Canadian Journal of Philosophy* **2**: 485–93. [Reprinted in EPH.]
1973. "Conceptual Change". In *Conceptual Change*, P. Maynard & G. Pearce (ed.), 77–93. Dordrecht: D. Reidel. [Reprinted in EPH.]
1973. "Reply to Quine". *Synthese* **26**: 122–45. [Reprinted in EPH.]
1973. "Givenness and Explanatory Coherence" [abbreviated version]. *Journal of Philosophy* **7**: 612–24.
1974. "Ontology and the Philosophy of Mind in Russell". In *Bertrand Russell's Philosophy*, G. Nakhnikian (ed.), 57–100. London: Duckworth.
1974. "Seeing, Seeming, and Sensing". In *The Ontological Turn: Studies in the Philosophy of Gustav Bergmann*, M. S. Gram & E. D. Klemke (eds), 195–210. Iowa City, IA: University of Iowa Press.
1974. "Meaning as Functional Classification (A Perspective on the Relation of Syntax to Semantics)", *Synthese* **27** (special issue *Intentionality, Language and Translation*, J. G. Troyer & S. C. Wheeler, III (eds)): 417–37. [An expanded version of BEB.]
1974. "Reply to Dennett and Putnam". *Synthese* **27** (special issue *Intentionality, Language and Translation*, J. G. Troyer & S. C. Wheeler, III (eds)): 457–70.
1974. *Essays in Philosophy and its History*. Dordrecht: D. Reidel. [Includes items EAE, CAE, TE, IV, KTE, MP, SPB, NDL, LTC, KBDW, TTC, AE, AL, I, RM, CC, RQ.]
1975. "The Structure of Knowledge: (I) Perception; (II) Minds; (III) Epistemic Principles". In *Action, Knowledge and Reality: Studies in Honor of Wilfrid Sellars*, H.-N. Castañeda (ed.), 295–347. New York: Bobbs-Merrill.
1975. "Autobiographical Reflections: (February, 1973)". In *Action, Knowledge and Reality: Studies in Honor of Wilfrid Sellars*, H.-N. Castañeda (ed.), 277–93. New York: Bobbs-Merrill.
1975. "Reply to Donagan". *Philosophical Studies* **27**: 149–84.
1975. "The Adverbial Theory of the Objects of Sensation". In *Metaphilosophy* 6, T. Bynum (ed.), 144–60. Oxford: Basil Blackwell.
1975. "On the Introduction of Abstract Entities". In *Forms of Representation*, proceedings of the 1972 Philosophy Colloquium of the University of Western Ontario, B. Freed, A. Marras & P. Maynard (eds), 47–74. New York: North-Holland. [Reprinted in EPH.]
1976. "Volitions Re-affirmed". In *Action Theory*, M. Brand & D. Walton (eds), 47–66. Dordrecht: D. Reidel.

1976. "Kant's Transcendental Idealism". *Collections of Philosophy* 6: 165–81.

1976. "Is Scientific Realism Tenable?", *Proceedings of PSA* II: 307–334.

1977. "Berkeley and Descartes: Reflections on the 'New Way of Ideas'". In *Studies in Perception: Interpretations in the History of Philosophy and Science*, P. K. Machamer & R. G. Turnbull (eds), 259–311. Columbus, OH: Ohio State University Press. [Reprinted in KTM.]

1977. "Hochberg on Mapping, Meaning, and Metaphysics". In *Midwest Studies in Philosophy* 11, P. French, T. Vehling, Jr. & H. Wettstein (eds), 214–24. Minneapolis, MN: University of Minnesota Press4.

1977. *Philosophical Perspectives: History of Philosophy*. Atascadero, CA: Ridgeview Publishing. [A reprint of Part I of *Philosophical Perspectives*.]

1977. *Philosophical Perspectives: Metaphysics and Epistemology*. Atascadero, CA: Ridgeview Publishing. [A reprint of Part II of *Philosophical Perspectives*.]

1978. "Some Reflections on Perceptual Consciousness". In *Crosscurrents in Philosophy: Selected Studies in Phenomenology and Existential Philosophy 7*, R. Bruzina & B. Wilshire (eds), 169–85. The Hague: Martinus Nijhoff.

1978. "The Role of Imagination in Kant's Theory of Experience". The Dotterer Lecture 1978. In *Categories: A Colloquium*, H. W. Johnstone, Jr. (ed.), 231–45. University Park, PA: Pennsylvania State University Press.

1979. "More on Givenness and Explanatory Coherence". In *Justification and Knowledge*, G. Pappas (ed.), 169–82. Dordrecht: D. Reidel. [Reprinted in *Perceptual Knowledge*, J. Dancy (ed.), 177–91 (Oxford: Oxford University Press, 1988).]

1979. "Sellars' Notes for The Ernst Cassirer Lectures", 16, 18 and 19 April, Yale University. [Published in KTM.]

1980. *Naturalism and Ontology* [The John Dewey Lectures for 1973–74]. Atascadero, CA: Ridgeview Publishing. [Reprinted with corrections in 1997.]

1980. "On Reasoning About Values". *American Philosophical Quarterly* 17: 81–101.

1980. "Behaviorism, Language and Meaning". *Pacific Philosophical Quarterly* 61: 3–30.

1980. *Pure Pragmatics and Possible Worlds: The Early Essays of Wilfrid Sellars*, J. F. Sicha (ed.). Atascadero, CA: Ridgeview Publishing. [Includes items PPE, ENWW, RNWW, CIL, LRB, LCP, QMSP, SSMB, IM.]

1981. "Foundations for a Metaphysics of Pure Process" [The Carus Lectures]. *The Monist* 64: 3–90.

1981. "Mental Events". *Philosophical Studies* 39: 325–45.

1982. "Sensa or Sensings: Reflections on the Ontology of Perception". *Philosophical Studies* 41 (Essays in Honor of James Cornman): 83–111.

1983. "Conditional Promises and Conditional Intentions (Including a Reply to Castañeda)". In *Agent, Language and the Structure of the World: Essays Presented to Hector-Neri Castañeda. With His Replies*, J. E. Tomberlin (ed.), 195–221. Indianapolis, IN: Hackett.

1983. "Towards a Theory of Predication". In *How Things Are*, J. Bogen & J. McGuire (eds), 281–318. Dordrecht: D. Reidel.

1988. "On Accepting First Principles". In *Philosophical Perspectives, 2, Epistemology*, J. E. Tomberlin (ed.), 301–14. Atascadero, CA: Ridgeview Publishing.

1989. *The Metaphysics of Epistemology: Lectures by Wilfrid Sellars*, P. V. Amaral (ed.). Atascadero, CA: Ridgeview Publishing.

2002. *Kant and Pre-Kantian Themes: Lectures by Wilfrid Sellars*, P. V. Amaral (ed.). Atascadero, CA Ridgeview Publishing. [University lectures on *The Critique of Pure Reason* and its historical framework: Descartes, Leibniz, Spinoza, and Hume, May–June 1976. Includes a reprint of APM.]

2002. *Kant's Transcendental Metaphysics: Sellars' Cassirer Lectures and Other Essays*, J. F. Sicha (ed.). Atascadero, CA: Ridgeview Publishing. [Includes a reprint of KTE, MP, KBDW, TTC, I, BD, KTI, IKTE, SRPC, OAFP, and the unpublished OAPK and CLN.]

# References

Alston, W. P. 1971. "Varieties of Privileged Access". *American Philosophical Quarterly* 8: 223–41.

Alston, W. P. 1989. "What's Wrong with Immediate Knowledge?". In his *Epistemic Justification*, 52–78. Ithaca, NY: Cornell University Press.

# Wilfrid Sellars

Alston, W. P. 2002. "Sellars and the 'Myth of the Given'". *Philosophy and Phenomenological Research* **65**: 69–86.

Astington, J. 1996. "What is Theoretical about the Child's Theory of Mind?: A Vygotskyan View of its Development". In *Lev Vygotsky: Critical Assessments: Future Directions, vol. IV*, P. Lloyd & C. Fernyhough (eds), 401–18. New York: Routledge.

Aune, B. 1975. "Sellars on Practical Reason". In *Action, Knowledge and Reality*, H.-N. Castañeda (ed.), 1–26. Indianapolis, IN: Bobbs-Merrill.

Aune, B. 1977. *Reason and Action*. Dordrecht: D. Reidel.

Aune, B. 1978. "Sellars on Practical Inference". In *The Philosophy of Wilfrid Sellars: Queries and Extensions*, J. C. Pitt (ed.), 19–24. Dordrecht: D. Reidel.

Aune, B. & W. Sellars n.d. "Correspondence between Wilfrid Sellars and Bruce Aune", www.ditext.com/sellars/csa.html [accessed May 2005].

Baron-Cohen, S. 1999. "Evolution of a Theory of Mind". In *Evolution of the Hominid Mind*, M. Corballis & S. Lea (eds), 261–77. Oxford: Oxford University Press.

Baron-Cohen, S. 2000. "Theory of Mind and Autism: A Fifteen Year Review." In *Understanding Other Minds*, S. Baron-Cohen, H. Tager Flusberg & D. Cohen (eds), 3–20. Oxford: Oxford University Press.

Bonevac, D. 2002. "Sellars vs. the Given". *Philosophy and Phenomenological Research* **64**(1) (January): 1–30.

Braithwaite, R. B. 1953. *Scientific Explanation*. Cambridge: Cambridge University Press.

Brandom, R. 1994. *Making it Explicit: Reasoning, Representing, and Discursive Commitment*. Cambridge, MA: Harvard University Press.

Brandom, R. 1997. "Study Guide to 'Empiricism and the Philosophy of Mind'". In *Empiricism and the Philosophy of Mind*, W. Sellars, 119–81. Cambridge, MA: Harvard University Press.

Broad, C. D. 1933. *An Examination of McTaggart's Philosophy*, vol. 1. Cambridge: Cambridge University Press.

Carnap, R. 1937. *The Logical Syntax of Language*, A. Smeaton, Countess von Zeppelin (trans.). London: Routledge & Kegan Paul.

Carnap, R. 1939. *Foundations of Logic and Mathematics*. Chicago, IL: University of Chicago Press. [Reprinted as "Theories as Partially Interpreted Formal Systems", in *Readings in the Philosophy of Science*, B. A. Brody & R. E. Grandy (eds), 5–11 (Englewood Cliffs, NJ: Prentice Hall 1989).]

Carnap, R. 1969. *The Logical Structure of the World*, R. A. George (trans.). Berkeley, CA: University of California Press. [Originally published as *Der Logische Aufbau der Welt* (Leipzig: Felix Meiner Verlag, 1928).]

Carroll, L. 1895. "What the Tortoise said to Achilles". *Mind*, New Series, **4**(14) (April): 278–80.

Carruthers, P. & P. Smith 1996. *Theories of Theories of Mind*. Cambridge: Cambridge University Press.

Castañeda, H.-N. 1976. "Some Reflections on Wilfrid Sellars' Theory of Intentions". In *Action, Knowledge and Reality: Critical Studies in Honor of Wilfrid Sellars*, H.-N. Castañeda (ed.), 31–5. Indianapolis, IN: Bobbs-Merrill.

Castañeda, H.-N. 1983. "Intending and the Logic of Intentions: Reply to Wilfrid Sellars". In *Agent, Language and the Structure of the World: Essays Presented to Hector-Neri Castañeda, With His Replies*, J. E. Tomberlin (ed.) 195–221. Indianapolis, IN: Hackett.

Castañeda, H.-N. & W. Sellars n.d. "Correspondence between Hector Castañeda and Wilfrid Sellars on Philosophy of Mind", www.ditext.com/sellars/corr.html [accessed May 2005].

Chisholm, R. 1966. *Theory of Knowledge*. Englewood Cliffs, NJ: Prentice-Hall.

Chisholm, R. 1955–56. "Sentences about Believing". *Proceedings of the Aristotelian Society* **56**: 125–48. [Reprinted in the published correspondence with Sellars, ITM: 510–20.]

Churchland, P. 1981. "Eliminative Materialism and the Propositional Attitudes". *Journal of Philosophy* **78**: 67–90.

Cornman, J. 1970. "Sellars, Scientific Realism, and Sensa". *The Review of Metaphysics* **23**: 417–51.

Cornman, J. 1971. *Materialism and Sensations*. New Haven, CT: Yale University Press.

Dancy, J. (ed.) 1988. *Perceptual Knowledge*. Oxford: Oxford University Press.

Davidson, D. 1974. "On the Very Idea of a Conceptual Scheme". *Proceedings and Addresses of the American Philosophical Association* **47**, 5–20. [Reprinted in D. Davidson, *Inquiries into Truth and Interpretation*, 183–98 (Oxford: Oxford University Press, 1984).]

Davidson, D. 2000. "Interview". *The Dualist* **7**: 60.

Davidson, D. 2001. *Subjective, Intersubjective, Objective*. Oxford: Oxford University Press.

# Bibliography

Davies, M. & T. Stone (eds) 1995. *Folk Psychology: The Theory of Mind Debate*. Oxford: Blackwell.

Davies, M. & T. Stone (eds) 1995. *Mental Simulation: Evaluations and Applications*. Oxford: Blackwell.

Delaney, C. F., M. J. Loux, G. Gutting *et al*. 1977. *The Synoptic Vision: Essays on the Philosophy of Wilfrid Sellars*. Notre Dame, IN: University of Notre Dame Press.

deVries, W. & T. Triplett 2000. *Knowledge, Mind, and the Given: Reading Wilfrid Sellars's "Empiricism and the Philosophy of Mind"*. Indianapolis, IN: Hackett.

deVries, W. n.d. "Sellars, Animals, and Thought", www.ditext.com/devries/sellanim.html [accessed May 2005].

Dretske, F. 1995. *Naturalizing the Mind*. Cambridge, MA: MIT Press.

Duhem, P. 1954. *Aim and Structure of Physical Theory*. New York: Atheneum.

Dunn, J. M. & N. D. Belnap 1968. "The Substitution Interpretation of the Quantifiers". *Noûs* 2: 177–85.

Eddington, A. S. 1928. *The Nature of the Physical World*. New York: Macmillan.

Fales, E. 1996. *A Defense of the Given*. Lanham, MD: Rowman & Littlefield.

Feigl, H. & W. Sellars (eds) 1949. *Readings in Philosophical Analysis*. New York: Appleton-Century-Crofts.

Firth, R. 1964. "Coherence, Certainty, and Epistemic Priority". *The Journal of Philosophy* **66** (October): 545–57.

Fodor, J. D. 1980. *Semantics: Theories of Meaning in Generative Grammar*. Cambridge, MA: Harvard University Press.

Garfield, J. L. 1988. *Belief in Psychology*. Cambridge, MA: MIT Press.

Garfield, J. L. 1989. "The Myth of Jones and the Mirror of Nature: Reflections on Introspection". *Philosophy and Phenomenological Research* **50**: 1–26.

Garfield, J. L., C. C. Peterson & T. Perry 2001. "Social Cognition, Language Acquisition and the Development of the Theory of Mind". *Mind & Language* **16**: 526.

Geach, P. T. 1951. "On What There Is". *Proceedings of the Aristotelian Society,* supplementary volume **25**: 125–36.

Goldman, A. H. 1992. "The Given". In *A Companion to Epistemology*, J. Dancy & E. Sosa (eds), 159–61. Oxford: Blackwell.

Goldman, A. 1989. "Interpretation Psychologized". *Mind and Language* **4**: 161–85.

Goldman, A. 1993. "The Psychology of Folk Psychology. *The Behavioral and Brain Sciences* **16**: 15-028.

Gordon, R. M. 1986. "Folk Psychology as Simulation". *Mind and Language* **1**: 158–71.

Gordon, R. M. & J. Barker. 1994. "Autism and the 'Theory of Mind' Debate". In *Philosophical Psychopathology: A Book of Readings*, G. Graham & L. Stephens (eds), 163–81. Cambridge, MA: MIT Press.

Gordon, R. M. 1995. "Sympathy, Simulation, and the Impartial Spectator". *Ethics* **105**: 727–42.

Gordon, R. M. 2000. "Sellars's Ryleans Revisited". *Protosociology* **14**: 102–14.

Grice, H. P. 1957. "Meaning". *The Philosophical Review* **66**(3) (July): 377–88.

Grice, H. P. 1969. "Utterer's Meaning and Intention". *The Philosophical Review* **78**(2) (April): 147–77.

Gutting, G. 1977. "Philosophy of Science". In *The Synoptic Vision: Essays on the Philosophy of Wilfrid Sellars*, C. F. Delaney *et al* (eds)., 73–104. Notre Dame, IN: University of Notre Dame Press.

Gutting, G. 1982. "Realism vs. Constructive Empiricism". *Monist* **65**: 336–49.

Harris, P. 1989. *Children and Emotion*. Oxford: Blackwell.

Heal, J. 1986. "Replication and Functionalism". In *Language, Mind, and Logic*, J. Butterfield (ed.), 135–50. Cambridge: Cambridge University Press.

Hempel, C. 1965. *Aspects of Scientific Explanation*. New York: Free Press.

Hempel, C. 1966. *Philosophy of Natural Science*. Englewood Cliffs, NJ: Prentice-Hall.

Hooker, C. A. 1977. "Sellars' Argument for the Inevitability of the Secondary Qualities". *Philosophical Studies* **32**: 335–48.

Jacquette, D. 1994. *Philosophy of Mind*. Englewood Cliff, NJ: Prentice Hall.

Kant, I. 1967. *Groundwork of the Metaphysics of Morals*, H. J. Paton (trans.). New York: Barnes and Noble.

Kant, I. 1929 [1782/1787]. *Critique of Pure Reason*, N. Kemp Smith (trans.). New York: St. Martin's Press.

Kripke, S. 1976. "Is There a Problem about Substitutional Quantification?". In *Truth and Meaning*, G. Evans & J. McDowell (eds), 325–419. Oxford: Clarendon Press.

Kukla, R. 2000. "Myth, Memory and Misrecognition in Sellars' 'Empiricism and the Philosophy of Mind'". *Philosophical Studies* **101**: 161–211.

Lance, M. 1996. "Quantification, Substitution, and Conceptual Content". *Noûs* **30**: 481–507.

Lange, M. 2000. "Salience, Supervenience, and Layer Cakes in Sellars's Scientific Realism, McDowell's Moral Realism, and the Philosophy of Mind". *Philosophical Studies* **101**: 213–51.

Langford, C. H. 1949. "The Institutional Use of *The*". *Philosophy and Phenomenological Research* **10**(1) (September): 115–20.

Lear, E. [n.d.] "The Jumblies". www.nonsenselit.org/Lear/ns/jumblies.html or www.poetry-archive.com/l/the_jumblies.html [accessed May 2005].

Lycan, W. 1987. *Consciousness*. Cambridge, MA: MIT Press.

Lyons, J. C. [n.d.] "Externalism and the Sellarsian Dilemma", http://comp.uark.edu/%7Ejclyons/papers/ESD.PDF [accessed June 2005].

Marion, M. 2000. "Oxford Realism: Knowledge and Perception I". *British Journal for the History of Philosophy* **8**(2): 299–328.

Marion, M. 2000. "Oxford Realism: Knowledge and Perception II". *British Journal for the History of Philosophy* **8**(3): 485–519.

Marras, A. (ed.) 1972. *Intentionality, Mind, and Language*. Champaign, IL: University of Illinois Press.

Marras, A. 1972. "Introduction". In *Intentionality, Mind, and Language*, A. Marras (ed.), 3–27. Champaign, IL: University of Illinois Press.

Marras, A. 1973. "On Sellars' Linguistic Theory of Conceptual Activity". *Canadian Journal of Philosophy* **2**: 471–83.

Marras, A. 1973. "Reply to Sellars". *Canadian Journal of Philosophy* **2**: 495–501.

Marras, A. 1973. "Sellars on Thought and Language". *Noûs* **7**: 152–63.

Marras, A. 1976. "Sellars' Behaviourism: A Reply to Fred Wilson". *Philosophical Studies* **30**: 413–18.

Marras, A. 1977. "The Behaviourist Foundation of Sellar's Semantics". *Dialogue* (Canada) **16**: 664–75.

Marras, A. 1978. "Rules, Meaning and Behavior". In *The Philosophy of Wilfrid Sellars: Queries and Extensions*, J. C. Pitt (ed.) 163–87. Dordrecht: D. Reidel,.

Marras, A. & W. Sellars n.d. "Correspondence Between Wilfrid Sellars and Ausonio Marras", www.ditext.com/sellars/csm.html [accessed May 2005].

McDowell, J. 1998. "Having the World in View: Sellars, Kant, and Intentionality". The 1997 Woodbridge Lectures. *Journal of Philosophy* **95**: 431–91.

Merriam-Webster 2003. *Merriam-Webster's Collegiate Dictionary*, 11th edn. Springfield, MA: Merriam-Webster.

Meyers, R. G. 1981. "Sellars' Rejection of Foundations". *Philosophical Studies* **39**: 61–78.

Millikan, R. 1984. *Language, Thought, and Other Biological Categories*. Cambridge, MA: MIT Press.

Millikan, R. 1993. *White Queen Psychology and Other Essays For Alice*. Cambridge, MA: MIT Press 1993.

Mitchell, P. 1997. *Introduction to Theory of Mind: Children, Autism, and Apes*. Oxford: Oxford University Press.

Morris, C. W. 1938. "Foundations of the Theory of Signs". *International Encyclopedia of Unified Science* **1**(2) (O. Neurath (ed.)). [Reprinted (Chicago, IL: University of Chicago Press, 1970–71).]

Muilenberg, G. & R. C. Richardson 1982. "Sellars and Sense Impressions". *Erkenntnis* **17**: 171–212.

Nagel, E. 1961. *The Structure of Science: Problems in the Logic of Scientific Explanation*. New York: Harcourt, Brace & World.

Palmer, F. R. 1981. *Semantics*, 2nd edn. Cambridge: Cambridge University Press.

Papineau, D. 1993. *Philosophical Naturalism*. Oxford: Blackwell.

Peirce, C. S. 1960. *Collected Papers*, 8 vols, C. Hartshorne & P. Weiss (eds). Cambridge, MA: Harvard University Press.

Pepper, S. C. 1926. "Emergence". *Journal of Philosophy* **23**: 241–5.

Perner, J., T. Ruffman & S. Leekam 1994. "Theory of Mind is Contagious: You Catch it from your Sibs". *Child Development* **65**: 1224–34.

Pitt, J. C. (ed.) 1978. *The Philosophy of Wilfrid Sellars: Queries and Extensions*. Dordrecht: D. Reidel.

Pitt, J. 1981. *Pictures, Images and Conceptual Change: An Analysis of Wilfrid Sellars' Philosophy of Science*. Dordrecht: D. Reidel.

Bibliography

Premack, D. & G. Woodruff 1978. "Does the Chimpanzee have a Theory of Mind?". *The Behavioral and Brain Sciences* **4**: 515–26.

Prichard, H. A. 1950. "Perception". In his *Knowledge and Perception: Essays and Lectures*, 52–68. Oxford: Oxford University Press.

Quine, W. V. O. 1948. "On What There Is". *Review of Metaphysics* **2**(5) (September): 21–38. [Reprinted in *From a Logical Point of View: 9 Logico-Philosophical Essays* (Cambridge, MA: Harvard University Press, 1953).]

Quine, W. V. O. 1951. "Two Dogmas of Empiricism". *The Philosophical Review* **60**(1) (January): 20–43. [Reprinted in *From a Logical Point of View: 9 Logico-Philosophical Essays* (Cambridge, MA: Harvard University Press, 1953).]

Quine, W. V. O. 1969. "Epistemology Naturalized". In his *Ontological Relativity and Other Essays*, 69–90. New York: Columbia University Press.

Quinton, A. 1955. "The Problem of Perception". *Mind* **64**: 28–51.

Rorty, R. 1967. *The Linguistic Turn*. Chicago, IL: University of Chicago Press.

Rosenberg, J. F. 1980. *One World and Our Knowledge of It*. Dordrecht: D. Reidel.

Rosenberg, J. F. 1982. "The Place of Color in the Scheme of Things: A Roadmap to Sellars' Carus Lectures". *The Monist* **65**: 315–35.

Rosenberg, J. F. 2000. "Perception and Inner Sense: A Problem about Direct Awareness". *Philosophical Studies* **101**: 143–60.

Rosenberg, J. F. 2002. *Thinking About Knowing*. Oxford: Oxford University Press.

Rosenberg, J. F. 2003. "Sellarsian Seeing: In Search of Perceptual Authority". In *Perception and Reality*, R. Schumacher (ed.), 262–85. Paderborn: Mentis.

Rosenberg, J. F. 2005. "Ryleans and Outlookers: Wilfrid Sellars on 'Mental States'". *Midwest Studies in Philosophy* **28** (*The American Philosophers*).

Rosenberg, J. F. n.d. "Sellarsian Picturing", unpublished manuscript.

Russell, B. A. W. 1905. "On Denoting". *Mind* **14**: 479–93.

Russell, B. A. W. 1910. "Knowledge by Acquaintance and Knowledge by Description". *Proceedings of the Aristotelian Society* **11**: 108–28.

Russell, B. A. W. 1912. *The Problems of Philosophy*. London: Williams and Norgate.

Seibt, J. 1990. *Properties as Processes: A Synoptic Study of Wilfrid Sellars' Nominalism*. Atascadero, CA: Ridgeview Publishing.

Sicha, J. 1974. *A Metaphysics of Elementary Mathematics*. Amherst, MA: University of Massachusetts Press.

Solomon, W. D. 1977. "Ethical Theory". In *The Synoptic Vision: Essays on the Philosophy of Wilfrid Sellars*, C. F. Delaney *et al.* Notre Dame, IN: University of Notre Dame Press.

Sosa, E. 1997. "Mythology of the Given". *History of Philosophy Quarterly* **14**: 275–86.

Sosa, E. 2003. "Are There Two Grades of Knowledge? Part II: Knowledge, Animal and Reflective: A Reply to Michael Williams". *Proceedings of the Aristotelian Society*, supplementary volume **77**: 113–30.

Suppe, F. (ed.) 1977. *The Structure of Scientific Theories*, 2nd edn. Champaign, IL: University of Illinois Press.

Triplett, T. & W. deVries unpublished. "Sellars's Principle of Observation Knowledge".

van Fraassen, B. 1975. "Wilfrid Sellars and Scientific Realism". *Dialogue* **14**: 606–16.

van Fraassen, B. 1977. "On the Radical Incompleteness of the Manifest Image (Comments on Sellars)". In *PSA 1976, Volume II*, F. Suppe & P. Asquith (eds), 335–43. East Lansing, MI: Philosophy of Science Association.

van Fraassen, B. 1980. *The Scientific Image*. Oxford: Clarendon Press.

Wellman, H. M. 1990. *The Child's Theory of Mind*. Cambridge, MA: MIT Press.

Williams, M. 2003. "Are There Two Grades of Knowledge? Part I: Mythology of the Given: Sosa, Sellars and the Task of Epistemology". In *Proceedings of the Aristotelian Society*, supplementary volume **77**: 91–112.

Wisdom, J. 1931. "Logical Constructions (I)". *Mind* **40** (April): 189–93.

Wittgenstein, L. 1961. *Tractatus Logico-Philosophicus*. London: Routledge & Kegan Paul.

# *Index*

$\phi_2$-ings  309
σ-ing  310
σ-ings  242, 243

*a priori–a posteriori* distinction  61, 62
abandoning the framework of common
  sense  274, 275, 298
absolute processes  237–40, 241–4
  purely and occurrently qualitative  240,
    310
abstract entities  58, 67, 68, 75, 88
  and meaning statements  28, 29
  and scientific realism  18
  awareness of  185
  names of  33, 76, 81
  relations to  55, 79, 88
abstracta  55, 68, 181, 200
  avoiding reference to  29
  commitment to  18, 89
  and names  74, 77
  ontological status of  67
  Platonistic realm of  180
  properties as  237
  reference to  76
abstractionism  4, 5, 31, 95, 110, 172, 192
accepting a proposition  164, 166
acquaintance  214
action  40, 44, 45, 126, 183, 202, 246–51
action vocabulary  310
  vs. observation vocabulary  248
adverbial analysis of sensation  216, 304–
  5
agency  139, 140
agreement in attitude and identity of
  intention  262
Alston, William  124, 295, 296, 301
Amaral, Pedro  291
analogical predicates  208
analogy in theory construction  178
analytic behaviourism denied  175
analytic–synthetic distinction  61, 62

animal behaviour, explanation of  187
animal representation system  199
animals  185, 186, 188, 190
  and knowledge  129, 132
  psychological concepts  296
anti-materialist, Sellars as  235
aperspectival phenomena  278
appearance claims  104–6
appearance theories  99, 103, 104, 112
appearance–reality distinction  114
applying a theory  194
applying psychological concepts to others
  193
Aristotelian categories  60
Aristotelian hylomorphism  10
Aristotelian inference  190
Aristotelian representational systems  190
Aristotelian theory of mind  172
Aristotelianism  227
Aristotle  2, 9, 58, 60, 301
artifacts  273–5
Asquith, P.  298
Astington, Janet  301
atomism  138
atomistic paradigm  306
attributions of psychological states rest on
  know-how  198
Aune, Bruce  253, 311
Austin, J. L.  24
authority  120–22, 138
authority of first-person knowledge,
  explanation of  176
auxiliary symbols  84
aware of sensum  233
awareness  42, 88
  as linguistic  185, 190
  of necessities  64
  of rules  40–44, 46
  prelinguistic  190
awareness of logical space  188
  ambiguity of  191

report, correctness of 295
reporting role
for concepts of sensation 211
for theoretical terms 156
reporting vocabulary, most basic 205
representation relation 270
representational or propositional states 189
representational system 199
and intrasystemic moves 286
language-like 199
map as 301
representational systems 31, 45, 53, 187, 189–91
logic-using 301
vs. languages 31
Richardson, Robert 227, 307
Rorty, Richard 23, 285
Rosenberg, Jay 50, 288, 304, 305
Ruffman, T. 301
rule-following 41, 46, 132, 183, 190, 288
and language 187
rule-governed behaviour 40–43, 128, 131, 135, 141
rule-governed practices 277
rule-governed vs. law-governed 40
rule-obeying agents 128
rule-obeying behaviour 40, 42, 46
rules 26, 32, 39, 40, 44, 127, 128, 131–3
and Humean systems 190
as real 42
epistemic 141
for the use of words or concepts 21
formation and transformation rules 31
linguistic 25
of language 39, 127
philosophical claims as 20
rules of action 43–5, 126, 127
rules of criticism 43, 44, 48, 126, 127, 187, 190
Russell, Bertrand 3, 23, 25, 293
Ryle, Gilbert 24, 304
Rylean metalanguage 182
Rylean metalinguistic concepts, inadequate 182
Ryleans 176, 177, 180–83, 206, 283, 284, 299
coherence of 300

satisfaction relation 70
and truth 288
scepticism about other minds 97
scheme of classification normatively grounded 280
science 97, 98, 142, 148, 156, 161, 216, 269
and language 24
not itself a picture 270
science and consciousness 240, 241
scientific activity and societal norms 273
scientific change 149
scientific framework
practical reality of 272

prescriptive dimension of 273
scientific image 9–14, 21, 64, 225, 297
and noumenal world 269
and the sensibles 227
empirical reality of 269
greater empirical reality of 272
transcendental ideality of 269, 270
scientific method 2
scientific objects
empirically more real 271
identity and individuation conditions 273, 312
practical reality of 273
practically ideal 271, 273
transcendentally real 270
scientific progress 147
scientific realism 142, 201, 298
scientific realists and the sensory 241
scientific reasoning 169
scientific treatment of perception 212
scientism 281
second-order predicates 117
second-order probability statements 298
seeing, propositional vs. objectual 214
seeing as 215
seeing of 214, 233
limits of 215
seeing that 215
seeing to be 215
seeing vs. looking 105
seemings 220
Seibt, Johanna 309
self-reports, justificational structure of 194
self-description in psychological vocabulary 177
Sellars, Roy Wood 2, 16, 17, 19, 97, 240, 241, 303
Sellars's myths, tensions between 284
semantic language, analysis of 180
semantic properties independent of intentionality 180
semantical rules 47, 48
sensa 13, 235, 243, 305, 308
sensation as non-conceptual 120
sensation reports, justifying acceptance of 220
sensations
a categorial feature of 232
a transposition of the sensibles 234
referents of our perceptual takings 232
sensations explain appearances 231
sense data 13, 99, 100, 103
and microtheory of sentient organisms 210
and neutral monism 242
sense-datum approach to sensing 305
sense-datum theory 99–103, 216
sense-impression inference 222
sense-impression predicates 225
sense impressions 5, 177, 206–17
as theoretical entities 308